Life in School

There can be little doubt that pupils' own interpretations of what happens in their schools represent a crucial link in the educational chain. We need to understand how pupils respond to different forms of pedagogy and school organization, and why they respond in the ways they do, in order to increase the effectiveness of our schooling.

In the ten years prior to first publication ethnographic studies of pupils in schools had increased in number and importance. They had come to represent a leading area of inquiry which is still of relevance to practising and student teachers today. However, this material was not easily accessible, being widely distributed across educational and sociological journals and books. Originally published in 1984, this book collects together significant contributions to the field in a single volume, and will still be of relevance to practising and trainee teachers, and students of sociology and education.

Life in School

The Sociology of Pupil Culture

Edited by

Martyn Hammersley and Peter Woods

Routledge
Taylor & Francis Group

First published in 1984
by Open University Press

This edition first published in 2020 by Routledge
2 Park Square, Milton Park, Abingdon, Oxon OX14 4RN

and by Routledge
52 Vanderbilt Avenue, New York, NY 10017

Routledge is an imprint of the Taylor & Francis Group, an informa business

Publisher's Note
The publisher has gone to great lengths to ensure the quality of this reprint but points out that some imperfections in the original copies may be apparent.

Disclaimer
The publisher has made every effort to trace copyright holders and welcomes correspondence from those they have been unable to contact.

A Library of Congress record exists under ISBN: 0335104193

ISBN: 978-0-367-42292-9 (hbk)
ISBN: 978-0-367-82336-8 (ebk)
ISBN: 978-0-367-42301-8 (pbk)

Life in School

THE SOCIOLOGY OF PUPIL CULTURE

Edited by
Martyn Hammersley and Peter Woods

Open University Press

Milton Keynes

Open University Press
Celtic Court
22 Ballmoor
Buckingham
MK18 1XW

and
1900 Frost Road, Suite 101
Bristol, PA 19007, USA

First published 1984
Reprinted 1987, 1989, 1993

British Library Cataloguing in Publication Data

Hammersley, Martyn
 Life in school
 1. Educational sociology—England
 2. School children—England
 I. Title   II. Woods, Peter
 370.19'34   LC191.8.G72E5

 ISBN 0-335-10419-3

Text design by W.A.P.
Cover design by Paul Clark.

Typeset by Gilbert Composing Services, Leighton Buzzard, Bedfordshire.

Contents

Acknowledgements

The Open University Press would like to thank the following for permission to reproduce copyright material. All possible care has been taken to trace ownership of the selections included and to make full acknowledgements for their use.

Reading 1: C. Lacey, *Hightown Grammar*, Manchester University Press, 1970; pp. 49–73.

Reading 2: S. Ball, *Beachside Comprehensive*, Cambridge University Press, 1981; pp. 23–52 and 292–295.

Reading 3: P. Woods and the *British Journal of Sociology*, Vol. 27, No. 2, 1976; pp. 130–149.

Reading 4: P. Willis, *Learning to Labour*, Saxon House, 1977; pp. 11–21 and 33–43.

Reading 5: M. Fuller, in R. Deem (ed.) *Schooling for Women's Work*, Routledge and Kegan Paul, 1980; pp. 52–65.

Reading 6: L. Measor, in M. Hammersley and A. Hargreaves (eds.) *Curriculum Practice: Some Sociological Case Studies*, Falmer Press, 1983; pp. 171–191.

Reading 7: S. Ball, in P. Woods (ed.) *Pupil Strategies*, Croom Helm, 1980; pp. 143–161.

Reading 8: J. Beynon, '"Sussing out" teachers: Pupils as data gatherers'. © John Beynon, 1984 (this volume).

Reading 9: V. J. Furlong, in M. Stubbs and S. Delamont (eds.) *Explorations in Classroom Observation*, Wiley, 1976; pp. 24–44. ©V. J. Furlong, 1976. Reprinted by permission of John Wiley and Sons, Ltd.

Reading 10: M. Hammersley and G. Turner, in P. Woods (ed.) *Pupil Strategies*, Croom Helm, 1980; pp. 29–49.

Reading 11: D. H. Hargreaves, *Social Relations in a Secondary School*, Routledge and Kegan Paul, 1967; pp. 119–139.

Reading 12: H. Gannaway, in M. Stubbs and S. Delamont, *Explorations in Classroom Observation*, Wiley, 1976; pp. 51–67. © H. Gannaway, 1976. Reprinted by permission of John Wiley and Sons, Ltd.

Reading 13: E. Rosser and R. Harré, in M. Hammersley and P. Woods (eds.) *The Process of Schooling*, Routledge and Kegan Paul, 1976; pp. 173–177.

Reading 14: C. Werthman and *Berkeley Journal of Sociology*, Vol. 8, No. 1, 1963; pp. 39–60.

Reading 15: P. Woods and *Journal of Curriculum Studies*, Vol. 10, No. 4, 1978; pp. 309–327.

Reading 16: A. Pollard, 'Goodies, jokers and gangs'. © Andrew Pollard, 1984 (this volume).

Reading 17: B. Davies, *Life in the Classroom and Playground*, Routledge and Kegan Paul, 1982; pp. 60–113.

Editors' introduction

Ten years ago studies of pupils' experience of school were almost a novelty. In Britain, the sociology of education had been dominated by the issue of equality of opportunity, being focussed largely on the relationship between social class background and school achievement (Halsey, Floud and Anderson 1961; Craft, 1970). While there had been some social psychological work on pupils (Fleming, 1959; Blyth, 1965) there had been very little empirical research documenting pupils' perspectives and adaptations. The only major exceptions were an isolated American article by Carl Werthman—'Delinquents in school' (Werthman, 1963; reproduced as Reading 14 in this volume) and the pioneering studies of Hargreaves (1967; Reading 11) and Lacey (1970; Reading 1).

The major stimulus to the blossoming of British research on pupils in the 1970s and 1980s was undoubtedly the injection into the sociology of education of interpretive approaches, especially symbolic interactionism and social phenomenology. These theoretical approaches, with their emphasis on identifying the meanings embedded in actions (Blumer, 1969) and on the importance of tapping the perspectives of groups low in the 'hierarchy of credibility' (Becker, 1967), led sociologists of education to treat the investigation of pupils' experience of school as a major research topic. This went along with the widespread adoption of ethnography as the method most appropriate to the description of people's perspectives and activities. In these respects the work of Becker *et al.* (1961, 1968) on university students was particularly influential.

As a consequence of these changes in the theoretical complexion of the sociology of education, there is now a considerable body of published work on pupils, covering many aspects of their attitudes and behaviour: their responses to organizational arrangements such as streaming, banding and setting; their orientations towards school transfer, entry into a new class, and the process of subject and occupational choice; their relations with one another as lads or ear 'oles, friends and foes, swots and dossers. At the same time some attention has also been given to variations in their adaptations towards school according to class, gender and race.

Despite common theoretical and methodological origins, the literature reveals considerable diversity in approach. Some researchers, notably Ball (1981; Reading 2), have followed the model of Hargreaves and Lacey quite closely, looking in particular at the extent to which the streaming and banding of pupils by school produces a polarization in their attitudes towards school values and thereby affects their academic and behavioural performances. Top streams or bands, the argument runs, tend to develop a pro-school, conformist culture, bottom streams an anti-school, counter-culture. While this work recognizes the influence of social class background documented by earlier research in the sociology of education (Westergaard and Little, 1967), it stresses the effects of institutional organization on pupils' orientations towards, and level of achievement in, school.

The roots of an alternative, and sometimes conflicting, approach are to be found in the work of Werthman. While his work pre-dates that of Hargreaves and Lacey, Werthman specifically criticizes explanations of pupils' behaviour which attribute it to membership of particular social classes or to the organizational structure of schools. Werthman stresses the rational appraisal which pupils (or at least the gang members he studied) make of their situation and the resulting contextual variability of their behaviour. He claims that both academically successful and less successful pupils engage in classroom deviance but that this occurs only in some lessons and not others. Whether deviance occurs depends, he argues, on the pupils' assessment of the fairness of the teacher's treatment of them, particularly as regards the distribution of grades. He claims that the gang members he investigated assessed the basis on which each teacher allocated grades, their response to him or her depending on the outcome of the assessment.

The rational and active character of pupils' interpretations of school and the contextual variability of their behaviour have been major themes in many subsequent studies. Particular attention has been given to the ways in which pupils make sense of school, not least how they interpret the behaviour of teachers (Rosser and Harré, 1976; Reading 13; Gannaway, 1976; Reading 12; Beynon, 1984; Reading 8). Closely associated with this has been interest in pupils' efforts to negotiate classroom rules and work rates with teachers (Ball, 1980; Reading 7; Woods, 1978; Reading 15). This has led some to challenge the view that pupils can be conceived of as either pro- or anti-school, and various efforts have been made to produce more sophisticated accounts of pupils' modes of adaptation (Hammersley and Turner, 1980, Reading 10; Turner, 1983).

Equally important, of course, are pupils' relations with one another. Here the pioneering work was done by Hargreaves (1967), and an example of this is included here (Reading 11) in his account of the rise and fall of Clint as leader among the anti-school pupils at Lumley Secondary Modern School. Subsequent studies have tended to be of younger children focussing on the making and breaking of friendships (Davies, 1982, see Reading 17) and the formation of gangs (Pollard, 1984, Reading 16).

Most of the work on pupils inspired by interpretive approaches has focussed at a micro level of analysis, being either primarily descriptive or being concerned with the formal characteristics of pupils' interpretations and activities inside and outside the classroom. There has, however, also been some research on pupils located in a more macro framework, notably that of Willis (1977, Reading 4) Corrigan (1979) and Anyon (1981). Willis argues that 'the lads' he studied actively created their own counter-culture in school. This culture was not so much a response to failure at school—as Hargreaves, Lacey and Ball argue—as a development of the working-class culture available to them in their homes, stimulated by the (to them unacceptable) authority claims made by teachers. Willis argues that this counter-culture contains both penetrating insights into the nature of capitalist society and also ideological limitations. Its effect, ironically enough, is to prepare 'the lads' for manual work. Despite its critical and oppositional edge, the school counter culture helps in the production of a docile force of manual labourers.

This body of work, predominantly Marxist in orientation, is most usefully viewed against the background of recent theorizing about the functioning of schools in the reproduction of capitalist social relations. Early reproduction theories, such as those of Bowles and Gintis (1976) and Althusser (1971), tended to portray pupils as passive recipients of messages built into the structure and content of schooling in much the same manner as structural functionalists such as Parsons (1959) had done earlier. For a variety of reasons (Hargreaves, 1982), more recent Marxist writers have come to stress the role of pupil resistance to schooling, noting how this varies across different social classes and types of school regime (Anyon, 1981). Historical depth has also been added through the work of Humphries (1981) who has documented the orientations towards school of working-class children early in this century by means of life-history interviewing.

If social class is the keynote of these approaches, another important stimulus to research on pupils has been the growth of interest in the effects of gender. One result of this has been the appearance of a range of studies investigating the perspectives and activities of girls in schools designed to complement earlier studies which had for the most part focussed on boys (McRobbie and Garber, 1976; Davies, 1976). Equally important, though, is the growing attention now being given to the effects of gender-related messages built into schooling and to gender-based differences in responses to them. Of interest here are the effects of both the 'official' and the 'hidden' curriculum. Inspired by feminism, this work is concerned with the social construction and development of feminine and masculine identities, the way these are shaped by family socialization, teaching, and pupil cultures, and how they contribute to differentiation in the curriculum, and of life chances generally (Deem, 1980; Stanworth, 1983; Measor, 1983; Reading 6). The influence of ethnicity on pupils' perspectives and adaptations has received much less attention. The pioneering work of Fuller (1980, Reading 5; 1983) is important, but much still remains to be done in this area.

There can be little doubt that pupils' own interpretations of school processes represent a crucial link in the educational chain. Unless we understand how pupils respond to different forms of pedagogy and school organization and why they respond in the ways that they do, our efforts to increase the effectiveness, or to change the impact, of schooling will stand little chance of success.

The wealth of material now available on pupils is obviously an important resource for anyone seeking to investigate the process of education. However, this material is not easily accessible, being widely distributed across educational and sociological journals, readers and books. It was for this reason that we felt that it would be useful to collect together some of the most important contributions to this field in a single volume. Of course, choosing what to include in a reader is always a difficult task. The selection obviously reflects our own priorities, preferences and prejudices. Nevertheless, we have sought to include a representative sample of currently available, good quality research on pupils' perspectives and adaptations. We hope that this selection will provide a useful introduction for those interested in the area.

References

Althusser, L. (1971) 'Ideology and ideological state apparatuses' in Althusser, L. (ed.) *Lenin and Philosophy and Other Essays*, New Left Books.

Anyon, J. (1981) 'Social class and school knowledge', *Curriculum Inquiry*, Vol. 11, No. 1.

Ball, S.J. (1980) 'Initial encounters in the classroom and the process of establishment' in Woods, P. (ed.) *Pupil Strategies*, Croom Helm.

Ball, S.J. (1981) *Beachside Comprehensive*, Cambridge University Press.

Becker, H.S. (1967) 'Whose side are we on', *Social Problems*, Vol. 14, pp. 239–47.

Becker, H.S. *et al.* (1961) *Boys in White: Student Culture in Medical School*, University of Chicago Press.

Becker, H.S. *et al.* (1968) *Making the Grade*, Wiley.

Beynon, J. (1984) '"Sussing out" teachers: pupils as data gatherers', this volume.

Blyth, W.A.L. (1965) *English Primary Education: A Sociological Description*, Vol. 1, Routledge and Kegan Paul.

Bowles, S. and Gintis, H. (1976) *Schooling in Capitalist America*, Routledge and Kegan Paul.

Blumer, H. (1969) *Symbolic Interactionism*, Prentice Hall.

Craft, M. (1970) *Family, Class and Education: A Reader*, Longman.

Corrigan, P. (1979) *Schooling the Smash Street Kids*, Macmillan.

Davies, B. (1982) *Life in the Classroom and the Playground*, Routledge and Kegan Paul.

Davies, L. (1976) 'The view from the girls', *Educational Review*, Vol. 30, No. 2.

Deem, R. (1980) *Schooling for Women's Work*, Routledge and Kegan Paul.

Fleming, C.M. (1959) *The Social Psychology of Education*, Routledge and Kegan Paul.

Fuller, M. (1980) 'Black girls in a comprehensive school', in Deem, R. (ed.). op. cit.

Fuller, M. (1983) 'Critical qualifications and qualified criticisms' in Barton, L. and Walker, S. (eds.) *Race, Class and Education*, Croom Helm.

Gannaway, H. (1976) 'Making sense of school' in Stubbs, M. and Delamont, S. (eds) *Explorations in Classroom Observation*, Wiley.

Halsey, A.H., Floud, J., and Anderson, C.A. (1961) *Education, Economy and Society*, Free Press.

Hammersley, M. and Turner, G. (1980) 'Conformist pupils?' in Woods, P. (ed.) *Pupil Strategies*, Croom Helm. (Also this volume.)

Hargreaves, A. (1982) 'Resistance and relative autonomy theories: problems of distortion and incoherence in recent marxist analyses of education', *British Journal of Sociology of Education*, Vol. 3, No. 2.

Hargreaves, D.H. (1967) *Social Relations in a Secondary School*, Routledge and Kegan Paul.

Humphries, S. (1981) *Hooligans or Rebels?: An Oral History of Working-class Childhood and Youth, 1889-1939*, Blackwell.

Lacey, C. (1970) *Hightown Grammar*, Manchester University Press.

McRobbie, A. and Garber, J. (1976) 'Girls and subcultures', in Hall, S. and Jefferson, T. (eds) *Resistance Through Rituals*, Hutchinson.

Measor, L. (1983) 'Gender and the sciences' in Hammersley, M. and Hargreaves, A. (eds) *Curriculum Practice: Some Sociological Case Studies*, Falmer. (Also this volume.)

Parsons, T. (1959) 'The school class as a social system', *Harvard Educational Review*, Vol. XXIX, pp. 297-318.

Pollard, A. (1984) 'Goodies, jokers and gangs', this volume.

Rosser, E. and Harré, R. (1976) 'The meaning of trouble' in Hammersley, M. and Woods, P. (eds) *The Process of Schooling*, Routledge and Kegan Paul. (Also this volume.)

Stanworth, M. (1983) *Gender and Schooling*, Women's Research and Resources Centre, in association with Hutchinson.

Turner, G. (1983) *The Social World of the Comprehensive School*, Croom Helm.

Westergaard, J. and Little, A. (1967) 'Educational opportunity and social selection in England and Wales: trends and policy implications' in *Social Objectives in Educational Planning*, OECD, reprinted in *Craft 1970*.

Werthman, C. (1963) 'Delinquents in school: a test for the legitimacy of authority', *Berkeley Journal of Sociology*, Vol. 8, No. 1, pp. 39-60. (Also this volume.)

Willis, P. (1977) *Learning to Labour*, Saxon House.

Woods, P. (1979) *The Divided School*, Routledge and Kegan Paul.

Woods, P. (1978) 'Negotiating the demands of schoolwork', *Journal of Curriculum Studies*, Vol. 10, No. 4, pp. 309-327. (Also this volume.)

PART ONE

School Organization
and Social Divisions

1 Differentiation and sub-cultural polarisation

C. LACEY

[. . .] This [paper] provides [. . .] a model of differentiation and sub-culture formation within [Hightown Grammar School]. The approach will be in three stages:

1 A description of some of the sociological characteristics of boys entering the school.
2. (a) A descriptive analysis of some aspects of the informal structure that developed in one class in the school, with particular reference to two case studies.
(b) An attempt to establish a model which describes the passage of pupils through the school.
3 An attempt to verify the model through the use of quantitative indices—in particular, the concepts of differentiation and polarisation which are developed in 2 (b).

The overall aim is to provide a picture of the stratification and subsequent sub-culture development, associated with academic streaming.

The intake

[. . .] Hightown Grammar School is a highly selective institution. It is important, therefore, for us to investigate the ways in which the selection affects the composition of the newly recruited first-year classes. Their composition affects the subsequent subcultural development of the group. The particular factors that will concern us are:

(a) The way selection restricts the intake to a particular type of student.
(b) The way selection isolates the successful candidate from his fellow pupils and friends at his junior school.

The effect of selection on the intake
The evidence I have been able to gather[1] supports my contention that the new intake to a grammar school will consist largely of 11 year olds who have been accustomed to playing what I have called 'best pupil' role in their junior schools and who, in their new environment, are often separated from their former school friends. The extent to which this is true of any grammar school will, of course, depend on a large number of factors, such as the percentage of grammar school places available and the number and size of junior and grammar schools in the catchment area.
[. . .] The local education authority of Hightown sends 15–20 per cent of its 11 year olds to grammar schools each year. Evidence from a variety of sources—junior school reports, autobiographies, and the statements of junior school teachers— clearly shows that these contingents include the vast majority of top scholars, team

leaders, school monitors, head boys and teachers' favourites. For example, in the 22 junior school reports of the 1962 intake that recorded a class position, only one boy was placed in the bottom half of the class (20/34). Similarly, of the 41 junior school reports of the 1959 intake recording class positions, the lowest position recorded was 19/39, and this was accompanied by the remark 'Tries hard, keen and interested'. In short, they are the 'best pupils'.

How selection isolates the successful candidates
The boys entering Hightown Grammar are selected from a large number of junior schools. Table 1.1 shows that the selection test tends to scoop a few pupils from each school. Over half the boys come from schools that send six or fewer pupils.

Table 1.1 *Hightown Grammar School intake, 1962, classified according to size of Junior School Contingents. Mean size: 3.5 boys per contingent*

	Size of contingents				
	1–3	4–6	7–9	10–12	Total
Number of junior schools	24	5	4	2	35
Number of pupils	42	25	30	21	118

The relative isolation of pupils from their former schoolmates is only partially illustrated in Table 1.1. When the boys arrive at Hightown Grammar they are divided at random into four classes, which further increases the likelihood of their being separated from former schoolmates. These classes are also house groups, and the pupils in them remain together for prayers, school meals and registration as well as lessons.

The degree of isolation of the first-year boy is illustrated by the responses to a 'friendship' questionnaire, asking whether boys had friends in their first-year class who had attended the same junior school as themselves. Fifty-eight boys out of 118 questioned had no friend from the same junior school in their class. Thus almost half the first-year intake spend the great majority of their time at school in a class where they are isolated from previous friends.

This isolation[2] means that there is no basis for a common identification other than membership of the school. Combined with their 'best pupil' background, it has the initial consequences for the boys of:

1 high commitment to the school and its norms,
2 rivalry among themselves.

Both are manifested in a number of ways. First-year boys adhere rigidly to school uniform, caps and blazers are proudly displayed, and they attend school functions and clubs in disproportionate numbers. Their behaviour in the classroom is characterised by eagerness, co-operation with the teacher and competition among themselves. 'Please sir, Willy Brown is copying my sums' is a remark that could only come from a first-year boy.

I once tried to measure the response rate to a narrative and question-and-answer lesson given by a history teacher. So many responded to each question that I could not record them. As the tension mounted, boys who did not know the answers looked around apprehensively at those who did. The latter, in a state of high excitement, smiled triumphantly at the ignorant ones, and stretched their arms and bodies to the utmost as they eagerly called 'Sir!' 'Sir!' 'Sir!' every time the master glanced in their direction. When he said 'All right, Green, you tell us,' there were quiet sighs and groans as those who had not been called upon subsided into their seats. The whole performance was repeated as soon as the next question was asked.

During such spells, the desire to participate was so great that some boys would put up their hands and strain for notice, even though they had no idea of the answer. If asked to give it, they would either make a gesture implying that they had suddenly forgotten, or subside with an embarrassed and confused look, to the jeers and groans of the rest of the class, who would then redouble their efforts to attract attention.

The type of enthusiasm characteristic of a first-year class was occasionally found in second- or third-year forms, but there were a number of observable differences. The second and third years were more likely to 'play dead' and allow five or six people to 'do all the work'. If the master succeeded in getting a larger proportion to participate, there was always a residue of boys who hardly took part at all or who did so only by giving obviously wrong or facetious answers. There was a possibility that the form would use any excitement of this kind to sabotage the lesson or play the fool: a boy might stretch so hard as to fall out of his desk, another accidentally punch the one in front as he put his hand up, and the form's 'funny man' would display his wit in response to an ambiguous question—sometimes isolating the teacher by referring to a private class joke.

First-year forms are thus widely regarded by teachers as the easiest and most rewarding to teach. They are typically allocated to young, inexperienced masters or those who have difficulty with discipline. Misdemeanours are largely the result of high spirits, over-eagerness or forgetfulness rather than conscious malice. Hopes are high and expectations as to school performance and subsequent careers unrealistically rosy.

The model

The informal structure: two case studies
As soon as the highly selected first-year population meets at the Grammar School and is allocated to the four first-year classes, a complex process of interaction begins. It takes place through a variety of encounters. Boys talk and listen to each other; talk and listen to teachers; listen to conversations; notice details of accent, gesture, clothing; watch others at work and at play in various situations and in innumerable different permutations.

During the first few days much of this interaction appears to take place in a fairly random way, influenced mainly by the physical and organisational arrangements. Soon, patterns of selection begin to emerge. Various initial interactions yield information and experience, which are retained by the individual and provide some basis for the interpretation and partial control of other interactions. This partial control is extremely important because it soon gives rise to a recognisable, although unstable and changing, structure.

When I started observing the first-year classes in March 1963, the members of each class had been together for only about six months, but each class already had a definite structure of which the pupils clearly had detailed knowledge. When a master called a boy to read or answer a question, others could be seen giving each other significant looks which clearly indicated that they knew what to expect. On one occasion, for example, a master asked three boys to stay behind after the lesson to help him with a task calling for a sense of responsibility and co-operation. He called out 'Williams, Maun and Sherring'. The class burst into spontaneous laughter, and there were unbelieving cries of 'What! Sherring?' The master corrected himself. 'No, not Sherring, Shadwell.' From the context of the incident, it was clear that Sherring's reputation was already inconsistent with the qualities expected of a monitor.

On another occasion, Priestley was asked to read, and the whole class groaned and laughed. A fat boy, he had been kept down from the previous year because of ill-health (catarrh and asthma) and poor work. He grinned apprehensively, wiped his face with a huge white handkerchief and started to read very nervously. For a few moments the class was absolutely quiet, then one boy tittered; Priestley made a silly mistake, partly because he was looking up to smile at the boy who was giggling, and the whole class burst into laughter. Priestley blew his nose loudly and smiled nervously at the class. The teacher quietened them and Priestley continued to read. Three lines later a marked mispronunciation started everyone laughing again. This performance continued, with Priestley getting more and more nervous, mopping his brow and blowing his nose. Finally, the master snapped, with obvious annoyance, 'All right, Priestley, that's enough!'

This short incident, one of several during the day, served to remind Priestley of his structural position within the class and to confirm the opinions and expectations of both class and teacher towards him. His behaviour was consistent with his performance in the examination at the end of the autumn term when he was ranked twenty-ninth out of thirty-three.

During this period of observation, I also noticed the significance of the behaviour of another boy, Cready. Cready first attracted my attention because, although his form position was similar to Priestley's (twenty-sixth), he habitually associated with a strikingly different group. He behaved very differently in class and had a markedly different reputation.

Cready was a member of the school choir. It so happened that the English master, whose classes I was observing, was also the music teacher, and he had arranged the class so that the members of the school choir sat in the row next to the piano and his desk (row 4). To be a member of the choir, one had to have a good voice and be willing to stay in school to practise during lunch time and at four o'clock, once or twice a week, for certain periods of the year. In the next two rows were members of the first-form choir. To be in this a boy had only to be willing to sing. In the last row (row 1) were boys who could not or would not sing at all.

During the first three lessons I observed, Cready answered four of the questions put to the class. On two of these occasions, he had discussed the answer with the boy next to him before putting up his hand. If Cready got an answer wrong he was never laughed at. Priestley answered two questions in the same period. He got one of them wrong and was laughed at by the class. As I observed later, if Priestley attempted to discuss an answer with the boy next to him, he was reprimanded.

Table 1.2 illustrates how the seating arrangements in the class affected the pattern of interaction with the teacher.[3] A sociogram for the class showed an apparent inconsistency. During lessons, Priestley was frequently in the middle of a

Table 1.2 *Record of teacher-pupil interaction: average for three lessons*

Type of interaction	Row number			
	1	2	3	4
Answers to questions (per boy)	0.5	0.7	1.3	3.6
Rebukes per boy	1.6	1.2	0.5	0.4
Questions from boys (totals)	3	1	2	10

group of mischievous boys. If there was a disturbance, he was in it. I expected him to be fairly popular with some of the boys who led him into trouble, but none of them picked him as a friend. He chose five boys as his friends but only one reciprocated.

The other boys used Priestley to create diversions and pass messages, and because he was so isolated he was only too pleased to oblige. He could never resist the temptation to act as if he were 'one of the boys'. But when he was caught out they deserted him and laughed at rather than with him. He was truly the butt of the class.

These incidents, seen in the context of the structure of the class, show how he had fallen foul of the system. He was not in control of his own situation, and anything he tried to do to improve his position only made it worse. His attempts to answer questions provoked laughter and ridicule. His attempts to minimise the distress it caused—a nervous smile round the room, a shrug of the shoulders, pretending that he had either caused the disturbance on purpose or did not care—served only to worsen his position with the teacher.

He compensated for social and academic failure by learning the stocks and shares columns of the *Financial Times* every week. This enabled him to develop a reputation in a field outside the sphere in which the school was competent to judge. He would emphasise its *real* importance to his future career and thus minimise the effect of his scholastic failure. Even this did not improve his standing at the school, least of all with the staff. It merely explained his laziness, bad behaviour and lack of concern with school work. 'Oh, Priestley. He's just biding his time with us—from what I hear his future is assured anyway. He's just lazy,' said the English master.

If I had had to forecast the future performance of these two boys on the evidence, I would of course have expected Cready to do better in the following examinations and Priestley, if anything, worse. Their positions in class in the first and second-year examinations were as shown in Table 1.3. The second-year forms, 2E, 2A, 2B and 2C, were streamed; 2E was the top form and 2C the bottom.

Table 1.3

	First-year exams				Second-year exams			
	Form	Autumn	Spring	Summer	Form	Autumn	Spring	Summer
Priestley	1A	29	30	26	2C	12	27	16
Cready	1A	26	10	10	2E	11	12	10

It is interesting to note their family background. Priestley was Jewish[4], second in a family of three, and lived in an area of expensive detached houses. His father was a clearance stock buyer. Cready, on the other, lived on a council estate, was fourth out of six in the family, and his father was a quality inspector in an abrasives factory.

Cready and Priestley did not, therefore, conform with the established correlation between academic achievement and social class. Cready, a working-class boy from a large family, was making good, while Priestly, an upper middle class boy from a smaller family, was failing academically. This negative case highlights an important point: there is a degree of autonomy in the system of social relations in the classroom which can transcend external factors and even differences of intelligence. External factors, such as social class, and intelligence have to be fed through the internal system of relations within the classroom. If the possessor of advantages in the external system fails to feed them in correctly (some factor in the internal system might intervene) they can be misunderstood or even ignored. On the other hand, positive rewards can come from skill in manipulating internal relations;[5] they can make up for lack of external advantages, and even intelligence, as measured by an IQ test.

The positions of Cready and Priestley are only explicable in the light of this type of analysis of the system of social relations inside the classroom. The system is open to manipulation by those who are sensitive to its details. Hence Cready, who had all the major external factors stacked against him, was able to use the system of social relations to sustain and buoy himself up. He was friendly with some of the most prestigeful and successful members of the class. He built up a reputation for reliability, neatness and helpfulness with his form master in his work and in attendance at the choir.

Despite all the advantages he brought to the situation, Priestley had fallen foul of the system. Although separated from his friends in the second year, he shared their contemptuous view of first-formers. His overbearing and rather condescending attitude to many of his new first-year classmates lost him their sympathy and friendship. His attempts to gain influence by playing the fool or 'acting up' in class, which would have been appropriate in a second-year group, estranged him further. He was not only failing but also speedily losing any motivation to succeed in the sphere in which the school was competent to judge him.

It should be reiterated that this is not an attempt to disprove the established correlations between social class and academic achievement, but to highlight the fact that there are detailed social mechanisms and processes responsible for bringing it about, mechanisms which are not completely determined by external factors. Studying them will enable us to add a new dimension to our understanding of the general process of education in schools.

Differentiation and polarisation
I now suggest a model which describes the passage of pupils through the grammar schools. Two terms should first be explained: differentiation and polarisation. By *differentiation* I mean the separation and ranking of students according to a multiple set of criteria which makes up the normative, academically orientated, value system of the grammar school. Differentiation is defined here as being largely carried out by teachers in the course of their normal duties.

Polarisation, on the other hand, takes place within the student body, partly as a result of differentiation, but influenced by external factors and with an autonomy of its own. It is a process of sub-culture formation in which the school-dominated, normative culture is opposed by an alternative culture which I refer to as the 'anti-group' culture. The content of the anti-group culture will, of course, be very much influenced by the school and its social setting. For example, it may range from a folk music CND group in a minor public school to a delinquent sub-culture at a secondary modern school in an old urban area. In Hightown Grammar School it fell between these extremes and was influenced by the large working-class and Jewish communities of Hightown.

Differentiation. There are a number of scales on which a master habitually rates a boy. For the purpose of the analysis, two will be considered:

(a) *Academic scale.*
(b) *Behaviour scale.* This would include considerations as varied as general classroom behaviour and attitudes; politeness; attention; helpfulness; time spent in school societies and sports.

The two are not independent. Behaviour affects academic standards not only because good behaviour involves listening and attending but because a master becomes favourably disposed towards a boy who is well behaved and trying hard.

The teacher therefore tends to help him and even to mark him up. I have found in my own marking of books that when I know the form (i.e. the good and bad pupils), I mark much more quickly. For example, I might partly read an essay and recognise the writing: 'Oh, Brown. Let's see, he tries hard. Good, neat work, missed one or two ideas—seven out of ten.' Or 'This is a bit scruffy—no margin, not underlined; seems to have got the hang of it though. Who is it? Oh, Jones, that nuisance—five out of ten!'[6]

Polarisation. There is another reason why good behaviour is correlated with academic achievement. A boy who does well and wishes to do well academically is predisposed to accept the grammar school's system of values, that is, he behaves well. The system gives him high prestige, and it is therefore in his interest to support it; the correlation between membership of the choir and performance in class illustrates this point (see Table 1.2). He is supporting his position of prestige. On the other hand, a boy who does badly academically is predisposed to criticise, reject or even sabotage the system where he can, since it places him in an inferior position.[7]

A boy showing the extreme development of this phenomenon may subscribe to values which are actually the inverted values of the school. He obtains prestige for cheeking a teacher, playing truant, not doing homework, for smoking, drinking and even stealing. As it develops, the anti-group produces its own impetus. The boy who takes refuge in such a group because his work is poor finds that the group commits him to a behaviour pattern which means that his work still stay poor—and in fact often gets progressively worse.

The following extracts from an essay entitled 'Abuse', written by a first-form boy for his housemaster, illustrate a development of anti-group values which is extreme for a first-year pupil:

> I am writing this essay about abuse in the toilets . . . What they [the prefects] call abuse and what I call abuse are two different things altogether.
>   All the people where I live say I am growing up to be a 'Ted' so I try to please them by acting as much like one as I possibly can. I go around kicking a ball against the wall that is nearest to their house and making as much noise as I can and I intend to carry on doing this until they can leave me alone . . . It seems to me the Grammar School knows nothing about abuse for *I would much rather be a hooligan and get some fun out of life than be a snob always being the dear little nice boy doing what he is told* [my italics].

In [the first] section above, we saw that at the beginning of the first year the pupils constitute a relatively homogeneous, undifferentiated group. They are uniformly enthusiastic and eager to please, both through their work and their behaviour. The pupils who are noticed first are the good ones and the bad ones. Even by the spring term, some masters are still unsure of the names of quiet pupils and the undifferentiated middle of the classes they teach.

It is somewhat rare for an anti-group to develop in the first year. Although one or two individuals may develop marked anti-group values, they are likely to remain isolates. In the 1962 first year, I was able to recognise only one, Badman, the author of the essay. He wished to be transferred to a secondary modern school.

The usual course of events associated with a marked degree of (relative) failure in the first year is for the child to display symptoms of emotional upheaval and nervous disorder, and for a conflict of standards to take place. Symptoms that occurred in the first year intake of 1962 included:[9]

> Bursting into tears when reprimanded by a teacher.
> Refusal to go to school or to particular lessons, accompanied by hysterical crying and screaming.

Sleeplessness.
Bedwetting.
Playing truant from certain lessons or from school.
Constantly feeling sick before certain lessons.
One boy rushed to the stage in assembly clutching his throat and screaming that
he could not breathe.
Consistent failure to do homework.
High absence record.
Aggravation of mild epilepsy.

The fifteen cases recorded probably represent all the instances of major disturbance,
but a large number of minor ones probably never become known to the school.

The individual cases cannot be discussed here, but their general significance is
important to the model under discussion. We have seen that the eleven-plus selects
the 'best pupils' from the top forms of the junior schools. These forms have been
highly differentiated in preparation for the examination. Often, the pupils have
been 'best pupils' for some time and have internalised many of the expectations
inherent in that position. Their transfer to the grammar school means not only a
new environment, with all that such a change entails—new classmates, new
teachers and new sets of rules—but also for many of them a violation of their
expectations as 'best pupils'. It is when this violation of expectations coincides with
'unsatisfactory' home backgrounds that the worst cases of emotional disturbance
occur.

In the second year the process of differentiation continues. If streaming takes
place between the first and second years, as it did in the year group I studied, it helps
speed the process and a new crop of cases of emotional disturbance occurs. In the
1963 second year most of them were associated with boys who were failing to make
the grade in the top stream and boys who were in the lower half of the bottom
stream. Early on, the symptoms are mainly individual; later, after a prolonged period
of interaction and the impact of streaming, they are expressed mainly in group
attitudes. After six months in the second year this bottom stream was already
regarded as a difficult form to teach because, to quote two teachers, 'They're
unacademic, they can't cope with the work'; 'Give them half a chance and they'll give
you the run-around'.

The true anti-group starts to emerge in the second year, and it develops markedly
in the third and fourth years. It is then that strenuous efforts are made to get rid of
anti-group pupils. Considerable pressure is put on the headmaster by the teachers
who take the boys. He in turn transmits it to the board of governors. In most cases,
application to leave will also be made by the boys and their parents. In Hightown, the
board of governors was often loath to give permission for a boy to leave or transfer,
for two reasons:

1   the governors were also the governors for the secondary modern schools in the
    area and could not readily agree to passing on disciplinary problems from the
    grammar school to the secondary modern;
2   they were generally suspicious of grammar school teachers and felt reluctant to
    risk an injustice to a pupil who was often a working-class boy.

Nevertheless, some requests cannot easily be refused, for example, cases of ill
health, family hardship or consistent truanting. There are also a number of cases of
unofficial leaving: the boy has actually left school and taken a job, but is still being
marked as absent in the register. It is difficult to estimate the extent of the total loss
accurately, but, from each of two intakes which have been thoroughly investigated,

14

C. LACEY

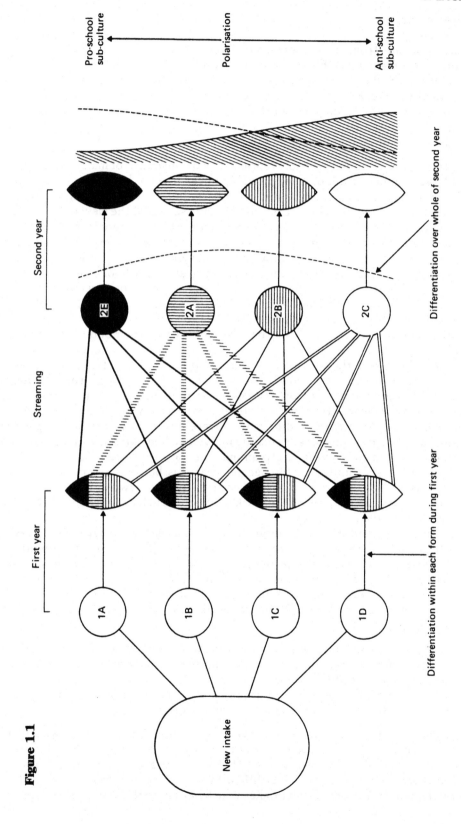

Figure 1.1

somewhere between ten and fifteen pupils left or were transferred to secondary modern schools before taking O level or reaching the age of 16.

A similar process can be observed in the sixth form and results in a crop of leavers in the first-year sixth. The extent to which differentiation develops and is internalised in the sixth is illustrated by a remark made to the economics master. He had just rebuked a boy in the Upper Sixth Modern and told him that unless he worked harder he would not pass economics A level. 'Well, the way I look at it is this. If some of the boys in the General form [the bottom stream in the sixth] can get it—and they usually do—then I should be all right.'

Quantitative indices

The indices developed below are prepared from two questionnaires completed by all members of the 1962 intake. One questionnaire was given at the end of the first year and one at the end of the second. The indices are designed to illustrate the processes of differentiation and polarisation. On both occasions the boys were asked who had been their close friends over the last year. They were asked to restrict themselves to boys in the school and to six choices, unless they felt they definitely could not do so.

The first and second years
There was virtually no difference in the average number of choices *received* per boy in the four *unstreamed* first-year classes (Table 1.4).

Table 1.4   *Average number of friendship choices received per boy in each first-year class**

Form	Choices per boy
1A	4.1
1B	4.1
1C	4.2
1D	4.5

*The choices are 'received' from boys in their own form and from the other first-year forms.

When the boys were streamed on academic criteria at the end of the first year, these *same* friendship choices were related to the new forms 2E, 2A, 2B, 2C (Table 1.5, column (a)).

Table 1.5   *Average number of friendship choices received per boy at the end of first year and second year, for each of the second year classes*

Form	Average number of choices per boy in each class	
	(a) First year*	*(b) Second year*
2E	4.8	4.8
2A	4.5	4.6
2B	3.9	4.0
2C	3.3	4.3

*The choices in column (a) were made at the end of the first year and are the same as those averaged in Table 1.4, but they have been averaged for the classes the pupils were about to enter.

The choices in column (b) were made at the end of the second year and are averaged for the classes in which the pupils have spent the year.

Not only do the figures reveal striking differences, but these differences are related to academic achievement. At the end of the first year, the higher up the academic scale a boy was placed, the more likely he was to attract a large number of friendship choices.

At the end of the second year, the boys were asked the same question. The response was equally striking. Column (b) of Table 1.5 shows that the year spent among a new class of boys has hardly changed the overall positions of 2E, 2A and 2B, although the actual friendship choices for any one boy will have undergone considerable change. However, 2C has undergone a substantial change. The increase from 3.3 to 4.3 for 2C represents an increase of something like thirty choices, in a class of thirty boys. That the new popularity of boys in 2C is brought about by the growth of a new set of norms and values or the beginnings of the anti-group sub-culture is demonstrated by Table 1.6. The boys of 2C have become popular for the very reasons they were unpopular in the first year.

The boys of 2E and 2A who, according to our hypothesis, *should* be positively influenced by the academic grading, since they are successful in relation to it, show that it does have a marked positive influence on their choice of friends (e.g. 2D make 26 choices in to 2A, fourteen choices into 2B and only seven into 2C). There is no element in the organisation of the school that could bring this about. Similarly, 2A make 28 choices into 2E, sixteen into 2B and only six into 2C.

Table 1.6 *Distribution of friendship choices according to class: second year, 1963 (1962 intake at end of second year).* Read *across* for choices made, *down* for choices received by each class

Form (number in each class in brackets)	2E	2A	2B	2C	Others	Total of choices made	Percentage of choices in own class
2E (31)	91	26	14	7	12	150	60.7
2A (31)	28	94	16	6	14	158	59.5
2B (28)	20	17	63	23	20	143	44.0
2C (30)	9	4	18	92	13	136	67.7
Total (of choices received)	148	141	111	128	58	588	

In 2B a change takes place. Their choices into 2E and 2A have the expected form but there is an unexpectedly large number of choices into 2C—23, more than into 2E or 2A. Similarly, the boys of 2C show a marked tendency to choose their friends outside 2C from 2B, rather than from 2E and 2A. There must be a basis, other than the school-imposed academic values, on which these friends are chosen. This alternative set of norms and values I have already referred to as the anti-group sub-culture.

Table 1.7 shows that, in the second year, academic achievement is related to social class. To some degree this is a problem of working-class and middle-class culture. That it is not the whole answer is demonstrated by reminding ourselves of Table 1.5, which shows clearly that anti-group development took place between the end of the first year and the end of the second. If it were solely a social class phenomenon, it would have been apparent at the end of the first year.

This analysis is confirmed by another set of data which are, in many ways, complementary to the first. The second-year questionnaire asked 'What boys do you find it difficult to get on with?' Once again, the subjects were allowed to give up to

Table 1.7 *Distribution of the sons of non-manual and manual workers between the four second-year streams*

Form	Non-manual-manual ratio	Ratio
2E	18:14	1.3
2A	18:13	1.4
2B	13:14	0.9
2C	8:23	0.3

six names unless they felt they could not possibly confine themselves to six. This time, however, many boys refrained from putting any names down and only a few put six. Enough names were mentioned to establish a pattern of unpopularity. Once again, the largest number of choices were made into the informants' own class (see Table 1.8). The number of choices into other forms was always less than seven, with

Table 1.8 *Distribution of choices of unpopular boys: second year, 1963*

Form	2E	2A	2B	2C	Others	Prefects	Total of choices made	Average number of choices received
2E	38	4	4	26	3	0	75	1.71
2A	5	33	1	9	22	1	51	1.45
2B	7	4	24	20	1	0	56	1.14
2C	3	4	3	42	3	6	61	3.23
Totals (of choices received)	53	45	32	97	29	7	243	

one notable exception: 2C received 26 from 2E, nine from 2A and 20 from 2B, so receiving the highest number of unpopularity choices—97 compared with 53 for 2E, the next highest.

The preponderance of choices into 2C is explained by the anti-group development in 2C. These boys are now regarded as bullies and 'tough eggs' who, in Badman's terminology, would rather be hooligans and have a good time than be nice little boys. They are aggressive, loud-mouthed and feared by many who are successful in terms of the dominant school norms.

An expectation that is altered by academic streaming is the school leaving age. Boys who are successful will expect to continue after O level at 15 or 16 into the sixth form. At the end of the first year the boys were asked 'At what age would you like to leave school?'

The results demonstrate the overall optimism of the first year. Only 25 per cent wanted to leave at the end of the fifth year, 75 per cent desiring a sixth-form career. In practice, only something like 50 per cent ever achieve this. When the figures are broken down into the second-year classes, they reveal, even so, considerable foresight (see Table 1.9).

Even the relatively low value of 2E compared with 2A is fairly realistic in that, since 2E take the GCE at the end of four years, compared with the normal five for 2A, 2B and 2C, many will expect to complete their sixth-form career at $17\frac{1}{2}$ compared with the normal $18\frac{1}{2}$. The fact that, at this stage in their school career, they had not been told officially that they would be going into 2E next year affects

Table 1.9 *Average age at which boys in each class would like to leave school*

Form	Before streaming at end of first year	After streaming at end of second year
2E	17.4	17.4
2A	17.7	17.3
2B	17.3	17.4
2C	17.0	16.7

the situation only marginally. By this time the process of structuring and differentiation had gone on long enough for most boys to know whether they would go into 2E or not. In the same questionnaire, 28 of the 32 boys who eventually went into 2E indicated that 2E was the second-year class of their choice.

By the end of the second year, the averages of the desired leaving ages revealed a number of puzzling features. 2E remained the same, while the average age for 2A fell below 2B. 2B's average, in fact, increased to the same level as 2E's; 2C's average value decreased, but not as much as one might expect. The situation has been complicated by an additional factor, which I call 'streaming reaction'.

When the top seven or eight boys from each first-year house group are put into 2E, it is obvious that most of them will not be able to maintain a high position there. In fact, Table 1.10 shows that only two were able to keep up their position; the rest

Table 1.10 *Examination performance before streaming compared with performance after streaming*

Form	Number of boys who were placed higher in second year than first year	Number of boys who maintained same place in second and first years	Number of boys who were placed lower in second year than in first year
2E	0	2	28
2A	7	4	16
2B	17	2	6
2C	15	0	2

were all placed lower than in their first-year classes. The tendency was not so marked in 2A, with only sixteen boys doing less well. It was reversed in 2B and 2C.

The depressing effect of streaming reaction on the Express form is unlikely to influence their estimates of the length of their school careers to any great extent, because all the E stream are expected to go into the sixth form and they are reminded of this constantly throughout the year. 'All of you will be expected to go on into the sixth form and *many* of you will, I hope, go on to university,' would be a typical remark. Streaming reaction is very pronounced in the E stream, but it takes a different form (see below).

2C is also affected by its polar position. It is not much to a boy's credit to have got a higher place in class if the class is 2C. Masters discussing 2C with me put it bluntly. 'There's not one boy in the class who has any sort of academic ability. In fact, most of them shouldn't be in the school at all. It's not fair on them and it's not fair on the school.' Similar comments were frequently made to me in front of the class and were obviously audible to the front rows of boys. Hence the low prestige of 2C minimised the correcting effects of streaming reaction with respect to leaving age.

It was in 2A and 2B that the reaction had its maximum effect. The relative positions of the two forms were for a long while ambiguous, since the Head had not made it clear.[10] Some masters thought 2A and 2B were on the same level, others that 2A was better than 2B. Only one thought 2B was academically better than 2A, but it is significant that he was able to make the mistake and persist in it for a considerable length of time. In these two classes, then, streaming reaction was a major factor in affecting the length of time the boys wanted to stay at school.

Another instance of 'streaming reaction' is shown in the personal assessment of success (Table 11.1). The boys were asked 'Do you consider that the past year at

Table 1.11 *Personal estimate of success in second year*

Form	Regarded the past year as a success	Couldn't say	Regarded the past year as unsuccessful
2E	19	1	11
2A	24	—	7
2B	21	—	7
2C	24	2	4
Totals	88	3	29

school has been a success?' The difference between 2A and 2B is not significant, but the difference between 2E and 2C is—especially when one considers the way the staff assess the 'success' of the two forms in tackling academic tasks. The difference can be accounted for only by the past experience of the two groups, the different sets of standards they have acquired and the way in which their new experiences measure up to those standards. This view is confirmed by an analysis of the experience of the eleven boys who regarded themselves as unsuccessful in 2E. On average, they dropped sixteen places in their second-year examinations compared with their first-year ones. The rest of the class dropped eight places on average. During the year two of these boys had been considerably disturbed emotionally, crying in lessons, crying before school and refusing to come to school. A third went through a similar period and his father wrote to the school complaining that 'the boy is utterly demoralised'. The only other category of boys to yield so large a number of disturbed cases in the second year was the bottom of 2C!

Finally, Table 1.12 shows another area of activity that is affected by streaming. The boys were asked to estimate the average amount of time they spent on homework each evening. Streaming gave rise to distinctly different climates: 2E estimated spending almost twice as much time on their homework as 2C. Although there is considerable overlap in the estimates given by individual boys in the four

Table 1.12 *Estimated length of time spent on homework before and after streaming*

Form	Estimated average time spent each night: first year	Estimated average time spent each night after streaming: second year
2E	1 hour 3 minutes	2 hours 0 minutes
2A	1 hour 4 minutes	1 hour 43 minutes
2B	1 hour 10 minutes	1 hour 18 minutes
2C	1 hour 1 minute	1 hour 7 minutes

classes (which, of course, deserves further analysis), the table does give a convincing demonstration of another aspect of the process of differentiation.

The third and fourth years
The study of the continuation of these processes in the third, fourth and fifth years could not be conducted in the same way. The school changed its policy with respect to streaming in 1964, so that although the E stream continued unchanged into 3E and 4E, the others were reorganised into sets. This meant that at the end of the second year 2A, 2B and 2C disappeared and the pupils were re-sorted into three unstreamed classes, 3P, 3Q and 3R. The new groups stayed together for some of the major academic subjects but were 'set' for a number of subjects that entailed specialisation or were difficult to teach to groups of mixed ability. The specialised options meant that pupils from all three classes could choose, or were directed to, various subjects. For example, they were able to take metalwork, physics or music, but not two of the three.

The second type of setting meant that pupils were sorted according to academic ability into 'sets' that came into being for that subject only, e.g. mathematics. Both types of set cross-cut the unstreamed classes P, Q and R, so that no one grouping contained the same pupils for more than a fraction of the timetable. The intense interaction restricted to a group of thirty boys, all with similar academic (and frequently social) characteristics and faced with similar problems by the school system, which had been the major feature of the old system, no longer existed. At this stage in the study it was impossible to launch the intensive period of field work that would have been required to tease out the effects of the reorganisation.[11]

The tables presented here are, therefore, constructed with the aim of showing how the processes described in the first and second years continue into the third and fourth. The change of organisation mentioned above makes the interpretation of the tables difficult, and they are given in an abbreviated form. More detailed analysis of these two years has had to be restricted to the E stream alone.

Table 1.13 *Distribution of friendship choices according to school class, third year, 1964 (1962 intake, end of third year)*

No.	Form	3E	3P	3Q	3R	Others	Total
30	3E	88	8	13	14	9	132
30	3P	14	67	29	27	12	149
27	3Q	13(14.4)	28(31.1)	76(84.5)	21(23.2)	2(2.2)	140(155.4)
27	3R	9(10)	14(15.6)	13(14.5)	82(91.1)	14(15.6)	132(146.8)
		124	117	131	144		

Note: numbers in brackets are corrected for number of pupils in the class; standard used 30 pupils/class.

Table 1.14 *Distribution of friendship choices, as in Table 1.13: Class numbers standardised at 30 and percentaged*

Form	3E	3P	3Q	3R	Other	Total
3E	66.5	6.0	9.8	11.0	6.8	100.1
3P	9.4	45.5	19.5	18.0	8.1	100.0
3Q	9.3	20.0	54.5	15.0	1.4	100.2
3R	6.8	10.6	9.9	62.2	10.6	100.1
	92.0	82.1	93.7	106.2		

As expected, the choices made between 3P, 3Q and 3R were more numerous than those between 3E and 3P, 3Q and 3R. The 'setting' of 3P, 3Q and 3R meant that the chance of meeting and maintaining old second-year friends in subject sets was quite high. In addition, the formation of 3P, 3Q and 3R was more recent than the formation of 3E.

The proportions of choices made by pupils of classes 3P, 3Q and 3R into 3P, 3Q and 3R, discounting the choices made into their own classes, are: 19.5 per cent, 18.0 per cent, 20 per cent, 15 per cent, 10.6 per cent and 9.9 per cent. The average proportion, 15.5 per cent is much higher than the average proportion of choices made by 3P, 3Q and 3R into 3E and vice versa—8.7 per cent. This is a dramatic reversal of the situation in the second year, when connections with 2E were more numerous (14 compared with 17.3).

There is evidence that the reversal was brought about by factors additional to those mentioned above. For example, the overall popularity of the E stream has also declined dramatically (see Table 1.15).

Evidence from informal interviews, questionnaires and direct observation confirms the hypothesis that the reversal has a secondary cause in the spread of

Table 1.15 *Average number of friendship choices received per boy in each third-year class, 1962 intake*

3E	4.1
3P	3.9
3Q	4.9
3R	5.3

elements of what has been termed the adolescent sub-culture. By the middle of the third year,[12] a large minority of boys in 3R had extended their activities from collecting pop records to sporting Beatle haircuts and attending coffee bars and dance clubs in the town centre at night. 'Adolescent culture' and 'pop culture' activities spread through the year group from this nucleus and a similar group in 3Q, and was more markedly associated with anti-group pupils than with pro-school pupils.[13] 3P and 3E were the last forms affected. Even by the end of the third year, only a small number of 3E and 3P boys could be termed sophisticated or fully initiated into the culture. By the fourth year, most of the boys could be termed relatively sophisticated and even those who did not attend the 'hard core' coffee bars and dance clubs in town went to youth clubs or held record sessions, where they kept in touch with the latest developments in fashion, music and style.

The figures for the fourth year confirm this analysis, but point to a slight modification of the situation due to the much wider dispersion of the sub-culture

Table 1.16 *Average number of friendship choices received per boy in each fourth-year class, 1962 intake*

4E	4.6
4P	3.7
4Q	4.6
4R	5.0

(see Table 1.16). However, it is important to note that, although in the third year the spread of adolescent culture mores and activities modifies the effects of differentiation and polarisation, it is a *modification* and of fairly recent origin.[14] It represents a sphere of activity which has its centre of gravity outside the school and is free of school domination. Those that are least successful within the school are most attracted to it. [. . .]

Notes

[1] All the records from junior schools of the 1962 intake were burned in a fire in March 1963 which practically gutted the school office. At this time I had recorded notes for about half of them.

[2] Isolation in the sense that they are strangers to each other. They have shared no common experience and at this stage do not trust each other. For an extreme example of isolation caused by lack of trust and an uncertain external situation, see Pons, V. *Social Relations Among Captive Civilians in Kisangani* (forthcoming).

[3] The pattern holds good for other lessons I observed in this class. However, I do not wish to imply that such a relationship between seating, class position and interaction is typical of the school as a whole. Other classes had different patterns.

[4] There was a large minority of Jewish boys at the school—about one-ninth of the school population.

[5] Skills developed at one stage in the process—say junior school—are not necessarily appropriate at later stages.

[6] Thorndike, E. L. 'Constant error in psychological ratings', *Journal of Applied Psychology*, 1920, pp. 24–29. Thorndike refers to this phenomenon as the 'halo effect'. [See also:] Wickman, E. K. (1928) *Children's Behaviour and Teachers' Attitudes*, the Commonwealth Fund, New York, p. 52: 'It is likely that a teacher's unfavourable impression of a pupil provoked by a single kind of distressing behaviour, would cause her to rate the child more rigidly on the other items of troublesome behaviour than she would another child concerning whom she had formed a favourable impression.'

[7] For a fuller exposition of this argument specifically related to delinquency, see Cohen, A. (1955), *Delinquent Boys: The Culture of the Gang*, Free Press, New York.

[9] Jackson, E. E. (1962) 'Status consistency and symptoms of stress', American Sociological Review Vol. 27, No. 4, p. 469. Jackson finds that 'status inconsistency' (as measured on three ranks—education, occupation and race) is associated with symptoms of stress. The stress symptoms listed above refer to change in status over time rather than ongoing status inconsistency. However, there is an important similarity in the situations. The unsuccessful first year pupil experiences 'status inconsistency' in the sense that his internalised status (from 'best pupil' role at junior school) is not consistent with his new status at the grammar school.

[10] At the end of the first year there was a change of headmasters. The ambiguity existed for longer than would normally have been the case owing to the administrative disruption this caused.

[11] Data have been collected but they must await the chance of a second period of fieldwork and the development of new techniques.

[12] In the second year, only two or three boys had been to coffee bars and these were not regular visits.

[13] See Sugarman, B. (1967), 'Involvement in youth culture, academic achievement, and conformity in school', British Journal of Sociology, Vol. XVIII, No. 2.

[14] When I started the study at Hightown Grammar School, many of the activities now common in the fourth year were confined to relatively small groups in the fifth and sixth forms. Club-going and many of the attitudes that go with it were new phenomena which spread down the school to the fourth and third years.

Banding, identity and experience

S. BALL

[. . .] The banding system was introduced at Beachside in the first-year intake of 1969 to replace 'fine streaming'[1] This cohort and each subsequent first year, until 1973, were divided into three broad bands of ability. In the second-year cohort with which we are concerned, there are ten forms in all; band 1 consists of four parallel forms; band 2 also of four parallel forms; and band 3 of two forms, one of which is designated as remedial. The forms are all labelled and referred to by initials taken from the names of their teachers; 2FT being the band 1 form of Miss Foot, 2MA the remedial band 3 form of Mrs Mather, etc. Each form is timetabled separately for academic subjects, with the exception of Mathematics which is 'set' within the bands. There is grouping within the bands between forms for Games and Technical subjects.

The most important consequence of the introduction of the system of banding, as far as the teachers were concerned, was the emergence of problems of discipline and control in band 2 lessons. The headmaster explained in an inverview that the replacement of streaming with banding had brought about a considerable increase in misbehaviour and disruption of lessons by pupils.

> 'It took only one year to become aware of the second band mentality in the middle band, with a very low level of participation and involvement in the activities of the school. There even seemed to be more rejection in the middle bands than there was in the middle streams previously.'

The band 2 forms represented for the staff what one teacher described as a 'behavioural and disciplinary blackspot'. There were few teachers taking band 2 forms who did not report to me at one time or another the difficulties of 'order and control' that they had. Thus, in the banding system it is not the pupils at the very 'bottom', the band 3 forms, that present most problems to teachers, as is the case with streaming. Although some band 3 pupils were difficult to control, the teachers suggested that these forms in general were more docile and more easily manageable than band 2 forms.[2] The misbehaviour of the band 3 pupils tended to be defined and dealt with by teachers in terms of emotional problems of maladjustment, rather than as belligerence[3] Band 2 pupils, on the other hand, were frequently 'in trouble' in lessons or around the school; band 2 forms were often 'kept in' by their teachers and particular pupils were 'sent' to the deputy headmaster on many occasions. Some impression of the amount of 'trouble' that the band 2 pupils got into, and the differences between the bands in getting into trouble, can be gained from the analysis of the detention book presented in Tables 2.1–2.3,[4] although the record of detentions was only begun after I had been at the school for two terms. Table 2.1 shows the detention record of the cohort prior to the one with which we are primarily concerned, but the pattern of differences between band 1 and band 2 forms is equally marked. As we shall see, the number of detentions recorded per pupil is roughly equivalent to the number received by the case-study cohort in their third year. Third-year forms were normally considered to be the most difficult to control. The differences between the bands are very clear in both years (see Tables 2.2 and 2.3), the band 2 forms receiving significantly more detentions than band 1. In the 1973–4 statistics, third-year band 2 forms receive 65 per cent of all third-year detentions, and the second-year band 2 forms receive 85 per cent of all second-year

Table 2.1 *Third-year forms. Detention record 1973–4*

		No. of detentions	No. of pupils in the form	Detentions per pupil
Band 1	3CF	24	31	0.77
	3AG	5	34	0.15
	3WK	0	33	0.00
Band 2	3DI	128	33	3.88
	3FH	76	34	2.24
	3PQ	155	34	4.56
Band 3	3LO (remedial)	38	12	3.17
	3RE	125	10	12.50

detentions; in the 1974–5 statistics, the band 2 forms receive 76 per cent of all detentions. There is also a clear difference in each case between the ordinary band 3 and the remedial band 3 forms in the number of detention received. A further indication of differences in being 'in trouble' between bands, at a much less serious level, is in the frequency of rebukes by teachers in lessons. In a small proportion of the lessons I observed I made use of the Flanders interaction-analysis grid[5]. A mark

Table 2.2 *Second-year forms. Detention record 1973–4*

Band 1	2CU	13	32	0.41
	2FT	2	35	0.06
	2ST	9	33	0.27
	2GD	2	34	0.06
Band 2	2WX	39	33	1.18
	2BH	19	35	0.54
	2TA	108	33	3.27
	2LF	31	35	0.89
Band 3	2UD	8	18	0.44
	2MA (remedial)	2	14	0.14

Table 2.3 *Third-year forms. Detentions recorded 1974–5*

	Third year	1st half-term	2nd half-term	3rd half-term	4th half-term	5th half-term	Total	No. of detentions per pupil
Band 1	3CU	6	1	0	2	13	22	0.69
	3FT	0	0	0	4	2	6	0.17
	3ST	1	3	0	5	0	9	0.27
	3GD	3	1	0	0	5	9	0.27
Band 2	3WX	15	42	33	60	35	185	5.61
	3BH	8	35	25	40	17	125	3.57
	3TA	6	35	51	1	17	110	3.33
	3LF	25	32	31	36	27	141	4.03
Band 3	3MA (remedial)	3	0	1	5	4	13	0.93
	3UD	6	39	6	18	49	118	6.56

is made on the grid, in the appropriate category, at frequent and regular intervals during the process of a lesson to record the communication events just completed. Even in this small sample of twenty-four lessons, a clear difference between bands emerged in the proportion of the teachers' time spent in 'criticizing or justifying authority'. In band 1 forms, only 1.5 per cent of lesson time was spent in such justification, whereas in band 2 forms it occupied 12.5 per cent of lesson time—a figure which suggests that a great deal more time in band 2 lessons is devoted to the maintenance of discipline.

The selection of two forms

The selection of the two forms on which I based my detailed examination of band 1 and band 2 was made primarily on the basis of convenience and availability. There was a minimum of clash between the timetables of the two forms, so that the same subjects were not always being taught at the same time; and both of the form teachers were very willing to co-operate with me.[6] Both of the banded forms I chose appeared to be generally typical of their band, although every school form is always in some way unique. I have attempted to make clear in my analysis those ways in which these forms were unusual or different from the rest of the band.

Once I had decided upon these forms I began to 'follow' them. I observed as many of their lessons as possible, as regularly as possible; I called into their form rooms at lunch and break-time, and spoke to them in corridors. Generally, I tried to get to know the pupils, and once I had established a rapport I began to interview individuals, and to talk about them to their teachers and the pastoral staff. I was also given access to their school files and records. Later in the year some of the pupils began to keep diaries for me, and during the summer holidays I was able to meet some of them in the town and on the beach. The two forms I chose were 2TA and 2CU.

2CU was the band 1 form of Mrs Culliford and 2TA the band 2 form of Mrs Tanner. From the very beginning of observation these forms appeared very different from each other in their work-performance and their behaviour in lessons. The general conduct of their lessons by the teachers was also very different. Teachers found 2CU generally easy to control, each 'to teach', co-operative, lively (in the positive sense in which teachers used the word), enthusiastic, and interested. On the other hand, 2TA were described as difficult to control, difficult to teach and to get to work, unco-operative, lively (in the negative sense in which teachers used the word), dull and uninterested. In each case these descriptions were typical of the band as a whole. My observations in other band 1 and 2 lessons demonstrated a similarity between all the band 1 forms and all the band 2 forms in terms of attitude, behaviour and teacher-pupil relationships.[7]

The lessons of 2CU were usually dominated by the teacher, who was the central focus of activity in the classroom; the form listened quietly when their teacher spoke, responding when required, in an appropriate manner (by putting up their hand and thus acknowledging the teacher's right to call upon them, or not, to make a contribution). In many lessons it was possible to hold 'class discussions', where members of the form and the teacher were able to exchange views or ideas with the attention of the rest of the form. That is to say, activity in 2CU lessons was invariably 'task-oriented', directed towards some end, or involving some endeavour, defined as appropriate by the teacher.

The lessons of 2TA differed from this in many ways; the level of noise was normally higher than in band 1 lessons, except when disciplinary threats were used or in lessons with a 'strict' teacher.[8] The teacher's position as the central focus of activity was a great deal more tenuous and problematic. Individually or in groups, pupils would attempt to diverge from the task-activity of the lesson or actually to challenge the teacher as focus of the lesson. Outbreaks of non-task-oriented behaviour, defined as inappropriate by the teacher, were frequent, and it would typically be necessary for the teacher to re-establish the receptivity of the form as a whole or of particular groups of pupils many times during a lesson. Their lessons were slow getting under way and difficult to organize. This may be seen from the following transcript and notes of a 2TA English lesson:

2TA English with Mrs Bradley: lesson notes
The pupils are arriving singly or in small groups while the teacher waits. The time between the first arrival and the last is over four minutes. While the teacher waits for the last arrivals to sit down, the noise being made by the form is considerable. Corina Newnes is the last to come in.
Teacher 'Where have you been?'
Corina 'Mr Dawson kept me behind.'
Teacher 'What for?'
Corina 'To talk to me.'
Teacher 'Well, this is my lesson now. You should be on time.'
Corina sits down, the teacher addresses the whole class.
Teacher 'All right, let's have some quiet.'
This is shouted over the noise of the class; the teacher is standing at the front of the room with one hand on her hip; she looks displeased. '2TA,' she shouts more loudly; the noise is considerably reduced. 'Peter, I am waiting for you. [To the whole class] I told you last week that I wanted you here on time. It is nearly ten minutes gone now. If it happens next week . . . Peter, I've told you once, what did I just say?'
Peter 'If it happens next week.'
Teacher 'Right, now stop talking to Sammy and listen to me . . . if it happens next week we will stay behind at four o'clock to make up the time we've lost.'
Two of the girls at the back are talking and writing on a small book.
Teacher 'Dorothy, bring your books and sit here.' The teacher indicates the empty desk at the front, next to one of the boys.
Dorothy 'You moved me last week.'
Teacher 'Well, I'm moving you again, come on.'
Grudgingly, Dorothy gets up, making her chair scrape noisily on the wooden floor, and picks up her books slowly; she goes to the front and stands behind the empty desk.
Dorothy 'Ugh, I'm not sitting next to him.'
She gestures at Wally who is sitting next to the empty desk; several of the class laugh and the teacher looks angrily around the room; her gaze returns to Dorothy.
Teacher 'You sit where I tell you.'
Dorothy 'Not next to him.'
She pulls the empty desk away from Wally's until there is a six-inch gap, and sits down. The teacher seems to be about to say something to her and then changes her mind; she picks up a book from her desk instead.
Teacher 'We began last week to look at . . .'

Teachers found it almost impossible to organize discussions in 2TA lessons, and even question and answer sessions tended to deteriorate into noisy shouted responses. Few members of the form would listen to their fellows' contributions, and many pupils took such opportunities to talk amongst themselves or to 'muck about'. In some lessons with young and inexperienced teachers, 2TA could get completely beyond control. In extreme cases the pupils would run around the classroom virtually ignoring the teacher's rebukes or threats or attempts to 'teach'. The maintenance of quiet and keeping the pupils working involved special effort in 2TA's lessons.

2TA Biology with Mr Kramer: lesson notes
The pupils are working individually on answering questions written on the board; the teacher is going round the room to look at books and answer queries. As he pauses at each bench to look at the pupils' work he looks round the room to check that all is well; at frequent intervals during his talk with the pupils his head pops up and down like a gopher from a hole, to recheck the class.

Teacher 'Wally, get on.'
He looks down, up again.
Teacher 'Jim, your own book. Belinda, you too.'
Down again and up.
Teacher 'Come on, you three, on your own, please.'
Down again and up, and down and up again.
Teacher 'Put that scarf away, Nigel, do I have to separate you three?'
He stares at them for a second or two.
Teacher 'Are you eating, Max?'
The boy nods.
Teacher 'Put it in the bin.'
Max 'Can't I swallow it?'
Teacher 'No, in the bin. Are you eating as well, Peter?'
Peter No, sir.'
Teacher 'All right, get on. What's wrong with you, Dorothy?'
Dorothy 'I want you to see my work.'
Teacher 'All right, I will be there in a second. I think you can get on without talking, Kathy.'

The lesson continues with the constant barrage of comment and rebuke from the teacher which keeps down the non-task oriented behaviour to a low level.

These two extracts from observation notes may be contrasted with the notes made from observation of a typical 2CU lesson, in this case Chemistry. Here the teacher's talk is exclusively concerned with the subject matter of the lesson, and there is not a single instance of 'criticizing or justifying authority'.

2CU Chemistry with Mr Baldwin: lesson notes
The lesson begins with twenty minutes of 'administration-talk' from the teacher. Books are returned and he comments on the homework, on writing up experiments, especially the method, and he explains the rationale of the marking. 'So if you got a bad mark for this homework it was not necessarily because the experiment or your conclusion were wrong, but that it was not written up correctly.'
  The form is silent and attentive throughout the whole of this time. The teacher now begins some experiments with CO_2 to show its qualities as a fire extinquisher; the form is gathered round the bench at the front but are orderly, without pushing one another or talking. The teacher asks questions as he goes along, hands are raised, he chooses a respondent and the rest of the form listens to the answer given.
Teacher 'Why wouldn't I use water in this case?' He looks up. 'Chris . . .'
The lesson ends with the writing up of what was seen; the bell goes, but the class continues to work as if nothing had happened.
Teacher 'Off you go when you are ready.'
The pupils leave in ones or twos. Several remain for more than five minutes of their break-time to finish writing.

Band identities

It is clear from these transcripts that there are stark differences between the classroom behaviour of the two forms as they were in the second year. But I want to look back now at these forms as they were in the first year, in order to illustrate the changes in the pupils' behaviour between the first and second years. This is necessarily a retrospective view, as I began my study at Beachside in the same year as the new first-year cohort became mixed ability. In order to study the band system it was therefore necessary to choose second-year forms.

It is important first of all to look at the way in which the pupils are allocated to their bands in the first year. This takes place on the basis of the reports and recommendations of the primary school teachers and headmasters of the four schools that provide Beachside with pupils. Almost all of the pupils who enter the first year at Beachside come from the four 'feeder' primary schools within the community: North Beachside, South Beachside, Iron Road and Sortham. In the cohort with which we are concerned here, the original distribution by school and allocation to bands is as presented in Table 2.4 below. There is no significant relationship between primary school of origin and the allocation to bands. The process of negotiation of recommendations and allocation to bands was done by the senior mistress at Beachside. Where the numbers of pupils recommended for band 1 was too large, the primary headmasters were asked to revise their recommendations until an acceptable distribution of pupils in each band was obtained. When they arrived at the secondary school, the pupils went immediately into their banded classes.

> 'The primary school heads sent us lists with their recommendations for band 1, band 2 and band 3; it was up to us to try and fit them into classes. If there were too many in the one band, then we had to go back to the primary heads to ask if all the list was really band 1 material and that way the bands were allocated and then they were broken into classes alphabetically. There was a lot of movement between the classes at the end of the first term, but very little movement between bands.'
> (Senior mistress)

Thus Beachside carried out no tests of its own; the primary schools acted as selecting institutions, and Beachside, initially at least, as the passive implementer of selection. Three of the four primary schools did make use of test scores in the decision to recommend pupils for bands, and these were passed on to Beachside on the pupils' record cards, but these test scores were not the sole basis upon which recommendations were made. Teachers' reports were also taken into account.

Banding and social class

The possibility of biases in teachers' recommendations as a means of allocating pupils to secondary school has been demonstrated in several studies. For instance, both Floud and Halsey (1957) and Douglas (1964) have shown that social class can be an influential factor in teachers' estimates of the abilities of their pupils. The covariance of social class and 'tested ability' in this case is examined below.

The practice adopted by the majority of social researchers has been followed here, in taking the occupation of the father (or head of household) as the principal

Table 2.4 *Allocation of pupils to bands according to primary school*

	S. Beachside	N. Beachside	Iron Road	Sortham	Others	Total
Band 1	33	36	37	11	4	121
Band 2	32	16	52	13	4	117
Band 3	17	7	15	4	4	47
Total	82(29%)	59(21%)	104(36%)	28(10%)	12(4%)	285(100%)

Table 2.5 *Distribution of social classes across the case-study forms 2TA and 2CU*

	I	II	IIIN	Total non-manual	IIIM	IV	V	Total manual	Unclass
2CU	5	10	5	20	12	—	—	12	—
2TA	2	3	2	7	15	8	3	26	—

indicator of pupils' social class background. Although this is not an entirely satisfactory way of measuring social class, the bulk of previous research seems to indicate that, in the majority of cases, the broad classification of occupations into manual and non-manual does correspond to the conventional social categories—middle-class and working-class. For the sake of convenience, I have adopted these social class categories when describing the data of this study.[9] [. . .]

[. . .] It was not surprising [. . .] to find that, as analysis in other schools has shown, there is a significant relationship between banding and social class. If the Registrar General's Classification of Occupations is reduced to a straightforward manual/non-manual social class dichotomy for the occupations of the parents of the pupils, then the distribution of social classes in 2TA and 2CU, the case-study forms, is as shown in table 2.5. There are 20 children from non-manual families in 2CU compared with 7 in 2TA, and 12 from manual families in 2CU compared with 26 in 2TA. This is a considerable over-representation of non-manual children in 2CU; a similar over-representation was found in all the band 1 classes across this cohort and in previous banded cohorts.[10] Thus on the basis of reports from junior schools, the tendency is for the children of middle-class non-manual families to be allocated to band 1 forms, whereas children from manual working-class homes are more likely to be allocated to bands 2 or 3.

[. . .] One of the main platforms of comprehensive reorganization has been that the comprehensive school will provide greater equality of opportunity for those with equal talent. Ford (1969) suggests that the most obvious way of testing whether this is true is 'by the analysis of the interaction of social class and measured intelligence as determinants of academic attainment'. If the impact of social class on educational attainment is greater than can be explained by the covariation of class and I.Q., then the notion of an equality of opportunity must be called into question.

There were no standard I.Q. tests available for the pupils at Beachside,[11] but, as noted above, three of the four 'feeder' primary schools did test their pupils. There was a great variety of tests used, for reading age, reading comprehension, arithmetic and mathematics. Each pupil's record card noted a selection of these test-scores, but only in a few cases were results available for the whole range of tests.

The clearest picture of the interaction between social class, test-scores and band allocation was obtained by comparing pupils who scored at different levels. Taking N.F.E.R. Reading Comprehension and N.F.E.R. Mathematics, the covariation of social class and test-scores within band 1 and band 2 is shown in Table 2.6 and 2.7. By extracting the 100–114 test-score groups the relationship between social class and band allocation may be tested. This suggests a relationship between banding and social class at levels of similar ability. Taking the Mathematics tests-scores, there is also a significant relationship. Altogether, the evidence of these test-scores concerning selection for banding was far from conclusive; the result is to some extent dependent upon which test is used. It is clear, however, that social class is significant, and that ability measured by test-score does not totally explain the allocation to bands. This falls into line with the findings of Ford (1969) and others that selection on the basis of streaming in the comprehensive school, like selection under the tripartite system, tends to underline social class differentials in

Table 2.6 *Banding allocation and social class, using the N.F.E.R. Reading Comprehension Test*

	Band 1		Band 2	
Test-score	Working-class	Middle-class	Working-class	Middle-class
115 and over	3	7	1	0
100–114	10	12	16	2
1–99	5	1	24	5
	18	20	41	7

N.F.E.R. Reading Comprehension Test (scores 100–114)

	Working-class	Middle-class
Band 1	10	12
Band 2	16	2

$X^2 = 8.2$ d.f. = $p < 0.01$. $C = 0.41$.

Table 2.7 *Banding allocation and social class, using the N.F.E.R. Mathematics Test*

	Band 1		Band 2	
Test-score	Working-class	Middle-class	Working-class	Middle-class
115 and over	5	8	0	0
100–114	15	13	15	3
1–99	1	0	25	1
	21	21	40	4

N.F.E.R. Mathematics Test (scores 100–114)

	Working-class	Middle-class
Band 1	15	13
Band 2	15	3

$X^2 = 4.28$ d.f. = 1 $p < 0.05$. $C = 0.29$.

educational opportunity. However, my work with these results also suggests that, to some extent at least, findings concerning the relationships between test-performance and social class must be regarded as an artefact of the nature of the tests employed, and thus the researcher must be careful what he makes of them [. . .]

Banding and band stereotypes

[. . .] The fact that the pupils came to the secondary school pre-selected, sorted out into bands, may have been important in making the allocation 'real' to the Beachside teachers. As the band allocation of the pupils was a 'given', a label imposed from outside prior to any contact with the pupils, the teachers were 'taking', and deriving assumptions on the basis of, that label, rather than 'making' their own evaluation of the relative abilities of individual pupils.[12] Each band-label carries its own particular status within the school and the staff hold preconceived and institutionalized notions about the typical 'band 2 child', the 'remedial child', etc. To a great extent these typifications are based on what the teacher knows about the bands in terms of their status identity. From the teacher's point of view the behaviour of band 2 forms is 'deviant', contravening their expectations of appropriate classroom behaviour These labels are consistent and embedded aspects of the system of meanings shared by all the teachers, and are not dependent upon the identification of particular forms or pupils. Once established, the typification 'band 2 form' or 'band 2 pupil' merely awaits the arrival of each new cohort in the school. I am not suggesting that the 'label' of being band 2 in itself creates a 'deviant' identity and is the cause of the 'deviant' acts described previously. But the label of being band 2 imposes certain limitations upon the sort of social identity that may be negotiated by the band 2 pupil. When persons are subjected to a process of categorization, they are subject also to the imputation of various social identities by virtue of their membership of that category. In this case, it is an identity that involves a status-evaluation and allocation to an inferior position in the status-hierarchy of the school. Band 2 forms, as we shall see, are considered to be 'not up to much academically' and most teachers find them 'unrewarding' to teach. Certainly, by the beginning of the second year in the careers of the case-study forms, it is a label that denotes a behavioural stereotype. The teachers hold stereotypical images of band identity (which I shall refer to as the 'bandness' of pupils). That is, they tend to jump from a single cue or a small number of cues in actual, suspected or alleged behaviour, to a general picture of the 'kind of person with whom one is dealing'.

In one sense, stereotyping may be understood quite straightforwardly in terms of the demands of a complex interaction situation. The classroom involves one individual interacting in various ways with 35 other individuals, and stereotyping may be necessary for the teacher to be able to order his expectations of, and thus predict the actions of, the pupils.[13] The reality of everyday life commonly involves stereotyping in terms of which others are 'dealt with'. That is, people apprehend others through patterns built up from previous experiences. But in regard to individual pupils in the banded classroom, stereotyping by the teacher may also be considered as a reaction that is based upon a selective perception or incorrect assessment of pupils, derived from preconceived notions of band behaviour. In their attempts to make sense of, and derive meaning from, social situations, people tend to organize data about other people in their environment. They tend to do so by making interpretations and inferences from what they 'know' and what they can see in front of them. Once such interpretations and inferences are made, further information is sought to confirm and strengthen them, and contradictory information tends to be overlooked.

The normal way of discussing pupils among the staff was in terms of singular and unitary characteristics, categorical identification that tended to become a pejorative label. Thus, with regard to projects:

> 'the band 1 child, who is intelligent, loves doing projects but the lower-band child will just copy chunks out of a book and cover about four sides.'
> (English teacher)

The band 1 child is 'intelligent' and by implication here the band 2 child is not. Yet the discrimination between band 1 and band 2 in the original allocation of pupils makes no such distinction; these differentiating perceptions are socially constructed. The original sum-variable basis of allocation to bands, recommendations made by the primary school indicating pupils of more or less ability, is here transformed into a zero-sum perception: band 1 pupils have ability; band 2 pupils do not. Cohen (1972, p. 12) makes the point that

> Society labels rule breakers as belonging to certain deviant groups and, once the person is thus typecast, his acts are interpreted in terms of the status to which he has been assigned.

In this way the band stereotypes were an important aspect of the shared meanings of the staff in their perceptions of and interactions with pupils. As Cohen indicates, 'the deviant or delinquent is always portrayed as a certain type'. As labels, the stereotypes of band identity provide a framework within which the pupil must negotiate his social identity in the school. Thus the band to which he is allocated is an important constraint upon the range of possible social identities available to him. For example, 'brilliant pupil' is an identity that is not normally available to the 'band 2 pupil' because of the sorts of notions that accompany that label. However, [. . .] there is still the possibility that *some* pupils may negotiate identities that supersede these constraints, at least in the early stages of their band career.

The framework of identities which derive from the band-labels can be seen in the following composite band-profiles, constructed from teachers' descriptions. These are the stereotypical notions that the teachers hold about the bands. As such they are also situational-expectations, that is, expectations about 'what this form is going to be like'. These stereotypes are constraints which the teacher brings into the classroom and with which the pupil has to deal.

The band 1 child
'Has academic potential . . . will do O-levels . . . and a good number will stay on to the sixth form . . . likes doing projects . . . knows what the teacher wants . . . is bright, alert and enthusiastic . . . can concentrate . . . produces neat work . . . is interested . . . wants to get on . . . is grammar school material . . . you can have discussions with . . . friendly . . . rewarding . . . has common sense.'

The band 2 child
'Is not interested in school work . . . difficult to control . . . rowdy and lazy . . . has little self control . . . is immature . . . loses and forgets books with monotonous regularity . . . cannot take part in discussions . . . is moody . . . of low standard . . . technical inability . . . lacks concentration . . . is poorly behaved . . . not up to much academically.'

The band 3 child
'Is unfortunate . . . is low ability . . . maladjusted . . . anti-school . . . lacks a mature view of education . . . mentally retarded . . . emotionally unstable and . . . a waste of time.'

It is apparent that by the beginning of the second year the majority of the teachers 'see', that is make sense of, the classroom in terms of these preconceived notions. They act as a 'filter' upon the teacher's perceptions of the pupils. And yet they derive from a fairly arbitrary line of demarcation between pupils; the importance of these stereotypes is perhaps best seen in terms of the borderline child who would be differently perceived in each band according to the point at which the allocation line is drawn. Keddie (1971, p. 139) also makes the point that 'what a techer knows about pupils derives from the organisational device of banding or streaming'.

Maddock (1977, p. 575) takes this even further. From a study of the relationship between streaming and pupils' identitites in an Australian High School, he concludes that

> Teachers conventionally typify pupils by locating them somewhere along the academic/non-academic continuum. On the basis of an assumed hierarchy of pupils, ordered according to their ability to handle 'academic work', various forms of knowledge, or various approaches to what is supposed to be a common body of

knowledge are presented to pupils or, more precisely, to groups or categories of pupils .
. . High School streams, with a differentiated distribution of school knowledge, have
given rise to sub-worlds within the total reality of the school. Within these sub-worlds,
the pupils tend to identify themselves, and are identified by others, as academic or non-
academic types.

I want to emphasize that I am not arguing that the method of grouping pupils
absolutely determines their level of academic achievement or their behaviour.
Clearly, one view of the banding is that it merely mirrors the real differences
between pupils in terms of ability and behaviour and thus reproduces and describes
an empirical reality. From this perspective the processes described here can be said
to represent the inevitable playing out of those differences. Inasmuch as the
differences between pupils are related to processes of categorization at work in the
primary school, it should not be unexpected that teachers in the secondary school
also find these typifications of relevance to them.[14]

But the fact remains that the estimated potential of the 2TA pupils based on the
reports from their junior schools, which led to their being allocated to band 2, was
such as to label them 'failures' in a system that had not given them the opportunity
to show their worth (despite the rhetoric of equality of opportunity). This system
required them to respect it and to accept from it values which stressed the
importance of hard work, enthusiasm, good behaviour and academic striving—even
though, by assigning them to band 2, the system had assumed and accepted that
they would be lacking in these qualitites. Whereas it was suggested to the children
that they were placed in band 2 so that they could be given work more suited to their
abilities, what actually happened (in an institution whose staff were working
towards the achievement of fairly specific educational attainments that these
children were not expected to be able to obtain or even to attempt) was that the
teachers simply expected them to be pupils of low, second-rate ability. As one
Human Studies teacher put it, 'Band 2 lessons are essentially dull for both teachers
and pupils.' For these children, their secondary school careers had begun with a
decision which meant that they were to strive for rewards in a race from which they
had already been disqualified. But despite this they were to try their hardest to run
as fast as the winners, and expect to be punished if they did not keep to the rules.[15]

The teachers' own descriptions of the early behaviour of 2TA show that the form
did not appear initially to conform to the stereotypes applied to them. During their
first term at the school, known then as 1TA, the form was described to me, by the
teachers most closely involved with them, their form teacher and year tutor, in
these terms:

'The promise was there, they were keen and enthusiastic school boys and girls, running
to lessons; worried about work. But towards the end of the first year some of the girls
were beginning to put their eyes on boys higher up the school.'
(Year tutor)

'They were delightful, for the first six months they were one of the forms that
everyone talked about as being lively and enthusiastic. Then the rot set in and they
began to assert themselves as individuals and they began to lose their form identity.'
(Form teacher)

By the second and third terms 1TA had already begun to demonstrate an
unwillingness to accept the authority of their teachers and to indulge in behaviour,
both inside and outside school, that involved them more and more frequently being
punished or reprimanded. Their reputation as a 'problem' form began to develop
from this time on.

Banding, behaviour and attitudes

Some measure of the beginnings of anti-school behaviour by members of the form can be gained from remarks in their personal files. These comments are presented chronologically; the first was recorded in the middle of the second term in the first year, and they cover the period up to the end of the first term in the second year. Both boys and girls are involved.

> 'Stealing from shops.'
> 'Rude to staff, mother asked to visit school.'
> 'Mother worried about boy friends, anxious that she be kept off the streets.'
> 'Cheeky and unco-operative in lessons.'
> 'On report.'
> 'Rudeness and bad behaviour.'
> 'Nuisance in assembly.'
> 'Spitting.'
> 'Swearing at member of staff.'

Comments like these are notably absent from the files of band 1 forms. In 1CU only one boy received any such remarks on his file over the same period. During the second and third years the number of such comments increased in frequency and distribution in the files of band 2 and 3 forms. But other data available on the first year of these forms are scarce; no detention records were kept at this time and the school did not maintain very comprehensive written records of its pupils.

The declining standard of behaviour of the band 2 forms described by the teachers during the first year continued into the second year. Some of the pupils in 2TA were now very frequently 'in trouble', both informally in face to face conflict with teachers and formally in detention. Sometimes the whole form was kept in on 'informal' detentions, as a result of misbehaviour or disobedience in lessons, rudeness to teachers or failure to do work. The example presented below is a typical classroom incident.

> *Second-year Maths (setted group); lesson notes*
> The group contains eleven pupils from 2TA. There is a lot of talking; the teacher issues a continuous stream of individual rebukes.
> *Teacher* 'When we do something together you've got to listen.'
> She is explaining how to do multiplication with a slide rule. Corina is turned completely round talking to the girls behind her. The teacher stops and waits.
> *Teacher* 'We are waiting for the same old people.'
> The teacher begins talking and then stops.
> *Teacher* 'We are not carrying on until you are all absolutely quiet—we are still waiting for those people who keep us waiting every lesson. Corina stop talking.'
> She is still turned with her back to the teacher.
> *Teacher* 'Corina!' [shouts]
> Corina still does not turn round or stop talking.
> *Teacher* 'All right, get outside—do as I tell you.'
> The teacher is red and ruffled, but Corina gets up and walks out, slamming the door behind her. Minutes pass. Corina is outside the door with her nose pressed against the glass; she opens the door and walks away.
> *Teacher* 'Corina—Michael, close the door please.'
> A few minutes and Corina lets it open again. The teacher writes some calculations on the board, then goes outside to speak to Corina. (She was eventually sent to the year tutor and later transferred out of this Maths group.)

A further illustration of the progressive change in the school behaviour of the band 2 pupils, and the emergence of differences between them and the band 1 pupils, is their record of attendance over the first and second years (see Tables 2.8 and 2.9). The average number of absences per pupil in band 1 is always at a lower level than in band 2, but the difference between them increases from 1.44 per pupil in the first

Table 2.8   *First year: average number of sessions absent
per pupil in each term*

	Term 1	Term 2	Term 3
Band 1	6.23	7.54	7.29
Band 2	7.67	10.55	9.82
Band 3	10.24	11.71	10.91

Table 2.9   *Second year: average number of sessions absent per pupil in
each term*

	Term 1	Term 2	Term 3
Band 1	7.23	11.21*	7.86
Band 2	12.33	12.83	14.17
Band 3 2MA (remedial)	19.75	17.29	22.56
2UD	10.64	16.95	16.22

*The sharp increase in band 1 in this term is accounted for by a
flu epidemic that hit the school and made a considerable impact
on attendances for four weeks.

Table 2.10   *Case-study forms: average number of
sessions absent per pupil in each term*

	Term 1	Term 2	Term 3
ICU	7.53	9.45	8.10
ITA	6.66	7.70	9.47

	Term 4	Term 5	Term 6
2CU	8.13	11.64	9.15
2TA	12.59	13.22	12.64

term to 3.01 in the second and 2.53 in the third. The band 3 absences are presented separately in Table 2.9 to show the difference in pattern between the remedial and non-remedial form. As far as the other bands are concerned, by the end of the second year the average number of absences in band 2 is nearly twice that of band 1, the difference being 6.31 per pupil. The level of absences in band 1 has increased very little from the first year.[16] Taking the two case-study forms independently over this period, the figures are as shown in Table 2.10. The 1TA pupils begin in the first two terms of the first year with a better attendance record than 1CU. But as with the general trend, the number of sessions of absence per term per pupil increases steadily term by term, although here the differences between the forms are less great than across the whole cohort. These indicators generally suggest that the adaptation of the 2TA pupils to the pressures of secondary schooling was different from that of the pupils of 2CU. This is 'visible' in terms of their behaviour in lessons, but it is also manifest in their attitude towards the school generally, towards their teachers and towards schoolwork, and in the extent of their involvement and participation in extra-curricular school activities and clubs, sports teams, societies and choirs, etc. I asked the pupils in both forms to write down for me all the clubs or teams they belonged to, and the extra-curricular activities they did at school. Only 5 members of 2TA said that they took part in any such school activity, and only 2 said they were connected with any club or organization outside school. In 2CU, on the other hand, 21 people were involved in extra-curricular activities, and 7 in clubs outside school. 2TA pupils mentioned a total of 10 activities and clubs altogether, while 2CU pupils could muster 43.

Because participation of this kind is not obligatory, the pupil involved is seen as being committed to the school in the widest sense [. . .] It is interesting to note that information regarding involvement in school activities and the holding of posts of responsibility is requested and normally included in headmaster's reports for university application. (Out-of-school activities can thus be seen to have a selective function.) Furthermore, King (1973) notes that the experience of joining school clubs is expected by teachers to result in the generation of lasting interests and the modification of behaviour in approved directions.

It was clear that the interests and attitudes of many of the 2TA pupils were developing in quite another way. Indeed, the increase in disruptive behaviour in the classroom seemed to be accompanied by a general disenchantment with school and all activities associated with it. A teacher who had been responsible for the first-year football team explained that one of the boys in 2TA, Donald Gaskell, 'used to be the best footballer in the first year, but now he's no longer interested and he's lost his figure'. The keeness and enthusiasm reported from 1TA had almost completely disappeared in the second year. I asked the pupils in the two second-year forms to write down whether on the whole they liked or disliked school. 48 per cent (17) of the pupils in 2TA said they disliked school on the whole, while 52 per cent (18) liked it, but only 13 per cent (4) of the pupils in 2CU expressed dislike, and 87 per cent (18) said they like school.

The work-habits of the pupils of the two forms were also different. I asked them how long they usually spent in doing their homework each evening. The pupils in 2CU were willing to spend three times as long on their homework as 2TA pupils[17]. The average time per pupil for 2TA was 16 minutes, while that for 2CU was 47 minutes.[18] In 2TA 13 pupils reported that they did no homework, but only one pupil in 2CU said this.[18] Homework is supposed to be set for two subjects each week-night and three subjects on Friday, and this work *was* set as it was due in most of the lessons I observed. However, some 2TA pupils were regularly 'in trouble' for not handing in their homework, and many others did it at school, quickly at lunch time or during pastoral periods in the mornings. For most of them it was a meaningless chore to be dispensed with as quickly as possible rather than something to be done carefully to ensure a good mark. Their unwillingness to do homework was symptomatic of their lack of interest in schoolwork and their reluctance to do any. However, the differences between the forms with respect to doing homework should not be taken to mean that the pupils of 2CU were wholeheartedly in favour of it and would always have done work at home if it were not specifically 'set'. One of the boys in 2CU who was most successful academically frequently urged me 'to do something about getting homework abolished' and 'put it in my book'. Few of 2CU would probably have done homework if it were not insisted upon, but almost all did it because it was. On the ocassions that extra, non-compulsory discovery-tasks were suggested by teachers, these were done by only a minority of the form.[19]

The doing of homework and doing it well represents further confirmation of the identification of the 2CU pupils with the school's values, stressing the importance of academic achievement, and thus the reinforcement of their self-image and status as pupils who are successful at school. Homework was a different sort of activity for the pupils from the different bands. The real difference between these forms in 'doing' homework was that most of the pupils in 2CU took time and trouble to do it 'well' and get as good a mark as possible, whereas most of the pupils in 2TA did homework in as little time as possible, with the least trouble, with little concern about the mark.

Academic performance

One of the major dimensions of the band stereotypes presented above is clearly concerned with the teachers' perceptions of the *'level' of academic performance* of which the pupils from different bands are capable. The marks obtained in homework and other assessable work is an indication of this 'level' to the teacher, and further indicates the sort of importance which the pupils attach to 'doing well'. At the end of each school year all forms have internal examinations, and although the first-, second- and third-band forms are set different examinations based upon work done during the year, it is useful to compare the results. While not strictly comparable in a quantitative sense, a qualitative comparison of the 'levels' of performance attained by 2CU and 2TA does provide an illustration once again of the differences between them. The level of marks obtained is a measure of the degree of 'academic excellence' achieved by the forms. As may be seen, at the extremes of very good and very bad marks the differences between them are dramatic indeed. For all subjects, except Maths (which was 'setted') and English (the department did not set a formal examination), the distribution of marks for the two classes was as follows:

Table 2.11

%	2TA	2CU
above 70	1	36
60–9	4	60
50–9	23	30
40–9	47	51
30–9	58	34
below 30	77	9

On the basis of these seven subjects, 2TA pupils only obtained 28 marks above half-marks (out of a total of 251 marks) compared with 126 marks above half-marks by 2CU pupils (out of a total of 219 marks).

Banding and differentiation

In every respect, in examinations, classwork and homework, 2CU performed at an academic level more acceptable to their teachers; so that not only was their behaviour in lessons well-perceived by staff but academically they were able to 'deliver the goods' as well in a far more satisfactory way. This is explained by an English teacher.

> 'They can both [band 1 and 2] attempt the same tasks but the quality of discussion is very different. The responses of the first band are more what a teacher, as an academic, would recognize as relevant. They know what the teacher wants and are able to give it to him.'

For the teacher of the band 1 form, the problems in the classroom are related to the teaching process, the organization and preparation of material, the coverage of the syllabus, and the preparation for tests and examinations; the major concern is normally with the maintenance of standards.[20] The great majority of the teachers' 'talk' and interaction with pupils in the classroom is concerned with subject material of work-tasks. In the case of the band 2 lessons, however, the teacher's major concerns in the classroom are problems of order and control. In some cases the 'order and control' problems in band 2 lessons are so great that work is virtually abandoned. 'Band 2 kids are often neglected and their lessons are the least prepared of the week', a year tutor said.

It is understandable that teachers should devote less care and energy to the preparation of lessons in which a great deal of time is spent maintaining or trying to maintain order and control, and in which little time goes to those tasks that the teachers consider valuable and worthwhile. Large numbers of pupils in the band 2 lessons expressed a considerable lack of interest in their school-work, made efforts not to have to do any work, and frequently tried deliberately to divert lessons away from work-activity. This may be interpreted as the outcome of the interaction between the expectations that teachers have of band 2 pupils, based on stereotypes, and the pupils' response to these expectations.[21] Several studies of stereotyping have shown that definitions of the situation that are held by actors who are reacting to 'deviant' behaviour, definitions which are themselves to a great extent shaped by stereotyped beliefs, can have so overwhelming an impact that the 'deviating' individual may find himself unable to sustain any alternative definition of himself. Schur (1971, p. 51) argues that stereotyping

> at the level of direct personal interaction significantly influences the expectations of others, causing serious problems of response and 'identity' management for deviators.

One Beachside year tutor commented in a similar vein that 'some teachers don't expect much from second-band forms, they accept anything for the standard of work'. The band 2 pupils are confronted by teachers who hold very negative perceptions of their intelligence and ability and likely attainment—'they are not up to much academically'. These perceptions have both attitudinal and practical consequences for the pupils' experiences of learning. That is, lack of enthusiasm for band 2 teaching is transmitted both in the teachers' attitude to the pupils and in their classroom management techniques, their organization of learning and their mediation of the syllabus. In these ways, the stereotypical notions of band-identity inherent in the teachers' perceptions of the pupils actually contribute to the increasing differences between band 1 and 2 pupils during the first and second years. Several of the teachers certainly attributed the changing attitudes and behaviour of the band 2 forms to the pupils' increasing awareness of inferior status.

> 'In the first year they started off fresh and the same, but by the end of the first year they began to realize that being in band 2 or 3 is not quite the same. And in the second year they click and in the third they switch off; it's tragic.'
> (Assistant year tutor)

> 'I had a band 2 form in the first and second year, they were tremendously self-motivated, really great kids, there was none of this 'we're at the bottom sod it' in the first year, it really came out in the third.'
> (Art teacher)

It is apparent that in the second year the teachers of band 1 and band 2 forms have well-established and very different expectations of them. Indeed, the social processes at work here appear to be essentially similar to the processes identified by Lacey (1970) and Hargreaves (1967) as *differentiation*-that is, the separation and ranking of pupils by the teachers. As Lacey suggests, this separation and ranking takes place along a number of dimensions or scales, but two appear to be most important, the academic scale and the behaviour scale. The academic scale relates to those qualities of achievement and performance in schoolwork which are consistently a part of the teachers' perception and evaluation of pupils; it includes things like numeracy and literacy skills, answering questions in lessons, and the neat presentation of book work. The behaviour scale 'would include considerations as varied as general classroom behaviour and attitudes; politeness; attention; helpfulness; the time spent in school societies and sports' (Lacey, 1970, p. 57).

In Hargreaves' terms the pupils are 'categorized' by their teachers and this begins from the moment that they enter the first year and join their banded forms. But beyond seeing them in terms of the allocated status of band 1, band 2 or band 3, the teachers are continually rating pupils in terms of the criteria listed by Lacey. [. . .] But the evaluation and separation of pupils by the teachers is only one part of the overall process of differentiation. The second aspect of the model, which Lacey suggests 'describes the passage of pupils through' the school, is *polarization*, the formation of sub-cultural groups. This

> takes place within the student body, partly as a result of differentiation, but influenced by external factors . . . It is a process of sub-culture formation in which the school-dominated, normative culture is opposed by an alternative culture which I refer to as the anti-group culture.
> (Lacey, 1970, p. 57)

Clearly, the changing patterns of behaviour of the band 2 pupils over the first two years may be interpreted as representing the emergence of the anti-school sub-culture to which Lacey refers. It is certainly the case that the behaviour of band 2 pupils in their lessons, as we have seen, presents a challenge to the normative school culture, whereas the behaviour of band 1 pupils normally does not. The situation facing the band 2 pupils is that they are perceived by their teachers as academically inferior to the band 1 pupils. This is inherent in the banding system. The band 2 pupils have low status and thus it is not in their interest to maintain a commitment to the school's values. The returns to them in terms of satisfaction are extremely limited; as we have seen, very few band 2 pupils achieve levels of performance in examinations that are considered to be acceptable by their teachers; neither do their teachers find band 2 lessons very rewarding to teach. [. . .] By the beginning of the second year, the existence of anti-school groups within the band 2 forms was clearly marked and the greater part of the disruption of band 2 lessons could be traced to these pupils. In Cohen's terms the emergence of these anti-school sub-cultural groups represents the adjustment of these pupils to the status problems with which they are confronted. He notes:

> One solution is for individuals who share such problems to gravitate toward one another and jointly establish new norms, new criteria of status which define as meritorious the characteristics they *do* possess, the kinds of conduct of which they *are* capable.
> (Cohen, 1955, p. 66)

Choosing friends

The description and analysis of the banded forms has concentrated so far upon the formal aspects of lessons and classroom behaviour. But the classroom as a social setting is made up of two worlds. One is the formal context of teacher–pupil interaction, of schoolwork and discipline, and the other is the informal context of social relationships among the pupils, of friendships and social groups. From the analysis of the distribution of friendship choices and the friendship groupings[22] of the banded forms it emerges that not only are the bands separate and distinct in the minds of the teachers, as two different types of pupils with different behaviour patterns and work capabilities, but the pupils also separate themselves out and hold

Table 2.12 *Distribution of friendship choices between pupils of different forms by band, amended for band size*

	Choice to:		
Choices from	Band 1	Band 2	Band 3
Band 1	67	21	3
Band 2	19	55	42
Band 3	6	30	24

stereotypical views of one another on the basis of their bands. The reality of this separation is borne out by the distribution of nominated choices of close friends. From the sociometric questionnaires that each of the second years forms completed for me, it was possible to plot the distribution of friendship choices between forms and between bands. Taking only those choices made outside the form group, the distribution by band is as shown in Table 2.12. The preference of band 2 pupils for band 3 rather than band 1 pupils is clear here; so too is the low level of choice between band 1 and band 3. In real terms, the vast majority of choices are made within bands. This can be explained in terms either of the constraints of the school organization, or of the normative requirements of the informal social structure among the pupils.

It is evident, then, that the way in which the pupils are formally grouped largely determines the patterns of pupil peer-groups by imposing constraints both on the nature and the range of contacts between pupils. Thus, pupils tend to choose for their friends those people with whom they have most contact and whom they know best. Overall, 78 per cent of the school friends nominated by pupils in this cohort came from within the same form. This is in line with the findings of Julienne Ford (1969), Lacey (1970), Hargreaves (1967) and Murdock and Phelps (1973), although none of these studies reported such a high percentage of 'within-form' choices. However, the preference of pupils for friends from the same band *can* also be related to the development of pro- and anti-school groups. 'It can be assumed that a person chooses for his friends those whom he respects and likes and those who he perceives to be like himself in some significant respects' (Lacey, 1970, p. 78). [. . .] Friendship groups are held together by common values and develop norms which limit the acceptable behaviour of group members and control entry into the group by defining the criteria of membership. Other groups and other pupils come to be seen in terms of how similar they are to other members of the group or how different they are from them. The problem with the previous argument, that the general level of distribution of friendship choices is affected by the limitations of contact between pupils, is that it does not explain why some other choices are made across the boundaries of the bands. The latter argument, however, does.

A few of the friendship ties that were made between bands were left over from junior school, but it often turned out that some secondary factor lay behind the maintenance of the tie, such as propinquity. Pupils who lived in the same street would have the opportunity to meet outside the school and to travel to and from school together. However, when I examined the friendship-group structures of 2TA and 2CU in terms of propinquity, only two of the six best-friend pairs lived close to one another (within a mile). The one significant basis of cross-cutting ties which I did discover was the friendship choices made between members of the various boys' sports teams in the second year. I am not suggesting that the tendency to choose outside form groups is actually encouraged by team membership, but that this is a basis of cross-cutting choice. Team membership and interest in sport are both opportunities to interact and the bases of shared interests. There were no other friendship networks of this kind extending across bands in the year-cohort. *All* other friendship choices made across bands were either reciprocating friendship pairs or unreciprocated choices made by individual pupils.

Separation between bands, however, is not simply reflected in the low level of friendship choice between them, but also in the negative and antipathetic attitudes that they entertain towards each other. These are some of the comments made by 2TA and 2CU pupils in interviews with me.

Kathleen Hopkins (2CU)	'I wouldn't want to be in a second band. I would try to get out if I was in one—they are thick.'
Dorothy Haines (2TA)	'They are not so friendly—they think they are better than us because they are in a higher band.'
Eddy (2CU)	'I don't like the people, they are a bit thick—simple.'
Belinda Hammet (2TA)	'They are stuck up—because they think they are so brainy.'
Smaldon (2CU)	'They are rough . . . tough kids in band 2.'
Kathy Forest (2TA)	'They're snobby, I don't like people in band 1.'
Fawcett (2CU)	'It's not easy to talk to them, they talk in a simpler way—they're only interested in football!'
Acre (2TA)	'They let you know they are in band 1 and how clever they are.'
Groome (2TA)	'Snobs—mainly it's the girls isn't it, in there, are poofy boys and they don't want to do nufink, they just stick around in class.'

Only two pupils in 2TA made favourable or neutral comments about band 1 pupils, and only six in 2CU made favourable or neutral comments about band 2 pupils.

Felton (2CU)	'I've got friends in band 2, I come to school with one and play with one sometimes.'

The existence of this mutual hostility can be seen in terms of Newcomb's (1947) findings, that barriers to communication are likely to lead to the formation of stereotypes, especially where differences in status are involved.

From this analysis, it is apparent that the *polarization* described by Lacey (1970) in the streamed Hightown Grammar is also an aspect of the process of relationships between the banded pupils in Beachside Comprehensive. This certainly suggests that the 'integrative function' so frequently attributed to the comprehensive school is not being achieved here. The negative implications of this segregation and mutual hostility become even clearer when the social class structure of the bands is taken into account.

Summary

This [article] has considered one banded year-cohort as a whole, as well as introducing two case-study forms. I have argued that *post factum* evidence indicates that 2TA, the band 2 form, has *become* different from the band 1 form, since the beginning of the first year and, further, that this can be related to the status-differentials that exist between the bands and to the assumptions that teachers make about the abilities and capabilities of the pupils in different bands. In particular I have indicated the importance of band stereotypes in the teachers' perceptions of, and behaviour towards, different forms. These stereotypes are an important component of the shared system of meanings of the Beachside staff, through which forms and pupils can be discussed and compared. I have also suggested that the social processes and social structures identified within this year-cohort are to a considerable extent represented by the concepts *polarization* and *differentiation*. [. . .]

Notes

1 That is to say, a system of streaming where each form-group was identified separately in an academic hierarchy in relation to every other form-group.

2 Although some band 3 forms in some years did present particular problems.

3 The band 3 forms were also smaller than forms in bands 1 or 2, and were taught by specialist members of the remedial department for a large proportion of their timeable.

4 It must be borne in mind that these figures only represent 'trouble' that has been 'processed'. Punishments carried out independently by teachers are not recorded here. And as with all official statistics there are unknown factors which may have contributed to the differences between groups. For instance, it may be that similar offences manifested both in band 1 and band 2 lessons were punished more harshly in band 2 because of policies of 'stamping out trouble' or 'not letting them go too far' operated by particular teachers.

5 See N. Flanders (1970), *Analyzing Teaching Behavior*.

6 I found that this was generally true of staff throughout the school; during the three-year field work period, only three teachers were reluctant to allow me to 'sit in' on their lessons. In each case, they were young probationary teachers who were finding problems in controlling the forms I had asked to observe.

7 These similarities are borne out in the quantitative measures presented later.

8 The notion of a 'strict' teacher was a category used extensively at Beachside by teachers and pupils, especially by the pupils. It normally referred to the particular ability of certain teachers to control and monitor the behaviour of the forms they taught in such a way as to reduce disruption and misbehaviour to an absolute minimum.

9 All responses that could not be straightforwardly fitted into the Registrar General's classifications—e.g. 'engineer', 'he works at Smith's Factory'—were consigned to the Unclassified category, as were the responses 'deceased', 'unemployed', 'I haven't got a father', etc.

10 The distribution of social class across the whole cohort is presented in table 2.13 N2.

11 I.Q. testing was abandoned by the Local Authority in 1972.

12 Within the mixed-ability cohorts, the same process of primary school recommendation was used to allocate pupils to ensure a reasonable distribution of abilities in each form. The subject teachers were unaware of the primary school recommendations in regard to individual pupils; assessments thus had to be 'made' rather than 'taken'.

Table 2.13   *Distribution of social classes across the second-year cohort, 1973–4*

	I	II	IIIN	Total non-manual	IIIM	IV	V	Total manual	Unclass.
2CU	5	10	5	20	12	—	—	12	—
2GD	4	8	5	17	12	—	—	12	4
2ST	—	2	3	5	14	3	—	17	8
2FT	2	6	10	18	11	2	—	13	3
Band 1	11	26	23	40	49	5	0	54	15
2LF	—	4	1	5	13	6	1	20	8
2BH	2	2	6	10	12	4	—	16	8
2WX	1	2	4	7	15	5	1	21	3
2TA	2	3	2	7	15	8	3	26	—
Band 2	5	11	13	29	55	23	5	83	19
2UD	—	2	4	6	6	5	—	11	4
2MA	2	2	—	4	5	4	—	9	2
Band 3	2	4	4	10	11	9	—	20	6

The questionnaire on which this table is based was not completed by nine pupils in the cohort. The relationship between banding and social class is significant $r^2 = 20$ d.f. $= 2$ p $< .001$.

13 This stereotyping may be considered and examined in another sense via the teachers' linguistic behaviour. The member's management of problems in any organization may be 'seen in the devices he uses to make them consistent, repetitive, normal and natural. By means of his linguistic behaviours the actor selects things which through meaning become social objects. That is they have potential for action when they are named, counted, assessed and ordered' (Manning, 1971, p. 224).

In this case the relevant lexicon of concepts and usages is that which refers to categories of pupils. Apart from the band labels, categories in normal use, applied to particular populations, were: 'remedial', 'bright', 'fast', 'slow', 'thick', 'dumb', 'less able', 'academic', 'less academic', 'problem', 'anti-school', 'pro-school', and 'average'. All of these categories appear to be concerned either with imputed academic ability or behavioural characteristics—that is, the same contours of relevance that are evident in all other aspects of the teacher–pupil relationship.

14 The emergence of these stereotypes of bandness is important to the school careers of these pupils in several ways, [. . .] but especially in the development of form reputations within the school, and as a label of capability with which the pupils must negotiate in making their option choices for examination courses at the end of the third year. [. . .]

15 In addition, the inferior status of the band 2 and 3 forms is both reflected in and exacerbated by the allocation of teacher resources [. . .]

16 The differences in adaptation of the different groups of pupils to the pressures and problems of schooling could be related to Merton's (1968) typology of modes of adaptation: conformity; innovation; ritualism; retreatism; and rebellion.

17 This, of course, relates to the amount given. Teachers did not expect band 2 pupils to do as much as band 1 pupils, but the difference was not of the magnitude of 3:1.

18 These figures may be compared with the times reported by the second-year grammar school pupils in Lacey's (1970) study, p. 68.

Table 2.14 *Estimated length of time spent on homework (after Lacey)*

Form	Estimated average time spent each night after streaming: second year	
2E	2 hours	0 mins
2A	1 hour	45 mins
2B	1 hour	18 mins
2C	1 hour	7 mins

19 The teacher in a 2CU Geography lesson, for instance, said, 'Perhaps you might also see what you can find out about the life of Captain Cook and we will spend a little while talking about it at the beginning of next week's lesson.'

20 When other problems emerge, the reaction of staff can be seen to be different from their reaction to the band 2 forms. [. . .]

21 Similar processes have been observed in American studies of academic stratification. For example, Wilson (1963) found in a study of 14 elementary schools in Southern California, that the normalization of diverging standards by teachers crystallized different levels of scholastic achievement. Teachers were seen to adapt their norms of success and their concepts of excellence to the composition of their student bodies. And in a review of a number of other similar studies, Passow (1966, p. 100) concluded: 'Teachers accept much less from low income children. The normalization of lower standards of performance in the less favoured socio-economic group provides the same kind of circular reinforcement for the group that normalization of past performance does for the individual student.'

22 This was done by the collection of sociometric data.

References

Cohen, A. K. (1955) *Delinquent Boys*, Free Press.
Cohen, S. (1972) *Folk Devils and Moral Panics*, MacGibbon and Kee.
Douglas, J. W. B. (1964) *The Home and the School*, MacGibbon and Kee.
Flanders, N. (1970) *Analyzing teaching Behaviour*, Addison Wesley.
Floud, J. and Halsey, A. H. (1957) 'Social class, intelligence tests and selection for secondary schools', *British Journal of Sociology*, **8**, pp. 33–9.
Ford, J. (1969) *Social Class and the Comprehensive School*, Routledge and Kegan Paul.
Hargreaves, D. H. (1967) *Social Relations in a Secondary School*, Routledge and Kegan Paul.
Keddie, N. (1971) 'Classroom Knowledge' in Young, M.F.D. (ed.) *Knowledge and Control*, Collier-Macmillan.
King, R. A. (1973) *School Organization and Pupil Involvement*, Routledge and Kegan Paul.
Lacey, C. (1970) *Hightown Grammar*, Manchester University Press.
Maddock, J. (1977) 'Academic stratification and the sustaining of identity types', *Sociological Review*, **25**, 3, pp. 575–84.
Manning, P. K. (1971) 'Talking and becoming', in Douglas, J. D. (ed.) *Understanding Everyday Life*, Routledge and Kegan Paul.
Merton, R. K. (1968) *Social Theory and Social Structure*, Free Press.
Murdock, G. and Phelps, G. (1973) *Mass Media and the Secondary School*, Macmillan.
Newcomb, T. M. (1947) 'Autistic hostility and social reality', *Human Relations* 1, 1, pp. 67–86.
Passow, A. H. (1966) 'Diminishing teacher prejudice', in Strom, R. D. (ed.) *The Inner City Classroom: Teacher Behaviours*, Charles Merril.
Schur, E. M. (1971) *Labelling Deviant Behaviour*, Harper and Row.
Wilson, A. (1963) 'Social stratification and academic achievement' in Passow, H. (ed.) *Education in Deprived Areas*, Columbia University Press.

3 The myth of subject choice

P. WOODS

I. INTRODUCTION

The study of subject choice urgently needs the attention of sociologists, who will not only illuminate the interactional processes that bear on subject choice, thus complementing the several personality studies that have been made, but will also, at the systems level, ask questions about the functions of the process within the general policy of the school and society at large.[1]

It was with this view that, while engaged in a long-term observation project in a Secondary Modern School, I undertook a study of the subject choice process. My engagement at the school enabled me to monitor the process through the summer term, and to follow it up the next year. I talked to all the pupils in the third year, at least once, in interviews ranging from $1/_2$ to 2 hours, and discussed freely with teachers from day to day. I sent a questionnaire to all parents of 3rd year pupils, and visited as many as I could before the end of term (25%). This involvement over a long period enabled me to cross-check results, follow up promising leads, and to explore in some depth the reactions of those concerned.

II. A Sociological Model of Subject Choice

In making sense of the data, I employed certain concepts. I was then able to link these in a general model which seeks to put the process into some sociological perspective.[2] For convenience and intelligibility I will give this theoretical framework here.

The first important concept arising from my discussion with pupils, was that of *group perspectives*. As used by Becker,[3] these refer to

> 'modes of thought and action developed by a group which faces the same problematic situation. They are the customary ways members of the group think about such situations and act in them . . . which appear to group members as the natural and legitimate ones to use in such situations'.

They arise when people face 'choice points', where previous thought and experience does not guide their actions, though if a particular kind of situation recurs frequently, the perspective will probably become an established part of a person's way of dealing with the world. They develop and gain strength as a result of group interaction and they are situationally specific. I shall show in section IV how, among the pupils, two broad 'group perspectives' developed.

The second key concept, focusing more on pupils' parents, discussed in section V, is *social class*. The relationship between social class and educational experience is well known, as is the culture clash between working class children and teachers.[4] My materials show that parental definitions of the situation differ along class lines, and thus the parental influences brought to bear on children in making their choices are both quantitatively and qualitatively different in accordance with these broad groupings. There is a strong connection between social class and the development of group perspectives. Underpinning these are different frames of reference and self-conceptions,[5] which are products of the position a family occupies within the overall class structure.[6] How these frames of reference are stabilized and reinforced by the child's experience of others within the school (thus facilitating the development of group persepctives) has been discussed by others.[7]

However, school decisions such as subject choice are triangular affairs, involving children, parents and teachers. I found the latter important as *choice mediators* operating within a framework of *institutional channelling*. These concepts owe a great deal to the work of Cicourel and Kitsuse.[8] As against explanations of academic attitudes and achievements mainly or directly in terms of class-related differentials and peer group culture,[9] Cicourel and Kitsuse in their study of the American 'Lakeshore High School' presented an alternative view which saw the differentiation of students as a consequence of the administrative organization and decisions of personnel in the school. The counsellor's role in students' ultimate admission to college was shown to be crucial. Assignment to college and non-college courses was dependent upon the interpretations of a student's ability and aptitude by admissions personnel; since parents knew little about college entrance requirements, his opportunities were to a great extent decided by counsellor's perceptions of him.

Cicourel and Kitsuse explain their counsellor's actions in terms of motivation in celebration of the self within the framework of professionalization, and in the self-fulfilling outcomes of bureaucratic structures. There were other factors bearing on teachers in my account, which I term *critical area influences*. To a great extent they direct and constrain teacher actions and thus serve to modify the Cicourel and Kitsuse conclusions above, at least in relation to this particular school. I shall expand on this in section VI.

How I relate these concepts together in a general model is illustrated in Fig. 3.1. Differences in social class origins produce different educational experiences. These are reflected in school structure, which is serving societal rather than individual aims, and hence feeds back into social structure. From all of these, singly and collectively, values, attitudes and actions form. Group perspectives develop in reaction to 'pedagogical orientation', which includes aims, methods and organization of teaching, themselves determined by teacher philosophies and ideologies and sustained or intensified by critical area influences (these are frequently mediated by the headmaster). The particular pedagogical orientation dominant in a school then bears on life in the school (culture) and the school's organization (structure). Most educational decisions in school, including subject choice, are made within this framework.

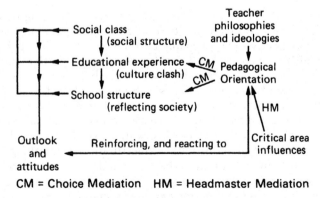

CM = Choice Mediation   HM = Headmaster Mediation

Figure 3.1   *A social structural model of subject choice*

III.   The School's System of Subject Choice

All pupils are required to complete a form expressing their choice of subjects. The rhetoric behind the scheme is governed by four crucial criteria:

1 Prevailing custom, which allows choice.

2 Prevailing state of knowledge and current patterns of educational career, largely dictated by the extended examination system, the requirements of further education and employers and the disposition of pupils. Thus there are the traditional subjects, and traditional groupings available (e.g., Sciences, Arts, Commerce, Non-examination subjects); English, Maths and Games are considered so important as to be compulsory.

3 Type of child. All the pupils had been unsuccessful at the eleven-plus examination and it was considered that six examination subjects were the optimum number for them.

4 Resources (size of school, number of teachers, space and equipment).

IV.   The Pupils: The Development of Group Perspectives

I asked each pupil his or her reasons for each of the original choices.[10] Table 3.1 summarizes the results. There appear to be two main factors, an affective one (liking or disliking) and a utilitarian one (career and ability), and they seem to hold in roughly equal proportions overall. However, there are some interesting differences within, illustrative of two basic group perspectives. The positive reasons (liking, good ability) are much stronger in 3a and 3b than in 3c, where good ability is hardly a factor at all. 'Liking for subject' includes of course a strong teacher element. The like/dislike teacher categories are for responses indicating direct personal reasons. This was a factor in only 7 per cent of cases, with nearly three times as many girls being involved as boys. The like/dislike of subject response focuses on the subject as

TABLE 3.1   Pupils' reasons for choices

Forms	Nos	Liking for subject	Dislike of others	Job	Good ability	Poor ability at others	Liking for teachers	Dislike of teachers	Others
3a Boys	15	29	5	15	19	1	1	2	8
Girls	21	29	26	44	5	5	11	2	
Total	36	58	31	59	31	6	6	13	10
3b Boys	14	18	9	12	23	6	1	3	10
Girls	20	31	17	13	8	5	3	1	5
Total	34	49	26	25	31	11	4	4	15
3c Boys	15	13	6	10	3	13	0	1	2
Girls	15	9	22	8	0	·3	0	1	2
Total	30	22	28	18	3	16	0	2	4
All Boys	44	60	20	37	45	20	2	6	20
All Girls	56	69	65	65	20	13	8	13	9
Total	100	129	85	102	65	33	10	19	29

mediated by the teacher. But this response begs a further question—why do they 'like' certain subjects? The interviews showed these reasons to fall into two types which point up the contrast between 3a and 3c more vividly. Thus the former tend to like subjects for official, supportive, traditional educational reasons, the latter for unofficial, counter-cultural, social reasons. Thus the first type might like a subject because the teacher makes it interesting, is well-organized, can keep order, and gives them to feel that they are learning something; the second type for almost directly opposite reasons, such as having few demands made on them, having great freedom and even 'having a muck-about'.

Another striking result, again indicative of group perspectives, was the difference in number of responses among forms. The average number of responses per pupil decreases with stream, with a big drop in 3c. I take this, as with their reasons for likes and dislikes, to be a reflection of their basic attitudes to school. For 3c, it is largely characterized by estrangement from its main objectives. As one of the teachers said to me 'You won't find many of their parents [i.e. of 3c pupils—P.W.] here tonight [at the headmaster's talk—P.W.], they know it's not for them'. Such pupils alienated from the school's processes, go through the organizational motions that are required of them, inventing their own rationale for existence. It is hardly surprising then that when faced with making a decision of their own relating to the school's processes, many were lost. It was an unreal situation for them.

Example 1
Dave: I filled that form in in about 20 seconds. *(laughs)*
P. W.:   Did you ask anybody's advice about what to do?
Dave: I didn't 'ave time. See, I filled my paper in, I took it 'ome, see what me dad think, an' I forgot all about it, an' then, oh, (deputy head) came in and gi' me another form an' I filled it in quick so I wouldn't lose it, because I've got a bad memory, I always forget things an' I just filled it in quick.
P. W.:   Did you talk about it amongst yourselves?
Dave and Philip: No.
Kevin: We just said what we were doing.

Example 2
P. W.: What subjects did you choose?
Paul: The non-exam ones.
P. W.: Why did you choose those?
Paul: Because I ain't no good at anything so I chose those.

Examples 3 and 4
Malcolm, though with three of his friends, seemed to know very little about the process, what was required of him, as well as how he met it. Though he had chosen four subjects, he was unable to say why he had chosen them. Sheila did the same as her sister because 'She was no good at anything'; in fact her sister filled in the form for her, and she was unable to remember the subjects she had chosen, even when shown the list.

Example 5
Gary: I only done two out of these, I didn't fill the other two places in.
P. W.: Why is that?
Gary: All the others I'm not any good at.

Example 6
P. W.: What subjects have you chosen, Susan?
Susan: I dunno. I forget. (*I show her the form*). I think it was (4 subjects).
P. W.: Why did you choose those?
Susan: I dunno.

P. W.:   Did you ask anybody's advice?
Susan: Yeah, I asked Mr. Lewis's. First of all, I put all sciences down because I want to be a
           nurse . . . and he said they're no good . . .
P. W.:   Why did he say that?
Susan: I dunno.

Example 7
Claire: I'm doing the non-exam course.
P. W.:   Why?
Claire: Because I don't like any of the other courses.
P. W.:   Why do General Science non-exam rather than General Science exam?
Claire: Because that's an exam course in't it?
P. W.:   How do you know you won't like it?
Claire: I don't like Science anyway.
P. W.:   Why put down for it then?
Claire: Well I 'ad to pick something, din't I?

These suggest the nature of the non-event it was for many pupils. In example 1,
Dave turns the procedure into material for his own use, as he does for many other
events relating to school. He makes a laugh of it. Examples 2, 3 and 4 illustrate the
problems set up by pupils' lack of success by the school's single criterion of ability.
Examples 3, 4 and 6 perhaps give some idea of the massive vagueness or
unawareness that some of these pupils displayed. Example 7 shows the unerring
logic of a pupil with a sound grasp of the situation.

   For these pupils then, there is not much 'choice'. Inasmuch as they 'choose' at all, it
is a diffident, social, counter-cultural choice. They employ the following kind of
dichotomous model:

Kinds of subjects

1	Hard work	Easy
2	Examination	Non-examination
3	Nasty, horrible	Fun
4	Boring	Interesting
5	Without friends	With friends
6	Control	Freedom

   There is a sense of immediate gratification, and jocular acceptance of ultimate
destiny. Years of interactions, tests and examinations have taught them their place.
By the time of the 3rd year, these processes have completed the sifting, and groups
have worked out their *modi vivendi*. They may choose only within their pre-ordained
route, and for some in 3c, as we have seen, that means no choice at all.

   For another group of pupils, mostly found in 3a, subject choice, like all other
school decisions, is a real and positive affair, and is defined in school terms. For them,
society is a contest system and they are in the contest with a chance. Comparative
success in assessment and selection mechanisms reinforced by social factors (like
within-group pressure and parental encouragement), will have cued them in to this.
This means they do see the future in progressively structured terms, and they do
believe their choices have relevance to their future careers. Thus they are much
more likely to think in terms of career, ability, examination success, and other
factors that promote it. Here is an example of the sort of reasoning involved:

Stephen: I chose Chemistry instead of Geography because someone advised me it would
           be better for the R.A.F. than Geography. I thought Geography would be better,
           but the bloke next door thought Chemistry. He knows a bloke in the Air Force,
           pretty important, and he was talking to Mum and Dad one night and he said
           Chemistry was more important. I would much rather do Chemistry myself than
           Geography because you can't do Geography 'O' level, but you can Chemistry.

P.W.:	Why Physics?
Stephen:	Well, the only other one I thought of was English Literature and I'm not really interested in that, so I chose Physics.
P.W.:	The others are out are they?
Stephen:	Yeah—General Science—I'm already doing Chemistry. I'm not interested in Biology, so I might as well do Physics and specialize in something else rather than do General Science.
P.W.:	Tell me about Technical Drawing.
Stephen:	Well, I wanted to do both that and History, I just couldn't make my mind up.
P.W.:	What was hard about it?
Stephen:	Well if I join the R.A.F., I want to be a draughtsman, so Tech. Drawing is obviously the one to do. But I'm interested in History and I enjoy it. I put History and I enjoy it. I put History down first then thought again and changed it later.
P.W.:	Did you talk to anybody about it?
Stephen:	No. I told Mum and Dad I was thinking of changing it, and they said we won't say yes or no either way.
P.W.:	And why Woodwork in group 6?
Stephen:	Well I'm not good at Metalwork, I don't do Needlework or Housecraft, I'm no good at Music, shan't mention French. I quite enjoy Woodwork, but I'm not much good at it.

Contrast this with the replies given on pp. 48-49. The close commitment to school values, the logical and ebullient application to the task in hand, the instrumental reasoning tinctured with the educational reciprocation all point to this pupil's close approximation to the 'ideal', and emphasizes the distance the others are away from it. His major criteria in choosing are:

Job-related	Non-related
Good ability	Poor ability
Good learning situation	Poor learning situation
Interest	No Interest

The existence of two polar sub-cultures in the school and their connection with school organization is well documented.[11] My study again illustrates the connection with school structure, but further shows the existence and illustrates the different perspectives of these two broad groups of pupils confronted with the specific problem of subject choice. They employ different interpretative models, distinguished by instrumentalism on the one hand, and social and counter-institutional factors on the other. These underwrite the more general and potentially misleading affective factor of 'liking' or 'disliking', which applies to some degree to both groups. The values and attitudes which provide the bases of these group perspectives derive in large part, I suggest, from position in the social class structure.[12]

V. Parents: Some Differences Emerging from Social Class

Conversations were held with six pairs of parents on subject choice, and on the basis of these a questionnaire was devised and sent to all parents of all 3rd year children in the middle of the summer term when pupils were resolving their choices. Replies were received from 73 per cent of homes. Also I visited 25 per cent of homes of all 3rd year children before the end of the summer term.

Parental advice
The responses were analysed by form. Unfortunately, insufficient precise detail of

TABLE 3.2 *Parents' projected advice to children*

	Very important			Quite important				Of some importance			Not very important			Not at all important		
	3a	3b	3c	3a	3b	3b	3c	3a	3b	3c	3a	3b	3c	3a	3b	3c
Ability	23	21	22		8	24	8	2	3	0	0	0	1	0 . 0		0
Interest	19	28	27		12	16	7	2	1	0	0	0	0	0	0	0
Best teachers	8	9	15		8	7	8	12	20	8	3	9	0	2	1	1
Own choice	15	19	27		11	20	3	7	5	3	0	1	0	0	0	0
Good job	20	25	26		7	13	4	6	7	3	0	1	0	0	0	0
Teacher advice	12	13	9		18	17	10	2	13	8	1	1	2	0	0	3

father's occupation was available for it to be of use. However, the connection between social class and stream is so well known for us to assume reasonably that it holds in this case, an assumption well supported by the interviews.

The questionnaire replies supported the social structure model in some respects, in that 3c parents in making certain different responses from 3a showed that they do hold different, less supportive attitudes towards school. Their replies on how they would advise their children, and on what influenced them as parents were particularly revealing in this respect. Table 3.2 summarizes the replies on projected 'advice to children'.

Fewer thought 'teacher advice' as important as some of the others, but 3c parents thought it even less so than others. 3c parents would be more inclined than others to say 'do those subjects you want to', and they also put more emphasis on doing subjects with the best teachers, and (compared with 3a) 'interest'. These results are consistent with a model implying a differential fit between outlook of parents of different class, and aims and ethos of school. The 'own choice' and 'teacher advice' differences in particular suggest less involvement and perhaps suspicion of teachers among 3c parents. More of these proportionately also put more emphasis on 'interest'. Interviews showed that 3a parents were inclined to be more involved, and to use more complex reasoning. Thus they would be less likely to settle first for interest, best teachers, or own choice and would more closely accord with the school's policy of 'guided choice', reasoning their way through a complex set of factors; while the replies of parents in the lower form accord with the 'drop-out' syndrome shown by many of their children. This squares with replies to question 1 which asked if their children consulted them about what subjects to choose. Table 3.3 shows there are signs of less consultation in 3c than in 3a.

This was supported by pupils' own responses, and reflected in attendance rates at the parents' meetings convened at the School to discuss the matter. Stronger attachment to unofficial functions of the school by 3c parents is also suggested by the replies on school aims. A much larger proportion of 3c parents attached great importance to 'keeping children occupied till they go out to work', than did other parents.

TABLE 3.3 *Parental consultation: parents' views*

	3a	3b	3c	Totals
Yes	26	33	21	80
No	7	13	15	35
Totals	33	46	36	115

TABLE 3.4 *Perceived influences on parents*

	Very influential			Quite influential			A little			Not very influential		
	3a	3b	3c	3a	3b	3c	3a	3b	3c	3a	3b	3c
Reports	10	12	3	17	22	19	4	8	9	2	0	5
Examinations	11	12	2	15	22	15	4	6	13	3	0	2
Own knowledge	25	23	23	7	14	11	0	3	1	1	1	0
Family knowledge	10	9	18	8	11	9	3	7	3	9	13	5
Teachers	11	13	5	19	22	13	2	5	7	1	1	8
Child's view	12	17	7	16	20	23	4	4	2	1	2	3
Other children	0	2	4	2	12	9	6	10	10	17	17	10

On influences bearing on their views of their child's suitability for certain groups of subjects (see Table 3.4) fewer 3c parents reckon they are influenced by school reports, examination results or teachers' recommendations (i.e. a 'school' factor). With others, most of them claim to be strongly influenced by a 'personal' factor (own knowledge of the child, knowledge of the rest of the family). This again squares with the social, uncommitted outlook of their children and a distancing from official policy and processes.

TABLE 3.5 *Distribution of types of parental influence*

Type of influence	Middle class			Total	Working class			Total
	3a	3b	3c		3a	3b	3c	
Compulsion	0	2	0	2	0	0	0	0
Strong guidance	1	3	0	4	1	0	1	2
Mutual resolution	2	1	0	3	1	4	1	6
Reassurance	3	0	0	3	0	1	2	3
Little/Nil	0	0	0	0	0	1	2	3
Total	6	6	0	12	2	6	6	14

From my interviews with pupils and parents, I identified five types of parental influence:

1 Compulsion
2 Strong guidance.
3 Mutual resolution.
4 Reassurance.
5 Little or nil.

Table 3.5 shows how these were spread among the 27 homes that I visited. Though numbers are small, the trend towards stronger counselling for the middle-class child is clearly visible.

Compulsion

This seems to have been used in cases where parents greatly feared their child was in danger of selecting the 'wrong' route with all its disadvantageous consequences. I only found middle class parents using it, and it is another instance of how the middle class child who, for whatever reason might have adopted the social, counter-cultural model, can be cushioned against a possible fall into the drop-out zone. (If this cushion is lacking, teachers might provide an alternative one. See p. 56.)

Linda, for example, who wanted to be a hairdresser, and had wanted the non-examination course, was coerced into opting for Commerce by her mother, because she 'wanted her to work in an office'. Many such parents showed a high degree of status consciousness, being very sensitive to the difference between the two main routes. Jane, daughter of a managing director, told me she would have preferred to carry on in the same way rather than be forced to choose. Her father explained to me at length the reasoning behind *his* selection on her behalf.

Strong guidance contains an element of persuasion, often subtly concealed in the continual involvement typical of the middle-class parent

> It goes back over a period of time. There's been a careful channelling of opportunities as they've presented themselves. From experience of life, I'm biassed towards a child going into secretarial work, because if you're not academic, the only alternative is factory work. It goes back two or three years really. I would say if you don't get good results you'll land up in a factory on the line, and you've seen them factory girls in their hair nets. Sara actually made her own choice—I think I influenced her unknowingly. She told me she wanted to be a secretary, and that's what I've wanted her to do! None of the subjects on the bottom line would be helpful to her in the sort of occupation I wanted her, so I chose housecraft for her, for general use, later.
> (Factory manager)

Having steered the child on the right courses, middle-class parents can then provide resources to see that he or she gets accepted, as when the estate agent's wife advised her son, who had done such a poor examination that he should by that teacher's rule have been automatically excluded, to apologize to the teacher and promise to try hard in the future. This he did, and was accepted to the annoyance of some who had scored higher. 'Why didn't you do what he did?' I asked one of these. 'I'm unlucky in things like that', he said.

Mutual resolution, with reassurance, was the most common form among those I interviewed. Working-class families were well represented here. However, though they might show as much concern as middle-class families, their guidance tended to be less well informed. Middle-class parents told me in detail how they monitored their children's thinking on the matter, making sure that they themselves were well informed, by, for example, frequent consultations with teachers; then employing this knowledge, and that of the child, and of the world in general to feed gently into the decision-making process when requested. By contrast, working-class parents seemed as puzzled as their children. To many of these, school is an alien though desirable agency, where professionals practice their considerable expertise behind well-defined boundaries. They have little idea of their own child's achievements and capabilities or of the career prospects and how they are associated with educational routes. Another 'disadvantage' for working-class parents was that they tended to be less instrumentally oriented than middle-class, though every parent I met thought primarily of the child's future career. *Reassurance* also differed along class lines, middle-class parents supporting their children through confidence in them to make the best choices, working-class parents supporting their children as they would in any enterprise as part of the socio-emotional bond between them. As the table shows, I only found working-class parents giving *very little* or *no* advice.

In this section I have shown that there are different kinds and amounts of parental advice and influence operating on the different groups of pupils identified previously. These show a connection with social class.[13] Middle class parents are likely to be more involved with school processes, show more complex reasoning in accordance with school criteria in advising their children, be more persuaded by 'school' factors. Working-class parents display less 'involvement', are less instrumentally oriented, possibly entertain suspicions of school and teachers, have less consultation with teachers and their own children, are more likely to be persuaded by 'personal' factors. Middle-class parents tend to give strong guidance, be well informed, critical and coercive, instrumentally oriented and status conscious. Working-class parents tend to give less guidance, and to be uninformed. Indications have been given of the subtle ways in which class can work towards differential opportunity, for example, through 'knowledge of the world' and 'how to handle men'. It also operates of course through the teachers.

VI. The Teachers: Choice Mediators

Teachers of course acknowledge that there is not a completely free choice, but there is a belief that the advice and guidance offered is given in the best interests of the pupil. This is a view I wish to contest in this section. As with Cicourel and Kitsuse's Lakeshore High School, this school's structure is determined by what happens at the end of the pupil's career, in this case the taking (or not) of examinations. Pupils are streamed and/or put in sets in the early years to facilitate optimum overall academic performance as defined by skills and knowledge deemed useful in the 5th year examinations. As at Lakeshore, early decisions can be crucial. Of one 5L group I was able to trace back, 27 out of 31 had come through the school in the bottom stream. This institutional channelling creates its own effects,[14] and in association with the group perspectives that form within the channels and the development of teachers' typifications,[15] brings about a crystallization of opportunities at a very early stage.

This is vividly illustrated by one aspect of the subject choice process, the rechannelling of misdirected choices. Teachers view pupils' subject choice in a way akin to Fig. 3.2.

This shows four basic types of choice from the teachers' point of view. The 'system acceptive' type pupil is one who interprets correctly the school and its

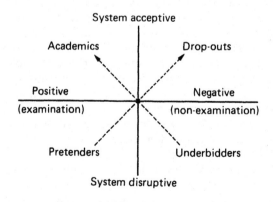

Figure 3.2

processes and his relationship to it, and hence the implications of the subject choice, be it for examination or non-examination subjects. The 'system disruptive' pupils however have misinterpreted the cues, and made unrealistic choices, selecting examination subjects when they should have chosen non-examination (by ability), or vice-versa. The problem for teachers then becomes one of moving pupils along the lines indicated.

But who are these 'pretenders' and 'underbidders'? Table 3.6 shows the changes that were made from pupils' first choices to final allocation. 'Positive' changes are those from non-examination to examination subjects; 'negative' vice-versa; and 'neutral' are changes within the same standard. 44 per cent of the whole, and proportionately twice as many boys as girls had at least one subject changed from his or her original choice, and 60 per cent of these changes were 'negative' ones. Nearly half of these came from 3c, even though many in that form had already made negative choices and therefore did not come into the reckoning. Most of the rest came from 3b, which is here showing its 'in-between' status, having some 'good' pupils, some 'bad'. 3a had two or three 'bad' boys who blotted 3a's copybook. 62 per cent of the boys were involved in changes, compared with 30 per cent of the girls. Clearly the vast majority of those requiring rechannelling came from the lower part of the streaming structure.

There is another problem, again shown by Fig. 3.2 namely the line between academics and non-academics. There can be no appeal to an absolute standard in drawing this line just as with the line separating success and failure in the eleven-plus. It is determined by the teachers, each for his own subject, and as with the eleven plus, it might fall at different points, for much the same reason—resources. If more pupils choose one subject than another, more have to be excluded from that subject.

This points up the uneven nature of the redistribution problem. But teachers will already have exerted influence to try to achieve these results less brutally beforehand. Their teaching and assessment, culminating in the all-important examinations at the end of the 3rd year, gives most pupils a sound idea of their 'ability' at school subjects.

This is the most powerful factor underlying all others in the acceptance of pupils to subjects—i.e., teachers' definitions of success and failure.[16] We have already seen

Table 3.6 *Choices changes*

Form		Nos	No in form	Changes	Positive	Negative	Neutral
3a	Boys	5	15	10	2	5	3
	Girls	3	21	3	1	0	2
	Total	8	36	13	3	5	5
3b	Boys	15	17	24	2	12	10
	Girls	10	20	16	2	7	7
	Total	25	37	40	4	19	17
3c	Boys	9	15	15	0	13	2
	Girls	4	15	10	0	9	1
	Total	13	30	25	0	22	3
All Boys		29	47	49	4	30	15
All Girls		17	56	29	3	16	10
	Total	46	103	78	7	46	25

in the section on the pupils how many of them (and their parents) had internalized
these definitions, accepted the consequences and chosen 'realistically'.

To guard against 'unrealistic' choices, a teacher might use special pre-option
techniques. The teacher of one popular subject, for example, possibly anticipating a
big redistribution problem, gave a talk which had the effect of cooling out several
'pretenders'.

> *P.W.:*   Why didn't you choose subject 4 in that group?
> *June:*   We'd get too much homework.
> *Mavis:* Yeah! She don't 'alf put it on . . . 'you'll 'ave to work all the time'—an' homework!
>   You think 'oh I can't do that—oh!' Talking about it made me feel ill.

As with Cicourel and Kitsuse's counsellors, teachers' judgments are not based
simply on past achievement.

I asked the teacher of one 'popular' subject what were her principles of exclusion.
In making up the optimum number she employed three—

1 the 'best ones';
2 those who seemed to have the 'right' attitude;
and
3 from 3c, the three who seemed a 'cut above the rest'.

It was no good having problem people like John Church.

> He's too lazy, he lays around, and if he gets his pen out, he lolls around saying 'Oh
> Miss!' I can't take the risk, it spreads like a cancer. Who starts it initiates it, I don't know.
>   It's cruel I know, but what else can I do? I haven't time to motivate, inspire, correct for
> behaviour and so on, you must cut out all the miscreants and thickies. You just haven't
> got time. They do drag you down. Now Sharon Brown, nice girl, parents didn't want
> her in that form, I think once she gets out and in with this other lot, they'll pull these
> three [from 3c] up.

This teacher is articulating the system's rules, and by tidying up the
'misplacements' illustrates how the wedge is even more firmly driven between two
types of pupil. These two types, and who falls into them, are clearly identified, as is
their within-group influences. So also are the criteria for success, which include
apart from past performance, 'attitude' and a 'cut above the rest'. The social
undertones and divisiveness become explicit towards the end. Family background
can be decisive. It can rescue or condemn at the eleventh hour.

Apparent also is the classic dilemma of the upper secondary school
teacher—concern for the individual while operating within the constraints of a
structure which allows very little room for manoeuvre. There is an overlap among
'O' level, C.S.E. and non-examination routes. For teachers, these overlap areas can
be high tension generators, for there is pressure on the teacher to achieve a high
proportion of examination passes. Usually this might be interpreted, as Cicourel and
Kitsuse did with their counsellors, purely through the concept of professionalization. Here, however, a critical external influence increases the pressure; indeed,
for some teachers, could be held responsible for it. In the ordinary course of events, a
teacher might gain relief by ensuring that the overlap is as small as possible, ideally
non-existent, which would mean 100 per cent examination passes; or, of course, he
might not feel under any pressure, especially if his results are deemed reasonable.
But at this particular point in the school's history, numbers are seen to be very
important. For the school is about to become a Comprehensive, and to receive pupils
formerly admitted to the high status town grammar and high schools. The strain
towards better and better examination results is seen by the teachers[17] as a public

relations exercise in honour of the parents of such children to convince them of the school's credibility as a respectable academic institution. One of the effects on teachers is to cause them to monitor the selecting of subjects with great care. It is unavoidable, even in traditionally less constrained subjects like creative design.

> A lot choose Art, yes, and you know why don't you? I'm not fooled. I say to them, 'Why do you want to do Art?' I say, 'I know, but come on, you tell,' and they say, 'Huh, I don't want to do old Biology or whatever, all that homework and so on.' It's an easy option, and they go for it on both lines. My results this year were pretty poor which rather proves my point. But what I do is this. I pick those with most artistic ability and I like it to be seen to be fair. I don't spring this on them either. I tell them all at the beginning of the third year. I tell them they'll be judged on the quality of work that goes into their folders, and then towards the end of the year, I get them to lay it all out, so they can all see, and of course some are very good and some are pathetic. There's no other way, not if they want to take the exam. If they just want to skive they can do it somewhere else.

Here is 'justice' being seen to be done, and opportunity given for pupils to make their cases. With its free and informal atmosphere, and its different, non-exacting work-task, the 'Art' options are a natural attraction for the diffident counter-cultural chooser. But the Art teacher is subject to the same forces as his colleagues, and the same criteria must apply.

What direct counselling of children by teachers came to my attention also seemed directed towards the preservation of institutional channels, while expounding the rhetoric which legitimated it. In his address to the 3rd year pupils, for example, the headmaster showed a conservative selection-oriented, instrumental and elitist approach, emphasising the virtues of 'ability' and 'usage' as against 'interest', the essential link with the occupational structure, the functionalist need for 'all sorts', and the predicating of all considerations on the system as it stood. As might be anticipated, the diffident, counter-cultural choosers at least took in little, if any, of this advice. The same applies to the senior master's 'counselling'. Empowered with responsibility for running the scheme, he had more involvement in it overall than any other teacher. But his individual 'counselling' came at the end of the chain, and, as we have seen, was channel-restorative. It appears therefore that teacher mediation does not operate in the interests of the individual pupil, but is predicated rather on considerations of status, career and professionalisation, rendered particularly acute by the critical external influence of parental pressure. Mediation then takes the form basically of alerting pupils to the ideal-types (and their own approximations to them) which serve the purpose of those ends through the agency of 'good examination results'.

Why then have a system of subject choice at all? I would suggest that, within the system, schemes like this have four main functions:

1 There is some option within groups of subjects, if not of routes. However, we have seen that some groups of pupils have more option than others.
2 It does give some pupils and parents an opportunity to relate, to some extent, their school careers with prospective occupations. For those on the 'deviant' route, for whom school has a different meaning, it is an opportunity to select those subjects which best support that meaning, though there will be problems if a subject is also an examination one, as with Art, above.
3 It helps to consolidate the image of the school as a meritocratic and democratic institution.
4 It serves as a kind of hiatus in the school programme which can be used as yet another motivating device.

However, in a wider sense, the subject choice scheme is serving the implicit school policy of selection in as much as

1 subjects are grouped in accordance with recognized patterns associated with occupation career;
2 two broad channels allow for those who 'opt in' and those who 'opt' or are ruled out'. The non-examination provision can be viewed therefore as a form of social control:[18]
3 pupils are encouraged to choose those subjects in which they have most ability and which are most related to their likely future occupational careers;
4 in rationalizing the picture that emerges from the last point, teachers apply those criteria which promise to lead to the best overall examination results; priority is given to the elite;
5 'interest' and 'liking' are played down.

VII. Conclusion

The four within-system functions therefore are serving a system of sponsorship mobility behind a 'contest' mask.[19] There is an illusion of a range of choice, of selection of personnel delayed to the last moment (immediately prior to the commencement of examination courses), of a common starting line (everybody in with a chance), and of common fare (roughly the same subjects up to the end of the 3rd year). In fact, the range of choice is variable among the pupils, non-existent for some; the pupils have been 'channelled', that is to say selected (at eleven-plus, and no doubt earlier), and selected again (in the school's streaming arrangements, and possibly 'hidden' streaming before) long before they come to the 3rd year; different social origins lead to different educational experiences, the difference being reinforced by the prevailing pedagogical paradigm; and these differences have repercussions for what is taught to different groups. Despite meritocratic overtones, by the third year most pupils have developed group perspectives; they know their places, having internalized teacher definitions of success and failure and their application to themselves with the usual labels ('thick', 'dibby', 'lazy', 'pest').

For them, subject choice has different meanings. Generally speaking to the initiated, generally middle-class pupil it is his choice, and he makes it carefully with a view to job, ability and prospects. To the estranged, generally working-class pupil it is a line of least resistance, and even that at times presents problems. This scenario is complicated, but sharpened still further, by the changing status of the school wherein the unseen and unspoken influence of potential 'sponsoring' parents is felt by teachers to exert great pressure on them, through the mediation of the headmaster, to produce better and better examination results. While this ultimately might mean more joining the élite ranks of the examination pupils, it does not of course alter the basic division and the principles on which it rests; in fact it increases it, since teachers will feel compelled to sharpen their selective and pedagogic techniques to guard against the increased risk of 'contamination'.

With these powerful forces structuring their policies and activities, teachers 'mediate', choosing the arena, making the rules and providing most of the equipment (including the pupil's own view of himself) for the game of subject choice. For them, the game is to guide pupils into the right channels to get the bell of examination results to ring. The criteria they use are past achievement and future potential. For all of these factors, we know that there is a strong connection with social class, though it is not a simple one. The middle-classes are at home in this arena, the working-class strangers. It is in this sense, most powerfully, that pupils' subject choice is socially structured. But we have seen also how, even within these severe limitations, social factors such as degree and type of parental advice, within-group influences, cultural impressions on teachers (a 'cut above the rest') or simply parents' *savoir-faire* of the middle-class milieu, can exert an influence and indeed at times retrieve apparently lost situations.

'Progressive' measures in schools, such as team teaching and mixed ability classes, have come under fire from both right and left lately. To the former they are fomenting disorder and decay, to the latter they are merely scratching at the edges of an outmoded but curiously resilient system. Pupils' subject choice might be regarded as one of these so-called 'progressive' measures owing something to fashionable child-centred philosophies, and how one regards it might depend ultimately on one's political position. However one thing is clear. Changes in the subject choice system alone will not make a fundamental difference. Extending the range of choice can only be of benefit, but while the social structure of its intake and the school's general aims remain the same, changes in constraint will be of degree rather than of kind.

Acknowledgements

My greatest debt is to the pupils and teachers of the school, who gave so generously of their time. I am particularly grateful to those teachers at the school who read and made comments on an earlier draft of this paper. Their reactions cannot be included here, but will be incorporated in the larger study of which this paper is a part. My thanks are due too, to my colleagues D. F. Swift and I. R. Dale for their comments on the first draft. I am solely responsible of course for the views expressed and the faults that remain.

Notes

[1] To date, the field has been the preserve mainly of psychologists interested in correlations between personality factors and subject choice. The most well-known one perhaps is Liam Hudson's famous distinction between divergent and convergent thinkers, and their predisposition for Arts and Science subjects respectively. See Hudson, L. (1966) *Contrary Imaginations*, Methuen; in a recent review of the literature, five times as much space is taken up with personality factors as 'other possible causes'. See Pitt, A. W. H., (1973) 'A review of the reasons for making a choice of subjects at the secondary school level', *Educat. Rev.*, **26**, 1 (November 1973); the most recent work on subject choice is policy research, taking for granted the general context of both school and society. See Reid, M. I., Barnett, B. R. and Rosenberg, H. A., (1974) *A Matter of Choice*, N.F.E.R.

[2] This follows the methodology recommended by Glaser, B. G. and Strauss, A. L. (1968) *The Discovery of Grounded Theory*, Weidenfeld and Nicolson.

[3] Becker, H. S. *et al.*, (1961) *Boys in White*, University of Chicago Press.

[4] For useful summaries and recent reflections on this position, see Section V of Eggleston, J (ed.), 1974 *Contemporary Research in the Sociology of Education*, Methuen.

[5] These terms are used by Ashton, D. N. (1974) 'Careers and commitment: the movement from school to work', in Field D. (ed.), *Social Psychology for Sociologists*, Nelson.

[6] Bernstein, B., 'A socio-linguistic approach to socialization: with some reference to educability', in Bernstein, B. (ed.), *Class Codes and Control Vol. I*, Routledge and Kegan Paul.

[7] E.g. Ashton, D. N. (1974) op. cit.

[8] Cicourel, A. V. and Kitsuse, J. I. (1963) *The Educational Decision-Makers* Bobbs-Merrill.

[9] As, for example, in Parsons, T., (1958) 'General theory in sociology', in Merton, R. K., *et al.*, *Sociology Today* Basic Books Hollinghead, A. B. (1949) *Elmtown's Youth*, Wiley, Coleman, J. S. (1961) *The Adolescent Society*, Free Press.

[10] Pupils were interviewed in friendship groups of 2 to 4 pupils previously ascertained by sociometry and observation. I have no doubt that this aided free and frank discussion. It might be argued that they would influence each others's responses. But I believe this to have been a beneficial influence, in that our discussions frequently drew upon discussion they had had amongst themselves on the subject, and they assisted each other's recall.

[11] Hargreaves, D. H. (1967) *Social Relations in a Secondary School* Routledge and Kegan Paul; Lacy, C. (1970) *Hightown Grammar*, Manchester University Press; King, R. A. (1969) *Values and Involvement in a Grammar School*, Routledge and Kegan Paul.

[12] See Bernstein, B. (1972) op. cit.

[13] It might equally be said that they show a connection with academic achievement, but of course I am assuming also a connection between *that* and social class. Also, as pointed out previously, I was able to establish from the interviews that the connection with social class predominated over connection with academic stream.

[14] For the effects of streaming see Jackson, B. (1964) *Streaming: an Education System in Miniature*, Routledge and Kegan Paul; Central Advisory Council and for Education (England) (1967) Children and their Primary Schools, Plowden Report, H.M.S.O.; Lunn, J. B. (1970) *Streaming in the Primary School* N.F.E.R.

[15] For teachers' knowledge of pupils based on institutional channelling, see Keddie, N., (1971) 'Classroom knowledge', in Young, M. F. D. (ed.), *Knowledge and Control*, Collier-Macmillan.

[16] For a discussion along these lines, related to subject choice in a girls' secondary school, see Beecham, Y. (1973) 'The making of educational failures', *Hard Cheese Two*, May 1973.

[17] It is important to note that the teachers did not feel this directly. Pressure was put on them by the headmaster, and from his words and actions they thought this the most likely, indeed the sole, explanation.

[18] Bernstein, B. (1971) 'On the classification and framing of educational knowledge', in Hopper, E. (ed.), *Readings in the Theory of Educational Systems*, Hutchinson.

[19] Turner, R. H. (1971) 'Sponsored and contest mobility and the school system', in Hopper, E. (ed.), op. cit.

4   Elements of a culture

P. WILLIS

Opposition to authority and rejection of the conformist

The most basic, obvious and explicit dimension of counter-school culture is entrenched general and personalised opposition to 'authority'. This feeling is easily verbalised by 'the lads' (the self-elected title of those in the counter-school culture).

[In a group discussion on teachers]

Joey   [. . .] they're able to punish us. They're bigger than us, they stand for a bigger establishment than we do, like, we're just little and they stand for bigger things, and you try to get your own back. It's, uh, resenting authority I suppose.

Eddie   The teachers think they're high and mighty 'cos they're teachers, but they're nobody really, they're just ordinary people ain't they?

Bill   Teachers think they're everybody. They are more, they're higher than us, but they think they're a lot higher and they're not.

Spansky Wish we could call them first names and that . . . think they're God.

Pete   That would be a lot better.

PW   I mean you say they're higher. Do you accept at all that they know better about things?

Joey   Yes, but that doesn't rank them above us, just because they are slightly more intelligent.

Bill   They ought to treat us how they'd like us to treat them.

[. . .]

Joey   [. . .] the way we're subject to their every whim like. They want something doing and we have to sort of do it, 'cos, er, er, we're just, we're under them like. We were with a woman teacher in here, and 'cos we all wear rings and one or two of them bangles, like he's got one on, and out of the blue, like, for no special reason, she says, 'take all that off'.

PW   Really?

Joey   Yeah, we says, 'One won't come off', she says, 'Take yours off as well'. I said, 'You'll have to chop my finger off first'.

PW   Why did she want you to take your rings off?

Joey   Just a sort of show like. Teachers do this, like, all of a sudden they'll make you do your ties up and things like this. You're subject to their every whim like. If they want something done, if you don't think it's right, and you object against it, you're down to Simmondsy [the head], or you get the cane, you get some extra work tonight.

PW

—   Yeah.

—   Yeah.

—   Most of them.

Joey   It adds a bit of spice to yer life, if you're trying to get him for something he's done to you.

This opposition involves an apparent inversion of the usual values held up by authority. Diligence, deference, respect—these become things which can be read in quite another way.

[In a group discussion]

PW   Evans [the Careers Master] said you were all being very rude [. . .] you didn't have the politeness to listen to the speaker [during a careers session]. He said why didn't you realise that you were just making the world very rude for when you grow up and God help you when you have kids 'cos they're going to be worse. What did you think of that?

Joey   They wouldn't. They'll be outspoken. They wouldn't be submissive fucking twits. They'll be outspoken, upstanding sort of people.

Spansky   If any of my kids are like this, here, I'll be pleased.

This opposition is expressed mainly as a style. It is lived out in countless small ways which are special to the school institution, instantly recognised by the teachers, and an almost ritualistic part of the daily fabric of life for the kids. Teachers are adept conspiracy theorists. They have to be. It partly explains their devotion to finding out 'the truth' from suspected culprits. They live surrounded by conspiracy in its most obvious—though often verbally unexpressed—forms. It can easily become a paranoic conviction of enormous proportions.[1]

As 'the lads' enter the classroom or assembly, there are conspiratorial nods to each other saying, 'Come and sit here with us for a laff', sidelong glances to check where the teacher is and smirking smiles. Frozen for a moment by a direct command or look, seething movement easily resumes with the kids moving about with that 'I'm just passing through, sir' sort of look to get closer to their mates. Stopped again, there is always a ready excuse, 'I've got to take my coat off sir', 'So and So told me to see him sir'. After assembly has started, the kid still marooned from his mates crawls along the backs of the chair or behind a curtain down the side of the hall, kicking other kids, or trying to dismantle a chair with somebody on it as he passes.

'The lads' specialise in a caged resentment which always stops just short of outright confrontation. Settled in class, as near a group as they can manage, there is a continuous scraping of chairs, a bad tempered 'tut-tutting' at the simplest request, and a continuous fidgeting about which explores every permutation of sitting or lying on a chair. During private study, some openly show disdain by apparently trying to go to sleep with their head sideways down on the desk, some have their backs to the desk gazing out of the window, or even vacantly at the wall. There is an aimless air of insubordination ready with spurious justification and impossible to nail down. If someone is sitting on the radiator it is because his trousers are wet from the rain, if someone is drifting across the classroom he is going to get some paper for written work, or if someone is leaving class he is going to empty the rubbish 'like he usually does'. Comics, newspapers and nudes under half-lifted desks melt into elusive textbooks. A continuous hum of talk flows around injunctions not to, like the inevitable tide over barely dried sand and everywhere there are rolled-back eyeballs and exaggerated mouthings of conspiratorial secrets.

During class teaching a mouthed imaginary dialogue counterpoints the formal instruction: 'No, I don't understand, you cunt'; 'What you on about, twit?'; 'Not fucking likely'; 'Can I go home now please?' At the vaguest sexual double meaning giggles and 'whoas' come from the back accompanied perhaps by someone masturbating a gigantic penis with rounded hands above his head in compressed lipped lechery. If the secret of the conspiracy is challenged, there are V signs behind the teacher's back, the gunfire of cracked knuckles from the side, and evasive innocence at the front. Attention is focused on ties, rings, shoes, fingers, blots on the desk—anything rather than the teacher's eyes.

In the corridors there is a foot-dragging walk, an overfriendly 'hello' or sudden silence as the deputy passes. Derisive or insane laughter erupts which might or might not be about someone who has just passed. It is as demanding to stop as it is to carry on. There is a way of standing collectively down the sides of the corridor to form an Indian gauntlet run—though this can never be proved: 'We're just waiting for Spansky, sir'.

Of course individual situations differ, and different kinds of teaching style are more or less able to control or suppress this expressive opposition. But the school conformists—or the 'ear'oles' for the lads—have a visibly different orientation. It is not so much that they support teachers, rather they support *the idea* of teachers. Having invested something of their own identities in the formal aims of education and support of the school institution—in a certain sense having foregone their own right to have a 'laff'—they demand that teachers should at least respect the same authority. There are none like the faithful for reminding the shepherd of his duty.

[In a group discussion with conformists at Hammertown Boys]

Gary   Well, I don't think they'm strict enough now [. . .] I mean like Mr Gracey, and some of the other teachers, I mean with Groucho, even the first years play him up [. . .] they 'the lads' should be punished like so they grow up not to be cheeky [. . .] Some of the others, you can get on with them all right. I mean from the very beginning with Mr Peters everybody was quiet and if you ain't done the work, you had to come back and do it. I mean some of the other teachers, say from the first years, they give you homework, say you didn't do it, they never asked for it, they didn't bother.

It is essentially what appears to be their enthusiasm for, and complicity with, immediate authority which makes the school conformists—or 'ear'oles' or 'lobes'—the second great target for 'the lads'. The term 'ear'ole' itself connotes the passivity and absurdity of the school conformists for 'the lads'. It seems that they are always listening, never *doing*: never animated with their own internal life, but formless in rigid reception. The ear is one of the least expressive organs of the human body: it responds to the expressivity of others. It is pasty and easy to render obscence. That is how 'the lads' liked to picture those who conformed to the official idea of schooling.

Crucially, 'the lads' not only reject but feel *superior* to the 'ear'oles'. The obvious medium for the enactment of this superiority is that which the 'ear'oles' apparently yield—fun, independence and excitement: having a 'laff'.

[In a group discussion]

PW   [. . .] why not be like the ear'oles, why not try and get CSEs?

–   They don't get any fun, do they?

Derek   Cos they'm prats like, one kid he's got on his report now, he's got five As and one B.

–   — Who's that?

Derek   Birchall.

Spansky I mean, what will they remember of their school life? What will they have to look back on? Sitting in a classroom, sweating their bollocks off, you know, while we've been . . . I mean look at the things we can look back on, fighting on Pakis, fighting on the JAs [i.e. Jamaicans]. Some of the things we've done on teachers, it'll be a laff when we look back on it.

[. . .]

Perce   Like you know, he don't get much fun, well say Spanksy plays about all day, he gets fun. Bannister's there sweating, sweating his bollocks off all day while Spanksy's doing fuck all, and he's enjoying it.

Spanksy In the first and second years I used to be brilliant really. I was in 2A, 3A you know and when I used to get home, I used to lie in bed thinking, 'Ah, school tomorrow', you know, I hadn't done that homework, you know . . .'Got to do it'.

–   Yeah, that's right, that is.

Spanksy But now when I go home, it's quiet, I ain't got nothing to think about, I say, 'Oh great, school tomorrow, it'll be a laff', you know.

Will   You still never fucking come!

Spansky Who?

Will   You.

[Laughter]

—   You can't imagine[inaudible] going into the Plough and saying, 'A pint of lager
           please'.
Fred   You can't imagine Bookley goin' home like with the missus, either, and having a
—   good maul on her.
—   I can, I've seen him!
—   He's got a bird, Bookley!
—   He has.
Fred   I can't see him getting to grips with her, though, like we do you know.

It was in the sexual realm especially that 'the lads' felt their superiority over the
'ear'oles'. 'Coming out of your shell', 'losing your timidness' was part of becoming
'one of the lads', but it was also the way to 'chat up birds' successfully. In an odd way
there was a distorted reflection here of the teachers' relationship to the 'ear'oles'.
'The lads' felt that they occupied a similar structural role of superiority and
experience, but in a different and more antisocial mode.

[In an individual interview]

Joey   We've [the lads] all bin with women and all that [. . .] we counted it up the other
           day, how many kids had actually been with women like, how many kids we know
           been and actually had a shag, and I think it only came to, I think we got up to
           twenty-four [. . .] in the fifth year out of a hundred kids, that's a quarter.
PW   Would you always know though?
Joey   Yes I would [. . .] It gets around you know, the group within ourself, the kids who
           we know who are sort of semi-ear'oles like . . .they're a separate group from us
           and the ear'oles. Kids like Dover, Simms and Willis, and one or two others like.
           They all mess about with their own realm, but they're still fucking childish, the
           way they talk, the way they act like. They can't mek us laff, we can mek them laff,
           they can fucking get in tears when they watch us sometimes, but it's beyond their
           powers to mek one of us laff, and then there's us [. . .] some of them [the semi-
           ear'oles] have been with women and we know about it like. The ear'oles [. . .]
           they've got it all to come. I mean look at Tom Bradley, have you ever noticed him.
           I've always looked at him and I've thought, Well . . . we've been through all life's
           pleasures and all its fucking displeasures, we've been drinking, we've been
           fighting, we've known frustration, sex, fucking hatred, love and all this lark, yet
           he's none of it. He's never been with a woman, he's never been in a pub. We don't
           know it, we assume it—dare say he'd come and tell us if he had—but he's never
           been with a woman, he's never been drinking, I've never known him in a fight.
           He's not known so many of the emotions as we've had to experience, and he's got
           it all to come yet.

Joey was an acknowledged group leader, and inclined at times to act the old
experienced man of the world. As is clear here, and elsewhere, he is also a lad of
considerable insight and expressive power. In one way this might seem to disqualify
him as typical of school non-conformist working-class lads. However, although
Joey may not be *typical* of working class lads, he is certainly representative of them.
He lives in a working class neighbourhood, is from a large family known as a fighting
family whose head is a foundryman. He is to leave school without qualifications and
is universally identified by teachers as a troublemaker—the more so that 'he has
something about him'. Though perhaps exaggerated, and though powerfully
expressed, the experiences he reports can only come from what he has experienced
in the counter-culture. The cultural system he reports on is representative and
central, even if he is related to it in a special way.

     It is worth noting that, in his own terms and through the mediations of the
group, Joey assumes both complete mastery and understanding of the school year
and its social landscape. He assumes that information will find its way to 'the lads' as
the focal point of that landscape. A clear hallmark of 'coming out' is the development
of this kind of social perspective and evaluative framework. It should also be noted

that the alternative standards constructed by 'the lads' are recognised by the teachers in a shadowy sort of way—at least in private. There were often admiring comments in the staff room about the apparent sexual prowess of particular individuals from younger teachers, 'he's had more than me I can tell you'.

Members of the group more conformist to school values do not have the same kind of social map, and nor do they develop an argot for describing other groups. Their response to 'the lads' is mostly one of occasional fear, uneasy jealousy and general anxiety lest they be caught in the same disciplinarian net, and frustration that 'the lads' prevent the smooth flow of education. Their investment in the formal system and sacrifice of what others enjoy (as well as the degree of fear present) means that the school conformists look to the system's acknowledged leaders, the staff, to deal with transgression rather than attempt to suppress it themselves.

[In a group discussion with conformists at Hammertown Boys]

Barry . . .he [one of the teachers] goes on about 'Everybody. . .', you know. I don't like things like that, when they say, 'Everybody's . . . none of you like this, none of you like this, none of you like that. You're all in trouble'. They should say, 'A few of yer. . .' Like Mr Peters, he does that, he don't say, 'Everybody', just the odd few. That's better, cos some of us are interested [. . .]

Nigel The trouble is when they start getting, you know, playing the teachers up [. . .] it means that you're losing time, valuable time, teaching time, and that, so its spoiling it for your, you know sometimes. I wish they'd just pack up and leave [. . .]

Barry It's better the way they've done it now [. . .] they've put them all together [CSE groups were not mixed ability groups]. It don't really matter whether they do any work or not . . . You just get on, get on well now [in the CSE groups], cos if anybody's talking, he tells you to shut up, you know, get on with the work.

PW [. . .] have you ever felt that you should try and stop them? [. . .]

Barry I've just never bothered with them [. . .] now, in the fifth, they should . . . you know, you don't just go around shouting at people in the classroom, you know, you just talk sensibly. [The teachers] should be more stricter.

Opposition to staff and exclusive distinction from the 'ear'oles' is continuously expressed amongst 'the lads' in the whole ambience of their behaviour, but it is also made concrete in what we may think of as certain stylistic/symbolic discourses centring on the three great consumer goods supplied by capitalism and seized upon in different ways by the working class for its own purposes: clothes, cigarettes and alcohol. As the most visible, personalised and instantly understood element of resistance to staff and ascendancy over 'ear'oles' clothes have great importance to 'the lads'. The first signs of a lad 'coming out' is a fairly rapid change in his clothes and hairstyle. The particular form of this alternative dress is determined by outside influences, especially fashions current in the wider symbolic system of youth culture. At the moment the 'lads' look' includes longish well-groomed hair, platform-type shoes, wide collared shirt, turned over waisted coat or denim jerkin, plus the still obligatory flared trousers. Whatever the particular form of dress, it is most certainly *not* school uniform, rarely includes a tie (the second best for many heads if uniform cannot be enforced), and exploits colours calculated to give the maximum distinction from institutional drabness and conformity. There is a clear stereotypical notion of what constitutes institutional clothes—Spike, for instance, trying to describe the shape of a collar: 'You know, like a teacher's!'

We might note the importance the wider system of commercial youth culture has here in supplying a lexicography of style, with already connoted meanings, which can be adapted by 'the lads' to express their own more located meanings. Though much of his style, and the music associated with it, might be accurately described as arising from purely commercial drives and representing no authentic aspirations of its adherents, it should be recognised that the way in which it is taken up and used by the young can have an authenticity and directness of personal expression missing from its original commercial generation.

It is no accident that much of the conflict between staff and students at the moment should take place over dress. To the outsider it might seem fatuous. Concerned staff and involved kids, however, know that it is one of their elected grounds for the struggle over authority. It is one of the current forms of a fight between cultures. It can be resolved, finally, into a question about legitimacy of school as an institution.

Closely related with the dress style of 'the lads' is, of course, the whole question of their personal attractiveness. Wearing smart and modern clothes gives them the chance, at the same time as 'putting their finger up' at the school and differentiating themselves from the 'ear'oles, to also make themselves more attractive to the opposite sex. It is a matter of objective fact that 'the lads' do go out with girls much more than do any other groups of the same age and that, as we have seen, a good majority of them are sexually experienced. Sexual attractiveness, its association with maturity, and the prohibition on sexual activity in school is what valorises dress and clothes as something more than an artificial code within which to express an institutional/cultural identity. This double articulation is characteristic of the counter-school culture.

If manner of dress is currently the main apparent cause of argument between staff and kids, smoking follows closely. Again we find another distinguishing characteristic of 'the lads' against the 'ear'oles'. The majority of them smoke and, perhaps more importantly , are *seen* to smoke. The essence of schoolboy smoking is school gate smoking. A great deal of time is typically spent by 'the lads' planning their next smoke and 'hopping off' lessons 'for a quick drag'. And if 'the lads' delight in smoking and flaunting their impertinence, senior staff at least cannot ignore it. There are usually strict and frequently publicised rules about smoking. If, for this reason, 'the lads' are spurred, almost as a matter of honour, to continue public smoking, senior staff are incensed by what they take to be the challenge to their authority. This is especially true when allied to that other great challenge: the lie.

[In a group discussion on recent brushes with staff]

Spike   And we went in, I says 'We warn't smoking', he says [. . .] and he went really mad. I thought he was going to punch me or summat.

Spanksy 'Call me a liar', 'I'm not a liar', 'Get back then', and we admitted it in the end; we was smoking [. . .] He was having a fit, he says 'Callin' me a liar'. We said we warn't smoking, tried to stick to it, but Simmondsy was having a fit.

Spike   He'd actually seen us light up.

Punishment for smoking is automatic as far as senior staff are concerned, and this communicates itself to the kids.

Spanksy Well, he couldn't do a thing [the deputy head], he had to give me three. I like that bloke, I think he does his job well, you know. But I was at the front entrance smoking and Bert comes right behind me. I turn around, been copped, and I went straight to him and had the cane. Monday morning, soon as I got in school, three I had . . . .You know he couldn't let me off.

Given this fact of life, and in the context of the continuous guerrilla warfare within the school, one of the most telling ways for 'the lads' to spot sympathisers, more often simply the weak and 'daft', in the enemy camp is to see which teachers, usually the young ones, take no action after an unequivocal sighting of a lighted cigarette.

Fuzz   I mean Archy, he sees me nearly every morning smoking, coming up by the

> Padlock, 'cos I'm waiting for me missus, sees me every morning. He ain't never said anything.
>
> *Will* He said to me in registration—
>
> *PW(interrupt-*
> *ing).* Who's this, Archer?
>
> *Will* Archy, yeah, he says, 'Don't get going up there dinner-time 'What do you mean like, up there?' He says, 'Up there, up that way, the vicinity like'. I says, 'Oh, the Bush', you know, but he's alright, like, we have a laff.

Again, in a very typical conjunction of school-based and outside meanings cigarette smoking for 'the lads' is valorised as an act of insurrection before the school by its association with adult values and practices. The adult world, specifically the adult male working class world, is turned to as a source of material for resistance and exclusion.

As well as inducing a 'nice' effect, drinking is undertaken openly because it is the most decisive signal to staff and 'ear'oles' that the individual is separate from the school and has a presence in an alternative, superior and more mature mode of social being. Accounts of staff sighting kids in pubs are excitedly recounted with much more relish than mere smoking incidents, and inaction after being 'clocked boozing' is even more delicious proof of a traitor/sympathiser/weakling in the school camp than is the blind eye to a lighted 'fag'. Their perception of this particular matrix of meanings puts some younger and more progressive members of staff in a severe dilemma. Some of them come up with bizarre solutions which remain incomprehensible to 'the lads': this incident involves a concerned and progressive young teacher.

[In a group discussion about staff]

> *Derek* And Alf says, er, 'Alright sir' [on meeting a member of staff in a public house] and he dayn't answer, you know, and he says, 'Alright sir?', and he turned around and looked at him like that, see, and er . . .and he dayn't answer and he says, in the next day, and he says, 'I want you Alf', goes to him and he says, 'What was you in there last night for?'. He says, 'I was at a football meeting', he says, 'Well don't you think that was like kicking somebody in the teeth?' 'No', he says. 'What would you feel like if I kicked you in the teeth?', he says. 'Saying hello like that down there', he says, 'what would you expect me to say?'. He says, 'Well don't speak to me again unless I speak to you first'. He says, 'Right sir, I won't say hello again', he says, 'even if I see you in the drive.'

Certainly 'the lads' self-consciously understand the symbolic importance of drinking as an act of affiliation with adults and opposition to the school. It is most important to them that the last lunchtime of their last term should be spent in a pub, and that the maximum possible alcohol be consumed. This is the moment when they finally break free from school, the moment to be remembered in future years:

[Individual interview at work]

> *PW* Why was it important to get pissed on the last day?
>
> *Spanksy* It's a special thing. It only happens once in your life don't it? I mean, you know, on that day we were at school right, you'm school kids, but the next day I was at work, you know what I mean?
>
> *PW* Course, you went to work the very next day.
>
> *Spanksy* Yeah, I got drunk, had a sleep, and I went to work [. . .] if we hadn't've done that you know, we wouldn't've remembered it, we'd've stopped at school [i.e. instead of going to the pub], it'd've been just another day. No, when we did that, we've got something to remember the last day by, we've got something to remember school by.

In the pub there is indeed a very special atmosphere amongst the Hammerton 'lads'. Spike is expansively explaining that although he had behaved like a 'right vicious cunt' sometimes, he really likes his mates and will miss them. Eddie is determined to have eight pints and hold the 'record'—and is later 'apprehended drunk', in the words of the head, at the school and ingloriously driven home by him. Fuzz is explaining how he had nearly driven Sampson (a teacher) 'off his rocker' that morning and had been sent to see the head, 'but he wasn't off or anything, he was joking'. Most important, they are accepted by the publican and other adult customers in the pub, who are buying them drinks and asking them about their future work. At closing time they leave, exchanging the adult promises which they have not learned to disbelieve, calling to particular people that they will do their plumbing, bricklaying or whatever.

That they have not quite broken loose, and that staff want to underline this, is shown when 'the lads' return to the school late, smelling of alcohol and in some cases quite drunk. In a reminder that the power of the school is backed ultimately by the law and state coercion, the head has called in the police. A policeman is waiting outside the school with the head. This frightens 'the lads' and a bizarre scenario develops as they try to dodge the policeman.

[Later in a group discussion]

> Will   I was walking up the drive [to the school], I was pulling Spike and Spanksy [. . .] I was trying to get these two alright, you know. Joey saw this copper comin' down the drive [. . .] I went into the bogs [at the bottom of the drive bounded at the back only by a fence]. I see the copper, 'If he don't see me like, I can jump over the fence and get scot free, like, nobody'll see me, I'll be alright'. Then I thought, 'Look well if he comes in or summat', so I undone my trousers like I was having a piss, as though I was late or summat. Then Bill come running in. I thought, 'Christ', and I climbed over the back fence, went creeping off [. . .] Simmondsy had seen Bill, he said, 'Ah, I want to see you two', he says, 'You two', and I dayn't think you know, I just went walking down.

Eventually 'the lads' are rounded up and delivered in an excited state to the head's study, where they are told off roughly by the policeman: 'He picked me up and bounced me against the wall'—Spike (I did not see this incident myself). The head subsequently writes to all of their parents threatening to withhold their final testimonials until an apology is received: in the case of Spike he wrote:

> . . . your son had obviously been drinking, and his subsequent behaviour was generally uncooperative, insolent, and almost belligerent. He seemed bent on justifying his behaviour and went as far as describing the school as being like Colditz . . . as is my practice, I wish to give the parents of the boys an opportunity to come and see me before I finally decide what action to take.[2]

Even sympathetic young staff find the incident 'surprising', and wondered why 'the lads' had not waited until the evening, and then 'really done it properly'. The point is, of course, that the drinking has to be done at lunchtime, and in defiance of the school. It is not done simply to mark a neutral transition—a mere ritual. It is a decisive rejection and closing off. They have, in some way, finally beaten the school in a way which is beyond the 'ear'oles' and nearly unanswerable by staff. It is the transcendance of what they take to be the mature life, the real life, over the oppressive adolescence of the school - represented by the behaviour both of the 'ear'oles' and of the teachers.

Some of the parents of 'the lads' share their sons' view of the situation. Certainly none of them take up the head's offer to go and see him.

[In a group discussion]

> Will   Our mum's kept all the letters, you know, about like the letters Simmondsy's sent [about the drinking] I says, 'What you keeping them for?' She says, 'Well, it'll

be nice to look·back on to, won't it', you know, 'show your kids like you know, what a terror you was'. I'm keeping 'em, I am.

[Individual interview at work]

PW   Did your old man understand about having a drink the last day of term?
Spanksy Oh ah [. . .] he laughed, he said, 'Fancy them sending a letter', you know. Joey's father come and had a little laugh about it you know.

No matter what the threats, and the fear of the law, the whole episode is 'worth it' to 'the lads'. It is most frequently recounted, embellished and exaggerated school episode in the future working situation. It soon becomes part of a personalised folklore. As school uniform and smoking cease to be the most obvious causes of conflict in schools as more liberal regimes develop, we may expect drinking to become the next major area where the battle lines are drawn.[. . .]

[. . .]

Boredom and excitement

PW   What's the opposite of boredom?
Joey   Excitement
PW   But what's excitement?
Joey   Defying the law, breaking the law like, drinking like.
Spike   Thieving.
Spanksy Goin' down the streets.
Joey   Vandalising [. . .] that's the opposite of boredom — excitement, defying the law and when you're down The Plough, and you talk to the gaffer, standing by the gaffer, buying drinks and that, knowing that you're 14 and 15 and you're supposed to be 18.

The 'laff', talking and marauding misbehaviour are fairly effective but not wholly so in defeating boredom - a boredom increased by their very success at 'playing the system'.

The particular excitement and kudos of belonging to 'the lads', comes from more antisocial practices than these. It is these more extreme activities which mark them off most completely, both from the 'ear'oles', and from the school. There is a positive joy in fighting, in causing fights through intimidation, in talking about fighting and about the tactics of the whole fight situation. Many important cultural values are expressed through fighting. Masculine hubris, dramatic display, the solidarity of the group, the importance of quick, clear and not over-moral thought, comes out time and again. Attitudes to 'ear'oles' are also expressed clearly and with a surprising degree of precision though physical aggression. Violence and the judgement of violence is the most basic axis of 'the lads' ascendence over the conformists, almost in the way that knowledge is for teachers.

In violence there is the fullest if unspecified commitment to a blind or distorted form of revolt. It breaks the conventional tyranny of 'the rule'. It opposes it with machismo. It is the ultimate way of breaking a flow of meanings which are unsatisfactory, imposed from above, or limited by circumstances. It is one way to make the mundane suddenly *matter*. The usual assumption of the flow of the self from the past to the future is stopped: the dialectic of time is broken. Fights, as accidents and other crises, strand you painfully in 'the now'. Boredom and petty detail disappear. It really does matter how the next seconds pass. And once experienced, the fear of the fight and the ensuing high as the self safely resumes its journey are addictive. They become permanent possibilities for the alleviation of boredom, and pervasive elements of a masculine style and presence.

Joey   There's no chivalry or nothing, none of this cobblers you know, it's just . . . if
you'm gonna fight, it's savage fighting anyway, so you might as well go all the way
and win it completely by having someone else help ya or by winning by the dirtiest
methods you can think of, like poking his eyes out or biting his ear and things like
this.

[. . .]

PW   What do you think, are there kids in the school here that just wouldn't fight?
Spike   It gets you mad, like, if you hit somebody and they won't hit you back.
PW   Why?
Eddie   I hate kids like that.
Spanksy   Yeah, 'I'm not going to hit you, you'm me friend'.
PW   Well, what do you think of that attitude?
Joey   It's all accordin' what you got against him, if it's just a trivial thing, like he give you
a kick and he wouldn't fight you when it come to a head, but if he's . . . really
something mean towards you, like, whether he fights back or not , you still pail
him.
PW   What do you feel when you're fighting?
Joey   [. . .] it's exhilarating, it's like being scared . . . it's the feeling you get afterwards . . . I
know what I'm fighting. . . it's that I've got to kill him, do your utmost best to kill
him.
PW   Do you actually feel frightened when you're fighting though?
Joey   Yeah, I shake before I start fighting. I'm really scared, but once you're actually in
there, then you start to co-ordinate your thoughts like, it gets better and better
and then, if you'm good enough, you beat the geezer. You get him down on the
floor and just jump all over his head.

It should be noted that despite its destructiveness, anti-social nature and apparent
irrationality violence is not completely random, or in any sense the absolute
overthrow of social order. Even when directed at outside groups (and thereby, of
course, helping to define an 'in-group') one of the most important aspects of violence
is precisely its social meaning within 'the lads' own culture. It marks the last move in,
and final validation of, the informal status system. It regulates a kind of 'honour' —
displaced, distorted or whatever. The fight is the moment when you are fully tested
in the alternative culture. It is disastrous for your informal standing and masculine
reputation if you refuse to fight, or perform very amateurishly. Though one of 'the
lads' is not necessarily expected to pick fights — it is the 'hard knock' who does this, a
respected though often not much liked figure unlikely to be much of a 'laff' — he is
certainly expected to fight when insulted or intimidated: to be able to 'look after
himself', to be 'no slouch', to stop people 'pushing him about'.

Amongst the leaders and the most influential — not usually the 'hard knocks' — it
is the capacity to fight which settles the final pecking order. It is the not often tested
ability to fight which valorises status based usually and interestingly on other
grounds: masculine presence, being from a 'famous' family, being funny, being good
at 'blagging', extensiveness of informal contacts.

Violence is recognised, however, as a dangerous and unpredictable final
adjudication which must not be allowed to get out of hand between peers. Verbal or
symbolic violence is to be preferred, and if a real fight becomes unavoidable the
normal social controls and settled system of status and reputation is to be restored
as soon as possible:

PW   [. . .] When was the last fight you had Joey?
Joey   Two weeks ago . . . about a week ago, on Monday night, this silly rumour got
around. It was daft actually, it shouldn've got around to this geezer that I was
going to bash him like and it hadn't come from me, so him not wanting to back
down from it, put the word out he was going to have me, we had a fight and was

stopped. I marked him up. He give me a bit of a fat lip, and he dropped the nut on me nose, hurt me nose, hurt me nose here. But I gouged his eye out with my thumb, split his head open, then after they pulled us off, I grabbed him and took him in the corner and I told him there that he knows I wasn't scared of him and that I know I wasn't scared of him, he warn't scared of me, that's an end of it. It was a sort of an . . . uh . . . he was from a family, a big family like us, they're nutters, they're fighters the Jones', and . . . uh . . . didn't want to start anything between 'em so I just grabbed him and told him what the strength is like.

In a more general way the ambience of violence with its connotations of masculinity spread through the whole culture. The physicality of all inteactions, the mock pushing and fighting, the showing off in front of girls, the demonstrations of superiority and put-downs of the conformists, all borrow from the grammar of the real fight situation. It is difficult to simulate this style unless one has experienced real violence. The theme of fighting frequently surfaces in official school work — especially now in the era of progressivism and relevance. One of Bill's English essays starts, 'We couldn't go Paki bashing with only four', and goes through, 'I saw his foot sink into his groin' and 'kicking the bloke's head in', to 'it all went dark' (when the author himself 'gets done in'). In the RSLA film option where pupils can make their own short films 'the lads' always make stories about bank robberies, muggings and violent chases. Joey gets more worked up than at any time in class during the whole year when he is directing a fight sequence and Spansky will not challenge his assailant realistically, 'Call him out properly, call him out properly, you'd say, "I'll have you, you fucking bastard" not "Right, let's fight".' Later on he is disgusted when Eddie dives on top of somebody to finish a fight, 'You wouldn't do that, you'd just kick him, save you getting your clothes dirty'.

The perennial themes of symbolic and physical violence, rough presence, and the pressure of a certain kind of masculinity expand and are more clearly expressed amongst 'the lads' at night on the street, and particularly at the commercial dance. Even though they are relatively expensive and not so very different from what is supplied at a tenth of the cost at the Youth Club, commercial dances are the preferred leisure pursuit of 'the lads'. This is basically because there is an edge of danger and competition in the atmosphere and social relations not present at the Youth Club. Commercial provision can be criticised at many levels, not least because of its expense and instrumentalism towards those it caters for. However, it at least responds to its customers' desires, as they are felt, without putting a moral constraint on the way they are expressed. In a sense 'the lads' do have a kind of freedom at the commercial dance. Its alienated and exploited form at least leaves them free from the claustrophobia and constriction of irrelevant or oppressive moral imperatives in official leisure organisations. It is possible for indigenous cultural forms to surface and interact without direction from above:

Spike   If there's a bar there, at a dance, it's good.

Will   Yeah, I think if there's a bar there you have to be more . . . watch what you're doing, not prat about so much, because some people what's got a bit of ale inside 'em [. . .] they see like a lot of birds there, and they think, 'I'll do a bit of showin' off', and they'll go walkin' round, like hard knocks you know [. . .] They just pick a fight anywhere.

Spike   Billy Everett, kids like 'im, he'll go around somebody'll look at 'im and he'll fucking belt 'im one [. . .]

PW   How do you start a fight, look at somebody?

Spike   No, somebody looks at you.

Will   That's it, just walk around so somebody would look at you.

Spike   Or if you walk past somebody, you deliberately bump into 'em and you swear blind that they nudged you.

PW	So if you're at a dance and you want to avoid a fight, you have to look at your feet all the time do you?
—	No.
—	Not really.
Spike	[. . .] Look at 'em, and fucking back away.
Fuzz	If you know a lot of people there, you're talkin' to them, you feel safer as well, if you know a lot of people.
Will	It's OK if you know a lot of them there.
Spike	If you go to a dance where you don't know anybody it's rough.
[. . .]	
Spike	The atmosphere ain't there [in the school youth wing] there ain't a bar for one. You drink fuckin' fizzy pop, and eat Mars bars all night.
Will	I think . . . this club might, if they'd got some new kids we'd never seen before.
Spike	It'd be good then.
Will	It'd be good then, 'cos there'd be some atmosphere and you know, you'd be lookin' at each other, then you'd go back and say, 'I don't like that prat, look at the way he's lookin' at us'. And there might be something goin' on outside after . . . but now you're always gettin' Jules [the youth leader] walkin' out or summat, you know.

Evening and weekend activities hold all the divisions of the school plus others— sometimes more shadowy, especially if they involve class differences — further projected onto clothes, music and physical style. Being a 'lad' in school is also associated with 'being out' at night and developing a social understanding not only of the school but also of the neighbourhood, town and streets:

Will	Classin' it like the modern kids, right, the kids who dress modern, right. There's the hard knocks, then there are those who are quiet [. . .] but can look after theirselves, like, dress modern and hang about with the hard knocks or summat. Then there's the money givers, kids who you can blag money off, who'll buy friendship. Then you get into the class of the poufs, the nancies [. . .]
PW	Pouf doesn't mean queer.
Will	No, it means like ear'oles, do-gooders, hear no evil, see no evil [. . .] I think the hard knocks and that like reggae, d'you know what I mean, reggae and soul, they don't listen to this freaky stuff, then the poufs, the nancies, they like . . . the Osmonds, y'know, Gary Glitter.
PW	[. . .] weirdos, freaks, hippy types [. . .] how do they fit into that, Will?
Will	Yeah, well, I dunno [. . .] you find a lot of those freaks are brainy an'all.
Spike	T'aint our scene like [. . .]
Fuzz	I mean take for instance you go down The Plough when the disco's on [. . .] when there's all the heavy music, and you see the kids with their hair long, scruffy clothes [. . .] jeans and everything, and you go down on a soul night, and you see kids with baggy trousers, you know, spread collar shirts, you can tell the difference.
[. . .]	
Will	I think you can feel out of it as well, 'cos I've been up the Junction, up town, it's a heavy place, got all the drugs and everything, and everybody was dressed really weirdo [. . .] and I felt I was out, well, I felt, well, out of it, you know what I mean, I felt smarter than the rest, as though I was going to a wedding, or I was at a wedding, and they was working on a farm.

It is the wider scope, extra freedom, and greater opportunities for excitement which makes the evening infinitely preferable to the day (in school). In some respects the school is a blank between opportunities for excitement on the street or at a dance with your mates, or trying to 'make it' with a girl. In the diaries kept by 'the lads', meant to record 'the main things that happen in your day', only 'went to school' (or in Will's case gigantic brackets) record school, whilst half a side details events after school, including the all important 'Got home, got changed, went out'.

However, although school may be bracketed out of many of these kids' lives, this 'invisibility' should not lead us to believe that school is unimportant in the form of what they do experience.

The pressure to go out at night, to go to a commercial dance rather than a youth club, to go to pubs rather than stop in, to buy modern clothers, smoke, and take girls out — all these things which were felt to constitute 'what life is really about' — put enormous financial pressure on 'the lads'. Shortage of cash is the single biggest pressure, perhaps at any rate after school, in their life:

[In an individual discussion]

> Joey   [. . .] after all, you can't live without bread, let's face it, fucking money is the spice of life, money is life. Without money, you'd fucking die. I mean there's nothing fucking round here to eat, you couldn't fucking eat trees, you couldn't eat bark.

All possible contacts in the family and amongst friends and casual acquaintenances are exploited and the neighbourhood scoured for jobs in small businesses, shops, on milk rounds, as cleaners, key cutters, ice-cream salesman, and as stackers in supermarkets. Sometimes more than one job is held. Over ten hours work a week is not uncommon. From the fourth form onwards, Spike thinks his work at a linen wholesaler's is more important than school. He gladly takes days and weeks off school to work. He is proud of the money he earns and spends: he even contributes to his parents' gas bill when they've had 'a bad week'. Joey works with his brother as a painter and decorator during the summer. He regards that as 'real' work, and school as some kind of enforced holiday. There is no doubt that this ability to 'make out' in the 'real world', to handle sometimes quite large cash flows (Spike regularly earns over twenty pounds a week, though the average for the others is something under five pounds) and to deal with adults nearly on their own terms strengthens 'the lads' self-confidence and their feeling, at this point anyway, that they 'know better' than the school.

There is even a felt sense of superiority to the teachers. They do not know 'the way of the world', because they have been in schools or colleges all their lives — 'What do they know, telling us . . .?' As the next chapter will show, there are also many profound similarities between school counter-culture and shopfloor culture. The emerging school culture is both strengthened and directly fed material from what 'the lads' take to be the only true worldliwise source: the working class world of work.

This contact with the world of work, however, is not made for the purposes of cultural edification. It is made within the specific nexus of the need for cash, and responded to and exploited within that nexus. The very manner of approaching the world of work at this stage reproduces one of its characteristic features — the reign of cash. The near universal practice of 'fiddling' and 'doing foreigners', for instance, comes to 'the lads' not as a neutral heritage but as a felt necessity: they need the cash. As Spanksy says, 'If you go out even with just enough money in your pocket for a pint like, you feel different', and it is only the part-time job, and particularly its 'fiddles', which offers the extra variable capacity in their world to supply this free cash. This particular form of early exposure to work helps to set the parameters for their later understanding of labour and reward, authority and its balances, and for a particular kind of contained resentment towards those who manage and direct them:

[In a group discussion on part-time work]

> Spike   [. . .] it was about eight o'clock in the morning, this was, he's [a butcher] got a telephone, he's got a big bag of ten bobs, and he'd left the two strings over the

telephone so that if I touched it, the strings'd come, you know. I opened the bag, got a handful of ten bobs out, zipped it up and just left it. He says, 'You've touched this fucking bag, the strings was over the telephone'. Well I couldn't say much [...] so he told me to fuck off [...]

Will   [...] like there was an outside toilet [at a greengrocers where he used to work] but it was all blocked with stinking vegetables and all this, and I used to put 'em [cauliflowers] on top of the cistern, you know [...] he says, I seen 'im counting 'em, and he says, 'Uh...there's one missing here'. I said 'I dunno' [...] He says, 'There's one missing here'. I says, 'There ain't. He says, 'There is'. I says, 'I must have put it in that one, 'ere' have one of 'em', and he dayn't count them, so I was alright. I thought he was laying a trap for me, like, I think it was a Friday night when that happened. The next day [...] I had to have a big fire up the back to burn all the rubbish and that, and I set fire to everything like and all the canal bank. It was like the railway bank like, round the back, it was all dry, bone dry, so I got this cardboard, this piece of cardboard box like that, and I threw it over there and set all the bank on fire to get him back like. And I went walking in, I says, 'Is the bank s'posed to be on fire?' [Laughter] He went mad he did. He says, 'Was it you?' I says, 'No, it must have been the butcher, 'cos they was having a fire.' And the fire engines come and everything.

There is some scope for getting money by saving it from dinner money, as well as some possibility for limited extortion from 'ear'oles' and younger boys — though 'blagging off' first and second formers is not highly regarded. Often the last — and sometimes earlier — resort for getting 'money in your pocket' is stealing. Shortage of cash should not be underestimated as the compelling material base for theft. In a very typical articulation of mixed motives, however, 'thieving' is also a source of excitement rather like fighting. It puts you at risk, and breaks up the parochialism of the self. 'The rule', the daily domination of trivia and the entrapment of the formal are broken for a time. In some way a successful theft challenges and beats authority. A strange sort of freedom — even though it is only a private knowledge — comes from defying the conventions and being rewarded for it. If you are 'copped', particular skills in 'blagging your way out of it' can be brought to bear, and renewed excitement and satisfaction is obtained if you 'get away with it'. Sometimes, of course, you do not 'get away with it'. Two of the Hammertown lads are put on probation for stealing car radios during the research. This is disastrous. Parents are brought into it, official reports written up, and all kinds of unspecified worries about the procedures of the court and the interminable proceedings of bureaucracy turn the original excitement to sickness. This is a moment, again, where the formal wins a decisive and irrevocable victory over the informal. The informal meanings do not survive a direct confrontation. Still, given the near universality of theft amongst 'the lads', there are very few convictions for theft. There are many more close scraps and the dread of 'being done' adds extra excitement and an enhanced feeling of sharpness and adroitness when you do 'get away with it':

[In a group discussion]

Bill   It's just hopeless round here, there's nothing to do. When you've got money, you know, you can go to a pub and have a drink, but, you know, when you ain't got money, you've either got to stop in or just walk round the streets and none of them are any good really. So you walk around and have a laff.

Joey   It ain't only that it's enjoyable, it's that it's there and you think you can get away with it...you never think of the risks. You just do it. If there's an opportunity, if the door's open to the warehouse, you'm in there, seeing what you can thieve and then, when you come out like, if you don't get caught immediately, when you come out you'm really happy.

Bill   'Cos you've showed the others you can do it, that's one reason.

Joey   'Cos you're defying law again. The law's a big tough authority like and we're just little individuals yet we're getting away with it like.

[. . .]

Fuzz   [. . .] we all went up the copper station [for stealing from a sportshop], he had all our parents in first. Then he had us lot in with our parents and he says, this copper, we was all standing up straight, you know, looks round, he says, 'You! How much pocket money do you get?' he says, 'would you like someone to pinch that'. He says 'NO', 'Have any of you got anything to say?' 'Yes, cunt, let me go' [under his breath]. 'You should say, "Sorry" ', he said, 'If anything hadn't've been returned, if a dart had been missing, you'd 'ave 'ad it'. Benny Bones had got two air rifles at his house, Steve had got a catapult and a knife, and I'd got two knives at home, and he said, 'If anything'd been missing!'.

[. . .]

Joey   I'd been doing it all night [stealing from handbags], and I was getting drunk spending the money, and instead of sitting there, doin' it properly, putting your hand down the back of the seat, I lifted the seat up and was kneeling down underneath, getting it out that way, and this bird comes back and says, 'What are you doing under there?'. I says, 'Oh, I just dropped two bob', and then her went on about it, so I just run off like, over the other side of the dance. Her went and told the coppers, and the police sat outside by the bogs. When I went out they just got me into this little cleaning room, and they got me in there and had all me money out. And she'd had four pound pinched, it was a lie really 'cos I'd only pinched three pound, and I'd spent nearly half of it, had a pound on me. If I'd've had four quid on me like, even if it hadn't been hers, I think they'd've done me. I didn't have enough money on me, so they couldn't do me.

Where the target is the school there is a particular heightening of excitement, of challenge to authority, of verve in taking well-calculated risks — and making money as well. Besides being a direct insult to staff, it also puts you absolutely beyond the 'ear'oles'. They have neither the need for the extra cash, nor the imagination to overcome conventional morality, nor the quickness and smartness to carry through the deed. The school break-in sums up many crucial themes: opposition, excitement, exclusivity, and the drive for cash:

X   I couldn't see how we was going to get copped [when they broke into the school some time previously]. If, you know, I could see how them others [the school had recently been broken into] was going to get copped, he was, just bust a door down and walked in. There was footmarks all over the place, smashed a window and shit all over the place, and pulling books off. . . .

Y   I mean we had gloves on and before we left the house we even emptied our pockets out to make sure there was nothing identifying. I left all my stuff at his house and he did, we just went then and I had a brown polo neck on, me jeans, gloves, you know, and he had all black things on.

X   All black, polish on my face. [Laughter]

Y   No. We was going to. Weren't we? We got the polish at your house, we was going to, but we thought, no.

PW   Were you nervous when you were doing it?

Y   Yeah.

X   Oh ar. Like this you know [trembling]. 'Cos it's . . . uh . . . I've always you know, I've pinched out of people's pockets you know, I've seen two bobs lying about and I've gone, but I've never done anything like that before. I enjoyed it!

Y   And I did, really enjoyed it!

X   And after you know coming down the road we were just in a fit, weren't we? We was that, you know , it was closely worked out.

Y   And we spent it all up The bleeding Fountain, day'nt we. Getting pissed down The Old Boat.

X   Oh ar . . .I saved ten bob for the ice rink, remember?
—   Yeah.
PW   Why did you want to break into the school rather than anything else?
Y   Got no fucking money [. . .]
X   We knew the school well and if you try and break in anything else like houses and
        that, you know, you're not sure if there's anybody in, it's a bit risky, you know
        what I mean, but the school you know there's nobody sleeping here, you know
        there's almost no way you can get copped . . . [. . .]   [. . .]

Notes

[1] It is now recognised that some teachers retained on school teaching staffs are seriously
disturbed and that this is a growing problem. See, for instance, Lawrence, J. (1975) 'Control
experiment', *The Guardian*, 18 March.

[2] Spike's letter of apology is carefully pitched to maintain his own dignity as well as to secure
his leaving certificate: I would like you to accept my sincere apologies . . . . The school *itself*
has nothing to resemble 'Colditz' in any way whatsoever . . . . I realise what I have done,
which might I add I find Stupid now, *but at the time not so stupid*, so I am now prepared to face
the consequence which you see fit' (my italics).

5 Black girls in a London comprehensive school

M. FULLER

In the areas of housing, the law, employment, education and welfare, black people and women continue to be disadvantaged in comparison with men and whites. The facts of racial and sexual disadvantage in Britain mean that, whatever their social class, black women and girls are in a doubly subordinate position within the social formation.

With regard to education, those people in Britain writing about academic aspirations and achievement of pupils have compared black and white pupils, and made similar comparisons between females and males. At the time when I began my research (in 1975) I was unable to find any instance of work which attempted to analyse simultaneously the bearing which pupils' sex and race might have in this area. With the single exception of Driver (1977), writing about the academic achievements of black pupils continues to treat them as a sexually undifferentiated group (see, for example, Little, 1978). Other writers, working in the interactionist and/deviancy tradition, and concerned to document and analyse the experiential world of the adolescent, inside and outside school, have been equally limited in their focus. Their efforts have been almost exclusively concentrated on white sub-cultures—with Sharpe (1976) being a notable exception—and the balance being heavily towards male (and white) adolescent experiences and cultural expressions. In other words, not only does this tradition in sociology treat the world of adolescence as essentially male, but it also considers adolescents to be racially undifferentiated.

What seemed to be clear was that black pupils were under-achieving academically,[1] and that black youth (and some parents) were increasingly disaffected from schooling (Dhondy, 1974). It seemed equally clear from the studies by Hargreaves (1967) and Lacey (1970) that similar anti-school and what were termed 'delinquent' sub-cultures among white boys were related to the pupils' social class. In the cases of both race and social class, disaffection from school and relatively poor scholastic performance were connected.

In the absence of specific work about them it was difficult to know where black girls came into this schema. If one assumed the primacy of social class and/or racial category in developing an anti-school stance, black girls could be straightforwardly accommodated, since there would be little difference between them and their male peers. But the fact of being female might alter this picture—by virtue of their sex girls are in a particular subordinate position. There are no *a priori* reasons for assuming a greater importance for either sex or race in this respect, and no certain guidelines as to the effect of an interaction between the two. From logic and guesswork only, the fact of being female could have rather different implications for black girls' sub-cultural response to schooling. Given an additive model of subordination, it would seem that black girls would be essentially like their male peers, only more so; i.e., even more disaffected than similar male pupils. On the other hand, and in line with the common view that females as a group are more conformist, less likely to rebel and generally less 'troublesome' in the school context

(Levy, 1972), black girls could be expected to demonstrate similar but less strongly manifested alienation from school. This is not something to be decided by logic; rather it is an empirical question, though not, as already indicated, one which has actually been given prominence by previous writers.

In this article I shall describe a small group of black girls (of West Indian parentage, though mostly themselves of British birth) who formed a discernible sub-culture in the comprehensive school in which I carried out research during 1975 and 1976. As part of a much larger study[2] involving male and female pupils from Indo-Pakistani, West Indian and white British family backgrounds I spent two terms in the school in daily participation and observation of pupils' school lives. At that time and subsequently, observational material was supplemented by interviews, questionnaires and the analysis of various school documents. The larger project aimed to examine in what ways pupils' and teachers' sex-structured their position within the school as well as the ways in which teachers' and pupils' relations with each other were structured by their respective notions of gender (i.e. masculinity/femininity). Hence the work took place in a mixed school. To confront adequately the question 'How much does sex matter in school?' some additional and equally important referent is required, so that inferences about sexual differentiation may be subject to alternative explanation.[3] For this reason the school selected was multi-racial, and the possibility of social class and race as alternative or additional explanations for differentiation among pupils was integrated into the analysis. This point has been laboured because in the ordinary way a study based on only eight people could hardly expect to be taken as a serious contribution to the sociological literature; although in our present state of ignorance concerning black girls and schooling, such considerations might be waived.

As I shall go on to argue, the existence and specific defining features of this sub-culture of black girls call into question some of our present assumptions and thinking, not only about black pupils but also about the development of school-based sub-cultures. I make this argument with greater confidence because what follows, while relating to a small and particular group, is informed by constant comparisons with other same-age peers within the school: male and female; white, Asian and black.

Torville School

The school was a ten-form entry comprehensive in the north London Borough of Brent, and the students, in their final year of compulsory schooling, were aged 15 to 16 years. The fifth year was divided into two parallel bands, one containing 128 pupils who followed a mixed curriculum of practical/vocational subjects with some more academic ones, and who would be expected to take some 'O' level or CSE exams; the other band (the one with which I worked) containing 142 pupils following a more thoroughgoing academic curriculum, with the expectation that they would take a rather larger number of 'O' level and CSE exams than those in the practical band.

The academic band contained significantly fewer girls than boys (with the reverse sex-ratio in the practical band). There were fewer West Indian girls in the academic than the practial band, as was true also of white British and Asian girls. Although there were in general more boys in the academic than the practical band, a greater proportion (and absolute number) of West Indian boys was to be found in the practical band. Relating this to other writers' work (e.g., Coard, 1971; Troyna, 1976), it is clear that the situation with regard to West Indian boys, but not with respect to girls, confirms the view that West Indian pupils are found in disproportionate numbers in the lower streams (or equivalent groupings) within school.

Within the fifth year nearly a quarter of pupils was of West Indian parentage, a further one in four were of Indo-Pakistani parentage, and just over half were white and British-born, with only a very few other white Europeans. Within the academic band the majority of West Indian pupils was British-born, whereas the majority of Asian students was immigrant (with by far the majority of these being of East African rather than Indian sub-continental birth).

The Girls

Five of the eight girls were British-born, three having migrated to Britain from Jamaica, two when aged 3, and one when aged 11. One of the British-born girls had spent four years in the West Indies as a small child (aged 2 to 6). Six lived in a two-parent family and two in mother-headed families. All had at least one brother or sister living with them, and in most cases considerably more than one. The mothers of six of the girls were permanently employed outside the home in full-time jobs, one girl's mother had a permanent part-time job, and in one case the mother took seasonal jobs according to availability. All six fathers were normally in permanent full-time jobs. The girls came from predominantly manual working-class homes (five) with two having a father in a manual but a mother in a non-manual job; one girl had both parents in non-manual employment.

Although the sub-culture comprised girls in the same age-group attending the same school, in many important respects it was not simply or mainly a school-based sub-culture, for in order to make sense of its structure and values it is necessary to look outside the school, to the situation of black minorities in Britain generally and also to the situation of women in comparison with men. The girls consciously drew on these when discussing themselves and the other girls in their group. In particular they drew on their knowledge and experience of the West Indies.

West Indian Roots

Most of the black students whom I interviewed had themselves visited the West Indies in the relatively recent past; all were closely connected with others who had also returned from visits, and were in other ways kept apprised of life in the West Indies. In large part it was their awareness of their Caribbean roots and the inferences which they drew concerning themselves as females in that society which underly and provided the basis both for the existence of the sub-culture and for an understanding of its values and particular style. The other part is contributed by the girls' interpretation of the fact of their female sex in British society.

From what they had themselves observed and gleaned from others' accounts the girls had constructed a picture of a physically demanding and financially unrewarding life for women in the West Indies, in comparison with which their present and future lives in Britain seemed favourable.

> Women back home were really masculine. They had to be. They had to go and fetch water, come back and do their washing and it was really dirty because they don't have washing machines. And they had to get down and really scrub, then after that they had really old fashioned irons and had to burn coal to do it, plus you've got to starch it, then wet it again and iron it. And the men just expect them to do that. So, I mean, they can't be really careful what they do.
> (Monica)

Foner (1976) suggests that older immigrant women whom she interviewed in London shared this perception. The girls drew a comparison between the life-styles of women and men in the Caribbean, typifying that of men as pleasanter and less arduous, even though male unemployment was high. Boys, during interview, also indicated that they believed this to be the case.

One very important ramification of this picture was that the girls did not easily envisage a future for themselves in the West Indies; on the contrary their awareness of their West Indian roots led them to believe that they would be better off in Britain. On the other hand a return to the homeland (by which was meant the West Indies) featured prominently in the boys' thoughts about the future, sentiments which were frequently given coherence by their understanding of Rastafarianism. Within the fifth year at Torville only boys displayed some of the externalia of Rastafarianism—the wearing of woolly hats in orange, green and black, modified 'locks', etc.—and had adopted its rhetoric. It may be that because the option of returning was less (psychologically) available to the girls that they found a Rasta identity that much more difficult to contemplate.

It should not be inferred from this that the girls dissociated themselves from their Caribbean origins or wanted to be anything other than black. None of the girls indicated in any way that she would prefer to be white, and indeed they were proud to be black. For example, Janice having explicitly defined herself as 'pure black' on several occasions in the interview returned to the theme of blacks who 'go on as if they are a white person', who are the opposite of 'pure black'. She also suggested that'. . . if a black goes over to white we regard them as traitors, but if a white person comes over to us, we accept them as a black'.

This positive acceptance of themselves as black echoes Ladner's (1971) findings in relation to Afro-American female adolescents. As was the case with many of the Asian and white girls interviewed, the black girls expressed considerable resentment towards their brothers because of what they saw as discrimination in favour of boys within their own families. The basis of their argument was that domestic tasks were unfairly allocated, so that the main burden of the shopping, child-minding, laundry and cooking not undertaken by their mothers fell on the shoulders of the girls in the family. Boys were not expected to contribute to these domestic tasks, or only intermittently, whereas commitments of this kind absorbed considerable amounts of the girls' time out of school. (The boys confirmed that they were not expected to help and only rarely undertook such 'womanish' work.)

The girls in Driver's (1977) study were also undertaking quite onerous domestic commitments. In his discussion of conflict with parents he seems to suggest that relations between girls and their parents are relatively harmonious despite these demands made on the girls. At any rate he does not mention conflicts except in the context of boys and parents. Among the girls at Torville this was the most frequently mentioned topic of arguments with parents, and it was patently a source of considerable friction between girls and their parents as well as between girls and their brothers.

In many cases this resentment extended to boys in general. And yet at the same time the discrepancy in the demands made on girls and boys seemed to provide one of the bases of the girls' greater confidence in their ability. They were inclined to interpret the boys' behaviour as evidence of inability to do even simple things, as signifying 'childishness', 'laziness', and so on. This interpretation seemed all the more plausible to them since it echoed the division of competence, as they perceived it, between their parents within the home. Thus Marcia:

> My dad helps around the house, he only helps with the good things—he never does the washing up . . . . He's not very good practically, my mum doesn't really approve of him

when he's doing his decorating. My mum did the back room actually because my dad did it in this paint and my mum didn't like it so . . . she's quite independent really. She's a lot better than my dad at things—he's good at the theory, but not on practical things.

Though they might envy the boys their greater freedom from domestic chores and freedom of movement the girls nevertheless expressed no desire to be boys, other than in 'idle talk'.

The girls were aware of racial discrimination, recounting incidents involving themselves and people whom they knew, and were conscious that such discrimination would probably continue. They were also aware from a number of sources of the high levels of unemployment locally and nationally which had double implications for them as young blacks. They had, as already described, experienced what they themselves interpreted as less favourable treatment because of their sex. The conjunction of all these—their positive identity as black but knowledge of racial discrimination in Britain, their positive identity as female but belief that both in Britain and the Caribbean women were often accorded less than their due status—meant that the girls were angry at the foreclosing of options available to them as blacks and as women.

Such a conjunction might be supposed to engender apathy and despair, but quite the reverse was the case. Discussing working-class pupils, White and Brockington (1978, p. 111) also note that 'Anger and frustration, consolidated and supported, is not wasted but can motivate to action'. The girls' forms of action and the import of their stance within school need to be understood as strategies for trying to effect some control over their present and future lives. Because they considered their futures were necessarily to be in Britain, these attempts included finding some *modus vivendi* with whites which did not undermine their identity as blacks.

Features of the Sub-culture

The sub-culture emerged from the girls' positive acceptance of the fact of being both black and female. Its particular flavour stemmed from their critical rejection of the meanings with which those categorizations are commonly endowed. Their consequent anger and frustration, unlike that of their black male peers, was not turned against themselves or translated into an automatic general dislike of whites or the opposite sex. Rather their feelings and understandings gave particular meanings to achievement through the acquisition of educational qualifications.

The girls were all strongly committed to achievement through the job market (cf. Ladner, 1971; Slaughter, 1972), being marked out from the other girls not so much by the type of jobs to which they were aspiring as by the firmness with which they held their future job ambitions, and by their certainty that they would want to be employed whatever their future domestic circumstances might be:

> I want a proper job first and some kind of skill so that if I do get married and have children I can go back to it; don't want just relying on him for money, 'cause I've got to look after myself. There must be something I can do.
> (Michelle)

and Monica's view of herself is very similar in this respect:

> I should go out to work because, really, if I don't start learning to get on with it, I maybe will just have to leave home, get married and depend on the husband and I don't want that at all . . . the picture of myself is an active one, always doing something, I don't know what. Maybe I'll be a housewife or something like that, but I always picture myself working.

They were also strong believers in the value of education and educational qualifications as a necessary preparation for the 'good' jobs which they hoped to obtain—or more accurately, perhaps, they took such a belief for granted. They were confident of their ability to achieve the academic qualifications which they were aiming for, both in the short term (i.e. 'O' level and/or CSE) and in the longer term ('A' level and/or a variety of examinations to be taken at college, polytechnic or university).

This optimism extended to their wider life-chances. Conscious of actual incidents of racial discrimination and the possibility of discrimination against them because of their colour and sex, and aware of the high levels of unemployment locally and nationally which had double implications for them as young people and blacks, the girls nevertheless believed that in the job market there was much that they could do to forestall ending up in low level, dead-end jobs, or finding themselves unemployed on leaving school. They spoke of this in terms of being 'ambitious', but equally, ensuring that whatever ambitions they had were not deflected.

As will be clear, acquisition of academic qualifications was an integral part of this sense of control over their future. What was less immediately obvious was the underlying relationship of academic qualifications to the girls' sense of self-worth. In a very real sense they perceived the obtaining of academic qualifications as a public statement of something which they already knew about themselves but which they were also certain was given insufficient public recognition: that they were capable, intelligent and the equal of boys.

> I think people trust you more when you're a boy; they say you're more reliable, you're more trustworthy. Because my dad always says that, he says you can take a boy and you can show him a trade, but you can take a girl and the next minute their heads are all filled up with boys, that she just doesn't want to know. So I'm going to show him, you see!
> (Beverley)

That is, their sense of self-worth did not derive from the acquisition of academic qualifications nor, in the future, from obtaining a 'good' job; rather their pursuit of these ends was given meaning by their existing knowledge of their own worth and their understanding that this was often denied. During interviews most of the girls said they thought boys considered themselves superior to girls, an idea which they viewed with amused disbelief or sceptisicm:

> Most West Indian boys definitely aren't going to let a woman dominate them or tell them what to do, they firmly believe that they're the boss and she has to do everything . . . . They just have this thing that they are the superior ones and women are inferior. This equality business—I don't think that it would ever work in the West Indies, don't think they'd accept it, might here. And I don't think the West Indian boys growing up here, I don't think they're going to accept it either because they always talk about it as a load of rubbish anyway, because as far as they're concerned they're superior and they're not going to be equal with a woman, or anything like that.
> (Christa)

The written word does not readily convey the tone in which Christa spoke, but what was clear was that she, together with most of the other girls, did not take it as self-evident that males were superior or deserved to be taken more seriously than herself.

To this point in their careeers the girls' confidence appeared well-founded; they had passed a greater number of 'O' level and CSE exams, and at rather higher grades than had the black boys. The black girls achieved a mean of 7.6 passes at this level compared with 5.6 for the black boys, an achievement which put them second only to Asian boys in performance in 'O' level and CSE. Similarly, while all the girls had remained in full-time education for at least one year beyond the statutory school-leaving age, only two of the black boys had done so. Where girls had left school or college to take up employment, all mentioned that they were also continuing their education by day release or block release schemes or by attending college in the evenings; only one boy mentioned that he was continuing his education in any way.

So far the picture drawn seems to be that of the girls as archetypal 'good' pupils—ones who have high aspirations and achieve well in public examinations—but this was far from the truth in most other aspects of their lives in school. Unlike other pupils who were similarly pro-education, the black girls were not pro-school. That is to say, their intolerance of the daily routines and their criticisms of much that went on inside the school were marked. They shared with some other pupils a view of school as 'boring', 'trivial' and 'childish', and yet at the same time were markedly different from these same pupils in that they had high aspirations and a high degree of academic success. Despite their critical view of school the black girls did not define it as 'irrelevant' (as did other pupils who found school boring, etc.), because of the particular importance which they attached to academic achievement. Quine (1974) discusses a similar orientation among the boys in his study of two Midland comprehensive schools.

Most high aspirers and achievers in the school were concerned to demonstrate their seriousness of purpose to teachers and other pupils by certain kinds of classroom behaviour: punctuality, a modicum of attention to lesson content, and a 'respectful' (by no means always deferential) attitude towards teachers, in addition to actually doing the work set. Whether they actively courted a good reputation in other ways or not, such pupils tended to be seen as 'good' pupils. The reverse of this behaviour was taken by both teachers and pupils to indicate a lack of interest in school and was associated with a reputation as a 'bad' pupil.

The black girls conformed to the stereotypes of the good pupil only in so far as they worked conscientiously at the schoolwork or homework set. But they gave all the appearances in class of not doing so, and in many other ways displayed an insouciance for the other aspects of the good pupil role. They neither courted a good reputation among teachers nor seemed to want to be seen as 'serious' by the staff or other pupils. Eschewing behaviour which would bring them into serious conflict with teachers (for example, truanting, direct challenges to a teacher's authority, grossly disruptive behaviour within the classroom), the girls were frequently involved in activities which exasperated the staff and which were yet not quite clearly misdemeanours requiring comment or action on their part. The following examples drawn from field notes represent incidents which occurred with some frequency: openly engaging in some 'illegitimate' activity (reading a magazine, chatting, doing homework for another subject) so that it appeared that the girls were not listening or not working, yet when questioned by the teacher they could show that they had, in fact, taken in what had been said or had actually completed the work assigned; arriving technically late for a lesson but actually seconds before the teacher, who could see their late arrival; handing in work for marking when it suited them rather than immediately it was asked for; complying with a teacher's request somewhat slowly and with a show of complete uninterest, and so on. Studying delinquent pupils (some of them black) in an American high school, Werthman (1963) describes somewhat similar behaviour. Neither meek and passive nor yet aggresive, and obviously confrontationist in their stance towards teachers, the girls were something of a puzzle to some of their peers and teachers.

Three themes emerged in their discussions of the stance they adopted within school. First, to be seen as a 'good' pupil (i.e., showing too much eagerness in class, appearing to take school too seriously) risked the discovery of their academic and job ambitions and consequently invited ridicule and possibly more from those peers with whom the girls most frequently compared themselves—black boys:

> I find that most boys do have ambitions but they're influenced by their friends, so they never get put into practice anyway . . . I think the girls are more ambitious but if they want to do something they don't feel embarrassed about it except when boys, when they hear you're doing 'O' levels, they won't come out with it and say you're a snob but they treat you a bit differently and you can feel it . . . I think West Indian girls might feel a bit funny about that.
> (Joan)

> I've always got my head in a book. I don't think they (boys in school) like it because they are always commenting on it and they say 'You won't get anywhere', and sometimes I think they don't want me to learn or something like that, you know; but I spoke to my mum about it, and she said I shouldn't listen and I should keep working hard.
> (Marcia)

In this way their classroom behaviour may be seen as a conscious smoke-screen to confuse others and enable the girls to retain the friendship of their peer group without giving up their aspirations.

Second, to be viewed by teachers as a 'good' pupil was inconsistent with the girls' own view of themselves. 'Good' pupils were boring, were unable to have 'fun', and were in other respects 'immature'. To behave in class like them would invite comparison with people from whom the girls expressly distanced themselves.

Third, the girls believed that other highly aspiring pupils placed too great an emphasis on teachers' opinions in relation to pupils' success: insofar as public examinations were marked by people who did not know the candidates personally, pupils could expect to pass exams on the quality of their work rather than on the quality of their relationship with the teachers who taught them. Very few other pupils discussed pupil-teacher relationships in this way.

The black girls' behaviour within the classroom is, I suggest, intimately connected with their positive identity as black and female. It seems reasonable to suppose that in coming to a sense of their own worth the girls had learnt to rely on their own rather than others' opinion of them. Their weighing up of the potential relevance and importance of teachers was part of a more general stance towards others. The girls were relatively sophisticated in judging who did and did not matter in their pursuit of academic qualifications, for example, so that one could say they adopted a somewhat 'strategic' political stand in relation to other people, including whites generally and white authority in school specifically.

To some extent this can also be seen in their social relationships with other pupils. The girls appeared to treat poor relationships as a resource of essentially individualistic achievement aims rather than as a source of pleasure and/or confirmation in its own right. The girls came together as a result of each of them trying to cope with the difficulties of proving their own worth. This was to be expressed through the acquisition of paper qualifications, not through the living out of a particular peer-based life-style. In a sense the confirmation of the girls' sense of identity could not come from either their peer group or from adults, but only from their own efforts. For this reason the sub-culture was not a readily discernible entity, marked out from others by a particular and visible style. Or rather their style was not the *raison d'être* of their coming together.

Unlike pupils in other 'academic' sub-cultures described in the literature (e.g., Hargreaves, 1967), the girls did not confine their friendship choices only to other academically inclined pupils, but showed a fluidity of friendship choices among other black but 'non-academic' girls in the school. This indicates, I suggest, that the girls had discovered or assumed that they had little in common with other pupils (white or Asian) who, like them, had high aspirations. That the black girls in the academic band at Torville made their choices of friends from among both academic and non-academic black girls, is partly due to the relatively small number of black pupils from whom to choose. (Similar ethnocentrism in friendship choices is reported by Durojaiye, 1970; Bhatnagar, 1970; Troyna, 1978). The girls' choice of friends does also underline the central importance of both their sex and ethnicity in the girls' identity.

This can also be discerned in their assessment of certain teachers. As already indicated, the girls did not automatically define teachers as adversaries, despite the fact that they behaved in ways which might have been interpreted as giving insufficient respect to teachers, and despite the fact that the girls were critical of many aspects of their daily life in school. Alone among the pupils, a few of the black girls indicated that they greatly admired certain teachers, whom they would like to emulate. As can be seen from the following passage from an interview with Beverley, the reasons for this admiration stem from the fact that the particular teachers in question are thought to demonstrate qualities (of persistence, struggle against convention, etc.) which have a particular resonance with the girls' own current situation. In other words, the teacher is admired not because she is a teacher or because she is white, nor even despite these factors, but only because she has succeeded in the job market. In this respect the teacher's sex is the salient point.

In reply to my question 'What is it about Miss G that you admire?' Beverley replied:

> Because she's a careers woman. She succeeded in life at a time in her days when women were expected to sit around... she rebelled against that and she's got what she wanted, got her own car, got her own flat, completely independent, goes where she likes when she likes, she's got her own money, you know, she's well paid. And now she's succeeded and got what she wants out of life, she's getting married—everything has kind of worked out for her... she can be very serious and hard-working but at the same time she can be good fun, you see.

What is also clear is that this particular teacher is a living demonstration that success and femininity can be reconciled, and that success and solemnity are not synonymous. No matter that the girl's perception of the 'olden days' may be inaccurate and the difficulties to be overcome exaggerated, the teacher's example is taken to heart since struggle and resourcefulness (Ladner, 1971) are important aspects of the girls' ideas about themselves. As the following incident illustrates, the girls' persistence is already well-developed:

> When I first went for the job, I was very crafty when I wrote the letter. I put that I was a student and they thought I was coming from university, and I did it in perfectly good English so they wouldn't think that it was a foreign person. And then when I went and they actually saw that I was coloured I think they were a bit shocked, so they kept stalling and said come back tomorrow. They said the person isn't in, can you come back next week, and I wouldn't give in. Every time they said come back I'd go back and I'd go back. My dad was backing me all the way and in the end I got through.
> (Christa)

This kind of persistence is much admired and is a source of considerable pride:

> Michelle and I are the same really, we have this thing to succeed, determined, you know. If anything gets in the way we kick it out the way and get on.
> (Annette)

Summary and Discussion

In trying to describe and understand the sub-culture of black girls in a particular school it has been necessary to make frequent comparisons with other people in and outside Torville school itself. There are two reasons for this. First, as is common in the development of an in-group identity, the girls saw themselves as a separate group by comparing themselves with other blacks (Rosenberg and Simmons, 1972) and contrasting themselves with others. Second, very few features of the sub-culture on their own were unique to the girls, although the specific configuration of values, attitudes, behaviour and self-perceptions did mark them out as quite distinct from other pupils in their year.

Because this sub-culture of West Indian girls contrasts with the general picture of West Indian disaffection from school and low attainment, it would be helpful to know just how prevalent or typical such a sub-culture is of West Indian pupils generally. The majority of writers do not differentiate between boys and girls, and from internal evidence it would appear that much of the work has been based on males, with perhaps the implicit assumption that what is established for males is more or less an accurate representation of the whole group. Because of this lack of differentiation or failure to specify the sex-class of those being studied, it is not possible to give an accurate estimate of the typicality of the sub-culture described of black pupils in general. For very similar reasons, that in the literature on adolescence, schooling, and sub-cultures very little specific attention has been paid to girls in their own right (a lack noted by McRobbie and Garber, 1976; Ward, 1976; among others), it is not possible to gauge just how frequently such a sub-culture may be found among girls. However, Lambart's account of her work in a girls' grammar school is particularly instructive, since her description of the Sisterhood (a group of third-year pupils) suggests a very similar conjunction of academic attainment and non-conformity to the rules, regulations and routines of school (Lambart, 1976, pp. 157-9):

> They had a sense of fun bordering often on mischief; and they were careful of the 'respect' they have to teachers ... despite its deviance, the Sisterhood existed as a focus for girls with more than average ability.

The relationship between academic performance and behaviour within school of the black girls at Torville and Lambart's Sisterhood contrasts with that described for boys by Hargreaves (1967) and Willis (1977). I would argue that this calls into question the necessary equation of academic striving and success with conformity, an equation which the work of Werthman (1963), Holt (1964) and Jackson (1966) in any case indicates is not universal.

Since it is frequently argued that teachers' expectations[4] serve to depress the attainment of certain groups of pupils (including females and blacks), it is particularly interesting that the black girls' achievement was not related to whether teachers saw them as good or bad pupils. Nor was there any relationship between teachers' perception of the girls as pupils and the girls' classroom activities, which contrasts with Driver's (1977) finding of a considerable overlap (particularly in relation to black boys) in the West Midland school he studied.

A radical analysis of schools and schooling points to an underlying ethnocentrism and middle-class bias in the structure, organization and curriculum of all schools. As Reynolds (1976) points out, this leads to viewing school as a battleground of opposing values in which pupils demonstrate their resistance to alien and oppressive race and class values by refusing to conform. It becomes only too easy to assume that academic striving and achievement are synonymous with subscribing (conforming) to these values, and to see school failure as necessarily indicative of rejection of those same values. Apart from the fact that neither Reynolds nor Quine (1974) could find evidence of such polarized stances in the schools they studied, conformity and deviance within the school are rarely global, but are situation-specific (Werthman, 1963; Furlong, 1976). Moreover, if further research confirms the disjunction between academic orientation and within-school behaviour, noted by Lambart (1976) and in the present study of Torville school, it may be that the pro-education pro-school connection and its polar opposite (anti-education, anti-school) emerge as somewhat specific rather than universal tendencies—specific to boys (and perhaps only a proportion of these) and/or more typical of particular types of school.

In this article I have described a group of black girls whose acute awareness of their double subordination as women and black was accompanied by a refusal to accept the 'facts' of subordination for themselves. As a strategy for present and future survival the girls had adopted a programme of 'going it alone' in which those aspects of schooling to do with acquiring qualifications had an important part. No more tolerant of the 'irrelevant' aspects of schooling (e.g., the daily routines) than their black male peers, the girls were in some ways a good deal more effectively independent of adult authority than any other group of pupils (male or female) in the school.

Wilkinson (1975, p. 305) argues that:

> [Black] youth are unlike their white counterparts not only with respect to placement in the social structure and their definitions of the dynamics of inter-racial relations, but also with respect to the type of attitudinal orientation which emerges from their cultural experiences. They are different in the collective symbolism and self-oriented definitions of who they are and what they wish to become. For they still must contend with social issues that never confront white youth.

Miles and Phizacklea (1977, p. 495) elaborate this theme, arguing that 'it is the unique experience of blacks of racial exclusion that is the essence of black ethnicity'. As I hope has been demonstrated in this chapter, when racial exclusion is overlaid and combined with sexual exclusion, it becomes necessary to begin to recognize that black ethnicity may take different forms and point to differing strategies for females and males.

Acknowledgements

The research on which this chapter is based was carried out while I was employed at the Social Science Research Council Research Unit on Ethnic Relations. This chapter does not represent the views of the SSRC, nor does it necessarily reflect those of the members of the SSRC Unit. I should like to record my thanks to Annie Phizacklea for comments on an earlier draft of this [article], and to Sarah Pegg who typed the manuscript.

Notes

[1] The extensive literature in this area is treated in Fuller (1976).
[2] See Fuller (1978).
[3] The same argument would apply whether the main focus were social class or racial category. In other words, analysis of sexual differentiation is not a special case, but the use of constant comparison is desirable in most research.
[4] The classic text here is Rosenthal and Jacobson (1968).

References

Bhatnagar, J. (1970) *Immigrants at School*, Cornmarket Press.

Coard, B. (1971) *How the West Indian Child is Made Educationally in the British School System*, New Beacon Books

Dhondy, F. (1974) 'The black explosion in schools', *Race Today*, February.

Driver, G. (1977) 'Cultural competence, social power and school achievement: a case study of West Indian pupils attending a secondary school in the West Midlands', *New Community*, Vol. 5, pp. 353–9.

Durojaiye, M. (1970) 'Race relations among junior school children', *Educational Research*, Vol. 11, pp. 226–228.

Foner, N. (1976) 'Women, work and migration: Jamaicans in London', *New Community*, Vol. 5, pp. 85–98.

Fuller, M. (1976) 'Experiences of adolescents from ethnic minorities in the British state education system', in Bernard, P.J. (ed.) *Les travailleurs etrangers en Europe occidentale*, Moulton.

Fuller, M. (1978) 'Dimensions of Gender in a School', Ph.D. thesis, University of Bristol.

Furlong, V. J. (1976) 'Interaction sets in the Classroom', in Hammersley, M. and Woods, P. (eds.) *The Process of Schooling*, Routledge and Kegan Paul.

Hargreaves, D. (1967) *Social Relations in a Secondary School*, Routledge and Kegan Paul.

Holt, J. (1964) *How Children Fail*, Penguin.

Jackson, P. (1966) 'The student's world', *The Elementary School Journal*, Vol. 66, pp. 343–57.

Lacey, C. (1970) *Hightown Grammar*, Manchester University Press.

Ladner, J. (1971) *Tomorrow's Tomorrow—The Black Woman*, Doubleday.

Lambart, A. (1976) 'The sisterhood' in Hammersley, M. and Woods, P. (eds) *The Process of Schooling*, Routledge and Kegan Paul.

Levy, M. (1972) 'The school's role in the sex-role stereotyping of girls', *Feminist Studies*, Vol. 1, pp. 5–23.

Little, A. (1978) 'Schools and race' in Commission for Racial Equality *Five Views of Multi-racial Britain*, CRE/BBC.

Mcrobbie, A. and Garber, J. (1975) 'Girls and subcultures' *Cultural Studies*, Vol. 718, pp. 209–22.

Miles, R. and Phizacklea, A. (1976) 'Class, race, ethnicity and political action, *Political Studies*, Vol. 27, pp. 491–507.

Quine, W. (1974) 'Polarised cultures in comprehensive schools', *Research in Education*, Vol. 12, pp. 9–25.

Reynolds, D. (1976) 'When teachers and pupils refuse a truce: the secondary school and the creation of delinquency' in Mungham, G. and Pearson, G. (eds) *Working Class Youth Culture*, Routledge and Kegan Paul.

Rosenberg, M. and Simmons, R. '1972) *Black and White Self-Esteem: The Urban School Child*, American Sociological Association.

Rosenthal, R. and Jacobson, L. (1968) *Pygmalion in the Classroom*, Holt, Rinehart and Winston.

Sharpe, S. (1976) *'Just like a Girl': How Girls Learn to be Women*, Penguin.

Slaughter, D. (1972) 'Becoming an Afro-American woman' *School Review*, Vol. 80, pp. 299–318.

Troyna, B. (1978) 'Race and streaming' *Educational Review*, Vol. 30.

Ward, J. (1976) *Social Reality for the Adolescent Girl*, Faculty of Education, University College of Swansea.

Werthman, C. (1963) 'Delinquents in school', *Berkely Journal of Sociology*, Vol. 8, pp. 39–60.

White, R. and Brockington, D. (1978) *In and Out of School*, Routledge and Kegan Paul.

Willis, P. (1977) *Learning to Labour*, Saxon House.

6 Gender and the sciences: pupils' gender-based conceptions of school subjects

L. MEASOR

One of the most influential sets of factors which has an impact upon the curriculum is that of gender. Girls perceive and react to the curriculum differently from boys. In this article I shall document some of these gender-based differences in attitude and reaction in the physical and domestic science areas of the curriculum; and attempt to trace out some of their consequences. The data on which the paper is based were drawn from interviews with and observations of first year pupils at a large, urban comprehensive school during 1979 and 1980.

Girls and physical science: current explanations

For once, we know more about the girls, since girls' reactions to natural science have been the subject of official concern and HMI reports. The basic fact that girls do less well in science than boys and that fewer girls take the subject when the time comes for option choosing is now well known. Inevitably, as a result, fewer girls get examination passes in the physical sciences. As HMI have recorded:

> Although the physical sciences and biology are normally available to both boys and girls at school, at the upper secondary level, one third of girls do no science at all, and over half do no physical science beyond the third year.
> (HMI, 1980)[1]

There are also some important differences *within* the general science area: girls take biology more than chemistry, and chemistry more than physics. Thus, according to DES figures:

> 50% of boys did physics in the 4th and 5th year while only 12% of girls did. Conversely nearly half of all girls in the 4th and 5th years study biology while 28% of all boys take this subject.
> (DES, 1975)

In recent years, the issue has attracted a considerable amount of research attention (summarized in Kelly, 1981). At first explanations concentrated on 'within-school' factors. It was suggested that the problem lay in the poor provision of equipment and inadequate staffing of girls' schools. Renee Short, for example, argued in the House of Commons in 1955 that all would be well when mixed schools replaced the single-sex ones (Kelly, 1981, p. 99). Ironically, however, once mixed schools became widespread[2] it became clear that:

> Girls are more likely to choose a science in a single sex school than they are in a mixed school, although in a mixed school a higher percentage of pupils may be offered these subjects.
> (DES, 1975)

The DES survey therefore looked at other ways schools failed to provide equal opportunities for boys and girls and speculated upon their effects on girls' performance in science. Girls, it was argued, were often denied the opportunity of taking craft subjects, where the skills they learned could feed usefully into science. In addition to such curricular influences, teachers attitudes, expectations and reactions were also said to have helped turn girls off science. Moreover, these expectations could well be reflected in the differential treatment given to boys and girls in science lessons (Galton, 1981). Lastly, given that the majority of science teachers, and especially senior teachers, are male, girls are often not provided with role models of scientifically competent females (Blackstone 1976, Sharpe 1976).

A second set of explanations involved ideas of differential abilities between boys and girls. J. A. Gray, for instance, argued that such sex differences have an inherent biological basis which cannot and should not be tampered with (Kelly, 1981, p. 43). Social learning theorists like Mischel (1966) and Bandura (1971) have suggested that early socialization, rather than biological inheritance, is responsible for these differences in ability. Early socialization lays down rules about and provides role models for sex-appropriate behaviour and actions (Kelly, 1981; Saraga and Griffiths, 1981).

Recent research, including Kelly's own, confirms this view that achievement in science is an aspect of sex role learning. 'The characteristically low achievement of girls in science', she argues, 'is an aspect of the feminine sex role—that is learned behaviour which is appropriate for females in our society.' (Kelly, 1981, p. 73). Kelly takes what she calls a 'cognitive approach' to sex role learning which 'conceives of the child as an active participant in structuring his or her experience and formulating sex role concepts'. (Kelly, 1981, p. 74). Society is seen as presenting 'an image of feminine and masculine to the child' and the child 'puts together a cluster of the attributes that they label male or female, and they try to copy the appropriate cluster'. This approach moves away from the social learning theories which see society as crudely imposing sex role stereotypes upon the individual. The child is regarded as essentially self-socializing, first developing categories and then fitting him or herself into these categories. This is important for science, the argument runs, because science, or at least physics and chemistry, is conventionally seen as masculine (Haste, 1981).

As an HMI report noted, pupils see science as 'leading to qualifications relevant to traditional male oriented occupations' (HMI, 1980, p. 9). It is not just that science is male dominated, but that in some way it is seen as 'masculine'. Consequently girls tend to reject physical science as part of their desire to become and be seen as 'feminine'. Science, then, like certain other areas of the school curriculum has become invested with gender characteristics to which pupils react. These pupil perceptions are critical at puberty and in early adolescence, when individuals are consumed with a concern to establish themselves as feminine or masculine. As Kelly puts it:

> Each sex, when educated with the other, is at puberty almost driven by developmental changes to use subject preference and where possible subject choice as a means of ascribing its sex role.
> (Kelly, 1981, p. 102)

If this argument is correct, the early adolescent years are crucial in the process of girls' disaffection from science. Contrary to some assertions of HMI (1980, p. 22) that 'combined science courses . . . with 11–13 year old pupils were generally successful in arousing the interest of the majority of pupils, both boys and girls, it seems that early adolesence is precisely the age and stage when girls are most likely to switch off from science, for it is during these years that sex role differentiation is most intense.

Science as a resource in the negotiation of gender identities

The research project from which this article derives dealt specifically with the years 11–13, and involved an eighteen-month period of observation of pupils at 11 plus to the end of their first secondary school year. In the area in which the research was carried out the age of transfer is 12 plus, so pupils were studied at both middle and upper school. The intensive character of the research allowed these issues and reactions to be documented in far greater depth than was possible for the HMI team. The science course the pupils followed was the integrated Nuffield Science scheme, where all the sciences are combined. Its approach is a problem-solving one, with an emphasis on practical and experimental work.

Even while they were at middle school pupils showed a clear gender difference in reactions to the idea of doing science at the new school. They already knew something of the science curriculum at the upper school, through the latter's induction scheme for its new pupils. They had visited the school several times, and been shown around the remarkably well equipped labs where pupils were working. In addition, the science department had put on a display of its wares and the tricks of its trade in the school's lecture theatre, which was suitably darkened for the occasion, thus heightening the atmosphere. There were tug-of-war experiments which involved a vacuum cup and two teams of excited middle school children pulling each other's jerseys out of shape. Hamsters, rabbits and gerbils were produced together with two goats, one of which ate the head of department's tie. The animals belonged to the school, and it was made clear that they were looked after entirely by the pupils. There were biological experiments which involved electric wiring of pupils, and rapid exercise which made light and heat meters react. Finally, the chemists put on a pyrotechnic display of flashes, sparks and explosions caused by chemicals, static electricity and batteries.

Most children thought the display, which closely resembled a successful Christmas pantomime, had been wonderful; though some of the girls had been rather afraid. The boys gave excited reports of the flashes and bangs:

> *Keith:* Gary put his hand up to spark off a flame with his finger with the help of a Van der Graph machine—he nearly burnt his finger off!
> *Pete:* I really liked that science lesson, we all stood up to see what happened.
> *Phillip:* Those experiments were great.
> *R:* Which ones did you like best?
> *Phillip:* The hydrogen one or was it helium. He lit it in Bruce's hand. Great!

Bruce, the boy actually involved in the experiment, repeated with mingled pride and humour:

> As for that chemistry man, he nearly blew my hand off on Monday.

Such reactions to the experiments can be contrasted with those of the girls. As one of them remarked, 'I don't like fire, and my friend Anne, she don't like fire neither'. The girls displayed anxiety about their ability to cope with the new science subjects, which they saw as difficult. In the words of one girl, Sue, 'I am worried about their way of doing physics, and I am no good at it, the hard part'.

The boys, by contrast, were looking forward to the chance of working with the new and sophisticated equipment they had seen.

Keith: Well, there is more of a chance to learn there, because in this school they haven't
          got the proper apparatus and that. Like in science, we have been told about these
          experiments; but we haven't been able to do them, there they have got science
          labs and everything.

As we might expect, given the statistics that more girls choose to do biology than
boys, their response to this subject was different. Far from being fearful, the girls
reacted very positively to the animals that had been brought in during the science
department's 'show'. There had been appropriate 'Ooohs' and 'Aaahs', especially to
the baby chicks, and the girls commented enthusiastically about the prospect of
looking after those animals.

However, there was another aspect to their reactions to biology lessons which
also demands attention. At middle school the girls had heard a story that in the
secondary school science lessons they were required to dissect a rat later in the year.
The responses of the boys and the girls to this prospect were very different. The
boys said 'Yes, that's really good' and by and large gloried in the gory nature of the
experiment, discussing eye-balls and lungs and other anatomical parts of childhood
grotesquerie. The girls reacted differently, and judged it 'not very nice'. In a more
detailed analysis of this data elsewhere we have already suggested that this
differential response was an important element of sex role learning; and that it
implied a gender code of behaviour (Measor and Woods, 1983). Clearly, at this point
in their anticipatory socialization, pupils displayed a gender-based difference in
attitude.

These reactions and responses were maintained during the first term at
secondary school, when the pupils found themselves in a Nuffied Science scheme
which involved them in doing experimental work each week. The girls did not enjoy
or find themselves drawn to the activity. It is important to understand what their
objections were. The girls protested about the smells that were produced in their
science lessons. One project had involved making and mixing substances, the
substances were then tested, and the testing included smelling them. Some of the
substances had been particularly nasty. Jenny said, 'I felt sick' and insisted she really
could not finish the work. Sally reported that the project had given her a headache,
this was sufficiently bad for her to have to miss the disco that evening, which from
her point of view was serious indeed! Others found the activities generally
unappealing and even abhorrent.

Valerie: In science we had that thermometer thing, when we had to stick it in our
           mouths.... That was horrible, I was sick that night.... I think I stuck it down me
           froat too far. It was 'orrible'.

The other dominant reported reaction was fear. The girls admitted that they felt
some fear when confronted with the range of equipment and dangerous chemicals.
Acids were especially threatening:

R: Do you find science difficult?
Clair: Yes, because you have got all these acids, and you have got to remember which
          ones are harmful, and what they do to you. It is quite hard to do things, because I
          am scared of fire, and when I put on the bunsen burners I am really scared of them.
          I always think I am going to go up on fire.

This fear of fire and of the bunsen burners which had arisen in the response to the
induction scheme was a recurrent theme:

Amy: I think Ros is scared of the bunsen burner.
Rebecca: She is, when I had her for a partner, I did everything, she was too scared to do
          anything.

There was one particular experiment where pupils had to heat, melt and manipulate glass rods. Many pupils did in fact receive minor burns and the teacher cheerfully administered antiseptic cream, and encouraged them to continue. The girls remembered this with a particular sense of objection:

Sally: I didn't like it when we had to burn down that glass.
Amy: No I didn't like that, everyone burned themselves that day.

The girls contrasted their attitudes with those of the boys in this context:

Sally: The boys are a bit braver than girls.
Amy: Yes, they will do anything, whereas girls won't all the time, I am not scared of the bunsen burner . . . but . . . sometimes when we have to pick the bunsen burner up, when it is alight, I get a bit . . . once, we had to pick it up, and I nearly burned myself.

One day the experiment involved dropping water onto an alkali pellet, which then hissed and burned, and let off an unpleasant gas. Before they began the experiment the teacher explained in graphic detail the dangers of dealing carelessly with alkali, and cautioned care. The girls then stood at arms length clearly displaying their fear. Again, in discussing this, the girls contrasted their own attitudes with those of the boys:

Sally: With the boys it's 'You just do this'.
Rebecca: When we boil water, I mean to say it is going to overflow, so I just get scared sometimes I am going to burn myself.

Another source of objection from the girls was that they got very dirty in these lessons. In one experiment pupils had to drop carbon into a solvent and it produced a black substance which got all over their hands. Again this led to protests:

Sally: It made us all really dirty.

The others agreed with her, expressions of real disgust on their faces:

Ros: I was scared it was going to burn right through my fingers, like some awful acid or something.

Another afternoon the pupils were working with eye droppers and Indian ink. Ros spilt some on her hand. She inspected it anxiously complaining:

Ros: Oh no, look what I've done.
Teacher: That'll come off in a few days.

Ros was not in the least appeased though and explained to Amy:

Tonight I have to serve sweets at this little bazaar my mum is running. This won't look very good to people, will it?

The girls also stated that they felt squeamish and disgusted by some of the things they saw in science lessons. The teacher showed the class a brain, preserved in formaldehyde, placed in a jar. It was an example of teaching strategies which urge the teacher to bring concrete examples of material in the lessons into class. The girls in the class displayed a really strong reaction to the brain, demonstrating once more their squeamish sense of what is 'not nice'. Though their reaction did reduce somewhat when it was explained that the brain was not from a human being.

The rat, which had a starring role in the stories told at middle school, was to make its actual appearance in the middle of the summer term. The myth had got some of the details wrong, for it was a teacher who carefully did the dissection, not the pupils themselves. Nevertheless the gender messages and implications of the whole event were present. The girls displayed a squeamish sense of disgust and indignation at being asked to witness such impropriety.

> *Janet:* Just cutting up an egg, never mind a rat made me feel ill, because it is a cell, and I never knew that, and you see all the nucleus and the membrane, it's revolting, I haven't eaten an egg since.

Such activities are not only disgusting and objectionable to girls, they are labelled as specifically masculine, things for men. Girls signal their differences.

> *Jane:* I think science is a boys subject, most of the science teachers are male aren't they. I think the reason why they are male teachers is because of cutting up rats. I don't think a woman could face that.

Indeed science activities could serve as a resource in a positive way; to signal things girls did approve of doing and being. On one occasion the class had to look at the micro-organisms within pond water, under a microscope. Ros declared herself deeply revolted by them all, and by their wriggling movements. However, for other girls this experiment seemed to provoke more interest than many they had done, and the contrast is significant. Sylvia, for example, kept only one drop of water on her slide, and she declined to change it; although the instructions were to examine the whole range of creatures. Her slide had a particularly large and interesting being on it, which she called 'The Blodge'. Sylvia talked to her 'Blodge' and watched it attentively, and was very reluctant to return it to the common pool of water. She put it back very carefully, allowing all the drops to leave her slide to ensure it made it back safely.

Sylvia's reaction to this experiment, which involved looking after a creature, needs to be contrasted with the girls' reaction to dissecting and examining the rat. They displayed very different attitudes towards the two activities. One—the nurturing caring activity—is acceptable, the other—the clinical, 'cutting up' activity—is not appropriate. Again some clear gender messages are being communicated, about activities and attitudes that proper girls have and do.

In addition to this, girls also commented on their differences in handling and controlling some of the scientific equipment, which was a problem they had anticipated. Ros, for example, could not cope with the microscope. She declared she found it impossible, repeatedly insisting 'I don't understand this, I just don't'. She spent the entire lesson floating around the room, seeking aid and assistance; and incidentally ensuring that everyone knew she could not cope with this piece of equipment.

These data connect up with the view of the HMI that 'Girls had difficulties dealing with machinery, they were hesitant about experiments and practical work' (HMI, 1980, p. 16). Yet it is important to point out that such hesitancy was not evident in all subjects, across the board. Domestic science provides an illuminating point of contrast here. In needlework, it was Ros, despite her incompetence with microscopes, who was one of the first pupils to grasp the workings of the double needle electric sewing machine. She was in fact asked for help by others in the class, which is important, for it meant that everyone knew she was competent with this kind of a machine. Nor did any of the other girls seem to experience any great fear or difficulty in dealing with this machine. Similarly, there was no evidence of the fear of 'fire' and the bunsen burners that characterized physical science lessons when it came to lighting the gas in cookery lessons, or dealing with hot ovens and sizzling frying pans in domestic science lessons. It appears to be the case then that girls only have difficulty with *some* machinery and are only hesitant about *some* practical work. The difficulties and hesitancies seem to be pronounced only in curricular areas which are perceived as masculine.

There was another point of objection too, which is important if we are to gain an accurate picture of the girls' perspective. The pupils had been told very firmly that they must wear safety goggles during the experiments they did. This rule had been heavily impressed upon them in the first weeks of their time in secondary school. The defining characteristic of pupil response during this phase of what Stephen Ball has called 'initial encounters' (Ball, 1980) was a high level of conformity. Yet despite the fact that this rule was insisted upon, nevertheless some of the girls simply refused to wear the spectacles. The offending objects were large, plastic, unsize and unisex. One group of girls made an enormous fuss about wearing the spectacles, and made a range of silly jokes on the subject. One girl, Amy, stated that 'they really don't suit me', and decided she would not wear them, she was followed in this rebellion by a number of her friends. The context of this action should be emphasized. The girls were disobeying a very firmly given and strongly presented instruction given to them by their teacher, who happened to be the Headmaster. The girls did this in the second week at their new school, in a situation where circumspect conformity to the demands of the teacher was the norm. The same behaviour was repeated the following week:

Rebecca: I hate wearing these glasses they give me a headache, I had a headache until 4 o'clock yesterday.
Rosemary: Yes it really does give you a headache.

The dislike of wearing the goggles emerged as a central element in Amy's definition of the subject. 'I don't like science, 'cos you have to tie your hair back and wear goggles'. Appearance is of course, a central issue in the construction of a properly feminine image.

These views of natural science as essentially masculine, because of its awesome difficulty, its high technological complexity, its deafening noise, noisesome smells and dirt, were central not only to the girls' perceptions of the subject, but to the boys' perceptions as well, as the following extract illustrates:

R: Do you think girls work as hard as boys at school?
Bill: Well at what subjects?
R: Any.
Bill: Well, it depends on the subject. I mean they're gonna work hard at something like needlework aren't they?
R: Are they?
Bill: Well, they're gonna like it better than something like cutting rats up.
Ian: Boys know more about science than any of the girls in our class.
R: Do they?
Ian: Girls are scared they might get burned or something. You know . . . don't wanna get their hands dirty and things like that.
Mark: Yes girls have got better hands than boys ain't they.

The girls, then, had a strong reaction to their science lessons. They had a clear perspective that it involved things that they did not feel it was appropriate, or pleasant, or inviting to do. And the 'appropriateness' of that attitude was also recognized by the boys. Kelly's notion of a cluster of attributes that are conventionally labelled masculine or feminine becomes relevant in this context. The girls signalled their objection to the dirt and fumes and smells of science; and also to being asked to look less attractive. They displayed themselves as squeamish, frightened and weak, by their objections to science; and somewhat incompetent as well, especially in relation to certain kinds of complex machinery and technology. The activities in science contravened conventional views of what 'proper' girls should do, and therefore the girls resisted doing them. The pupils were reading sex-related characteristics into activities and things, and responding to them as a result. This response goes to make their sex-based identity clear to those around them. My suggestion is that the girls actively used aspects of the school to construct their identity, in this case their feminine identity. They are not therefore simply responding passively to school in terms of gender stereotypes. Science lessons provided an arena for the acting out of feminine susceptibilities in a public setting. They were a kind of backdrop against which signals could be displayed about feminine identity.

This argument is strengthened by data gathered from interviews with the girls about careers or jobs that they might do in the future. In these interviews the girls rejected any jobs connected with science since these were seen as essentially unfeminine.

R: Why do you think there aren't many girl scientists?
Ruth: Just because they don't sort of go in for that job, because, say you are doing acid and that, they don't because they have got very delicate skin and that.
R: There aren't many girls in engineering either.
Jacqui: No, because you sort of get all your hands greasy and that.
Ruth: And lifting things a lot, and a noisy background.
Jacqui: I want to be a secretary.
Ruth: Yes or a telephonist.

The girls contrasted their own preferred identity, that of secretary or telephonist, with the noisy, dusty, dangerous heavy male jobs. Such contrasts, and the public signalling of which direction they personally had chosen, made clear statements about sex role identity.

The girls did have one example of a woman who had gone into an occupation based on science, since one of their own science teachers was a woman. But, as Kelly (1981, p. 4) has commented, women science teachers may not be an acceptable or appropriate role model for female pupils, and this certainly was the case here. Mrs Lines was unpopular with the girls. She was strongly disapproved of. The image of a woman who had gone into science, it seemed, was poor:

Amy: Mrs Lines—she's too posh.
Ros: Did you know, she's a judo expert Mrs Lines.
Rebecca: Oh God, I didn't know that.
Ros: That's why she must wear trousers, isn't it?
Amy: Yes she's horrible.

There are class subjectivities in this perception, but additionally it was Mrs Lines' image of femininity which is commented upon. Her appearance was wrong, she wore 'trousers' not 'jeans' or even more acceptable 'straights', and her activities, in particular 'judo', brought an exclamation of disapprobation since they were not regarded as proper feminine ones. This connects with Ebutt's (1974, p. 20) findings on the picture girls had of women scientists: 'Lots of thick glasses, flat shoes, big feet, judo types with muscular calves and sensible clothes'. It is the flat chested, flat heeled syndrome.

The girls' comments are an interesting example of the way a rationale is developed to cover a problem or a gap in the girls' view of the world. Science is seen as not feminine, not appropriate to women, not something women do. Yet there is a woman, Mrs Lines who does it. A rationale is available to cover the problem, this woman cannot herself be very feminine, she is not a 'proper woman', after all she wears trousers and learns judo. There is no problem coming up with this rationale, it is an easily found explanation.

This data connects with other material on pupils, where the same mechanism was at work. The picture so far has suggested that all the girls disliked science. In fact there were two important exceptions to that, cases which provide useful further insights. The two girls who admitted liking science were girls who were seen by the others in their class as being very conformist. They were described as 'goody-goodies'. The image and identity of these girls has been described in more detail elsewhere (Measor and Woods, 1983), but it can be stated that they were seen and defined as less feminine than the other girls. This recalls Willis's (1977) argument, that conformist pupils are often seen as less sexual, as having a less clear gender identity. The two girls were clearly regarded as less attractive: 'she wouldn't go out with a boy' and 'no one would go out with her'. The boys agreed with the view, 'Me—go out with *her!*', pronounced incredulously. The two girls involved found themselves friendless and isolated in their class. The other negative case was a boy, Geoffrey, who admitted that he did not much like science, and that he too was afraid of fire and the bunsen burners. He was, in turn, taunted about his sexuality; criticized for not being masculine enough. His diffident behaviour in science went together with other problems: he couldn't finish the cross-country run, was completely unable to fight and so on. A conformist to the extreme at school, he was liable to tell a teacher if he heard of deviant infringements on the part of other pupils. All of which earned him the title of 'poofter' and he was rewarded with a fairly miserable existence.

Bearing in mind both the general pattern and the significant exceptions, then, it seems that sex-role learning plays a significant role in forming pupils attitudes to science. Sex-role differentiation it appears is centrally important in switching girls be emphasized: girls come to evolve their own perspective on the 'cluster of for girls, then by refusing and rejecting them the girls have a useful device for signalling their own gender identity. The active nature of this process again needs to be emphasized, girls come to evolve their own perspective on the 'cluster of attributes' they label as feminine, and they select and use aspects of the school context to throw their own feminine identity into clear relief. Science lessons are far from the only resource in this respect. Other areas of the curriculum, sport for example, are used for much the same purpose. But, given its association with educational and job opportunities, science is perhaps of particular concern.

In emphasizing the fact that girls take an active part in sex role differentiation, in the construction of a feminine identity, I would not want to imply that other pressures and constraints are unimportant. Much of the choice process is, in fact, subject to strong social pressures. The girls are, after all, adopting a traditional and non-innovative set of attributes as feminine. Images of women and the social roles of women are currently in flux, but there is very little sign that newer ideas have permeated the lives of these girls, at least at this stage in their development.

Group processes also are involved, they seem to amplify the effects. As a girl rejects science she also puts pressure on others to do the same, to show that they too are feminine. Science is a useful resource for signalling identity, for signalling femininity, but it is simultaneously a constraint. Given peer group pressures, it is not possible to like physical science *and* be feminine; and that constraint affects girls' academic careers and career opportunities. Science lessons are a fruitful resource, but ultimately they give girls an unhappy choice between expressing their sexual identity and making full use of their intellectual potential. There is now an interesting body of research (Spender, 1981; Sharp, 1976) which suggests that to succeed academically in any subject is to run the risk of being labelled unfeminine. In Spender's phrase girls 'learn to lose'. Our research supports that suggestion, but the data on science enables us to make a further point. The curriculum is not viewed uniformly, different areas of it have different gender implications. Failing at science, I would suggest, is even more crucial than failing anywhere else. Girls might well work quite hard in needlework, maybe even in English, but physical science is a kind of boundary, around which no negotiation is possible; though biological science has partially escaped this labelling process, presumably because it is seen as nurturant and acceptable for girls (Kelly, 1981, p. 24).

Boys and domestic science

A number of the issues surrounding girls and science can be usefully contrasted with boys' reactions when they were made to do something they did not regard as appropriately masculine. The argument is that sex-role learning affects girls' attitudes to a particular area of the curriculum. It ought then to be possible to see boys reacting to the curriculum on gender grounds as well. For this reason, I selected the conventionally 'feminine' subject of domestic science for close scrutiny, a subject which was taught at the secondary school to all first year pupils in mixed sex groups.

Even before the transfer to upper school, the boys had negative reactions to the idea of doing Domestic Science. They learned of their obligation to take the subject on their induction visit:

> A group of middle school pupils were taken into the needlework room. The boys eyed their surroundings uneasily and sneered at the dolls and furry toys on the display boards. The teacher explained the kinds of projects they would be doing at the school. The boys looked uninterested. The teacher asked for suggestions of objects the pupils would like to make. The suggestions all came from the girls. No boy put up his hand. (Fieldnotes, June 1979)

Later the boys commented on the domestic science area of the curriculum, and elaborated their views in an interview:

R: What do you think about doing needlework and cookery?
Phillip: Not a lot.
Keith: It's cissy.
David: Boys don't do needlework.
Ian: Girls have got better hands.
David: It's not the sort of thing boys do is it?
Keith: I don't really like needlework as much as other things like cutting up rats.

It is interesting that Keith chose the notorious and symbolic rat for his example of a 'properly' masculine phenomenon. The boys made clear prescriptive statements about domestic science, it was totally unacceptable to them. When boys were faced with activities that went against their sense of masculine convention they objected as strongly as the girls did to physical science, thereby displaying elements of their gender identity.

It is important to note, however, that cookery did not raise the same level of objections as needlework:

Keith: I don't mind cookery, I can cook.
Phillip: Oh cookery will be a laugh.
David: Loads of blokes are chefs.
R: Loads of men are tailors too.
David: Yes . . . but . . . .

Nevertheless it is significant that boys regarded cookery as a non-serious area of the curriculum, it was 'a laugh' unlike maths for example which was 'important, you need it for a job don't you.' It is not clear why there should be a gap in the way sewing and cooking are viewed in gender terms. The rationale the pupils used had something to do with adult occupations, and the fact that adult men made a living from the activity of cooking made it a not altogether inappropriate activity for them. A rationale of this kind seems to modify the 'intrinsic' quality of femininity in the activity.

It is additionally instructive to look in some detail at the ways the boys acted out their negative reactions to the subject area, and to compare it with the girls' reactions to science. There is an interesting body of research which suggests that the kind of resistance that girls employ in schools is different from that of boys (Llewellyn, 1980; Fuller, 1980). This research emphasizes the largely passive quality of the girls strategies. The data in this study certainly supports that conclusion, and perhaps points the way to some understanding of why that should be so. Most of the girls' resistance can perhaps best be termed 'work avoidance' strategies. Girls could quietly daydream and chat a lesson away, and in no way meet 'trouble' as a result; their resistance remained invisible to the teacher. The boys' tactics were more disruptive:

> One science lesson Valerie sat quietly drawing a very elaborate pattern, which she then carefully coloured in. Her 'front' of absorbed activity which also rendered her quiet enabled her to avoid any discipline message.
> (Fieldnotes, February 1980)

Girls would be slightly late for science lessons, and they would try to edge a little time off the end of them, packing up their things early for example. They would wander around the room and chat to people on the way. If they were challenged, they could claim that they were looking for equipment and again avoid trouble. Often a teacher would ask the rest of the class to help them in their search. In a quiet way, they tried to make time and space for their own interests within a lesson.

Girls could avoid answering questions, and keep out of class discussions if asked a question directly. They displayed a quality of shy quietness during verbal exchanges in class, it seemed that this shy quietness was in evidence especially in interactions between female pupils and male teachers. Girls could answer questions so quietly that they could barely be heard. On such occasions the teacher would usually sigh and pass on. The girls had answered after all. They had not been resistant and deviant, nor refused to meet a teacher's demand. They had only been shy and demure, and there is after all little objection to girls showing these qualities.[3] Girls repeatedly engaged in acts that were known to be deviant, albeit subtly and surreptitiously.

> *Pamela:* We just suck polos in science lessons.
> *Sheila:* We do, or the end of our pens—we all suck pens on our table, and don't take no notice.

Often the girls also attempted to assert the priority of their informal concerns within the science lessons, they chatted a lot about clothes and shoes for example. They would sit next to the windows so that they had a good view of the rest of the school, then they could discuss the attractiveness of the older boys, and the clothes of the older girls. Sometimes the girls would 'mess about' a bit, with Amy putting Tipp-Ex on Ros's nose and Rebecca tickling Valerie, for example. However, these more overt forms of deviance never amounted to head-on disruptive confrontation as in the case of the boys.

To some extent the boys used similar tactics in domestic science. They avoided work and procrastinated on projects, so that these never got finished. One boy, Pete, an 'ace deviant', was able to boast 'No, I ain't finished nothing all year, and I'm not bringing in my money to pay for it. I'm not robbing my mum of 75p for that rubbish'. Boys made time and space for themselves in the lessons, arriving late and attempting to pack up their things early. They would leave their work unattended, while discussing projects more dear to their heart. Ray and Matthew, for example, pored over racing tips for the Derby all one afternoon.

But, in addition to these tactics, the boys employed a further set, which were significantly more disruptive in their effects. They engaged in a lot of 'messing around' particularly in cookery which provided golden opportunities for this. There were ovens to turn off and on at inappropriate times, raisins to steal, cake mixture to put up other people's noses, and in their hair, eggs to drop on the floor and so on. Needlework too had a range of equipment that could be put to good use. You could stick pins into each other, threaten to cut off ties, and worse, with the scissors, push over the ironing boards, and throw material and kapok around the room.

In some cases the boys went further still, and made a series of challenges to the authority of the teacher. They asked silly questions to divert the paced progress of the lesson, they made jokes and engaged in repartee to create diversions. Such acts brought status to the perpetrator, especially if the joke had sexual connotations:

[Miss Blancke was attempting to teach macramé to a group of boys]

T: Make a knot in the end of that string.
Sean: How do you get knotted miss?

[Sustained laughter from the rest of the class resulted in disruption.]

Sometimes the boys challenged their teacher directly, and more than once questioned 'What do we 'ave to do this stuff for Miss?' All in all, this added up to a real problem for the teachers of these domestic science subjects. One probationary teacher of needlework freely admitted she found it difficult to control the boys and resented her training course for its neglect of the issue. The college course had made no suggestions for projects or curriculum material for boys. And two of the women who taught domestic science eventually refused the researcher permission to attend their classes, since discipline was proving so difficult for them, and they saw the researcher's presence as only making it harder. It is interesting that they were the only teachers in the school who did refuse entry to the researcher, so severe were the discipline problems.

In the case of both boys and girls, then, deviance is spread unevenly across the curriculum. While there are clearly a number of factors which have a bearing on where the deviance is sited, the data discussed here strongly indicated that one of the most important of these influences is gender and gender codes. That is to say, both boys and girls used areas of the curriculum as a resource to signal their sexual identities.

This signalling was emphasized further by the differing styles and types of deviance that boys and girls respectively employed. The boys strategies were more disruptive than those of the girls; being directed at the 'public arena' of the classroom, at the centre stage, to divert and control the flow and the direct of the lesson. The girls, meanwhile, employed more passive forms of deviance, withdrawing unostentatiously from the lesson, rather than challenging it publicly.

Lynn Davies (1979) has suggested that girls see themselves as quite as deviant as boys. This may well be true, but their deviance takes different forms. In eighteen months research, only two examples of girls engaging in the public style of resistance was recorded. On both occasions the challenges met with strong sanctions, both from the teachers and from other pupils. The two girls involved were not popular and were labelled by other pupils as 'big mouths'.[4]

It seems, then, that certain classroom strategies are designated as male, and the girls avoid them. There are peer group pressures at work, it seems that socialization is not only or even mainly carried out by adults. This is only part of the explanation of the girls' passivity. For the presentation of a passive front was, paradoxically, an *active* statement in the construction of a properly feminine identity. Loud challenges to the teacher, public disruptions and jokes intended for a class-wide audience seemed to be exclusively a male preserve. So were the noisier forms of messing around. By their very nature they signified masculinity to those involved. Pupils could use their hostility to one of the science subjects—'natural' or 'domestic'—to signal an interest in things masculine or feminine. At the same time pupils used strategies that were felt to be appropriate to their sex. This represented a strong message, a doubly loaded message.

Teachers and the sciences

Of course I would not want to suggest that gender differentiation in schools is simply a pupil-initiated phenomenon. Teachers no doubt also influence pupils, through their attitudes, expectations and interactions. In a sense they finish off and reinforce the messages that pupils have already learned through primary socialization. In our research there were examples of sex-stereotyped messages, and teachers did sometimes communicate to the girls that they were less welcome, less interesting, or less likely to do well in some subjects.

There were some clear examples of bias. The Headmaster would welcome his class with 'Come in my merry *men*'. One teacher, the head of the science department, always stood directly in front of the boys and talked to them almost exclusively. The class was divided on sex-segregated lines, the girls occupying one half of the room, the boys the other. Pupils had themselves moved into this pattern early in their first term at the secondary school. This teacher would sometimes return to the desk in the centre of the room, but then rapidly go back to the boys side of the room. He gave books out to the boys first, and the whole direction of his talk and his eye contact was with the boys. The girls resented this kind of treatment:

> *Vivien:* He always picks on the boys to do things.
> *Tina:* He doesn't think the girls are capable.

The Headmaster, who taught first-year science, found a need to issue a series of discipline messages to the girls. The discipline messages specifically emphasized their gender:

> I don't want to hear anyone talking while I am—Girls! Girls, girls, come on, clear up over there, don't leave it for someone else to do. Don't sit around talking. Good Grief, get your books open. You're a family of fuss pots you girls.

On one occasion, when the girls were having difficulty with an experiment, his attitude was less than supportive, 'We seem to be dividing into two groups, those who can do it—and the girls'. This was to recur, as in his sarcastic remark that 'We've got the women's lib thing going on here, women saying we're dozy, we're female, Help Us'. The Headmaster was also willing to make jokes which improved his chances of a 'matey' relationship with 'the lads', but which were at the expense of the girls. When he was explaining electricity and conductivity, he warned:

> So the moral is, if you are wearing nylons, don't step on electric wire, because you'll get a nasty shock up your backside.

The girls certainly felt there was discrimination:

> *Margaret:* I think the boys get more help with the science really, because I think the teachers think it is a bit of a waste of time for girls. A lot of teachers have the type of idea, that the girls, they are going to be housewives and stay at home all the time.
> *R:* All teachers?
> *Margaret:* The older ones might do, because they were brought up to it themselves.

There was very little attempt made to relate the physical sciences to girls' interests, a point made more generally by HMI (1980, p. 14). Examples used in science lessons tended to come from the 'male world' and were male-oriented. One example of a lesson on measurement can perhaps illustrate this:

> The teacher, in this case the Headmaster, was discussing measurement. He dealt with heat, measured by thermometers, with liquids measured in pints, like beer, and gallons, like petrol. The Head then went on to question whether any of the children had ever gone to France by car. This illustrated the difficulties caused by different forms of measurement; and the Head questioned how their *fathers* dealt with litres and kilometres. 'Have none of you got adventurous dads, that took the car to France?'

The social class models implied in this teacher's comment are interesting in themselves, but there are important gender implications too: of passive mothers who get taken places, if they are lucky. At one point the teacher did recognize the gap in his own teaching and curriculum illustration, and did introduce material from the world conventionally defined as feminine, but even here:

> What are we measuring in needlework . . . And I suppose in our male chauvinist world, it is still girls who do needlework, so I'll ask them for the answer.

As a teaching strategy, this raises any number of issues, but the point at stake here is that this was the only occasion in eighteen months of observation of combined science where a specifically 'feminine' example was used.

The ways that domestic science teachers reacted to the boys and their strategies is also a matter of some interest and contrast. Unlike the natural science teachers and their treatment of girls, the female needlework teachers did make specific provision for the boys. Indeed, the two teachers involved were acutely aware of the boys' feelings about domestic science, and they employed a range of strategies and devices to attempt to cope with, if not overcome, their resistance. They went so far as to change the name of their subject from needlework to 'fabrics'. The domestic sciences were administered by the craft department, and the latter purveyed the idea that in their first year pupils were learning craft skills and solving design problems upon a wide range of materials: paper, metal, wood, plastic, clay and fabrics. Within the subject, the teachers attempted to offer boys projects that had a 'masculine' feel to them. For example, the boys could design a football flag, or a banner, or a bag to take fishing tackle. Teachers certainly did not insist that the boys shared the girls' project, which was to make a rag doll with a frilly Victorian pinafore on it. The teacher changed the setting of the room so that there were pictures of football teams with their slogans and mottoes, for example, as well as girls' dress patterns up on the walls. The teacher had offered a wide range of objects to make and design, which fell into categories, 'banners, bags and toys' being three of them. The teacher held up examples of objects from each category. However, the only example of a toy she had was a doll:

> T: Or you could make a toy [held up the Victorian style rag doll in a Laura Ashley style smock].

There was a visible sneer from the boys.

> T: Ok, I know this is a doll, but you could make something else.

There is no criticism of the teacher's actions intended in this account, she was recognizing an attitude, derived from community culture, and social pressures, which sex stereotype a particular curriculum area, and particular objects. She employed a range of strategies in order to break this down, and in some measure she succeeded. Whatever the outcome of her efforts, though, it is interesting that there was no equivalent compensatory action for girls in the natural science lessons, no attempt to offer projects and examples of a more 'feminine' kind. Instead, as I have suggested, teachers sometimes did and said things that made matters worse. Science laboratories tend to be fairly austere places, except for those devoted to biology. They are not, for example, covered with posters about things that traditionally interest girls.

Perhaps the domestic science teachers were not committed non-sexist egalitarians, eager to 'switch boys on' to needlework. They probably only hoped to contain the situation, and remove some of the possibilities of disruption.

As Elliot has pointed out:

> Boys are seen as the source of the fun and laughter, but also the confusion in the classroom. The dynamics of the classroom are radically affected by the presence of boys. Even a seasoned teacher can be dictated to by the dominant elements of the class. (Elliot in Spender, 1981, p. 105)

Thus the constraints operating on the domestic science teachers were largely those of maintaining discipline. In this sense the strategies used might be seen as belonging to Hargreaves' model of 'coping strategies' (Hargreaves, 1978; Pollard, 1982). For natural science teachers, however, the threat of disruption does not exist to the same extent, since the girls' disaffection is less threatening to teacher control.

In addition, the fact that the girls switch off to physical sciences is a well known and accepted fact amongst the teachers interviewed:

> *The Headmaster:* There's no sexual discrimination here, but at the end of the second year, when it comes to option choosing, all the girls get out of science.

The HMI (1980) and the DES (1975) reports both acknowledged that teachers seemed to expect and accept this reaction amongst their female pupils. Some teachers lamented the fact but perceived it as socially acceptable, it did not contradict basic values and social reactions. These expectations may have constrained their attitudes, and in turn shaped the strategies they used with girls. Teachers' expectations and prejudices then interact with those of pupils, as well as community attitudes, to make a very solid wall of resistance to any change.

Conclusion

In conclusion, then, the data from this research clearly supports the view that sex-role differentiation is an important factor in understanding pupil reactions to the curriculum. Particular school subjects do seem to act as one potent resource for pupils in their attempt to sort out and establish their gender identity at the early adolescent stage. Both boys and girls select out curriculum areas to act as marker flags for their identities. Learning theory has tended to assume a gender-neutral pupil, but it does seem that gender needs to be put into the study of the curriculum.

There may be some policy implications to be derived from this analysis, about ways to 'switch girls on' to science. Certainly there is a case for removing what the HMI called 'the inadvertently discriminatory behaviour on the part of teachers' (HMI, 1980, p. 18). If we accept some of the speculations about girls' reluctance to engage in the 'public verbal arena' of the classroom, then this again has implications for teachers' tactics. Girls are not likely to be as willing as boys to join in open class discussion, they may go so far as to choose to withdraw from answering questions. There are teacher strategies to get round these problems, for example girls could be asked questions directly, and addressed by name. There must also be consideration given to the notion of educating girls in single-sex groups, for science at least.

The other major possibility of curriculum change involves trying to create what Allison Kelly has called a 'feminine science' (Kelly, 1981, p. 92), designing chemistry projects which show how nylon stockings are made, or doing experiments in which perfume is mixed, rather than carbon dioxide released in a mass of inky black vapour. However, this does raise some difficult issues. Such changes might keep girls more interested in the subject, though similar tactics were not markedly successful with the boys in needlework because of the strength of social pressures. Moreover, such a strategy does suggest that girls have a very restricted field of interests and activities, and that they are incapable of dealing with the 'larger things of life'. That was not however the reaction to the idea of introducing football banners for the boys in needlework: that seemed simply reasonable, a thoughtful attempt to accommodate the boys. The contrast raises some crucial questions about the nature and the status of different kinds of knowledge in our society. It seems clear that there is a 'sexual division of knowledge' and that it ties up with notions about gender-appropriate subjects for both boys and girls (Deem, 1980, p. 7). This means that we need to take account of gender in any work upon curriculum or curriculum innovation, and equally to attempt to grasp the very powerful forces which militate against change.

Acknowledgement

The author would like to acknowledge the financial support of the SSRC in the project from which this paper derives.

Notes

[1] HMI surveyed twenty-one schools, and fifteen of these were studied in more depth. They attempted to find schools which represented 'a social and geographical diversity' and visited the schools for three or more days, in parties of two or three Inspectors, one of whom was a woman. The schools were all fully comprehensive up to the age of 16, and had not been a girls school in the previous decade.
[2] Figures taken from 1975–76 DES Survey of all school leavers in England and Wales.
[3] Girls occasionally produced what teachers regarded as 'insolent answers', but these usually stemmed from a teacher challenging a girls' passive work avoidance strategies.
[4] These data correspond with Mandy Llewellyn's (1980) picture of Sandy, a girl who was also seen as acting in ways inappropriate for 'proper girls', and who was labelled in exactly the same way.

References

Ball, S. (1980) ' "Initial encounters" in the classroom and the process of establishment', in Woods, P. (ed.) *Pupil Strategies*, London, Croom Helm.
Bandura, A. (1971) *Psychological Modelling: Conflicting Theories*, Aldine–Atherton.
Blackstone, T. (1976) 'The education of girls today', in Mitchell, J. and Oakley, A. (eds.) *The Rights and Wrongs of Women*, Penguin.
Davies, L. (1978) 'The view from the girls', *Educational Review*, Vol. 30, No. 2.
Deem, R. (1980) *Schooling for Women's Work*, Routledge and Kegan Paul.
DES (1975) *Curricular Differences for Boys and Girls*, Education Survey Q1, HMSO.
Ebbutt, D., 'Science options in a girls grammar school', in Kelly, (1981) op. cit.
Fuller, M. (1979) 'Dimensions of gender in a school', PhD Thesis, University of Bristol.

Galton, M. (1981) 'Differential treatment of boy and girl pupils during science lessons', in Kelly, A. (1981) op. cit.

Hargreaves, A. (1978) 'Towards a theory of classroom coping strategies', in Barton, L. and Meighan, R. (eds.,), *Sociological Interpretations of Schooling and Classrooms*, Nafferton.

Haste, H. W. (1979) 'The image of science', in Kelly, A. (1981) op. cit.

HMI (1980) *Girls and Science*, Matters for Discussion, No. 13, HMSO.

Kelly, A. (1981) *The Missing Half*, Manchester University Press.

Measor, L. and Woods, P. (1983) 'The interpretation of pupil myths', in Hammersley, M. (ed.) *The Ethnography of Schooling*, Nafferton.

Mischel, W. (1966) 'A social learning view of sex differences in behaviour' in Macoby, E. (ed.) *The Development of Sex Differences*, Stanford University Press.

Pollard, A. (1982) Towards a revised model of coping strategies, in *British Journal of Sociology of Education*, 3.2.

Savage, E. and Griffiths, D. (1981) 'Biological inevitabilities or political choices' in Kelly, A. (1981) op. cit.

Sharpe, S. (1976) *Just Like a Girl*, Penguin.

Spender, D. (1980) *Learning to Lose*, Women's Press, London.

Willis, Paul (1977) *Learning to Labour*, Saxon House.

PART TWO

Pupil Adaptations

7 Initial encounters in the classroom and the process of establishment

S. BALL

The ethnographic paradigm of classroom interaction research is now a well-established element of the sociology of education in Britain. There are now several collections of papers which represent the development and current state of work in this area (Chanan and Delamont, 1975; Stubbs and Delamont, 1976; Woods and Hammersley, 1977) as well as Delamont's (1976) exemplary introductory text. Most of the work, from the ethnographic paradigm, included in these various contributions to the field is founded to a greater or lesser extent upon a theoretical perspective derived from symbolic interactionism, although phenomenological and ethnomethodological perspective have also made themselves felt (e.g. Torode, 1976, 1977; Cicourel, et al., 1974; Payne, 1976). However, despite the growing body of empirical work on classroom interaction and the concomitantly increasing amount of theoretical commentary, surprisingly little attention has yet been given to the evolutionary and developmental nature of teacher-pupil relationships in the classroom setting. The tendency has been (with one or two exceptions in the American literature) to treat and portray classroom relationships as fixed and static patterns of interaction within which teachers select strategies or act out the constitutive rules or procedures which serve to structure this interaction. Little attention has been given to the ways in which strategies are tested or rules established and in my view this has tended to inhibit the development of a coherent formal theory of classroom interaction. In part, I want to argue, this state of affairs is an artifact of the nature of classroom interaction research itself and the constraints upon it. The problem is that most researchers, with limited time and money available to them, are forced to organise their classroom observation into short periods of time. This usually involves moving into already established classroom situations where teachers and pupils have considerably greater experience of their interactional encounters than does the observer. Even where the researcher is available to monitor the initial encounters between a teacher and pupils, the teacher is, not unreasonably, reluctant to be observed at this stage.

But the reasons for the teacher's reluctance are exactly the reasons why the researcher should be there. These earlier encounters are of crucial significance not only for understanding what comes later[1] but in actually providing for what comes later. However it should also be said that even in cases where the researcher is able to be present during these initial encounters, his conceptual and empirical grasp of the observed situation at this stage, if it also happens to be the start point of a research project, may be so underdeveloped as to render the complexities of these encounters virtually unintelligible.

Whatever the reasons for this neglect of initial encounters, and there may be other factors which I have overlooked,[2] it seems to me that this has resulted in an unfortunate distortion in the representation of classroom relationships in interaction research. As Hammersley (1978) puts it:

> We have studies of teacher strategies and of pupil strategies but nothing as far as I am aware on patterns of relationships between the two beyond the vague notion of negotiation.

In this article I want to take up the vague notion as it illuminates initial encounters between teachers and pupils in the classroom and in particular what I shall refer to as the 'process of establishment'. This is defined as an exploratory interaction process involving teacher and pupils during their initial encounters in the classroom through which a more or less permanent, repeated and highly predictable pattern of relationships and interactions emerges.

The data on which this largely exploratory article draws comes from two different sources and is of two distinct kinds. The greater part of the data on which the initial formulation of the article was based is taken from a participant observation study of a comprehensive school which was in the process of introducing mixed-ability classes to replace a system of banding (Ball, 1978). This includes classroom observation and transcript notes and the associated comments of the pupils and teachers involved. The second source of data is a small-scale interview study of PGCE students who were encouraged to describe their initial encounters with classes in their teaching practice.

First Encounters

The theoretical position in which this chapter is embedded is Mead's symbolic interactionism and specifically Blumer's (1969) formulation of this. A single quote (also quoted in the introduction to *The Process of Schooling* Reader: Hammersley and Woods 1976) will probably serve to illustrate the particular focus with which I am concerned. Here Blumer (1969) stresses the importance of realising and retaining the emergent and negotiative character of social interaction and concentrating upon processes and experience rather than structures and roles:

> Rather than viewing behaviour as a simple 'release' from a pre-existing psychological structure (such as drives, personalities, emotions or attitudes) or as a consequence of an external coercion by social 'facts' (cultures, structures, organizations, roles, power), the interactionist focusses upon emergence and negotiation—the processes by which social action (in groups, organizations or societies) is constantly being constructed, modified, selected, checked, suspended, terminated and recommenced in everyday life. Such processes occur both in episodic encounters and in longer-lasting socialization processes over the life-history.

What Blumer's work suggests, particularly in terms of episodic encounters like lessons, is the particular importance of the initial meetings between actors for the negotiation and emergence of social perspectives, and patterns and routines of social interaction. It is during these initial encounters that the negotiation of social parameters in the classroom setting is exposed to view in a way that they are not in later lessons. And one crucial aspect of this is the gathering of information on both sides.

Obviously it is often the case that both teacher and pupils can anticipate their initial encounters in a number of ways. Both carry with them previous experiences of classrooms and possibly specific information about each other from other sources and these are important as Goffman (1959) stresses

> Information about the individual helps to define the situation enabling others to know

in advance what he will expect of them and what they may expect of him. Informed in these ways, the others will know how best to call forth a desired response from him.

However, it was apparent from interviews with pupils, teachers and student teachers that a great deal of information relevant to the classroom, both for the pupils and the teacher, is actually gleaned from face-to-face contacts.[3] In practice, for the pupils, this involves such things as the level of noise the teacher will tolerate; the method that they are allowed to use in addressing him or her or attracting his or her attention; the amount of work demanded of them and the level of risk involved in this;[4] the acceptable form of presentation of work and numerous other features of the teacher's organisation and management of the classroom. Indeed a teacher will begin to give out cues and information to the pupils the moment he or she walks into the classroom—by style of speech, accent and tone of voice, gestures and facial expression, whether he or she sits behind the desk at the front or walks up and down and talks to pupils privately. As Garfinkel (1967) suggests 'members of a society do interpretative work on the smallest and most fleeting fragments of behaviour'. As yet, however, we know little about the social knowledge that pupils employ in recognising these cues as relevant or the interpretative procedures employed in making sense of them.

It was clear both from my observation and interviewing data that these initial encounters were recognised both by teachers and pupils as a distinct phase in the history of their interaction. For example:

> It's depressing to know that whenever you have a new class that for the first few lessons you're going to have fun and games until'you show them who's boss.
> (Maths teacher)

> They're scared, they don't know who you are, then they find out you're not a Harry Jones (teacher renowned for being very strict with pupils) or you haven't got the charisma of David Lortimer (teacher renowned for having excellent relations with pupils).
> (English teacher)

> **SB** What happens usually when you have a new teacher?
> **Band 2 pupil** We're nice to him the first day then real horrible, you have to get used to him first.
> **Band 2 pupil** The boys muck about to see if they can get away with being stupid.

From the pupils' point of view these initial encounters necessitate a testing out of the new teacher. This normally involves two stages, the first is a passive, and in a sense, purely observational stage. This is indicated by the first pupil quoted above, 'we're nice to him the first day', and was noted by all the student teachers I interviewed. For example:

> In the first lesson they were very quiet.
> (English student)

> They're quiet at first because they don't know where they stand.
> (Geography student)

> As a general statement the rowdiest forms are quiet in the first lesson.
> (Physics student)

This stage in the development of their relationships with pupils was referred to by some teachers and students as 'the honeymoon': it rarely appeared to last beyond the first lesson. Hargreaves (1975) refers to this as the 'Disciplinary Illusion'. After this the second stage is embarked upon, which usually involves at least some pupils in being 'real horrible'. This is when the pupils actually involved in what Wadd (1972) refers to as 'elementary escalation', playing up the teacher:

. . .to see if the teacher is prepared to defend the authority he is seeking to establish.

This stage of testing out through playing up the teacher is evident in the following observation notes collected in an early lesson of a new school year involving a religious studies teacher and a third year, band two class. The class arrives in groups of four or five over a two or three minute period. The teacher is already in the classroom and is standing at the front room with her arms crossed. She is pointedly 'waiting' for the class to arrive and to pay attention. Teacher:

> You're taking a long time to settle down. (This descriptive comment is clearly intended to reduce the volume of the noise being made by the pupils, and to indicate that the teacher wants their attention. This is the function of the teacher's talk here.)

Two boys, Keith and Charlie, are being particularly noisy and there is considerable confusion, Keith and Charlie are talking out loud and making comments across the room ignoring the teacher. The teacher shouts at the class to be quiet and then immediately sends Charlie out. The class is then threatened with 35 minutes detention and the amount of noise decreases considerably. Keith is now reading as instructed, but he seems intent on annoying the teacher. He turns round in his chair again and waves out of the window. The teacher again addresses the class as a whole.

> I'm very annoyed with you and I shall show you how annoyed I am by punishing you.

Keith begins to do some work but is still making noises in his throat. He is going as far as he can, pushing the teacher to the limits of her tolerance, the teacher's response is to delineate the steps towards that limit.

> That's your last warning Keith, any more and you shall be in detention.

He tests and pushes and she lays down the rules. What is expected, what is allowed, what is not, Keith is moved to the front, he is now quiet. The teacher calls for silence.

> I'm not satisfied with the standard of work, anyone who talks will be in detention for an hour tomorrow night.

The teacher asserts herself gradually and imposes her definition of the way the classroom should be, over the attempts to assert an alternative definition by some of the class. Her expectations of work and behaviour are made very clear. But the class were alert to the way in which she would treat Keith and Charlie, their behaviour tending to respond to the way in which these two were handled. When Keith is finally subdued the teacher is able to impose an unbroken rule of silence on the whole class.[5]

It is interesting to note that this pattern of information gathering and testing as observed and noted by the present writer in a British comprehensive school is almost exactly paralleled by Doyle's (1979) analysis of American classrooms based upon his observation of student teachers. Several points seem worth picking out. For example he notes the same two stage process whereby 'playing up' or misbehaviour, what Doyle refers to as 'behaviour tasks', are manifested only after a preliminary period of quiescence.

> After a brief period of hesitancy, behaviour tasks were usually initiated frequently over the course of the first day or so after the student teacher assumed the teaching role in the classroom. Many of these behaviour tasks, which varied over a fairly wide range, appeared to function as active tests of the ability of the student teacher to manage classroom routines and rule systems.

Furthermore, as in the lesson described above, Doyle found that rules or prohibitions uttered by student teachers were invariably subjected to testing out in practice.

> Verbalized rules were seldom accepted at face value. In almost all cases, students sought empirical evidence that the student (teacher) would actually follow routines and enforce rules. Behaviour tasks are an especially useful way for students (pupils) to obtain such evidence.

Finally, again as in the lesson described, Doyle also found that participation in this testing out process tended to devolve to a few pupils only in any class. The teacher's responses to these few, however, in the public arena of the classroom, may serve as indications to all the pupils in the class for their future behaviour.

> It is important to emphasize that in nearly all situations only a few students participated in behaviour tasks, at least initially. Moreover, it was not always clear that a particular behaviour task was a deliberate challenge to the student teacher's managerial skills. But classrooms are very public places and students often appeared to take advantage of all behaviour tasks to measure a teacher's classroom abilities. Some students, in other words, seemed to rely on others to test the rule system.

The pupils' information gathering and 'testing out' of the teacher may be considered conceptually as having two major purposes. Firstly the pupils find it necessary[6] to discover what parameters of control the teacher is seeking to establish over their behaviour. So for instance:

> I'm new and they know it and I think they're trying it on. I expect to have some problems in the first year, but I think they're pushing to see how far they can go. (Probationary English teacher)

It may be that the kinds of expectations evident in this comment have their own impact on classroom relationships by self-fulfilment in the strategies that teachers employ in anticipation of or in response to certain types of behaviour. This possibility seems even more explicit in the following remark:

> I know I expect some kids to be charming and interested and others to be difficult and very much a confrontation situation and I am very tight when I go in there. (Probationary History teacher)

Secondly, as noted above, the pupils find it necessary to explore in practice whether or not the teacher has the tactical and managerial skills to defend the parameters he or she is seeking to establish. So, for instance, as one 'successful' teacher explained:

> They know exactly where the red line is, and what will happen if they step over it, both in terms of work and behaviour. And I like this group. (Maths teacher)

It is important though to bear in mind that the relationship between the theory and practice of control is not always a simple one. Some teachers, and many student teachers, attempt deliberately to avoid imposing parameters of control on their pupils seek instead through establishing personal relationships to have the pupils exercise self-control in the classroom. Other teachers who do seek to impose parameters of control on their pupils find that they lack the appropriate tactical and managerial skills to do so. For example Kounin's (1970) study of discipline and classroom management discovered a close connection between the effectiveness of teachers' 'desists', that is control statements, and their 'withitness', and 'transition smoothness', ability to deal with 'overlaps' and provide a variety of work tasks for pupils, and monitoring and management of movement in the classroom. That is to say, those teachers who demonstrated skills in these areas proved to be more able to responded appropriately and effectively to the 'deviant behaviour' of their pupils than those who did not. As Doyle (1979) notes, 'students (pupils) appear to respect what might be called "tactical superiority"'. Thus the outcomes of the pupils' testing out' of their teachers are by no means a foregone conclusion. The outcome depends upon the nature of the teacher's response to the pupils' actions. From my observations it was evident that taking no action at all, or getting angry and losing self-control, or showing signs of confusion on the teacher's part, all typical of the inexperienced student teacher, demonstrated the kind of lack of tactical skill that would be taken advantage of even by pupils in the most pro-school oriented classes. The subsequent nature of the classroom relationships established between teacher and pupils and the nature of the pupils' behaviour, especially the amount of disruption and 'deviant behaviour', is highly dependent upon and emerges out of these processes of information-exchange and test and response in these initial encounters. Clearly this proposition is basic to the ubiquitous 'start as you mean to go on' and 'go in hard and ease off later' folk remedies for the beginning teacher (see Marland, 1975). Hargreaves (1975) notes that

> . . . most experienced teachers insist that the teacher must, if he is to survive, define the situation in his own terms at once. Basically this initial definition is not so much a statement of the rules that will govern the class, but rather a clear indication that the teacher is completely in charge and not to be treated lightly.

Hargreaves goes on, in considering classroom dicipline, to discuss the long-term establishment of a completed body of classroom rules in some detail. This, he says, 'takes some weeks to establish because the rules must be created and always clarified in relation to concrete incidents where the rules are applicable.'[7] Once they are established and routinised the social parameters of teacher-pupil interaction are less readily accessible to the researcher, as noted previously. Once routinised: 'Action becomes a symbolic medium. The occurrence of particular actions, and perhaps even more their absence, communicate messages.' (Hammersley, 1979)

Defining the Situation

I now want to go on to address two of the issues that seem to me to be raised by the discussion so far. Firstly, how can we make sense of the processes outlined above, in terms of symbolic interactionist theory? And secondly, why do these processes occur anyway? That is to say, how can we explain why the pupils find it necessary to identify and test out the parameters of control that their teachers seek to establish in the classroom? It may be that one answer will suffice for both questions.

Initial encounters between teachers and pupils in the classroom are it would seem problematic definitional situations *par excellence*. The mode of definition which is of concern here is what Stebbins (1977) refers to as *habitual personal definition*.

> the same category of situation holds roughly the same meaning for a particular class of actors participating in it, but in which each individual participant is more or less unaware that people like him who are having the same kinds of experiences elsewhere define them the same ways.

It is important to recognise the revelance of Stebbins's use of the phrase 'roughly the same meaning' here, we have already touched on some sources of diversity in the action orientations and the predispositions that different teachers carry with them, but aspects of the surroundings—and other environmental/institutional factors: class size; age and status of pupils; form of grouping (streamed, setted, mixed-ability, etc.); length and timing of lesson (note the interpretation of the teacher of 4B last two periods on Friday afternoon mentioned below); lesson topic; resources and materials to be used and location (particular strategies may be adopted for lessons timetable in the assembly hall, canteen or cloakroom)—can all contribute to definitions which are personally and situationally unique. As Stebbins (1977) outlines, the teacher's definition of the situation is a process involving perception of others and reflexive 'looking glass' perceptions of self. It is 'synthesis, interpretation and interrelation of salient predispositions, intentions and elements of the setting'. For the pupils' movement from lesson to lesson may require considerable adaptation and flexibility in terms of the diversity of the rules of behaviour and performance expected or demanded by the teachers. Hargreaves *et al.* (1975) faced this problem in attempting to establish a typology of classroom rules in their study of deviance in classrooms:

> . . .there are some general rules that are 'generally accepted' even though they are not written down. But these fuse into the individual preferences and judgements of teachers, who vary in what they will 'have' or 'stand for' or 'tolerate' within their classroom over which they exercise a legitimate authority.

However, it would be oversimplistic to interpret the adaptation of pupils to different classroom settings solely as a methodological process of learning and accumulating 'facts' about the classroom. It is more realistic to see this 'social knowledge' of the classroom as 'knowledge of relevance'. It is not a matter of learning situational/contextual rules, but forgetting for the moment transcontextual ones, whittling down a stock of knowledge to a core of relevant and/or acceptable strategies. From the pupils' point of view the action limitations of the classroom situation are virtually unknown in the lesson of a new teacher. Despite the traditional and institutional authority of the teacher as major significant other in the classroom[8] and the provision of institutional rules of behaviour, the interactional detail of classroom conduct is broadly left to the individual teacher to establish. As Waller (1932) points out, when a teacher faces a new class he faces an undefined situation:

> . . . and it is part of his job to impose his definition of the situation upon the class quickly, before any alternatives have an opportunity to be considered.

This definition of the situation is essentially a process. To quote Waller again:

> It is the process in which the individual explores the behaviour possibilities of a situation, marking out particularly the limitations which the situation imposes on his behaviour, with the final result that the individual forms an attitude toward the situation, or, more exactly, in the situation.

Clearly this process of defining the situation may be seen to relate to the information gathering and testing out by pupils described above. However, this does not necessarily reaffirm Waller's conflict model of the classroom. It is misleading to assume *sui generis* that the testing out by pupils of their teachers engenders a challenge to the definition of the situation that the teacher is seeking to establish. For some pupils 'testing out' may be important in that it enables them to acquire the knowledge necessary for them to conform, for instance knowledge of their teachers' conventions, for attributing 'achievement', 'success' and 'good behaviour'. They are concerned to know the teacher's conception of the lesson in the sense of being able to perform competently within it, rather than to challenge it. Indeed, even in the case of the lesson quoted earlier it is possible to suggest at least four interpretations of the pupils' actions:

(a) The pupils were seeking to arrive at a competent interpretation of the meanings of the situation held by the teacher.

(b) The pupils were seeking to negotiate a mutually acceptable and congruent definition of the situation.
(c) The pupils were attempting to challenge the teacher's competence or right to assert her definition over certain significant sub-sets of the classroom situation. (E.g. who has the right to initiate talk.)
(d) The pupils were attempting to challenge the teacher's competence or right to assert her definition over any aspect of the classroom situation.

In part at least the likelihood of one or another of these interpretations being correct will depend upon the previous educational careers of the pupils involved, and of the teacher, and thus the attitudes and purposes carried by the participants into the new classroom situation. Nevertheless, in all of these cases (except perhaps the first) the teacher's competence, what Wadd refers to as 'personal power', will have a crucial bearing on the definitional consequences. So too will the extent of the pupils' commitment to and sharing in the long-term purposes of the teaching encounter, in whatever way they perceived them. While the status of teacher presents the incumbent with a certain degree of official legitimacy, problems always revolve around the individual teacher's ability to 'bring it off' in the interactional sequences of everyday classroom life. While, as we have seen, the first lesson may be conceded by the pupils, the emergent social orderings appear to rely heavily upon how the teacher actually handles or manages his or her relationship with pupils during these preliminary interactions.

Clearly then there is always the possibility that the defining process of mutual testing, cue-reading, elaboration and modification may lead to an outcome that is satisfactory to neither teacher nor pupils. For example, a colleague described to me his strategy for dealing with 4B, last two periods on Friday afternoons, as 'playing for a draw'. As Stebbins (1977) illustrates, definitions are tried out by participants and then accepted, rejected or modified in response to the reaction of others in the negotiation process.

However the definition of the situation is of further relevance and importance in the classroom in regard to the possibility of the pupils being able to predict and routinise patterns of interaction. As I see it one of the major functions of the pupils' testing out of teachers is a guidance to the evaluation and selection of future possible actions. Pupils are concerned to know in advance what the teacher's reaction will be to certain types of behaviour. Will deliberate disobedience (or failure to hand in homework, or 'doing poor work') incur the teacher's wrath; involve a minor dressing down, being told to 'stop it', being sent out of the room or to the headmaster, being put on detention, given lines or will it be ignored. On the basis of this kind of anticipation of the teacher's response the pupil is able to weigh up the amount of satisfaction to be obtained from the commission of a 'deviant' act against the dissatisfaction likely to be involved in the teacher's response to it, if any. This may in fact account for pupils' often stated preference for 'strict' teachers.[9] Strictness usually also provides for a highly structured and therefore a highly predictable situational definition. Indeed beyond this, in general terms, Gergen and Gordon (1968) argue that personal consistency is a quality of person that is broadly supported by the values of Western culture. They report evidence from laboratory experiments which demonstrate that consistent persons are liked by others, while inconsistent persons are disliked.

However, the teacher's control of the pupils is not the only aspect of classroom interaction that requires the negotiation of definitions. Whereas control may be regarded as a persistent and background feature of the classroom setting, the organisation of learning by the teacher is often more prominent. The well-worn example of discovery learning provides many illustrations of this. In Doyle's (1979) terms the task accomplishments associated with discovery learning 'task structures' confront the pupils with high levels of risk and ambiguity compared with the task accomplishments associated with more straightforward 'memory task structures'. Doyle (1979) found that pupils who were confronted with potentially high risk, high ambiguity, learning situations adopted various interaction strategies to resist or reformulate these 'task structures'. In other words the pupils attempted to resist or renegotiate aspects of their teachers' definition of the situation.[10] And this resistance to risk-laden learning situations is not restricted to the school pupil: university students and teachers on in-service courses also, in my experience, actively seek to renegotiate 'task structures' with their tutors. So then equally in terms of 'task structures' what actually comes to pass in the classroom, may be seen to be the outcome of the relative capacity of the different actors to establish their definition of the situation over and against the definitions held by others. A further example of the role of the pupils' definitions of the situation, in terms of the legitimate use of authority by teachers, is provided by Werthman's (1963) study. Werthman was able to demonstrate the importance of the pupils's interpretations of teachers's activities as a basis for an organised and rational set of responses to the teachers' assignment of grades. Snyder (1971) also illustrates, in the case of college students, the ways in which students found it necessary and useful to employ strategies of manipulation and negotiation in order to cope with their undergraduate workload. The student

> . . .is forced to make judgements about what is relevant; he develops a method of study and fixes a way of budgeting his time. But it may also foster a sense of gamesmanship and make the encounter between student and professor a competitive rather than a cooperative one.
> (Snyder, 1970)

In terms of both control and 'task structure', once the establishment is completed[11] it will be maintained and reproduced by the actors' shared expectations of the situation. However the network of interdependency that is embodied in the situation will in itself be moving and changing over time, 'the association of people is necessarily in the form of a process in which they are making indications to one another and interpreting each other's indications' (Blumer, 1969). All actions have their intended and unintended consequences in this process and teacher-pupil relationships in the classroom may be expected to evolve and change over time as a result. The tentative and precarious nature of social order in the classroom, which is most apparent in initial encounters, is never totally suspended since the teacher will be continually testing inferences about the pupils' responses. However this natural form of group life, of designation, interpretation and redirection, is different in kind from the exploratory gestures and reactions evident in the process of establishment itself.

It is difficult to describe and account for the significance of establishment without accentuating the normative and authoritarian aspects of defining the situation that are involved. However in general terms it is *not unusual* that the traditional and institutional authority of the teacher will serve to legitimate his or her normative practice and his or her definition of the situation, to the pupils. It is *not unusual* for pupils to accept the teacher's definition of the situation. The problem is that it is the 'conflict model' of teaching, referred to previously, that is most commonly employed in observers' accounts of classroom processes. Its generality and appropriateness are assumed but not proven. This may be related to the problem of order that is fundamental to almost every sociological theory, and this is of course exquisitely vital to the understanding of life in classrooms. Several studies have addressed this question directly, Torode (1976) and Nash (1976) for instance, but the tendency has been to start from the problem of disorder and work back from there. The unusual is deployed as typical and, perhaps as a consequence, the typical remains unexplored. One of the reasons for this state of affairs is undoubtedly that many of the studies thus far available on the classroom interaction of teacher and pupils have tended to focus upon the interesting, but untypical, perspectives of anti-school pupils in their latter years of schooling (cf. Furlong, 1976; Gannaway, 1976; Birksted, 1976; Willis, 1978) Epistemologically this may be related back through the theoretical antecedents of much of the contemporary work on classroom interaction, Mead, Blumer, Becker, etc., to the work of the Chicago School, from whence the 'underdog perspective' is derived. A concern with the disenfranchised and alienated derived from this theoretical tradition melds well with the empirical tradition of mainstream sociology of education which concerns itself with explaining the failure of the working-class pupil.

In making reference to and use of this body of literature it is all too easy to forget that these cases may not be normal or representative. [...] In its crudest form the 'conflict model' merely sees the classroom regime as a matter of a single competition for ultimate supremacy, and this seems inadequate to explain or illuminate the primary school classroom; the first-year classroom in the comprehensive school; the top stream classroom; the O-level classroom; or the sixth-form classroom. 'The marshalling and developing of familiar themes' (Willis, 1978) in these particular circumstances require a more sophisticated and subtle model of explanation. I am not trying to suggest that teachers' and pupils' interests are always complementary. I would agree that this is unlikely in the classroom, given the range of different interests on both sides and the large number of pupils involved in most cases. And indeed the absence of overt conflict cannot be taken to mean that interests are complementary, it is more likely to mean that a working consensus has been negotiated. My criticisms are of the assumed ubiquity of conflict in much of the writing on classroom interaction and the often unexplicated nature of situations and incidents identified by observers as representing conflict.

Thus, to return to my major concern, while I want to argue that teaching is normally 'done' on the basis of the communal features of everyday life in classsrooms and 'picks its fruits', I would also argue that the convenience and comfort of this intersubjective state is often necessarily suspended in initial encounters.[12] The naively assumed and implicitly reaffirmed *sense* of community that *is normally* a part of everyday life in classrooms, *is normally* unavailable to teacher or pupils in their initial encounters. The classroom *is normally* a social environment where violations in the communicative and interactive process are assumed to be minor or unimportant and easily remediable (cf. Hargreaves *et al.*, 1975) it is an optimistic environment. The initial teaching encounter is, however, more often than not, a pessimistic environment.[13] The 'until further notices' that hold together the social patchwork of classroom life cease to be routine, or have not yet become routine. Distrust in the 'we-ness' of interaction becomes the order of the day, or disorder of the day, and it is intersubjectivity that provides the 'surprises'. The nature of the other is radically problematic here, that is to say the ratio of *assumption* to *appraisal* in the we-relationship and the *sense* of community in the classroom is shifted dramatically towards *appraisal*.

The initial encounters are necessarily situations of *performance*—participation on the part of the teacher (and perhaps as suggested earlier by some of the pupils too) and this is most evident in the deliberateness and reflexivity of involvement in these lessons. This deliberateness and reflexivity is particularly clear in the diaries kept by student teachers.

I felt a bit out of my depth—and in conflict internally, because I didn't want them to be totally silent or have to keep nagging at them. But I did want them to get down to some proper work. Conflict also re the learning situation, because I wanted them to choose what they'd do, but they were totally unable to behave while two groups did a bit of drama. In the end we wasted the whole lesson. Right at the end I broke—I told them I wouldn't tolerate so much noise, and said that if anyone didn't want to learn they should say so and leave the lesson. I promised dire, unknown, evil punishments if I didn't get order and quiet next lesson. I sent John out during the lesson and I had a word with him afterwards on his own; he promised to behave. Someone even came in because they were being so noisy—I felt I may be losing my self confidence.
(PGCE English student)

Initial encounters, then, constitute pessimistic social environments that necessitate, or are conducive to, the continual reflexive calibration of the congruence between the self and others. The doing of teaching requires the establishment of a communal we-relationship between teacher and pupil. I am saying that in initial encounters the teacher may find that the thesis of 'the natural attitude of everyday life' is empirically refuted (for some teachers or in some schools or certain classrooms it may be constantly refuted), although its reaffirmation is likely to be always more readily available to the 'strict' teacher (cf. Furlong and Gannaway). Even here though a *sense* of consociality in the classroom must be achieved and appraised. It cannot be assumed.[14]

Acknowledgements
I am indebted to Richard Tudor, Tony Bailey, Barry Cooper, Martyn Hammersley and Peter Woods for their comments on previous drafts of this paper.

Notes
[1] See Walker and Adelman (1976) for an account of the culture of the classroom which illustrates this.
[2] Another simple and rather facile reason for this neglect of initial encounters might be the fact that the school year begins in September but the university year does not normally commence until October.
[3] As Hargreaves, Hestor and Mellor (1975) have pointed out the classroom is just one of several social arenas 'at school' in which the pupils must become competent by constructing appropriate modes of interaction. The corridor, the assembly, the dinner canteen, and perhaps most of all the playground, require exploration and adaptation by the pupil. The focus of this chapter is, however, limited to the classroom and to the specifics of particular classrooms. It is not concerned with what is held in common between classrooms in a single institution but rather with what is idiosyncratic and therefore difficult for actors in different classrooms.
[4] Doyle (1979) in his paper discusses the importance of changes in pedagogy for pupils in terms of the increased 'risk' involved. That is the increased possibilities of failure that are inherent in forms of learning where the stress is upon understanding rather than memorisation.
[5] From my observations of this class group in other lessons and interviews with the pupils it was clear that Keith and Charlie based their social identities upon their roles as disrupters in the classroom. They derived status from their classmates in this way, by engaging in a continuing series of clashes with their teachers.
[6] There are a number of studies which explore the primacy of the teachers' ability to control in the dynamics of classroom interaction. Furlong (1976) Gannaway (1976) and Nash (1976) all stress in particular the importance of the pupils' perceptions of their teachers in this respect. However it may be that in certain circumstances 'control' is superseded by or subordinated to other factors, for example in my own research I came across a group of fifth-form pupils who were primarily concerned with 'respect' that they 'tested for' in their initial encounters with teachers.
[7] This article is asking 'how are rules established between teachers and pupils?' but it is also possible, and at some stage necessary, to examine 'the rules for establishing these rules'

which underlie the processes and experiences addressed in this article.

[8] For some pupils obviously there are other significant others to whom they refer when making decisions about ways of behaving in the classroom. But I would want to argue that in the typical classroom the teacher remains the *major* significant other, if only inasmuch that decision-making on the pupils's part will take the teacher into account, albeit as a negative reference point.

[9] Nash (1976) and Musgrove and Taylor (1969) among others have demonstrated, via widely differing techniques, the preference of pupils, of all kinds, for 'strict' as opposed to 'soft' teachers.

[10] This resistance to potentially high risk 'task structures', especially in school, can be related to the instrumental and essentially alienated orientations of pupils towards their academic labour and its products.

[11] The process of establishment may be regarded as completed at some stage in as much as it is recognised as a distinctive and identifiable phase in the history of teacher—pupil interaction in the classroom by the teachers and pupils themselves. The tentative and exploratory nature of interactions in this phase are regarded as qualitatively different in kind from later interactions.

[12] The formulation of this concluding section draws upon a theoretical argument outlined by Melvin Pollner in an oral paper delivered at a Schutzean studies *ad hoc* group meeting at the 9th World Congress of Sociology, held at the University of Uppsala, Sweden, 8—13 August 1978.

[13] This pessimism was clearly expressed in almost every one of the student teacher interviews I conducted and is also apparent in the comments of the probationary English and History teachers and the Maths teacher and the pupils quoted above. However one documented exception to this is the 'optimistic compliance' noted by Woods (1979) in the case of first-year secondary school pupils.

[14] This is an assumption often made by student teachers when they make their first forays into the classroom, an assumption that seems to lead inevitably to chaos and recriminations.

References

Ball, S.J. (1978) 'Processes of comprehensive schooling: a case study', unpublished D.Phil. thesis, University of Sussex. See S.J. Ball *Beachside Comprehensive,* Cambridge University Press, 1981.

Birksted, I. (1976) 'School performance: viewed from the boys', *Sociological Review,* 24, 1,pp. 63-77.

Blumer, H. (1969) *Symbolic Interactionism: Perspective and Method,* Prentice-Hall.

Chanan, G. and Delamont, S. (1975) *Frontiers of Classroom Research,* NFER.

Cicourel, A., *et al.* (1974) *Language Use and School Performance,* Academic Press.

Delamont, S. (1976) *Interaction in the Classroom,* Methuen. 2nd ed. 1983.

Doyle, W. (1979) 'Student management of task structures in the classroom', paper presented at the Conference on Teacher and Pupil Strategies, St Hilda's College, Oxford.

Furlong, V. (1976) 'Interaction sets in the classroom: towards a study of pupil knowledge', in Stubbs, M. and Delamont, S., op.cit.

Gannaway, H. (1976) 'Making sense of school', in Stubbs, M. and Delamont, S., op. cit.

Garfinkel, H. (1967) *Studies in Ethnomethodology,* Prentice-Hall.

Gergen, K.J. and Gordon, C. (eds) (1968) *The Self in Interaction, Vol. 1,* Wiley.

Goffman, E. (1959) *The Presentation of Self in Everyday Life,* Penguin.

Hammersley, M. (1978) 'Strategy or rule: two models of action' synopsis of paper presented at SSRC Conference on Teacher and Pupil Strategies, St Hilda's College, Oxford

Hammersley, M. (1979) 'What is a strategy? A critique of interactionist strategy analysis', unpublished manuscript.

Hammersley, M. and Woods, P. (1976) *The Process of Schooling,* Routledge and Kegan Paul.

Hargreaves, D. (1975) *Interpersonal Relations and Education* (revised ed.), Routledge and Kegan Paul.

Hargreaves, D., Hester, S. and Mellor, F. (1975) *Deviance in Classrooms,* Routledge and Kegan Paul.

Kounin, J.S. (1970) *Discipline and Group Management in Classrooms,* Holt, Rinehart and Winston.

Marland, M. (1975) *The Craft of the Classroom: A Survival Guide to Classroom Management in the Secondary School*, Heinemann Educational.

Musgrove, F. and Taylor, P.H. (1969) *Society and The Teacher's Role*, Routledge and Kegan Paul.

Nash, R. (1976) 'Pupil's expectations of their teachers', in Stubbs, M. and Delamont, S.,op.cit.

Payne, G. (1976) 'Making a lesson happen: an ethnomethodological analysis', in Hammersley, M. and Woods P. (eds)op.cit.

Snyder, B.R. (1971) *The Hidden Curriculum*. Alfred A. Knopf.

Stebbins, R. (1977) 'The meanings of academic performance: how teachers define a classroom situation', in Woods, P. and Hammersley, M., op. cit.

Stubbs, M. and Delamont, S. (eds) (1976) *Explorations in Classroom Observation*, Wiley.

Torode, B. (1976) 'Teachers' talk and classroom discipline', in Stubbs, M. and Delamont, S., op. cit.

Torode, B. (1977) 'Interrupting intersubjectivity', in Woods and Hammersley, M., op. cit.

Wadd, K. (1972) 'Classroom power', *Education for Teaching*, No. 89

Walker, R. and Adelman, C. (1976) 'Strawberries strawberries', in Stubbs, M. and Delamont, S.,op.cit.

Waller, W. (1932) *The Sociology of Teaching*, Wiley.

Werthman, C. (1963) 'Delinquents in school: a test for the legitimacy of authority', *Berkeley Journal of Sociology* 8, 1, pp. 39–60.

Willis, P. (1978) *Learning to Labour*, Saxon House.

Woods, P. and Hammersley, M. (1977) *School Experience*, Croom Helm.

Woods, P. (1979) *The Divided School*, Routledge and Kegan Paul.

8 'Sussing out' teachers: pupils as data gatherers

J. BEYNON

1 Introduction

In order to study initial encounters between teachers and pupils (and their impact upon each other) I observed a class (1Y) in all their lessons during their first half-term in Victoria Road, a boys' comprehensive school in South Wales. Lower School, in which the study took place, was a separate unit housing the first year and was isolated from the rest of the school. As the fieldwork got under way one of the aspects which immediately began to attract my attention was the rapid emergence of what I termed a form-wide 'fraternity' of pupils which would expand and contrast as occasions allowed. Within it, boys possessed different roles, namely: core members and instigators; 'jokers'; 'the sillies'; 'dumboes'/'spastics'; 'tactical muckers', or occasional participants; and a very small number of isolates and non-participants. In what follows I focus exclusively on the formation, behaviour and identity management of the boys who gathered around David King: they constituted the fraternity's core members mentioned above and were the principal instigators of 'mucking' and 'sussing' during these early days. I became interested in the strategies they employed to find out about classrooms and type teachers; the specific nature of the 'knowledge' they required; and the means they employed to (in their words) 'suss-out' teachers. To investigate these I engaged in participant observation; made audio-recordings of classroom interaction; and extensively interviewed pupil and teacher informants. The combative strategies utilized by the boys often had more than one simultaneous function (for example, 'playing' was both a means of 'sussing-out' a teacher and of rendering the boring bearable). However, their primary purpose (repeatedly testified to by the boys) during the opening week of term was to control, as well as facilitate pupil–pupil typing and the rapid creation of a viable alternative (and 'enjoyable') culture to offset the threatened domination by the official school procedures into which all pupils were then being 'grooved'.

'Sussing' revealed how individual teachers reacted to provocation and stress and whether they could uphold and put into practice (in acceptable, to the boys, ways) the claims they were making for themselves of being strict, 'no nonsense' teachers, who were both interesting, worth listening to and expert. In this heavily data-based paper I identify and comment on *six* major groups of 'sussing' strategies, namely:

1 Group formation and communication.
2 Joking.
3 Challenging actions (verbal).
4 Challenges (non-verbal).
5 Interventions.
6 Play.

2 Group Formation and Communication

King's 'sussing out' of the school and teachers, although partly dependent on his own restless energy and abrasive personality, was, nevertheless, an aspect of a wider group activity. Early in my fieldwork (towards the end of Week 1) I recorded:

> *Formation:* Blond–King–Long
> Blond rushed into the room, grabbed a seat and kept a space for King. To be a power in the class demands friends and support. The King group seem to have gone through three stages:
> (i)   King on own, exhibiting.
> (ii) King, alliance-making.
> (iii) The emergence of the core group and the development of 'outposts' through recruiting.

King immediately gathered around him two boys (Blond and Long) he had known in Junior School and who he found happened to be with him in 1Y. Many of the strategies they adopted had been tried, developed, and perfected in previous years. Bright was added to the group and the three boys sat together or in close proximity thereafter. The Bright-King-Blond pattern, with a few variations, remained constant across the curriculum. For example, in French, Blond sat on his own near the door and in Art the boys sat around a table and were joined by Long. Long acted as 'linkman' with 'the sillies', boys who were not direct members of the core group, but who were often 'recruited' to initiate activities or amplify and lend weight to challenges made by the core:

> *Formation:* Bright–King $\begin{smallmatrix}\text{Long}\\\text{Blond}\end{smallmatrix}$
> Long, in spite of his failure in swimming, is still a member of the group. Meanwhile Ginger and Roland Lloyd act as 'floaters': they can be recruited:
> (a) when they initiate an activity; or
> (b) to lend support to the group; or
> (c) to form a diversionary move.

Links could also be made with 'the spastics' (low status boys who, nevertheless, could be used by the core group if they happened to create a diversion intentionally

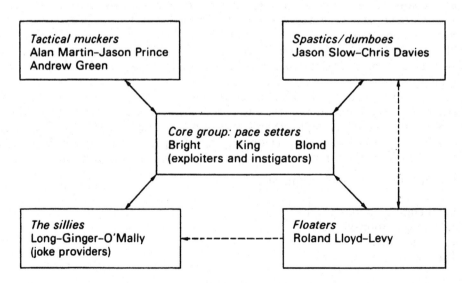

Figure 8.1 *The core group and recruitment*

or unintentionally by displaying stupidity) and with the 'tactical muckers' (my terminology), who were academically ambitious boys who could, nevertheless, at times join the core instigators. The composition of this core group only changed when the form was reshuffled (on the basis of a battery of attainment tests in Week 4) and Bright left the form and Ginger (class clown) was promoted into the inner sanctum (see Fig. 8.1).

Sitting with your mates in formation and communicating by means of eye contact appeared a prerequisite for the effective operating of the core and its subsidiaries. Their joint activities remained the sole means of retaliation and prevention of complete teacher domination as Lower School geared itself to shape pupils to its demands.

There were certain essential features of the core group which contributed to its effective initiation and issuing of challenges to teachers and these are now discussed.

2.1 Intra-group roles and activity

Early on in my fieldnotes I commented upon the composition of the King group:

> The group has now settled down. At the heart of it is King, aided and abetted by Bright, who is the more scholarly/clever of the two. Then come the side-kicks—Long, Blond, and contacts, notably Ginger and O'Mally, and just lately, Lloyd. Bright has won his spurs and appears to be King's first lieutenant, whereas Long has an honorary position, having had a long association with King in the same Junior School. Their 'fronts' complement each other: King is hard and 'mock-tough'—looking, a juvenile John Travolta; Blond is a good-looking boy with a smile which is interpreted as cheeky and challenging—he may be easily led and seems to be in King's grip; Long is mischievous and cheeky; Bright is quick, clever, witty. He often makes the cannon balls that are fired by King. Although he seeks King's praise and approbation, I sense he obtains considerable pleasure from being one step ahead of King. His school work is very good—he manages to fool and to work well. King, on the other hand, is a messy, slow worker. All his energy is directed towards being the form 'hardman' and, to some extent, the clown, although Ginger runs him a close second in the latter stakes.

I noted, too, the rapidity with which they started to function as a group:

> After a week the King group has an unity about it and an internal dynamism. King remains the centre, but appears to hand over the initiative to Bright at times. But it is King rather than Bright who kids in the class glance at and seek to impress. Teacher messages are passed through, processed by the group. A remark addressed to a member of the group is answered by any member of the group.

Members of the group complemented each other and sparked each other off, and a number of my comments focussed upon this intra-group dynamism:

> Early on the King group monopolize Mrs Paint's attention by fooling with drawings and not listening to her instructions. She talks about separating them next lesson. Tetley whistles and there is a lot of joking and intra-group chat. They scrumple up drawings, throw paint around, and attempt to implicate quiet kids. Testing teachers and each other. King shows drawing to others and raises a laugh. Holiday atmosphere—and laughter is a communal effort and production. They provoke and fire each other. 'Look at that!', and laughter at Bright's sketch. King and Long start throwing water around at the sink.

2.2 The domination by King

Many 'runs' or challenges originated with King, who led by example:

> King and Long are very matey. King is encouraging Long to act as he does—silly

and challenging teacher after teacher. Perhaps he sees Long as a frontman behind whom he can hide? He is making every effort to recruit Long to his banner.

Boys looked to King to notice and approve their activities:

> Jason Slow dismantles his desk, unscrewing the lid with his fingers. Robert Bright has brought a huge roneo size sketch pad to school. It is as big as his desk top and he keeps holding it up for the admiration of other kids. Both boys look to King for signs of approval for their activities.

King played a co-ordinating and orchestrating role:

> King subsequently builds on the play on names: O'Mally/Smelly and Pitt/Shit. The latter clearly resents it and is unwilling to be recruited by King and act as stooge/target for his humour. O'Mally, however, becomes a willing disciple and looks to King to 'use him' when necessary. He laughs, smiles and waves his arms in return. Like the good winger, he hovers out in the shadows, ready to exploit the long ball from King, key joker and strategist.

2.3   Drawing attention to each other

King referred to this as 'bundling in' and 'helping out your friends', so that one boy's run became a group and collaborative effort:

> *Mr Stern:*   What's your name? [Looks at the cover of the exercise book.] Ginger, is it? [For no apparent reason Ginger breaks into uproarious laughter. It is infectious, like the 'Laughing Policeman' song. He is joined by the lads—King, Bright, Long and Blond, as well as the 'second division' of O'Mally, Cooper, Tetley.] SHUT UP! [Mr Stern roars and slams Ginger's exercise book down on the desk with a sharp crack. The hubbub dies down.]

Boys publicized each other's activities:

> King at back, back to wall, pushing his desk to crush those in front. 'Look at Kingsy. He's a nut!' [Bright]. He calls for support on Blond and Long, who laugh to annoy.

2.4   Links outside form

Those associated with King were linked with troublesome pupils in other forms in particular with Freddie Wild, acknowledged by both staff and boys as 'looney of the year':

> King's links with Freddie Wild, the worst pupil in the year, are considerable. He lives near him and travels to school with him. One teacher 'broadcasts' about Wild in the staffroom: 'I walked into the form room and there was this character with his feet up on my desk laughing at me. He's been eating pears—the bin was full of them. He grinned at me like a Cheshire cat and offered me a pear. I nearly burst out laughing myself. I went spare, I can tell you!'

To be a mate of King was to become a member of a wider community and hierarchy of 'hards'.

2.5   Focus of teacher attention

Within a short time King and his group were the focus of teacher control utterances:

> 'King, that is your final warning. 'Hey, you, Bright, what are you writing?' [Mr New]. In Maths, he is moved down front. Similarly: 'King, you'd better come down here with me where I can watch you. You're too much of a fool to be left up there' [Mr Friendly]. Ginger fools with paper, makes a dart, and told to behave himself. Even so, he throws a dart at Bright who flights it back.

Teacher's attempts to separate King from other group members had little impact on curtailing his influence. In fact, by directing their control utterances at the group, teachers were inadvertently drawing attention to the group and, thereby, strengthening its power and influence in the life of the class.

2.6   Recruiting
The power of the core King group to challenge teachers and disrupt lessons was in no small part due to having 'sidekicks' or allies in other areas of the form who could be 'recruited' if necessary:

> Bright shouts out: 'Lloyd, stop messing about!' Recruiting/directing from home base.

These recruits could amplify the laughter or, if they created a disturbance of their own, facilitate the entry onto the scene of the King group, either to join the fun or create some separate incident of their own. Alternatively, they could draw attention to core group activities, 'publicize' them:

> In French the King group combine with the 'sillies' (Cooper, O'Mally, Ginger) and have a field day. Mrs Calm calls for a class response, either to answer a question she has asked in French, or to repeat something after her. King and Bright make high-pitched replies, and make a succession of funny noises. They interject other words and control the rhythm, forcing the class to say something quickly or slowly. The net result is that the class response is an absolute shambles, analogous to the singing at an international match when sections of the crowd sing different things at different speeds. All this is interspersed by open laughing at Mrs Calm and fits of lung-racking coughing initiated by King. Bright sometimes claps out a rhythm or hammers his desk. In spite of all this, the French lesson continues and Mrs Calm maintains reasonable control in that a considerable amount of work is, nevertheless, done.

2.7   Diversions
The boys both created and exploited diversions in order to fool around and 'stretch' teachers.

> King initiates a 'walkabout' and Long talks over teacher, thus dividing Mrs Paint's attention: You, sit down. And what is your name? [to Long].
> King: Me, miss.
> Mrs Paint: You! and you [pointing at Long], you're not a very polite boy. They're all talking to me and I've got to answer them and you start talking on top of everything.
> King: Yes, belt up, Long.
> Long: Sit down, King [both laugh].

Indeed, the strength of the group and its allies lay in making the most of diversions and encouraging 'mucking' by other sections of the form:

> King exploits the diversion created by Jason Slow. Exploits such situations and puts up 'smokescreens'.
> Great fuss/noise/disturbance as Ginger accuses Cooper of pinching his pen. Mr Piano sorts it out and tells Bright and King to sit apart after they made the most of the diversion.

Joking

3.1   Open Joking
Open joking, whether directed at staff or not, was both an attempt to raise a laugh and assess and judge teachers by their reactions. As such it was often interpreted by them as a threat to order and discipline. It took a number of forms:

3.1.1 *Jokes based on pupils' names*

These involved play on the surnames of two pupils and recurred throughout my time in the school:

(a) *Neil Pitt* (not a member of the King group)
Miss Floral: And your name?
Pitt: Neil Pitt, Miss.
King: Did you hear that? He asked her to kneel and shit! [uproar]
King/Bright: [shout out in high voices]   ˙
Teacher: Neil Pitt.
King/Bright: Neil Pitt!

(b) *O'Mally* (a King 'sidekick')
King giggles when O'Mally is asked by Miss Floral to spell out his name. 'He's called O'Smelly, Miss'. [laughter].
O'Mally and Ginger miss most of the period searching the yard for lost money. When O'Mally enters there are shouts of 'Smelly'. Mr Jovial shouts King down.
Long: He's called O'Smelly!

3.1.2 *Risqué Jokes*

Risqué humour was, without exception, directed at female teachers and therein lay its point and power to generate class laughter. The King group held the prerogative on risqué humour, perhaps because only its members were daring enough to make it public:

(a) Michelle joke again. Blond, King, Green and Long sit together in Art and make the most of it. (Miss, 'he's a woman', etc. from King). They laugh at O'Mally and King bellows out: 'Miss, Miss, he's called O'Tool, Miss'.

(b) *Miss Floral:* [issuing an order in Drama] Stand in the middle!
Long: And take your trousers off! [Laughter]. ˙

(c) *Ginger:* Miss, he [O'Mally] lets his mother load his bag . . .
Mrs Christian: Good grief, he's old enough to load his own bag.
Ginger: One old bag loads another, Miss. [Ginger and O'Mally roll around with laughter].
Mrs Christian: That is an incredibly rude, unkind, and unthinking thing to say.
Ginger: Yes, Miss.

3.1.3 *Lavatorial Humour*

As with risqué jokes, there was an element of daring and disrespect for the teacher on the part of the joke-maker. The laughter was a product of both embarrassment and a making explicit in front of teachers the taboo:

(a) *Mrs Calm:* What is the Louvre?
Long: A lavatory, Miss. [Laughter].

(b) *Miss Floral:* What could have made that story more interesting, better, exciting?
Ginger: Miss, he [O'Mally] said he [the giant in the story] had someone's bum on the end of the fork. [Laughter].
Miss Floral: Charming! You'd need a very big fork! [Laughter].

3.1.4 *Repartee and Wit*

The combined quick wit of the King group enabled them to answer back and create laughter at the teacher's expense and, in the process, negate any effective reply. More often than not the teacher had to acknowledge defeat and retreat as gracefully as possible:

(a) *Mr Jovial:* Now, what's your name? King, is it? [Laughter].
King: No, a Queen [Laughter and applause].
Mr Jovial: That' enough, okay, quiet.

(b) *Mrs Calm:* O'Mally, what is Corsican cheese in French [pointing to a poster upon which is written Fromage de Corsica]?
O'Mally: It's rubber, Miss [Laughter].

Other aspects of King's humour was an open incitement to riot and ridicule, as well as a means of 'creating a name' for himself:

(a) *Mr Pickwick:*   You twit, Long!
    King: [roaring with laughter] You twitling, twitling! Twitling! [He whistles like a bird].
(b) *Mrs Calm:*   What is your name? Comment appelles-tu?
    King: Toot! Toot! [A cacophony of toots/car horns, accompanied by laughter].
(c) *Miss Floral:*   Who would make a good leader? I suggest that as a form you need someone reliable and sensible as your form captain.
    King: Me, Miss. [Laughter].
    Miss Floral: Someone who is brainy, patient, and reliable.
    King: That's me, Miss. [Laughter].

3.1.5   Set Pieces
Although these were often effective as laughter-raisers and took the initiative momentarily out of the teacher's hands, they were jokes that had been told or read beforehand. They were less effective for being someone else's and well-rehearsed, rather than off-the-cuff:

> *King:*   If I don't play I'll play for Dow Corning instead. I don't mind. [Football for school or an outside team].
> *Ginger:*   Sir, Sir, they stopped me playing football in my last school and I was top scorer.
> *Mr Stern:*   Wait a minute! They stopped you playing football and you were top scorer?
> *Ginger:*   Yes, Sir, they stopped me playing because I kept scoring in the wrong end. [Laughter].

3.2   Covert Joking
I shall comment on this under three headings:

1   Underbreath *'backchat'* or *'lip'*, unheard by teachers, but by the group and its neighbours:
2   *Closed joking* by pupil participants from which the teacher was excluded, but towards whom the resulting laughter was directed:
3   *Michelle, a private (class-shared) joke*

3.2.1   'Backchat' and 'Lip'
One of the purposes of covert backchat was to insult staff without them realizing it. All they heard was the laughter of those who shared the remark. Unless the teacher was prepared to momentarily halt the lesson (either for the class as a whole, or for the group) and 'make a scene', then they had to leave it slip by and, rather lamely, settle for a general reprimand. In King's eyes this was 'putting one over' on the teacher, as well as being amusing:

(a) *Mrs Paint:*   You have to be careful if you are carrying a jar of paint because those chair legs stick out.
    King: And yours do! [Laughter].
(b) *Mr Jovial:*   What are you boys doing coming in here [through side door into hall] this way?
    King: We're late!
    Mr Jovial: I can see you're late. That's not what I asked you. What I want to know is who told you to come in this way. You don't come in this way.
    Long: We do if we're late.
    Mr Jovial: Who said so?
    Long: I dunno who he was. Fat man with glasses. [All this mumbled]. [Mr Jovial is rushed for time].

> *Mr Jovial:*   You'd better sit down over there. [Then to me] Another rule changed—
> they call it moving the goalposts.
> *King:*   [laughing to Long] Fat man with glasses!
> (c)   *O'Mally:*   Miss, I ain't got no pencil.
> *Mrs Fashion:*   You haven't a pencil. Where do learn your English.
> *O'Mally:*   Same place as you [muttered under breath]. [Laughter].
> *Mrs Fashion:*   Say 'I haven't a pencil. [Laughter].
> *O'Mally:*   You haven't a pencil. [Laughter].
> *Mrs Fashion:*   No! O I give up.

The 'putting one over' on the teacher was accomplished by means of the follow-up laughter even if the 'lip' was not primarily directed towards the teacher, but provided a 'pupil view' of things:

> *Pitt:*   What do we do on wet days?
> *Miss Floral:*   On wet days you play in what we call the barn [covered area].
> *Long:*   You run around the piss holes! [King laughs].
> *Miss Floral:*   I don't want any lip. That's enough.

3.2.2   Closed Joking

By this I meant the joke was 'closed' to the teacher and private to the pupils concerned, but was made public, much to the bafflement and bewilderment of teachers. This technique was one frequently employed by Michael Ginger as a tool for disrupting lessons:

> *Ginger:*   Sir! Sir! Sir!
> *Mr Stern:*   Yes, what is it?
> *Ginger:*   Sir, Peter lives in Ash Grove. [O'Mally, Cooper and Long collapse into laughter; members of the King group turn around and smile].
> *Mr Stern:*   Right, that's enough, get on quietly.

However, the outstanding example of 'having a secret' which could be used and about which teachers were ignorant was the Michelle joke.

3.3.3   Michelle: A Private Joke

The Michelle joke developed into a private, class joke, a resource constantly available to be tapped and occasion laughter. Its origins were in the first French lesson:

> *Mrs Calm:*   And what is your name?
> *Long:*   Michael, Michael Long.
> *Mrs Calm:*   The French for Michael is Michelle. Michelle. [King rolls around, keeps pointing at Long and bursting into a loud, raucous forced laugh.]
> *King:*   Michelle's a girl's name.
> *Mrs Calm:*   Listen, you've had your fun and now be quiet.

This rebuke, issued in an icy voice and accompanied by a steady stare has little impact. Throughout the rest of the lesson King continues to laugh and point at Long, who appears to share the joke and enjoy having such undivided attention.
Therefore, there are numerous references to it throughout my fieldnotes:

> (a)   Mrs Paint tells the King group to be quiet and then goes to have a 'quiet word' with them. They giggle and chatter amongst themselves.
> (b)   *Mrs Paint* [to Long] You've made him look as if he's got a cap on. [She alters the drawing. Long grins at King who makes faces behind Mrs Paint's back. Long burst out laughing.]
> *Long:*   It's his flat head!
> *King:*   Miss, he's a woman.
> *Long:*   King drew a woman, Miss. Me! [Laughter].
> [Mrs Paint looks baffled. King, Long, Blond and Bright all roar with laughter. King shows his drawing to his neighbours and invites laughter.]

It rapidly became part of a class mythology: that in an all-boys school there was, nevertheless, a girl in the form. Long proved to be a ready and willing recipient of King's humour and as a private joke (unknown to teachers) it allowed King to appropriate and turn to his own advantage a host of innocent teacher remarks:

(a) *Mr Changeable:* This is not a very big school.
    Bright: What, it's massive.
    Mr Changeable: There are no girls.
    King: Yes there is, Michelle [i.e. Long].
    [Laugher] He starts to sing, 'Michelle my belle'. etc.
(b) *Mr New* [English]: Long, your work is terrible.
    King: He's a woman, Sir! [Laughter].

In spite of its recurrence, even at the end of my fieldwork teachers were still 'in the dark' concerning the point of 'Michelle'.

4 Challenging Actions (Verbal)

These took a number of forms.

4.1. Stupid Questions
Asking stupid questions was, in a sense, an invitation to the teacher to joke with the pupil, to become a partner in raising a laugh. But it was also a challenge: the teacher could well appear to be the fool unless he was quick-witted enough to out-joke the pupil:

> Mr Bunsen explains how, when writing in the back of their exercise books, they should first turn the book upside down and work towards the centre, thus keeping the margin on the left-hand side.
> *Bright:* Do we write upside down? [Laughter].
> *Mr Bunsen:* If you want to pretend to be in Australia, Yes, twit head! [Laughter].

The acknowledged master of the stupid question was Michael Ginger. A member of the 'sillies' group he made his name as a joker, so much so that before half term he was 'promoted' to become one of King's closest accomplices. He was pleased to present himself publicly as a clown and draw laughter upon himself. When I asked him what he enjoyed most about school he said he liked 'being called a twit by teachers'!

(a) *Ginger:* What colour ink do we use to underline, Miss?
    Mrs Fashion: That is the stupidest question yet.
    Ginger: I know, Miss.
    Mrs Fashion: What is your name?
    Ginger: Michael Ginger.
    Mrs Fashion: Well, you're not a very polite boy, are you?
    Ginger: No, Miss.
(b) *Ginger:* Sir, Sir, Sir, I can't find Psalm 23.
    Mr Pickwick: Psalm 23 comes after 22, can't you count?
    Ginger: No, Sir. [Laughter].
    Mr Pickwick: [to me] God, 1Y! That means I'll be answering fool questions for half an hour and as limp as a rag at the end of it! One darn fool question after another!

4.2 Pseudo Information
This was an effective way of interrupting the teacher or breaking the silence as a class worked. It involved making public and passing on to the teacher a totally useless piece of information and eliciting a reply. Unless the teacher could 'out trump' the pupil then the subsequent laughter was, in part at least, at his expense:

Mrs Calm mentions King as a 'troublemaker'. Already his antics and reputation have made him a focal point for staff attention. I find myself watching him, too, and his emergence as a rebel has marked a shift in my fieldwork interests. Even if he asks a serious question of a teacher it is interpreted as 'playing up', 'fooling', 'being difficult'. King and Long now operate as a pair, one taking the lead whilst the other is the stooge:

King: He's making a noise at me, Sir.
Mr Union: He's what?
King: He's making a noise at me, Sir.
Mr Union: O dear, dear me! Does it hurt? [Long laughs].
King: No, Sir.
Mr Union: Well get on with it then. And you [to Long] you'll be making noises to me on your own after four o'clock in a minute!
[Long and King grin at each other and carry on working].

The pupil might 'invite' the teacher to reply but move immediately into an exchange with a pal, thus excluding the teacher and leaving him stranded, but nevertheless obligating to break back into the pupil patter:

Bright: Miss, King is pushing my chair [grins at King].
King: No! No, I'm not.
Bright: Yes, you are, you nutter!
Mrs Fashion: Do you mind, I'm the one who does the talking.

Most often it was just a mechanism to focus class attention upon oneself, to capture the initiative and 'set up a circus' (as one pupil, Bright, described it):

Bright: Miss, I'll have to miss a line because I've written too big. [Laughter]. Get lost, Kingsy!
Mrs Calm: Never mind, it's nearly time.
Bright: O good!

4.3   Build-ons
'Build-ons' were, in the boys' words, 'joining in with lip' and 'helping your friends'. They can best be described as gang jokes, initiated by one member and developed in public by one or more others. A good example occurs in my notes for Week 2:

Bright jogs O'Mally's elbow and, as a result, he splatters paint everywhere. Hoots of laughter and shouts of 'You idiot!' etc. Mrs Paint intervenes, is furious, and tells O'Mally off. His protests are ignored, much to Bright's amusement. Bright, referring to O'Mally's closely-cropped hair, says: 'O'Mally's a skinhead, Miss'.
King, quick to join in the fun, bellows out 'O'Mally's a skinhead, O'Mally's a skinhead'.
Bright: O'Mally is a hedgehog. Miss, Miss, O'Mally is a prickle!' [Laughter]. O'Mally is a prick!
Ginger: [not to be outdone]: Miss, he's got a head like a scrubbing brush.
King: Miss, O'Mally's a scrubber!
[Uproarious laughter].

Build-ons clearly depended upon quick wit: their effect lay in their speed off the mark before the teacher had time to intervene or take over the initiative again:

King leans back and hangs from the 4' wooden dividing board which runs around the room. He attracts attention and encourages other boys at the back to do the same.
Mrs Calm: What are you doing, King?
King: Hanging from the rail. [Laughter].
Mrs Calm: I can see that! But why? Why are you hanging from the wall.
King: Dunno.
Bright: He's a nut! He thinks he's a monkey [Laughter]

> *King:* Shut your face, Bright.
> *Bright:* Kingsy's a monkey nut! [Laughter]. The Monkey Nut Kid is big and strong [sings].

Within the group it was Bright who provided most of the impetus and quick thinking, although King often 'stole' from his companions:

> *Mrs Christian:* Now I'm sure you all like Turkish Delight.
> *King:* I wouldn't mind some, Miss.
> *Bright:* Neither would I, Miss. How old is she?
> *King:* [cackling and to himself] How old is she! Miss, Miss, I wouldn't mind some. Miss, how old is she? [Laughter].
> *Bright:* Shut up, I just said that!

Their crudest 'build-ons' were merely a form of verbal ping-pong between boys in order to stall the teacher:

> The lads fool and shout out. An outbreak of finger-clicking and finger-drumming. Chairs are tipped back and desks rattled. When the teacher focusses on a pupil (e.g. King), they implicate someone else: 'It's him, Miss', and 'No, it's not, it's him', etc.

4.4   Requests for Information

Requests for information already given were, sometimes, the result of not hearing and not listening. At other times, however, it was an effective way of 'needling' teachers, especially those in whose classes there was a lot of noise to start with. King described it to me as 'just joining in with the others, having something to say' and 'asking for the sake of asking':

> *Mrs Calm:* I'd like you to cover your books.
> *King:* Do we cover it, Miss?
> *Bright:* She just said, you nut!
> *King* [persisting]: Do we write our names, Miss?
> *Bright* [joining in]: Miss, Miss, what do we do, Miss?

It was most often just plain provocation:

> A teacher explains about the size of margin and drawing it in pencil. As he finishes
> *King:* Do we draw it in pencil?
> *Mr Bunsen:* Has anyone ever told you you are extremely provocative?
> *King:* Yeah! I dunno. What's 'provocative'?

4.5   Third Partying

The boys reverse the asymetricality of rights which usually exists between pupils and teacher by 'excluding' the latter (by placing them in the position of third party in a conversation) and obligating them to 'break back' into the exchange:

> Talk, in lesson time, about *Star Wars* and *Close Encounter.*
> *Mrs Fashion:* What is happening, David?
> [Bright whispers behind him and King turns around. They chat together]. You answer me, David, not your friend. How dare you be so cheeky!

This, then, was in direct contradiction of what the teachers were vigorously attempting to establish at the very outset of the boys' time in the Secondary School, namely what was regarded as the 'proper', deferential relationship between teacher and taught: and the norm that all public talk was to be regulated and controlled by teachers. As well as being a general challenge to teacher status, it was a calculated personal insult to the individuals concerned.

4.6   Answering Back and Open Cheek

'Giving lip', or answering back in a cheeky, cocky way, was noted by the King group to be the principal method of 'sussing out' and finding out about a teacher. In the first week, Mrs Paint was subjected to a barrage of open cheek:

(a)   Mrs Paint has told the class to divide into pairs and for one boy to draw his partner. King and Long work together. King sketches a monstrous face, doesn't look at Long, who sits grinning. Mrs Paint watches them from the side of the room. King shows his grotesque drawing to neighbouring pairs and much laughter, forcing Mrs Paint to intervene:
Mrs Paint: You, King are not looking at him at all. You're not drawing your partner, you've just drawn any face.
King: No, I'm drawing yours! [Long and King collapse into uncontrollable laughter].
Mrs Paint either doesn't hear or ignores the remark. She comes near and ends up drawing King for Long. With the teacher studying his face in order to draw him, King makes a funny face and plays up, like looking away and chatting to someone behind him. He is rapidly becoming a pupil whose 'authority' has to be obtained if you are to have any weight or standing in the pupil counter-culture. Long, with the teacher doing his work for him, sits back, arms folded, and pretends to nod off. The class is laughing *with* them at Mrs Paint, who is doing her best to remain calm and 'win over' King and Long.
(b)   *Long shouts out to Mrs Paint:*   Sir, Sir, King is throwing water around. [Laughter].
Mrs Paint: I'm Miss. My name is Mrs Paint.
Long: Hey, Mrs., King is throwing water around [in a very cheeky tone].

Mr Piano was subjected to similar treatment:

Mr Piano: The time will come when you get self-control, both of yourselves and the recorders. I think some of you need dummies, not recorders. I don't care if I take two periods, or more, over it, but in the end you'll learn to blow the recorders only when I say [pauses] blow. [King blows his recorder]. Stand up!
King: Me?
Mr Piano: Yes, you!
King: Why?
Mr Piano: Because I said so! Who told you to blow?
King: You did. You said 'blow'. [Laughter].
Mr Piano: I didn't!
King: Yes, you did!
Bright: Yes, you did! Sir.

A recurrent form of pupil answering-back was to 'draw out' the teacher and then to evaluate the comment upon their remark:

(a)   *Mr New:*   Long?
Long: 2nd May, '67.
Mr New: Sir!
Long: Sir?
Mr New: 2nd May, '67, SIR!
Long: Yes, that's right. [Laughter].
(b)   *Bright:*   Shouldn't there be an 's'?
Mrs Calm: No.
Bright: O that's alright then.

4.7   Chattering and Not Listening

This was as much a social activity as a means of exploiting a teacher suspected, or regarded as, weak. It served to consolidate and advertise a teacher's hardening reputation as incompetent (from the boys' point of view) and not worth attending to. Bright voiced the general opinion that 'good teachers' were the ones who not only had something 'interesting' to say, but who 'forced you to listen to 'em'. My references to chattering/not listening in Music, French, Welsh and Drama were legion:

> In Music, King talks and laughs when Mr Piano is teaching.
> *Mrs Fashion:*   There's someone in here talking when I am teaching. [King grins].

4.8   Challenging Comments and Statements

(a) At their simplest these were provocations, attempts to 'make the teachers lose their cool' [Blond].
> *King:*   Sir, you know that homework you set us?
> *Mr Union:*   Last night's homework. Yes?
> *King:*   Well, I didn't do it. [Laughter].
> *Mr Union:*   That's a good start, I must say!

(b) *Sloper:*   Miss, do we have Maths just once a week?
> *Miss Floral:*   No, we don't. You've got the M's mixed up.
> *King* [commenting]:   Stupid!
> Later Miss Floral makes a slight mistake in reading out the timetable.
> *King:*   She's hopeless!
> *Miss Floral:*   I'm getting a little tired of you already!

(c) *Long:*   Miss, Miss, French is boring.
> *Mrs Calm* [tired and more than a little defeated]:   I'm sorry you think that—I've got no reply I'm afraid.

At their most sophisticated, however, they placed the teacher in a most difficult position: a 'slap down' reply was not sufficient and a justification was demanded.

> *Miss Floral:*   What do you think Drama is about?
> *King:*   Drama is girls dancing about, Miss. [Laughter].

This 'challenge' was raised during Miss Floral's first lesson with 1Y when she was introducing them to Drama, which was new to many of them. King's answer was accompanied by a waving of arms and ballerina movements. It contradicted whatever definition of Drama the teacher could possibly hold since it dismissed it as merely fooling about. As a challenge it was highly successful in that it:

- forced a response from Miss Floral and placed the onus upon her to issue her definition and argue her case;
- did much to extend the reputation of King amongst his mates;
- raised a laugh and successfully interrupted the course of the lesson (instead of 'doing Drama', the class spent the next half an hour talking about it);
- raised sexist issues which were prevalent amongst the King group and the male-dominated school at large and were guaranteed to irritate Miss Floral.

A similar challenge was issued by King in the first RE lesson. Again it placed the teacher in a position in which she had to reply at length if she was to retain 'face', not only to voice an alternative view, but to justify it as being superior to King's:

> *King* [shouting out]:   Church is for sissies, Miss!

In putting forward such a radical criticism of both Drama and RE (or, at least, RE as Mrs Christian presented it) he was placing both teachers on the horns of a dilemma: if they ignored him then they were in danger of a personal and subject loss of credibility at the outset; on the other hand, to be forced to start off justifying your subject and its content at this early stage was, in itself, something of a defeat and retrograde step for both Miss Floral and Mrs Christian.

5 Challenges (Non-Verbal)

Issuing challenges was one of the chief means of 'sussing-out' a teacher and acquiring the necessary 'knowledge'. I have divided them (with the help of pupils) into verbal and non-verbal challenges. The latter are grouped under four headings:

1 Putting on a show.
2 Postural and gestural challenges.
3 Barging, hitting, and spitting.
4 Splattering and inking.
5 Noises.

5.1 Putting on a Show

(a) King and his group frequently 'put on a show' (as he termed it) for the class. He likened his relationship with Bright as Laurel and Hardy, and they worked closely together:
King and Bright are laughing and fooling in Drama, making a nonsense of Miss Floral's attempts at a lesson. She tells King to take the grin off his face and behave himself. In the ensuing improvisation he decides to play a dog and attempts to mount Bright. The class become completely unruly—gales of laughter, shouts, catcalls. He is forcibly prevented from giving a repeat performance by Miss Floral's vigorous intervention.
(b) King pretends to hug and kiss Bright. Laughs, purses lips, winks.
Similarly, they worked together to 'oggle' Mrs Fashion whom they held to be highly attractive and desirable:
Roland Lloyd talking-over, moved to front in Mrs Fashion's Welsh lesson:
['I don't like boys who always sit at the back'.] Bright/King oggle and fool. King turns around and draws in the air with his hands a woman's figure, enlarged and voluptuous. [Laughter].

Another aspect of 'putting on a show' was that King termed 'doing a mental'. This comedy involved drawing attention to himself by rolling his eyes and tapping his head, and was much appreciated by the class at large. It was not merely an effective way of retaining 'face', covering up for a mistake, but of using mistakes and turning them to his advantage:

(a) Those mistakes which King makes which are not exploitable (like not writing in block letters when requested to do so) he hides. However, some mistakes can be 'used', to his own advantage:
King: If your ink pen runs out what do you write in? Biro?
Mr Pickwick: I wish you'd listen you know! No, no!
King: Sorry, ink.
Mr Pickwick: PENCIL! [shouting].
King: Pencil. [He laughs, puts on a 'dumbo'/'mental' act, grinning and screwing his fingers to his head).
Bright: Kingsy's a nut! [Laughter, but *no* loss of face by King].
(b) Bright points out to King that he's missed out the first word. King announces his mistake to the form and gets a titter. 'What a silly billy I am', he says, with a touch of Mike Yarwood's Dennis Healey. [Laughter]. He rolls his eyes, taps his head and 'does a mental'.

In my chats with King he described other acts which he occasionally employed to enliven the day, impress his pals, and 'put one over' on teachers. Amongst these were:

(a) 'pretending to be asleep'; and
(b) 'playing Tarzan'.

(a) In the middle of Science, King yawns so loudly and so dramatically that Mr Bunsen stops talking.

>   *Mr Bunsen:*   I suggest you get to bed earlier, son. Otherwise I'll have to come up
>   there and give you a good shaking to wake you up, my lad.
>   King says nothing. Moments later he pretends to have fallen asleep sitting upright
>   in his chair. Laughter and whispers of 'Look at Kingsy' around the class.
> (b) King volunteers to stand in front of the class in a group in French and answer
>   questions asked by Mrs Calm. He swaggers up to the front, pumps up his chest,
>   beats it in Tarzan fashion and grins at the class.

5.2   Gestural and Postural Challenges

My field notes are littered with references to members of the King group 'trying it
on' by means of gestures and posture:

> 'Trying it on' early on—hands in pockets, smiling (when, from the teacher's point
> of view, there doesn't appear to be anything very much to smile about), resting
> hands on desk and twiddling thumbs in an exaggerated show of boredom, etc.
> Similarly swaggering up to the front, dragging feet, etc. punching people as you
> pass them. At this early stage of the year, teachers cannot allow any challenge to pass
> uncommented upon, and perhaps pupils utilize this, and the whole thing becomes
> an elaborate ebb and flow of advantage, like the early rounds of a boxing match
> when the fighters are probing for strengths and weaknesses.

Lounging around and not sitting up; desultorily obeying teacher's orders; feet on
desk; waving arms; combing hair; mock laughter and pointing—all these figure
in the repertoire:

(a) Backchat between Bright and King. Former combs his hair in full view of
    Mrs Calm.
(b) Bright is told to stand. He does so by perching on the corner of his desk. King
    laughs.
(c) Pulling blazer over his ears and waving arms as if drowning. [Bright].
(d) King, Bright, Ginger, fiddle with paper and throw paper balls at each other. King
    places his feet on the seat in front of him, then leans back and rests his feet on the
    desk.

These often served as preliminaries to bait and draw the teacher into further
confrontations:

(a) King leans back on his chair so that only the two back legs are on the ground. He
    yaps to his friend, Blond, pushing himself back into the desk behind, his arms
    levering himself back from his desk or holding to it in order to balance. He smiles
    as the teacher warns: 'You could have a nasty accident to your back, laddie, if you
    persist in doing that'. [Mr Piano, Music]. He leans back further and is generally
    bolshy, brash, showing-off and aggressive.
    Mr Piano: What school do you come from?
    King: [bellowing out]   Red Brick Junior.
    Mr Piano: [remaining quiet, calm]. You needn't shout. Sit properly in your chair,
    please.
    He stares at King, allows the silence to work, then continues, keeping his eyes
    on him and effectively preventing any 'follow up' fooling around.
(b) Ten minutes before the end of Mr Union's Maths' lesson, Blond packed his bag and
    sat back, arms folded, and stared vacantly out of the window. Mr Union asked him
    if he had finished the work and he replied he had. 'You've never finished in Maths,
    my lad'. Mr Union marked his work, found much of it to be incorrect, and told him
    to try again. This he did, but as soon as the bell sounded, he quickly packed his case
    and sat back again, arms folded, and grinned around at King and company who
    were still hard at it. Mr Union interpreted this as an act of open defiance since he
    had instructed the class on a number of occasions that he, not the bell, signalled
    when they were to stop working. Mr Union walked up to Blond, took his briefcase,
    walked back to the front of the class, held the case up high, called for the attention
    of the class, opened it, and poured the contents over the floor. Pens, pencils, books,
    discs, Blond's sandwiches and an apple rolled everywhere.

Mr Union: [shouted] You were warned, lad! I'll say no more! You were warned! I said I'd act if I caught you at it again. So you've got no complaints, you were warned. Come and pick up your junk! The rest of you now have my permission to pack up'.

Blond, red-faced, picked up his belongings. As the class filed out past a class lined-up ready to enter the room, King and Bright congratulated and consoled Blond. I heard Blond call Mr Union a 'fucking cunt'. Both he and Mr Union were visibly angry and flushed.

5.3   *Physical Challenges*

These were directed against fellow pupils, but often in the sight of teachers who were duty-bound to intervene. Barging, shoving and pushing when entering classrooms was a way of both impressing yourself upon other pupils as well as challenging staff:

> King barging. As he was being ticked off by a teacher, he grinned at another boy and waved.
> King barges and crashes into French. Mrs Calm sorts him out: Get back in line at once, please, and come back in properly.
> As he comes past her, she says: 'I don't want to see you barging and pushing like that again. Is that clear?
> *King:*   Yes, Miss. [He kicks over a bag and knees a boy as he passes].

Another form of physical challenge were open assaults on pupils in classes:

> In drama, the blindman's game. King barging and spitting on the floor.

5.4   *Spattering and Inking*

Ink and paint were readily available materials which the King group use as weapons:

> (a)   King flings ink around. Big boy has ink all over him. King wipes it into his desk, then places his inky hands around the neck of the boy in front of him.
> (b)   The King group throw paint around. Long paints his face, reddens his lips and cheeks and pretends to be Michelle. Great laughter. The table and floor is awash with water, paint and paper. King uses his brush to splatter his neighbours with water and paint. Huge fracas as Mrs Paint discovers the mess.

Although all this might be described as horse play or dismissed as youthful high spirits, it was an ever-present challenge to teachers to keep it within reasonable bounds. Only in Miss Floral's Drama and, to a lesser degree, Mrs Paint's Art lessons, did events move to such a pitch that it was the King group rather than the teachers who ran the lesson and determined its tempo and course.

5.5   *Noises*

'Noises' were intended to disrupt lessons and initiate 'band playing' (when whole groups of pupils took part). Tapping, desk-moving, floor scraping, and displays of drumming were one manifestation:

> (a)   Moving of desks (in Drama) an occasion/opportunity to have fun. Kids scrape desks along floor and make an enormous racket.
> (b)   *Mr Union:*   Thank you for tapping [to Roland Lloyd] I like it!
> (c)   Ginger knocks the underside of his desk—it catches on. Knockings and scrapings rise to a crescendo.

'Funny noises', on the other hand, included squeaks, tongue-clicking, falsetto singing, and whistling:

> Eye-contact—King/Bright flash signals, tempt, goad others into 'making runs'.
> Click tongues and alert the silly kids like Ginger, O'Mally, Cooper, etc.
> Shouting out in a high, falsetto voice:
> King leans back, his back against the wall, his seat balancing on two legs, looking
> bored. He starts to whistle, watching for staff reaction, seeing how long he can
> get away with it. After a while, he nudges Blond and Long and they whistle
> together.

In French, especially, funny noises became obvious because of Mrs Calm's emphasis
upon individual and class response, the major means of 'having a laugh' and pushing
the teacher to the limits:

> Public speaking in French allows King to draw attention to himself—grins, laughs,
> jokes when replying to Mrs Calm. Also, adopts a squeaky voice in class response—
> already establishing an image and reputation. Powerful member of a rapidly
> developing pupil culture.

The emphasis upon the oral meant that it was impossible for the teacher to pick out
and isolate the offender. Furthermore, it was an activity in which the
group could operate as a group:

> Roland Lloyd mucks around and Miss Floral appropriates his discs. In French,
> King leads the squeaky voice brigade. King raises the pitch of his voice and
> 'harmonizes' with the class response. In French the King group speak as a kind of
> barber shop quartet!
> *King* [to Bright]:   O good, we got French next. We can hold a choir practice!

6   Interventions

Interventions had to be loud and dramatic, forcing the teacher to stop whatever he
was doing:

> *Miss Floral:*   If you have ever been involved in a crowd scene . . .
> *Ginger* [interrupting]:   Mr, Miss!
> *Miss Floral:*   Yes? [annoyed].
> *Ginger:*   I have, Miss [Long laughs].
> *Miss Floral:*   You have what?
> *Ginger:*   I've been involved in a crowd scene [grinning broadly].
> *Miss Floral* [pauses]:   Who are you trying to impress?
> *Ginger:*   You, Miss. Miss, when he stuck his hand up I did.
> *Miss Floral:*   Did you!
> *Ginger:*   Yes, Miss.
> [Meanwhile, Bright, King, Long fool around. Roland Lloyd and O'Mally smile and
> laugh].

Interruptions could be broadly divided into four categories: shouting-outs; maniacal
laughter; bellowed/guttural singing (grossly and purposely out-of-tune); and what
boys termed 'parrots' (insistent, repetitious and insolent demands made of the
teacher):

6.1   Shouting-Outs
King led the way in shouting out without putting his hand up. He continued to do
this even after numerous warnings that he must wait his turn. It was partly
impetuosity and boundless energy on his behalf; partly habit; and also arrogance, a
belief that he was entitled to make demands of the teacher over and above the needs
of his classmates. It was also (on his admittance) a way of 'needling' some teachers:

> *King* [shouting out]:   Miss, do we underline it, Miss?
> Throughout the lesson he shouts out numerous questions and generally fools around.

His shouting-outs were often aimed at 'involving' the teacher as well as drawing attention to himself, a mixture of ego-building and pupil challenge:

> 'Smokes' his pen, closes book, and infers that others are copying from him by placing his arm around the book. Shouts out: 'Miss, he's copying, Miss', etc. [Laughter].

6.2   Maniacal Laughter

Bursts of maniacal laughter invariably resulted in the teacher momentarily losing control of the class to King and thus being obligated to recapture it:

> French is suddenly interrupted by King giggling hysterically for no apparent reason. He looks around for support. Similarly, when the teacher, Mrs Calm, asks Robert Bright his name, she receives a giggly response, with King throwing fuel on the fire.
> 'Trés bon, Marie'. He giggles and tries to involve Blond, who fiddles with his desk and laughs support. Laughter sweeps the class: when I asked King and Bright later what the joke was about he said: 'We were just laughing at nothing. You get carried away and then you can't stop'.

6.3   Bellowed Singing

This served the same function as an attention-drawer, interruption, and challenge:

> In the middle of the lesson King clicks his fingers and starts to sing *Summer Nights*. He projects a John Travolta image, both in his singing 'style' and appearance: dark, long sideburn 'flaps', older-looking and more mature physically than most kids in the form. He is a well-built boy, a young man amongst boys, although not the biggest boy in the class. He blinks and smiles a lot. His 'recital' gives rise to a great deal of laughter and attention, which he clearly relishes.

Occasionally songs would be adapted to the circumstances and become an insulting comment upon a teacher:

> Bright, eagerly assisted by Long, breaks into the Flump's song when Mrs Paint's back is turned: 'She's a Flump! She's a frump!' [Laughter].

6.4   Parrots (Repetitions)

Persistent repetitions of a question directed towards a teacher were termed 'parrots' by the boys. These could be the production of an individual or the cooperative effort of the group:

> *King:*   Do we write it down? Miss, do we write it down? Miss, do we write it down?

6.5   Verbal Attacks

Pupils whom the King group disliked or of whom they disapproved were verbally assaulted during lessons both as a means of asserting group and individual authority by, as Bright said to me 'giving them the verbal'. Eager, overtly enthusiastic kids were, from the outset, prime targets for these assaults.

> King coordinates his mates to humiliate a quiet, fresh-faced kid sitting nearby. Bright whacks quiet kid with a book.

Although teachers might be involved, the attacks were mainly directed by pupils at pupils:

   (a) *King:* What did he ask, Miss?
         Miss Floral: Who?
         King: Him with the funny-shaped head, Miss. [Laughter].
         Miss Floral: Shush!
   (b) *Mr Jovial:* Is it Jonathan Bott or Bolt?
         King [disdainfully]: It's Jonathan Belly. [Laughter].
         Mr Jovial: Keep your nose out of this, son.

The pupil population contained a wealth of material for the King group and early on in the term pupils were categorized in terms of their physical appearance, behaviour, and willingness (or reluctance) to be 'recruited'. They developed personal vendettas against two boys in particular: Lewis, (who they saw as a 'pet') and Tetley, a former member of the group who had been thrown out but who was intent upon impressing King and being re-admitted as one of his intimates. The former was a ready object for King's humour:

> *Mrs Paint:* [speaking to the son of a friend]: Clive, would you come here for a moment?
> *King:* O Clive, come here, Clive [mocking tone].

The material for King's humour lay in the boy's appearance: he was tall, fat, and red-haired, and each time he spoke in class King would bellow out "Here comes Frankenstein!'

> King plays with his pen-top, jamming it onto the end of his tongue, then sticking his tongue out at his neighbours and making a choking noise. Later he flashes his ruler at various targets, including Lewis, who he has nicknamed Frankenstein and whom he appears to enjoy taunting.

Similarly, quiet, shy, defenceless boys were picked upon and used as laugh-raising fodder by the boys:

> Roland Lloyd has played cards for most of today, undetected and uncorrected. Mr Piano asked Jason Slow if he was a fool: Slow didn't hear the question, and Lloyd told him to say 'Yes', which he did. This was the occasion for an outburst of laughing and hooting, and to Slow's confusion and Lloyd's pleasure. Later, the latter was told to stand in the front for persistent talking. He still continued to fool, smiling and gesturing at King.

6.6   Dramatic Entrances

During the first month late entries into lessons became a popular means of 'testing' teachers. They capitalized on the fact that in a traditional, rigidly organized school like Victoria Road (Mr Changeable, the Lower School Head, boasted that he ran the place 'like clockwork') a lesson 'started' when:

- the door was shut;
- the class was seated, silent, paying attention;
- the teacher started to talk.

Furthermore, a late entry, whilst it was guaranteed to affect all these conditions, was, by definition a challenge to teacher authority since movement around the school was strictly controlled and regimented (for example, boys were instructed to go to their classes and then ask to be excused, rather than arrive late). Staff had, therefore, either to deal with the latecomer on the spot or ease his passage into the lesson with the minimum of fuss and remember to investigate and reprimand later. In either case, initially at least, the latecomer held the upper hand. There were exceptions, however, when a teacher had been warned that a pupil would be late. These were invariably passed onto the class so that other pupils did not view the late entry as a challenge to teacher authority:

(a) 'Okay, Michael, sit down. I knew you'd be late today'. [Week 2].
(b) 'Two boys are going to be late because they have to see the Secretary. The rest of us can make a start'. [Week 2].
(c) *Mr New:* You've been to collect your medicine from the Staffroom Carl?
    Carl: Yes, Sir.
    Mr New: Okay, sit down, you've not missed much. [To me]. He's a walking dispensary, that boy! [Week 5].

A number of factors were essential to the success (in pupil's terms) of late entries:

(i) they should be noisy and dramatic, perhaps accompanied by preliminary door rattling or slamming:
    Late entrants: Blond enters noisily and leaves the door open. Mr Piano tells him to close it. He slams it shut.

(ii) they should interrupt the flow of the lesson (perhaps even re-direct it), and best of all, the teacher's early (and, presumably, guiding) remarks. This facilitated pupil 'follow-ups', endless questions concerning minor points made explicit prior to the latecomer's arrival, thus forcing the teacher to recap and repeat himself. In extreme cases they could lead to a 'take-over' by the latecomer so that the lesson was left far behind and the teacher had to reassert himself in order to make up for lost ground:

    A lot of noise and a dramatic, challenging late entrance by King just as the Drama lesson had started.

    Miss Floral: Where have you been, David?
    King: Chatting with my friend, Mr Changeable. Miss, Mr Changeable hugged me! [Laughter. King makes a kissing gesture]. He said, 'Hello David, how are you?' [His imitation brings the house down and there is loud applause].

(iii) they should raise a laugh or create the opportunity for a public exchange or slanging match between teacher and latecomer. In this case the latecomer had to be prepared to 'take the teacher on', using his wit, cheek and perseverance:

    King arrives late for Mrs Fashion's Welsh lesson. He makes a dramatic entry, laughing and letting the door crash shut after him. He stands in front of the class grinning broadly.
    Mrs Fashion: Where have you been?
    King: I've been to Mr Changeable about pears with Freddie Wild. [Laughter].
    Mrs Fashion: Pears with Freddie Wild! Come over here and explain what you mean. You didn't steal pears, of course! I suggest you start off your term better than going with Wild to steal pears.
    King [vehemently]: I didn't steal no pears!
    Mrs Fashion: Not 'no pears', but 'any pears'.
    King: I didn't steal no pears!

(iv) the location of teacher and late entrant.
    A late entrant was positioned with the teacher in front of the class, who acted as audience. He and the teacher are literally the only people on the stage and this could be used by the latecomer (through movement and gesture) to his advantage:

    Ginger comes in late. Laughs and makes a face behind the teacher as he passes.

(v) they should be supported by members of the class who are sympathetic and 'tuned-into' the latecomer's motives and intentions:

    Blond and Ginger chant and laugh as Long enters. 'Ding-a-dong, here comes Long'.

Late entries could create a scene which coloured the whole course and spirit of the subsequent lesson and could be enshrined and related as part of the oral tradition of the pupils' developing culture:

    Ginger [on King]: He came into our class late and made a rude sign at Miss Floral when she asked him why he was late. 'What are you doing?' she said. He told her to get lost and I agree with that. She's a right old . . . !'

Victoria Road was an overcrowded school in buildings which were nearly a century old. There were few, if any, spare rooms and there were numerous occasions when staff swapped rooms (for example, only some rooms could be blacked out). Invariably the King group seized these as opportunities to make spectacular group late entries, barging into classes other than their own:

> King and friends are told that the next lesson is to be held in Room I. They pretend not to hear and burst into Room II and play the innocents when apprehended.

6.7   Walkabouts

'Walkabouts', or 'Going for a walk', were regarded by them as one of the most effective ways of annoying and 'finding out' about a teacher, as well as being good fun. King himself rated it as one of the most successful strategies. A minority of the boys had come from Junior Schools in which a considerable degree of free pupil movement had been permitted. In Victoria Road, however, pupils were expected to sit down and remain seated throughout the course of the lesson (there were exceptions—in Drama and, sometimes, Art—but even here pupils had to be invited or granted permission to move about). Walkabouts, then, not only facilitated fooling by pupils, but were interpreted by teachers as either meaning:

(i)   Pupils had not yet been socialized out of their Junior School habits into the more rigorous mores of the Secondary School:

> King goes on a 'walkabout' later in Science to examine exhibits and smell samples laid out on benches. Later, tie-play—elaborate knots. Much laughing with Roland Lloyd who now has a punk hairstyle. Mr Bunsen furious and tells him never to walk around Lab. without permission.

(ii)   They were doing it in the full knowledge that it was forbidden and were, therefore, purposely setting out to disrupt and annoy:

   (a)   King rushes to the back in Geography. He pushes a desk into Blond, knocks on the wall with his ruler, and grins around ostentatiously. Robert Bright giggles and aids him. Elicit reprimands from Mr Jovial, who is near losing his temper.
   (b)   King, Long and Bright saunter around the room, hands in pockets, defiant.
         Perhaps what made walkabouts so desirable was not only the pleasure of being up on one's feet and taking a more active role in things, but that they could be 'explained away' if you were reprimanded and lead to a public 'dispute' with a teacher:
         Later King goes on a walkabout and fools around under the pretext that he is sharpening a pencil. Then Long wanders around to 'borrow a pencil' and Ginger 'to get some ink'. Blond ambles around the class after blotting paper. All answer the teacher cheekily.

7   Play

The King group 'played' a great deal in lessons.

> In Welsh I notice how fidgetting has become, for some pupils, a fine art. There is an immense amount and variety of handplay with pens, books, rulers, desks, clothing, rubbers, pockets.

Their games took the form of bag games; ruler flashing; pen play; things-that-come-to-hand play; bringing-things-to-school play; and disc play, and in chatting with the boys a number of functions of the play emerged:

(i) *To annoy.* Much play was underhand and a concerted attempt to ascertain how far you could go and just what you could get away with in the case of a particular teacher. Much of it was a clear-cut defiance of teacher authority at a time when staff were 'establishing themselves' with the classes.

(ii) *To entertain (both yourselves and friends).* Most of what went on in lessons was regarded by the boys as 'boring' and so the fun-making and time-wasting aspect of play was most important:

> It helps to pass the time.
> (King)
> Gives us something to do.
> (Long)
> Can be good fun.
> (Bright)

In another sense it was an attempt by the boys to capture and shape their surroundings, make them 'habitable' in their terms, and create in part their own working conditions. Disc play, for example was a powerful assertion of the emerging pupil culture, the meanings of which most staff were unaware.

(iii) *To interrupt the lesson.* A great deal of play threatened, if unchecked, to mess up the lesson and detract from the serious business of 'work' (as defined by teachers). It was geared to elicit a response from the teacher and provide material for 'making a scene'. Sometimes the play was of such a nature that it stopped the lesson and forced the teacher to act.

(iv) *Bolster image and reputation.* Play allowed pupils to impress their neighbours with skill and daring and 'put one over' on friends, enemy, and teacher.

(v) *To communicate.* Play was a means of linking-up and colonizing, so that individual 'games' became class activities and a boy's reputation was at stake if he did not participate. The King group often issued such challenges and acted in a 'follow-my-leader' capacity.

7.1   Fidgetting with pens

This took the form of making things out of pens; smashing and repairing them; cleaning and filling; 'smoking' a pen; using it as an implement to catch, push, poke, drop, roll, etc.:

> King, Long, Cooper, O'Mally often stand up and wander around the class with no apparent purpose in mind. There is almost constant pen/pencil-play amongst them—systematically smashing, bending, crushing pens, then attempting to repair and patch them up. Pens/cartridges/pencils/rulers—they are the occasion/topic for interrupting lessons, for not doing work, or for wandering around the room, or even the building, looking for parts, attempting repairs, or borrowing replacements.

My field notes were shot through with references to pen play. For example:

> King 'smokes' an ink carridge like a cigar. He then chews it and sticks out a bright blue tongue at Ginger, who turns around and cackles hysterically. Within seconds he has directed the attention of the class towards King's uproar.

7.2   Ruler Flashing

Ruler flashing could do a number of things: communicate; annoy; and momentarily halt a lesson. Elaborate games of 'chase' were held across the ceiling:

> Long flashing ruler onto ceiling. Then on to board upon which teacher is writing. When the teacher angrily turns around he looks a picture of innocence.

7.3   Bag games

These usually took the form of stealing and then hiding other kids' bags by passing them on. A 'pass-the-bag' game resulted in an outburst of laughter when the victim realized his bag had gone, or in absolute chaos as the victims tried to find and recover their possessions. Another form was the smashing up of your own or someone else's bag, or using it as a weapon to bash, dent, scratch someone or something. Bags were amongst the most prized possessions, decorated as they usually were with emblems of the owner's allegiance to a cause or football club (example: 'Man. United for ever', etc.).

(a)   The bag game starts up again. Bright surreptitiously takes King's brief case and hides it under a desk across the way from where he is sitting. King eventually discovers it is missing.
      King: Miss, Miss, Miss, my bag is missing. Someone's whipped my bag, Miss. [Bright quietly slides it back into place.].
      Bright: It's there, you idiot.
      King: Where?
      Bright [pointing]: There!

(b)   Bag-play initiated by O'Mally, supported by King. Knocking my mic. over or stepping on cable also popular. After school yesterday I watched O'Mally walk past a teacher's car dragging his open briefcase the length of the body, the metal strap buckles rasping the paintwork. From his look I'm sure he did it on purpose. When Mr Dancer tackled him today he said it was an 'accident'.

7.4   Bringing things to school

These included personal belongings (discs, keys, toys, knives, etc.) as well as cards and games.

(a)   Bright's tie-play impresses King, who starts doing it also. The object appears to be the production of the most elaborate tie knot. The game ends with King pretending to hang himself. With the end of his tie held high above his head he rolls his eyes and pretends to gasp for breath.

(b)   King has invented a new game—dropping books on his desk. He has spent much of the lesson playing with a key ring and a pile of plastic beer barrel discs. He was caught by Mrs Calm and reprimanded. Under his breath he called her 'a bitch, a bag'. It was uttered just loud enough for his immediate neighbours to hear and they sniggered. Mrs Calm, if she did hear, let it pass.

7.5   Finding materials

This took the form of fooling with objects and materials that came to hand in certain rooms for certain lessons: paint, blinds, recorders, books, projectors, desks, board rubbers:

(a)   King fools with projector. When Mrs Calm switches it on the picture is hopelessly out of focus. He follows it up by raising the blind in the middle of the slide show. Light floods the room and Mrs Calm is furious.

(b)   Ginger plays with the blind. He gradually darkens then lightens the room, watching carefully for the teacher's response.

(c)   *Mrs Fashion:*   Will you, David, stop playing with that board duster so I don't get silicosis from the dust!
      King grins and hammers the board duster one more time onto the desk, sending a cloud of chalk dust into the air.

7.6   Disc Play

The importance to pupils of collecting and playing discs (the plastic covers on the bung holes of beer barrels) in lieu of ball games (which were not allowed because of the sloping yard) was acknowledged by all:

Breaks and lunch hour are great. We play discs and muck around
[King].

Elaborate rules were devised for the conduct of disc games in the yard and it was not
long before desk-top disc play developed:

Disc-play in lesson time, a form of desk top football, hitting one disc into another using
a ruler as a kind of billiard cue.

In Week 3 I noted:

Discs are collected and a huge black market has developed. Gambling games take place
and an individual's importance is linked to the number of discs he has in his possession.
King has nearly three dozen. At points during the day he counts them, piles them up,
gloats over them, shows them off to other kids. Discs are amongst the hard currency of
the emerging informal pupil culture.

8 Conclusion

Finding out about Lower School staff by means of experimental testing ('sussing')
was an important feature of starting Secondary School for these boys. It allowed
them to provisionally 'locate' teachers through a process of retro/prospective
evaluation and planning. Neither was 'sussing' an accidental, hit-and-miss affair:
rather it was a purposeful, skilled accomplishment which was difficult for teachers
to handle; threatened their authority from the outset; and, also, helped boys
establish and consolidate reputations and a pecking order amongst peers (termed, by
them, 'bodybuilding'). 'Sussing' was the way of discovering degrees of teacher
tolerance; behavioural elasticity; and coercive powers, essential 'knowledge' which
could not otherwise be ascertained. This meant casting doubt and discrediting the
claims teachers were currently making about themsleves, and contradicting the
identities and procedural competence they were intent on fostering. In
concentrating on the core activists at the heart of the 1Y 'fraternity' I have
emphasized the importance to them of seeking and combining with like-minded
boys: 'sussing' was essentially a linked series or orchestrated, collaborative cheek
and challenges which aided both the typing of teachers and peers. Ironically these
pupil challenges simultaneously afforded 'hard' teachers the opportunity to deal
with troublesome pupils and establish themselves both in their eyes and in the eyes
of colleagues.

What emerges is the diversity of 'sussing' during the early weeks, a period
regarded, not surprisingly, as formidably demanding by all Lower School staff.
What is required is much more data on the settling-in strategies employed by pupils
(and teachers) in a range of schools and classrooms during this crucial period of
procedural establishment and induction into secondary schooling.

9 Interaction sets in the classroom: towards a study of pupil knowledge

V. J. FURLONG

Not all pupils 'know' the same things about their school lives. They do not all form the same commonsense judgments about their teachers or the curriculum; they do not all see other pupils in the same way. Because of this, a study of pupil experience or 'knowledge' of school life must begin by looking at the way some pupils come to share common perspectives, and how pupils influence each other in what they 'know'. In other words, we need a more detailed understanding of pupil interaction. Only when this process is fully understood will it be possible to go on to document what individuals or groups actually 'know'. This paper is therefore intended to provide the groundwork for a more detailed study of pupil knowledge.

The ways in which pupils influence each other, both in their behaviour and in their interpretation of their school experience, is of great interest to both teachers and parents. That interest is often expressed in phrases such as 'He's getting into bad company', or 'She's a good influence on her class.' Despite this interest, there has been relatively little research which examines pupils' informal school life. Most classroom observation, whether 'systematic' or 'anthropological', seems to be directed at throwing light only on the teacher–pupil relationship; this study is an attempt to redress that imbalance.

The field work was carried out in a secondary modern school in a large English city for two terms during 1972 and 1973. I had taught in the school since 1970. The data presented relate to one class of sixteen fourth-year girls, whose average age was fifteen.[1] The material has come from two main sources. First, notes made during my extensive observations of lessons with each of their ten teachers. I simply sat at the back of the class and wrote down what the girls did and said, concentrating in particular on situations where they communicated with each other. The second source of data was tape-recorded interviews with groups and individual girls.

Many of the quotations selected for this paper relate to one particular girl, whom I call Carol. (All names of pupils and teachers in this paper are, of course, pseudonyms.) In this way the reader can build up a consistent picture of interaction as it takes place in the classroom. For this purpose, any of the girls could have been chosen, for Carol is not seen to be in any way unusual.

Of the sixteen girls, thirteen, including Carol, were of West Indian origin, although most of them had spent the majority of their school career in England.[2] This class was considered to be below average intelligence and they occupied a 'one from bottom' position in the streaming system. The general assessment of the staff was that they were 'difficult' but not the 'worst' class in the school.

The paper is divided into two main sections. The first part is devoted to building up an understanding of what interaction is, and how it takes place in the classroom. Patterns of interaction are seen to be related to how individuals or groups define classroom situations: what they 'know' about them. The second section develops this model, illustrating Carol's typical pattern of interaction, and typical ways of looking at classroom situations.

I begin by comparing my approach with some of the existing work on pupil interaction, most of which has been based on a key theory of social psychology: that of groups. I argue that the results are less than adequate.

The social psychological approach

Various authors[3] have applied a social psychological model to the study of schools. The process of pupil interaction in the classroom is assumed to take place within the context of peer groups or friendship groups. It is suggested that these groups have a 'culture' of norms and values which colour the pupils' whole school experience.

This approach does not, however, examine how the pupils *themselves* see their social relationships. Researchers have not asked how pupils actually interact with each other in the classroom, or examined the different action they see as appropriate in different circumstances.

The studies by David Hargreaves (1967) and Colin Lacey (1970) are probably the best known in this field. Their analysis is simple. They both believe that social interaction can best be understood by using the concept of the informal group. They assume that friends will 'interact' more frequently than pupils who are not friends, and that in doing so they will develop their own norms and values. Interaction is therefore understood only in terms of group membership, and it is a simple task, using a sociometric questionnaire, to discover exactly who is in the group. (A sociometric questionnaire is a means of obtaining quantitative data on the preferences of individuals for associating with each other. For example, Hargreaves asked pupils to write down the names of the friends they went around with at school. Pupils who chose each other were assumed to form a peer group.)

Once Hargreaves and Lacey have plotted their different groups, they proceed to 'measure' the norms and values associated with each. They assume that these groups form 'cultures' which will be consistent in their approach to the school, and Hargreaves goes so far as to identify the 'central norms' of each of the classes he studied. For example, the main value of his 4B is seen as 'having fun' while the values of his 4C are characterised in terms of delinquency (Hargreaves 1967, p. 27).

Conformity to these central norms is explained in terms of 'social pressure' or 'power'. Conforming to the demands of the group culture is something the individual must do if he is not going to sacrifice his social status. Those who do not conform are called 'deviants'.

There are three major difficulties with this model. First, interaction does not just 'happen' in friendship groups but is 'constructed' by individuals. When classes are observed, it becomes obvious that who interacts with whom can change from minute to minute, depending on a great many circumstances. Pupil interaction in a classroom will not necessarily include all friends at the same time, and will often involve pupils who are not friends at all.

The second difficulty with this model relates to the idea that norms and values will be consistent. It would be obvious, even to the most casual observer of classroom behaviour, that there is no *consistent* culture for a group of friends. Even the most delinquent pupils will be well behaved in certain circumstances.[4] Teachers do not always invite the same amount of conformity or hostility, and some lessons allow for greater feelings of personal achievement than others. Classroom situations change in the meaning they have for pupils and, as they change, so will the pupils' assessments of how to behave.

Finally, the model suggests that there is a pressure on group members to conform to the group's demands. The culture is presented as an external reality, and social behaviour is shown not so much as an interaction between two or more individuals, but as one person responding to some reified group. The implication is that the individual has little choice in his action, as he is controlled by something outside him: the group.

This 'external' analysis of interaction is inadequate, because it misses the main point, that participants have to build up their own respective lines of conduct as they go along. They must continually interpret each others' actions, and therefore continually 'redefine' the situation for themselves. Norms and values are significant only in so far as they are interpreted by the participants during the interaction process.

I am therefore arguing for an alternative understanding of classroom interaction, where the pupils are seen to be continually adjusting their behaviour to each other, where those actually interacting are always changing, and where norms of behaviour are not consistent. In these circumstances it is impossible to use the necessarily static methods implied by the social psychological model. Questionnaires and paper-and-pencil tests become inadequate, and it is necessary to observe pupils' interactions as it actually happens in the classroom. It is also important to record what the pupils say about their classroom situations, and to try and understand how they form rules for interpreting these situations. Anthropological observations must therefore become the major tool of analysis and cannot simply be used to resolve ambiguities as Lacey for example suggested (1970, p. 98).

Interaction

The objective of this study, then, is to develop a more sensitive analysis of the way in which pupils influence each other, both in their understanding of their school experience and in the types of behaviour they consider appropriate. The assumption that this somehow 'happens' in groups is inadequate and it is necessary to study interaction as it takes place and as the pupils themselves see it.

By interaction, I mean situations where individuals come to a common 'definition of the situation' by drawing on similar commonsense knowledge, and make common assessments of appropriate action. That is, they 'see' what is happening in the same way and agree on what are appropriate ways to behave in the circumstances. This does not mean that those interacting will behave in the *same* way, simply that they behave in a way that can be interpreted by others as showing similar 'definitions of the situation'. Nor do pupils have to 'tell' each other how they see things, for their actions will symbolically tell this to the whole class.

In this way, running out of a class or shouting an answer to a teacher can be examples of interaction when the individual takes into account that he is being given support by smiles or laughter from others present. He knows by their support that they 'see' the classroom situation in the same way; they share the same commonsense knowledge about it. Here it is not enough to look at the individual on his own, for he is aware that his behaviour is a 'joint action'; that others are taking part; that he is interacting.[5]

The following example of interaction comes from my observational notes. The incident occurred after Carol had been told to leave the room because she had been rude to the teacher. My notes show her interacting with Valerie and Diane, and taking into account what they are doing in choosing her own action:

> She (Carol) wanders out slowly, laughing and looking round at Valerie and Diane, who laugh as well. She stands outside the door, looking through its window for a few minutes . . . trying to catch the eyes of the people inside the room.

While she is walking out of the room, Carol is aware of Valerie and Diane and is making continual non-verbal contact with them. Even when she is outside the door, she maintains this contact for a few minutes, but after a while she gives up and wanders off out of sight.

In this example, Carol is communicating with two other girls in the room, each of whom 'see' what is happening in the same way. They symbolically communicate this to her by the way they act (laughing and looking at her) and therefore support her action. These three girls who are choosing their behaviour together from a group or a set. To distinguish those taking part in this sort of grouping from any other, I am going to call it an 'interaction set'. That is to say: the interaction set at any one time will be those pupils who perceive what is happening in a similar way, communicate this to each other, and define appropriate action together.

Now consider this example of Carol interacting with a much larger group of girls; she is aware of them and directs what she says to them all. They are all part of an interaction set.

> (Eight of the girls are sitting round the same bench in the science lab. Carol and Diane run in thirty minutes late and sit down with them all.)
> Carol   (to the whole table): I went home to get some tangerines.
> Mrs Newman: Where have you been?
> Diane   (aggressively): Dentist . . .
> Mrs Newman: Where have you been?
> Carol   (aggressively): None of your business.
> (Mrs Newman ignores or does not hear this remark.)

The interaction set in the second example is much larger than in the first: nine girls are involved, as opposed to three.

The descriptions above show that the girls are aware of each other in choosing their behaviour. This awareness of others is implied in the way they describe classroom situations. For example, in an interview, Carol uses the term 'we' rather than 'I': 'We sneak out of the class, or ask to go for a drink of water . . . and we don't come back, we don't come back in again at all.'[6] This is a generalised classroom description, and Carol thinks in terms of herself and her friends; she does the same when describing specific situations; 'We had RE . . . We had that stupid teacher, and he just sits there and gives us these stupid books to read, so I just sit there reading them . . . so Anne says "Let's go out", so me, Jill, Linda and Diane just follow her out.'

A lot of Carol's classroom behaviour takes place in the context of an interaction set. She takes others into account in deciding how to behave, and is aware that they share a common definition of the situation. Similar observations were made for all the other pupils in the class. Each spends a great deal of her classroom time interacting rather than behaving individually.

Who is in the interaction set?
Consider the following descriptions of classroom situations, which show different interaction sets in operation. In the first, the set comprises Carol and Diane alone; they are late for the lesson and are talking to each other in the corridor. Angela tires to distinguish herself from them in the teacher's eyes by 'telling on them'.

> (When Mrs Alan comes in, Carol and Diane are missing, she asks where they are. Angela says they were in the last lesson.)
> Angela: Them lot are outside, Miss.
> (Mrs Alan goes out and sends in Carol and Diane who enter, laughing loudly, and start to sit down. They are followed in by Mrs Alan, who shouts, 'Stand at the front.' They continue to laugh and look round the room, though less confident than before. Other class members are no long laughing with them and Carol and Diane's eyes rove round the room, but come into contact with no one in particular.)

In this second example, the interaction set includes Carol and five other girls.

> Carol, Valerie, Diane, Anne, Angela and Monica sit round one of the benches in the science lab. There is continual talking throughout the lesson from these girls even though they carry on copying down the notes that Mrs Newman has written down on the board. At times the noise from these girls is so great that Mrs Newman can't be heard. The rest of the class, sitting round the other bench, are comparatively quiet.

It is obvious from these examples that quite different interaction sets are in operation. In the first situation Carol and Diane form a distinct unit. They are defined as an interaction set both by themselves and by others' assessment of their action, as shown by Angela's behaviour. In the second example, a much larger interaction set is in operation. Again, Carol, Valerie and Diane take part, but this time Anne, Angela and Monica participate as well, each legitimating the action of the others.

There are other situations which illustrate different patterns of classroom interaction. In the following example, which describes a test, the pattern of interaction continually changes.

> When the test begins, they slowly move to different seats without being told to . . . Linda does not know the answer to the first question and does not write anything. Diane whispers across the room to Carol, 'You doing it?' Carol holds up a blank piece of paper and giggles, she hasn't been able to do the first two questions either. Miss Lane asks the next question: 'Name a common cooking cheese' . . . Linda smiles, looks round the class and does not write anything. Next question: 'Name one use the body puts calcium to.' Linda behaves differently. She writes, then looks up to the ceiling for a moment, and then writes again. 'Name a common egg drink.' Linda and Jill's eyes meet; they both seem to know the answer and quickly look away, covering their papers from each other with their arms.

Here the girls are moving in and out of interaction, depending on whether or not they know the answers. When they know the answer they act alone, when they do not, they interact.

The changing pattern of interaction is reflected in the way the girls describe each other. For example, in an interview, Carol, Valerie and Diane discuss who they are 'friends with' in the class:

Carol: Yes we're all friends together, really . . . not Monica though, she's not really with us.
Valerie: No, she works too hard, she's too good.
Diane: Well, she used to be last year.
Carol: Well I suppose she is most of the time.

They seem confused about whether Monica is or is not a 'friend'; observations show that Monica interacts with these three girls only at certain times, but at others she has nothing to do with them, often sitting on the other side of the room.

Patterns of interactions can vary a great deal. Sometimes the girls act quite alone without obvious communication between them, apparently defining situations for themselves. At different times interaction sets form, involving varying numbers of girls and occasionally the whole class. Each interaction set relates to a specific definition; all of the girls interacting share the same commonsense knowledge of the situation.

Norms and values

A great many researchers have tried to study the 'culture' of different adolescent groups by trying to identify both the norms of behaviour and the underlying values to which members subscribe.[7]

I have already argued that action cannot be understood in terms of friendship groups, for these are not the same as interaction sets where membership can vary from minute to minute. Consistent groups do not exist in reality, and observation has also shown that there is no consistent culture for a group of pupils. Norms and values relate to specific definitions of the situations and to typical interaction sets, rather than to a particular group of friends. We have already seen that there is a great variety of behaviour in the class—a variety too great to be described in terms of a consistent 'culture' as the word has traditionally been used. This diversity is even more strongly brought out by the following descriptions of some girls going to two different lessons on the same afternoon.

> (The girls are standing in the corridor talking to me before the beginning of a commerce lesson.)
> *Mary:* Quick—Mrs Alan!
> (She runs violently into the class, smiling. The other girls all enter quickly and find their places and sit talking.)
> *Mrs Alan* (through the noise): Good afternoon 4G.
> *Girls in unison:* Good afternoon.
> (There is silence as they wait for the register to be taken, each girl answering her name as it is called. They then wait quietly for the lesson to begin.)

Contrast this with the beginning of the science lesson that followed immediately afterwards:

> The girls all enter the lab. Carol, Valerie, Diane, Debbie, Monica, Anne and Angela are talking, shouting and laughing. They find their places, and continue talking, all completely ignoring the teacher, Mrs Newman. She takes the register, but is not able to call out the name as there is too much noise, and she spends a considerable time looking to see who is there.

The way the girls behave in these two situations is quite different: different norms are being used, and different interaction sets are in operation. In the first example the whole class shares a common definition of the lesson, whereas in the second example, seven girls form one specific interaction set.

The following examples relate to history, but with two different teachers. They bring out just how varied behaviour can be:

> Carol, Valerie, Diane and Mary are sitting close together, though there is no visible interaction between them, verbal or non-verbal . . . Mr Marks moves to the back of the class and talks to me in whispers for the last ten minutes of the lesson. None of the girls show any signs of hearing us, they all seem too involved in their work to notice us.

As Mary says, in an interview: 'We all love it, it's our favourite subject . . . we all like history.'

During my period of observation, the history teacher, Mr Marks, left. Carol describes the incident with the new teacher who replaced him. 'I just started to laugh and he hold my collar until I get out of the chair so I hit him . . . then I push him and he fall down.' Extreme behaviour like this is very rare, but the girls are quite frequently rude and hostile to their teachers, and sometimes do not bother to turn up to lessons at all.

The idea that different norms and values are appropriate at different times is borne out by what the teachers wrote on a questionnaire about the pupils. Take for example the comments made about Carol by two teachers, Mr Marks, the history teacher, and Mrs Newman, who taught science.

> *Mrs Newman:* Carol is restless, awkward and often very noisy . . . I can get a lot more done
> when Carol isn't there.
> (Mr Marks wrote after he had left: 'amenable to discipline and not at all unintelligent'.)

Obviously these teachers saw very different 'sides' of Carol in their lessons and, for this reason, the girls' behaviour cannot be described as a 'culture' in the normal use of the word. The range is too great and at first glance, at least, their actions often look contradictory. Carol can arrive one day at a lesson and work quietly and well, and the next not bother to turn up at all for the same lesson.

I am not suggesting that the action of these girls is random: there are patterns and common ways of behaving, as will be shown below. Yet these patterns are much more complex than has been implied by other researchers. Norms of behaviour relate to specific definitions of classroom situations. People who interact regularly function with a limited number of typical definitions, and there will be typical patterns of action related to each. Before discussing norms and values for any one girl, therefore, it is necessary to examine how she sees situations, what she 'knows' about them, and who else shares that knowledge. Only in this light can her specifications be interpreted.

The individual and the set
A large proportion of the classroom behaviour of the girls observed took place in the context of interaction sets; there was a great deal of joint rather than individual action. In these cirumstances it is important to examine the relationship between the individual and the other interaction set memebers. Are pupils 'forced' to act in a certain way simply by being a member of an interaction set, or do they choose their action for themselves?

There are two ways of examining the relationship between the individuals and the set. The first is to look at the behaviour of pupils when they are not in interaction: when they define situations in a different way from those around them. The second method is to look at the variety of action that takes place in any one interaction set.

Individual action
Most of Carol's classroom behaviour is interactive, but sometimes she acts alone. On these 'individual' occasions she shows the same type of behaviour as when part of a set. What is different is not the behavioural content, but the times when Carol considers that behaviour appropriate Carol can be seen as having the same 'repertoire'[8] of classroom behaviour in individual or interactive situations. For example she can be just as hostile to a teacher when acting alone as when part of an interaction set. When she 'greeted' her new history teacher by pushing him over, she was acting alone. Other girls describing the same incident seemed slightly shocked by the extremity of Carol's action; they were not participating or supporting.

A quite different example of very individual action comes in a cooking lesson: 'Carol . . . works alone, all lesson; she talks to no one, not even Dorothy who is working at the same table.' In an interview, she explains how she sometimes acts alone: 'Valerie . . . and them lot sometimes start to muck about, you know, and I says to them all, "Why can't you lot behave?"—you know, start to tell them off. Sometimes I just sit down in the corner, you know—just sit down by myself.' Carol can therefore be extremely hostile and disruptive in some lessons, but at other times she is very work-orientated. In the examples above she was acting alone, defining situations for herself. Yet as is well documented below, she frequently shows exactly the same type of behaviour in interactive situations.

Particularly 'pieces' of behaviour can, then, be displayed in both social and individual settings. Action should therefore be considered not so much a product of a social situation, in some way 'manufactured' by it, but much more 'facilitated' by that situation. The choice of action remains with the individual, and belongs to her. Only the general situation is interactively defined.

Variety of action

Girls who assess situations in a similar way and define appropriate actions together do no necessarily act in the *same* way. When Carol and Diane run in late to a science lesson, it is Carol who makes most of the comments to the teacher, saying 'None of your business' when asked where they have been. Diane, on the other hand, is much quieter, and begins getting out books and finding out what they have missed. Despite the fact that they are in full communication with each other, each legitimating the action of the other, they negotiate different 'social identities', Carol being outspoken, and Diane being supportive. similar examples occur in less hostile situations. For example, Carol often shouts out answers to questions, or wanders round the room, while Diane and Valerie support her by watching and laughing. They seldom, if ever, take over this sort of action themselves.

Thus joint action does not always imply the same action. It simply demands behaviour that can symbolically communicate to another a particular definition of the situation; it must show that interactants have the same commonsense knowledge. Thus the range of any one individual's joint action can, theoretically at least, be quite varied, as long as it symbolically implies a common definition. It is the willingness to take others into account and share interpretations and definitions of situations that is important. Carol chooses her own action, but is dependent for support on others. She does not act in the same way as she would if she were alone, but decides how to behave in the light of commonly negotiated definitions of the situation.

Definitions of classroom situations

Goffman (1959) has suggested that definitions of the situation tend to be 'idealised'. That is, a group's or interaction set's definition of the situation is likely to differ to some extent from the individual's own. Establishing a common point of contact demands compromise from all. Action itself may be drawn away from what the individual wants to what is appropriate to the idealised definition. Goffman has also pointed out that most groups function with a limited number of 'typical' definitions: people 'see' situations in certain set ways. Of course, individuals can extract themselves from interaction, and groups as a whole can establish new definitions. Goffman is simply suggesting that this will not be the usual experience.

In this section, I illustrate some of the 'idealised' and 'typical' definitions of classroom situations that Carol often subscribes to. That is, I will examine some of the criteria she uses in making assessments of situations and show some of the more common interaction sets related to these.

Before proceeding, a number of points should be made. First, my objective will be to provide a series of simplified 'ideal/typical' definitions, so that the interaction sets associated with them can be specified. These definitions are not intended to be rigid categories for analysing behaviour, since real life situations would be unlikely to correspond to any of them exactly. Second, the pictures to be presented will necessarily be static. The more abstract knowledge Carol uses to move from one definition to the next is beyond the scope of this paper. Finally, it must be remembered that these definitions relate only to Carol and her interaction sets. It is not suggested that they have wider validity.

For Carol and those she interacts with, the most significant factor involved in making definitions of classroom situations is the teacher. Many of her criteria of assessment related to teachers, both in the way they taught, and in the methods they used for controlling the class. The following example comes from a group interview:

Question: When you work in class, is it because you like the subject, or is it the way the teacher teaches?
Diane: It's the subject.
Carol: Mmmmmmmmmm. It's the teacher as well, isn't it.

In another interview:

Carol:
Question: Why do you think you all muck about so much?
Carol: The teachers look for it, if you ask me.
Question: Why?
Carol: I don't like no subjects, they're boring, they make me feel like going to sleep.

Obviously, then the teacher was very important. How was he assessed?

'Strict' and 'soft' teachers
One of the major distinctions between teachers was between those who were seen as 'soft' and those who were 'strict' or 'tough'. Valerie often interacts with Carol; in an interview, she says:

'Some of the teachers are soft, you could stand up and they don't teach you nothing, they don't teach you anything that way.'
Question: What would you do if you were a teacher, and you came in and everyone was mucking about?
Valerie: Well it would depend on what sort of teacher I was. If I was a tough teacher, I'd go 'Sit down'. You know, once you hit one of them, the rest are frightened, and everybody just do the same thing just sit down.

As criteria of definition, though, 'soft' and 'strict' are not adequate. Take, for example, two teachers, Mrs Alan, who taught commerce, and Mrs Newman, who taught science. Both of them were characterised as 'soft' by Carol. But she and her friends responded quite differently when these two teachers told them off for something. In a lesson with Mrs Alan, Carol, Valerie and Diane had arrived late, and were instructed to stand at the front of the class. They were then severely told off. The three girls became extremely hostile, and made abusive comments to the teacher. Mrs Alan ignored these for a while, but when Carol called her an 'ignorant pig', she was asked to leave the room.

This example can be contrasted with Carol's interactive behaviour when being told off by Mrs Newman for coming in late. When asked where she had been, she simply said 'None of your business', and continued discussing what she had been doing with seven or eight of her friends.

Carol, Valerie and Diane seem to take the 'telling off' from Mrs Alan far more seriously than from Mrs Newman. Even though both teachers were thought of as 'soft', one seemed to pose a more serious threat to the girls than the other, and their response was different. Other girls in the class also defined these situations differently. In the first instance, the rest of the class was quiet, and avoided contact with Carol, Valerie and Diane. In the second case they eagerly participated, and were keen to listen to Carol's latest exploits. Obviously, some teachers were 'softer' than others!

'Learning a lot'

Carol made further distinctions between teachers. She readily admitted that while taught by Mr Marks, history was her best subject. 'You can't talk in Mr Marks' lesson, you just have to work . . . so after a while you work, and you enjoy it because you're learning a lot.' This may be compared with her comments on her new history teacher who came after Mr Marks had left. He was also 'strict', but 'he don't make sense, I don't understand nothing.' There is obviously an additional criterion being applied, for Carol seemed to be concerned about how much different teachers actually managed to teach her. For example,

> Question: What do you think about teachers who aren't strict, but who are really soft?
> Carol: Some of them are all right. I learn a lot from some of them . . . Mrs Alan's soft, but I learn a lot from her, because it's kind of funny the way she gives jokes.

Obviously, 'learning a lot' was important to Carol, but we must ask what she actually means by this. It seemed to be important that teachers 'explain'. 'Mr Marks would talk to us as well. Not talk them big words you know; talk words we understood.' But the new history teacher 'talks and writes things on the board, like diagrams, names, and you're supposed to keep them in your head, and then after he talks, it don't even make sense.' Also important was whether she was actually involved in doing something rather than just listening.

> Carol: I can't stand people talking when I'm not doing anything!
> Diane: Yes, like Mr Stacks, in art. He puts you to sleep. We have him on Wednesday, and he just talks and talks for two lessons.

Actually giving these girls a feeling of 'learning a lot' was extremely difficult for any teacher, whether defined as 'soft' or 'strict'. Linda probably best sums up the difficulty:

> 'I don't like doing maths. I can't do it, it's too hard. I don't know how to add. Well, I know how to add, but I don't know how to do the other sums. They're too hard anyway. I don't do nothing in maths lessons, I've always got a headache . . . I enjoy doing things I know, I can sit all morning doing that, but when something's hard and I don't really know how to do it, I don't *want* to do it. I don't even want to try. I get bored.'

Linda expresses her difficulty in trying to learn when she does not really understand. She must learn immediately or not at all. The whole class seemed to have very little interest in their subjects *per se* and were strongly dependent on the learning context provided by the teacher.

Members of staff who did not live up to Carol's particular criteria of assessement—that is those who 'can't teach you nothing'—were 'written off'. Carol approached their lessons 'knowing' that she was not going to learn anything.

Naturally, this is a simplified assessment of what classroom situations meant to Carol. Nevertheless, if particular lessons are looked at in terms of a combination of the simple criteria of definition (that is 'strict/soft', 'effective/ineffective'), then typical interaction sets and patterns of behaviour emerge.

Typical patterns of interaction

Teachers who were assessed as potentially 'effective' and able to provide some lessons where it was possible to 'learn a lot' were approached in a very different style from those who were considered 'ineffective'. Naturally, 'effective' teachers were not always successful in providing the right learning context for the girls, but when they were, a fairly standard pattern of interaction emerged.

'Successful' lessons

In lessons where the context enabled the girls to 'learn a lot', they would act as a unified group, and the whole class was included in the same interaction set. Although they were not always in verbal contact, each girl was aware that the others defined the lesson as one where they could 'learn'. In these circumstances it was irrelevant whether the teacher was 'strict' or 'soft'. Mr Marks was considered 'strict' and the whole class worked quietly and well. Miss Keene, on the other hand, was 'soft', yet in 'successful' lessons no one took advantage of this fact. Consider this example of a typing lesson with Miss Keene.

> (Miss Keene is teaching the girls how to file alphabetically. It is a revision lesson, though evidently the girls do not understand the principles fully.)
>
> Miss Keene: Carol, how would you file 'The Borough of East Hamilton'?
> Carol: Under H. (She obviously does not realise that the name is *East Hamilton*) . . .
> General question: How would you file Miss Mary Brown-Curtis? (Someone says 'C', not realising it is a double-barrelled name.)
> Carol: M. (She is going to the other rule they have just learnt which says that if it does not go under the surname as a person, it must be the name of a company, and therefore goes under the first name. She seems to be trying to apply rules as she understands them, but is still confused) . . .
> Miss Keene: 20th Century Films Limited.
> (Carol says 'C', then 'F', applying the rules she knows. But this is a new one. As 20th is short for twentieth it shoud go under 'T').

Here the girls are willing to take risks, struggle to understand and consistently keep applying rules to make sense of what they are being told even though they make a lot of mistakes. They take into account that others are behaving similarly in choosing to act in this way.

When the girls assess a lesson in this way, they will often ignore attempts to 'redefine' it. In the example below, everyone in the class but Debbie is working, and her attempts to communicate with the other girls are ignored.

> Debbie is eating an ice lolly. Mrs Alan tells her to put it in the bin, but Debbie refuses and turns round in her seat to face the rest of the class. Mrs Alan grabs the hat Debbie is wearing, and says: 'Right, you are in school to do as you are told. When you have put your sweet in the bin as I asked you can have your hat back.'
> Debbie: You give me that hat back. I paid for it. Give it back to me!
> As she says this she looks towards Diane and Carol, but they continue with their work. Debbie sulks for the rest of the lesson, making no attempt to do any work whatsoever. She is totally ignored by the rest of the class, who carry on working enthusiastically.

Here, it is only Debbie who sees her action as appropriate. The rest of the class are too interested in their work. They form an interaction set, but Debbie is left outside it.

Judgment of 'effective' teachers

Lessons as 'successful' as those shown above were very rare, but the ability of teachers to provide such a context, even occasionally, was extremely important in the girls' eyes. When a teacher was considered 'potentially effective' the girls seemed more likely to approach the lesson with an open mind, and reserve their judgment until they had seen the content of the lesson. Of course, with 'strict, effective' teachers, this was not so important, for as Carol says of History, 'you just have to work'. With 'soft, effective' teachers, specific lessons content becomes much more significant. An extreme example of the sort of assessment that took place was shown in domestic science. These lessons were often 'successful', particularly when the girls were actually cooking, rather than learning theory:

Valerie, Jill, Diane, Carol and Linda are all missing at the beginning of the lesson. Carol
rushes in and says to Monica: 'What have we got to do, write notes?'
Monica: Yes.
Carol: I'm going out then. (She runs out . . .)

Writing notes in domestic science was considered a 'non-learning' situation.

'Non-learning' situations

Two factors seemed to lead to a lesson being defined as a 'non-learning' situation.
The first was when teachers who were judged 'potentially effective' did not provide
an adequate learning context. The second was when teachers were considered
'ineffective'. In these latter circumstances the specific content of the lesson was
irrelevant. The judgment had already been made, and the girls would arrive
'knowing' they would not learn anything.

This was Carol's most frequent definition of the situation. Most lessons were not
able to provide her with the sort of learning context she wanted. Her interactive
behaviour at these times could be called mildly anti-authoritarian. It involved joking,
laughing, talking on topics such as boys and clothes, while at the same time, at least
nominally, carrying on with the classwork. The interaction set usually included nine
or ten girls. They were: Carol, Valerie, Diane, Debbie, Anne, Angela, June and
Monica, with Linda and Jill taking part when present.[9]

An example of this sort of interaction with a 'potentially effective' teacher comes
in a typing lesson. Carol is interacting with a large group of girls who all sit close to
each other. Although they are working they still manage to make jokes among
themselves.

Miss Keene has asked the class how to go about 'tabulating'. She says: 'How many spaces
do you go in?'
Various people shout out answers, all of which are wrong; eventually Debbie gives the
right answer. After it has been said, Carol jumps up and shouts out the right answer again,
looks round the room, and giggles.
Anne (out loud to the class): Oh, God, she waits till someone else has said it.
(All of the girls sitting near by laugh.)

It is this type of interaction that Carol is referring when she says of her class 'we're
all friends together really', and Valerie says 'You get a lot of fun, a lot of jokes in the
classroom.' Valerie points out that Carol is best at making jokes, but also says that
others are involved: 'She's good at making jokes (pointing at Carol) and she (Diane) .
. . and Anne and June . . . and this other girl Debbie, she's good at laughing'.

The next example comes from an RE lesson which Carol considers a 'waste of
time' and 'boring'. It is an example of how they behave when they consider the
teacher 'ineffective'.

Carol, Valerie, Diane, Jill, Debbie, Anne, Angela and Monica are sitting close together.
Debbie is playing with one of Carol's shoes; Valerie and Diane are reading comics and
Carol is combing her hair and occasionally making jokes quietly to those around her. By
and large no one in the class seems very interested in the content of the lesson . . .
eventually the teacher 'notices' that Valerie and Diane are reading comics and demands
to have them. Diane quietly gives hers up, but Valeries says 'Oh no sir, please don't take
it'. The teacher insists and takes it away until lunchtime. Carol immediately gets out
another magazine from her bag, turns round to Valerie and Diane, and they all start
looking at it.

When a particular teacher's lessons were defined in this way, it was fairly irrelevant
what specific material they presented. They always met the same style of
interaction. By Easter of her fourth year, with the typing and history teachers

leaving, Carol had 'written off' six out of her ten teachers in this way. Most of these assessments were shared by several of the other girls in the class.

'Bunking it'

Another response when it was not possible to 'learn' was to run out of the lesson or not bother to turn up at all—in their terms, they would 'bunk it'.

This involved a different interaction set, as only Carol, Valerie, Diane, Jill and Linda would 'bunk' lessons.

In an interview, Carol explained how 'bunking' was related to specific definitions.

> 'With Mr Marks in history, them lot sometimes say "Let's muck about", or "Let's bunk it", and I say "Yeah", and then I goes in the lesson and them lot comes in and calls me "snide". If I don't feel like bunking it, I don't. But now (i.e. with the new history teacher) if they tell me don't go to history, I don't go.'

She describes how they make the decision to miss a lesson:

> *Question:* When you and your friends say 'Let's bunk a lesson', who actually suggests it?
> *Carol:* When we don't want to go nowhere, like if we say we don't want to go to this lesson . . . Valerie comes up and says 'Let's bunk it.' Sometimes Diane do, sometimes I do. I say, 'Let's bunk it' and they all agree.

This interaction set is far more specific than the others described. Carol, Valerie, Diane, Linda and Jill were the only girls in the class who would 'bunk' lessons. They also formed a separate interaction set when teachers who were regarded as 'soft' tried to become 'strict'.

Teachers who become 'strict'

When a 'soft' teacher tried to become 'strict', for example if he threatened to discipline the girls in some way, a specific pattern of interaction emerged. This situation occurred regardless of whether teachers were considered 'effective' or not.

In the following example, Valerie and Jill had arrived late for science.

> *Mrs Newman* (to Valerie and Jill): Where have you been?
> *Carol* (aggressively): Shut your mouth.
> (This is said loud enough for Mrs Newman to hear, but she ignores it.)

Another time, Carol, Valerie, Diane, Jill and Linda arrived late for domestic science and became aggressive.

> *Miss Lane:* I think one of you ought to go and tell Mr Kraft *(Deputy Head)* where you've been.
> *Valerie* (aggressively): I ain't going nowhere.
> (She turns to talk to Carol . . .)
> *Carol* (to those round her): Where's Monica?
> *Linda:* Oh! she's at the front (of the class).
> *Carol:* Oh! look at that lot. She's too brainy for me. (They all laugh.)

In this example the girls who arrived late sat physically separated from the rest of the class and at each successive 'joke' they laughed heartily. Even though the rest of the pupils and probably the teacher could hear what they said, none of them laughed or made any comment.

Again, it was only Carol, Diane, Valerie, Jill and Linda who would interact in this manner. On these occasions, the rest of the class sat very quietly, seldom interacting with anyone but the teacher. Carol and her friends were defined as an interaction set by themselves and by the rest of the class.

I have shown that interaction sets represent shared knowledge among a group of pupils and are associated with regular patterns of behaviour. But the definitions presented above are necessarily incomplete, as is shown by the way Carol will sometimes, for no apparent reason, extract herself from a common definition and act alone. A very good example of this sort of 're-definition' came in a science lesson. The rest of the class were chattering and laughing in their usual way and not taking much notice of what the teacher was saying.

> Carol and Diane sit at the top of the bench, farthest from the board. They are correcting or finishing a diagram of a skeleton, and seem very engrossed in it. Carol says 'and this is the arm, the femur . . .'
> Eventually they put their folders away and then begin writing the notes written on the board.

Here, for some reason, the girls were willing to extract themselves from their typical definition of science and establish new appropriate behaviour. Obviously, additional criteria of assessment are being applied and a new pattern of interaction emerges.

Why is it that Carol will come to one science lesson and work very hard, while the next day she will take part in a common definition and 'bunk it' completely? Why is it that even with teachers who are assessed as 'able to teach', some lessons are more 'successful' than others? Obviously more detailed analysis of pupil knowledge is necessary before these questions can be answered with any certainty.

What can be said, however, is that 'how to define the situation' is a constant problem for these girls and one that demands continual negotiation. Unlike the successful grammar school pupil who knows how to look at his school experience, these girls constantly have to make sense of frustrating and often confusing situations. This, together with the fact that all interaction sets tend to function with a limited number of definitions, makes it progressively difficult for individuals to extract themselves from their usual way of seeing things. Attempts by teachers to reach these girls were effective only when they conformed to the girls' own standards of assessment. They no longer blindly accepted all teachers as the grammar school pupil might do. Presumably because of their own unsuccessful learning experience they had established their own criteria of judgment. They seemed to want to learn quickly, effectively and, at least to begin with, with the minimum of effort. Teaching these girls in the way they wished to be taught was something which many members of staff (myself included) found almost impossible.

Conclusion

Pupil knowledge about school life is differentially distributed. An interaction set presents a static picture of a group of pupils making the same commonsense judgments about classroom situations. Their behaviour is chosen in the light of what they agree they 'know' about that situation. The fact that different pupils take part in interaction sets at different times simply illustrates the point that they do not always agree about what they know. Teachers, subjects and methods of teaching mean different things to different pupils. A study of pupils' knowledge must take this fact into account and begin by specifying situations where pupils do agree. Only then would it be possible to ask what they agree about—what they know.

In describing some of Carol's definitions, I have already illustrated some of the things she knows about school life and pointed out which girls agree with her and when. Unfortunately, the whole concept of 'definition of the situation' is a static one:[10] What is now needed is an understanding of Carol's abstract knowledge so that we can tell how she goes about classifying situations in the typical ways I have shown.

Both teachers and researchers seem extremely ignorant of what school life means to pupils. The present study already brings into question some of the more popular beliefs amongst teachers about 'non-academic' adolescents. there is a common assumption that such pupils will only be interested in subjects that will be immediately relevant to their life when they leave school. It is for this reason that many time-tables are heavily laden with 'practical' subjects such as typing, domestic science, woodwork, metalwork, and (if all else fails) games. Yet the girls described in this paper were much more concerned with 'learning' no matter what the subject. History or typing could be of equal interest to them if they provided the sort of learning situation that they looked for. Further case studies of pupil knowledge will not only be of interest to sociologists, but may even be some practical use to teachers, both in preparing their material, and in understanding their pupils.

Perhaps the last words should be left with Carol herself:

Question: What do you think the teachers think of you as an individual?
Carol: I don't think they like me much . . . I'm not a good girl anyway . . . I don't blame them; if you've got a child and she's rude, you can't like her very much . . . I mean, if I was in their place, I wouldn't like *me* 'cos the way I act—you know, I won't learn, keep making jokes and muck about. I don't blame them, but I'm not worried at all you know!

Acknowledgements

I would like to begin by thanking the pupils of 4G for allowing me to observe their lessons and for their open and frank discussions with me; without them there would have been no paper. I am grateful to the Local Education Authority for allowing me to carry out the research, and to the staff of the school where I have worked for four years. The continued co-operation and interest of many teachers, particularly those who allowed me to observe their lessons, was a great help. I would also like to thank Dr Ed Sherwood and Dr Diana Leat for their encouragement and support throughout my research. For financial support, I am indebted both to the Social Science Research Council and to the Lawrence Atwell Charity, administered by the Skinners' Company. For comments on the first draft of this paper, I am grateful to Dr Diane Leat and to my wife Ruth.

Notes

[1] Because of the high proportion of 'immigrant' pupils, the staff/pupil ratio was considerably better than in many neighbouring schools. Most of the 'lower ability' classes comprised twenty pupils or fewer.

[2] About 50 per cent of the school population were classed as 'immigrants' by the Local Education Authority; i.e. they had not been born in Great Britain or Ireland. The majority of these 'immigrants' were West Indian. The remainder of the school were mainly working-class English or Irish.

[3] See for example Hollingshead (1949), Coleman (1960), Hargreaves (1967), Sugarman (1966, 1967, 1968) and Lacey (1970).

[4] See for example Lacey's (1970) discussion of a pupil called Short (p. 98), or some of the comments made to Hargreaves about maths (pp. 99–100).

[5] For a fuller discussion of 'joint action' see Blumber (1965).

[6] One of components of Bernstein's (1971) 'restricted code' is a strong sense of loyalty to the group, as it implied here.

[7] See in particular Cohen (1955).

[8] The notion of 'repertoire' in behaviour is developed in Goffman (1959).

[9] As part of the 'remedial group', Linda and Jill did not take all of their lessons with the other girls.

[10] This limitation on the usefulness of the concept of 'definition of the situation' characterises the distinction between enthnomethodology and symbolic interactionism. For a useful comparison of these two approaches on these lines, see Zimmerman and Wieder (1970).

References

Berstein, B. (1971) *Class, Codes and Control*, Routledge and Kegan Paul.

Blumer, H. (1965) 'Sociological implications of the thought of George Herbert Mead', *American Journal of Sociology*, Vol. **71**, pp. 535-44.

Cohen, A. (1955) *Delinquent Boys: the Culture of the Gang*, Free Press.

Coleman, (J. S.) (1960) *The Adolescent Society: the Social Life of the Teenager, and its Impact on Education*, Free Press.

Dale, R. (1973) 'Phenomenological perspectives and the sociology of the school', *Educational Review*, Vol. 125, No. 3, pp. 175-89.

Filmer, P. Phillipson, M. Silverman, D. and Walsh, D. (1972) *New Directions in Sociological Theory*, Collier Macmillan.

Goffman, E. (1959) *The Presentation of Self in Everyday Life*, Anchor Books.

Hargreaves, D. (1967) *Social Relations in a Secondary School*, Routledge and Kegan Paul.

Hollingshead, A. B. (1949) *Elmstown's Youth: the Impact of Social Class on Adolescents*, Wiley.

Keddie, N. (1971) 'Classroom knowledge', in Young, M. F. D. (ed.) *Knowledge and Control: New Directions for the Sociology of Education*, Collier Macmillan.

Lacey, C. (1970) *Hightown Grammar: the School as a Social System*, Manchester University Press.

Sugarman, B. N. (1966) 'Social class and values as related to achievement in school', *Sociological Review*, Vol. 41, pp. 287-302.

Sugarman, B. N. (1967) 'Involvement in youth culture, academic achievement and conformity in school', *British Journal of Sociology*, Vol. 18, pp. 151-64.

Sugarman, B. N. (1968) 'Social norms in teenage boys' peer groups—a study of their implications for achievement and conduct in four London schools', *Human Relations*, Vol. **21**, 41-58.

Werthman, C. 1963, 'Delinquents in schools; a test for the legitimacy of authority', *Berkeley Journal of Sociology*, **8**, 1 pp. 39-60.

Werthman, C. (1970) 'The functions of social definitions in the development of delinquent careers', in Garbedian, P. E. and Gibbons, D. C. (eds) *Becoming Delinquent*, Aldine.

Young, M. F. D. and Keddie, N. (1973) 'New directions: is there anything happening in sociology?', *Hard Cheese*, no. 2, May 1973, pp. 29-36.

Zimmerman, D. H. and Wieder, D. L. (1970) 'Ethnomethodology and the problem of order: comment on Denzin', in Douglas, J. D. (ed.) *Understanding Everyday Life: Towards the Reconstruction of Sociological Knowledge*, Routledge and Kegan Paul.

10   Conformist pupils?

M. HAMMERSLEY AND G. TURNER

In recent years, the study of pupil perspectives and adaptations has been one of the growth points in the sociology of education. However, from Hargreaves to Willis, the focus has been predominantly on deviant or anti-school pupils. We can only speculate about the reasons for this, but two seem particularly plausible. The first is the overwhelming concern in the sociology of education since 1945 with the explanation of failure at school, and particularly the failure of working-class pupils. One of the consequences of this is that school success has not been treated as in need of explanation: 'successful' pupils simply have the personal characteristics, cultural backgrounds, material circumstances, etc., which 'failures' lack. Another possible explanation for the relative absence of studies of 'conformist' pupils is that researchers have taken over the preoccupation of teachers with problem behaviour. Paradoxically reinforcing this, perhaps, is the influence of the sociology of deviance with its celebration of the deviant and exotic.[1]

This concentration on the deviant pupil has certainly advanced our knowledge of cetain kinds of pupil and indeed of those pupils whose activities are most fequently dismissed as irrational. However, it has involved a neglect of the majority of pupils, or rather an assumption that their behaviour can be satisfactorily accounted for in terms of some combination of pro- and anti-school orientations. Thus, even where 'conformist pupils' have come into focus the pro-school/antischool model has been retained, despite evidence of its shortcomings.[2]

In this [paper] we examine the notion of conformity and evaluate the adequacy of currently available models of pupil activity. It is our view that these models are oversimplified and the purpose of the [paper]—is to demonstrate this, show some of the resources that are available for the construction of a better model, and indicate the direction this might take.

Problems of the deviant-conformist scheme

Once we begin to look at, or for, 'the conformists', a cluster of questions arise, and principal among them is: conformity to what? In the literature these pupils are usually portrayed as a pale mirror image of the deviants: they simply conform to middle-class or school values and norms. Where the deviants, on most accounts, develop novel values and strategies for dealing with their situation, the conformists simply conform to the school's definition of the pupil role.

However, only a little observation of 'conformist' pupil behaviour suggests that, at the very least, this is simplistic. Indeed, the inadequacy of the model is visible even in the data reported by the studies that have employed it. Consider, for example, Hargreaves' comments about 4A at Lumley School, the class with the highest 'commitment to school' and to 'middle-class values':

> The boys expressed their concern for academic achievement in their impatience with those subjects they did not intend to take in the CSE, RE and Music in particular were subject to criticism and ridicule.
> (Hargreaves, 1967, p.13)

Furthermore,

> When they thought the lessons were inadequate in some way, the teachers were
> criticised.
> (Ibid., p. 14)

Clearly, the attitudes of 'pro-school pupils', or some of them anyway, are not
identical with those of teachers. Furthermore, it seems most unlikely that there is a
single set of values presented by the school and all the teachers. Nor, were there
such consistency, could we assume that it represented a single coherent 'middle-class'
world view. Indeed, we can expect different segments of the middle class,[3] and
teachers occupying different positions within the school, to promote rather
different values and norms. We might also reasonably expect to find, on the part of
particular teachers, 'official' and 'subterranean' values operating side by side.[4] Then
again, values are often internally inconsistent and, even if they are not, drawing
their implications for particular situations is always potentially problematic and
open to decision and negotiation. Thus, even if we assume that 'conformist' pupils
are totally committed to 'school values', there is much still to be explained
concerning how they construct lines of action in conformity with these values.

But there is no reason to assume this. For one thing, we must recognise the
ambivalence which underlies much social interaction,[5] and evidence for ambivalence
on the part of pupils can again be found even in the existing literature. Thus, Lacey
explicitly comments on the way in which pro-school pupils are committed to values
other than those promoted by the school, and how they engage in a kind of balancing
act which often relies for its success on the segregation of audiences.[6]

> Sherman was frequently top in 5B. He rarely misbehaved in class and was prominent in
> co-operating with teachers during lessons. On one occasion, however, I observed that
> after a lesson in which he was conspicuous for his enthusiastic participation, he waited
> until the master had left the room, then immediately grabbed an innocuous classmate's
> satchel and in a few moments had organised a sort of piggy-in-the-middle game. He
> passed the bag across the room, while the owner stood helplessly by, occasionally trying
> to intercept or picking up a fallen book. The initiation of this activity so soon after the
> lesson seemed to be a conscious demonstration of his status within the informal
> structure of the class. He was indicating that, although he was good at work, he was not
> a swot and would not be excluded from groups based on other than academic values.
> (Lacey, 1970, p. 87)

But secret deviance from school norms is unlikely to be the product simply of an
attachment to alternative values and a concern with maintaining face in terms of
those values. There are intrinsic long-term and short-term payoffs to be gained
from 'unofficial' actions. Conversely, we can expect that much conformity to school
demands is motivated as much by instrumental concerns, for example to get good
exam results and thus a 'good' job, as by attachment to school values for their own
sake. In other words, conformity may be a calculated strategy rather than simply the
product of successful socialisation into school values and norms.

Once we recognise the multiplicity of orientations which even 'official' school
values can produce, and also the existence of multiple alternative values and
interests, it becomes clear that the pro/anti schema does not adequately capture the
complex patterning of pupil perspectives.

An alternative: the adaptation model

The pro/anti model has its immediate origins in the work of Miller and Cohen on
delinquent subcultures.[7] There is, however, an alternative scheme available based

on the earlier work of Merton on anomie.[8] Merton was concerned to show that deviance is systematically generated by the mismatch between socialisation into common goals and the opportunities for individuals differentially placed within the society to achieve those goals by legitimate means.[9] He outlines five adaptations individuals could adopt towards the social order, each representing a unique combination of positive and negative orientations to the goals and means embodied in that order.

> We here consider five types of adaptation, as these are schematically set out in the following table, where (+) signifies 'acceptance,' (—) signifies 'rejection,' and (±) signifies 'rejection of prevailing values and substitution of new values.'

A TYPOLOGY OF MODES OF INDIVIDUAL ADAPTATION

Modes of Adaptation	*Culture Goals*	*Institutionalized Means*
I. Conformity	+	+
II. Innovation	+	—
III. Ritualism	—	+
IV. Retreatism	—	—
V. Rebellion	±	±

A number of people, most notably Harary (1966) and Wakeford (1969), have developed this model, and more recently Peter Woods has reworked it to relate to pupils in state secondary schools.[10] Woods's model provides for the six possible pupil orientations (see Figure 10.1).

The adaptation model, especially the Woods' version, clearly allows for much more variation in pupil orientation than the pro/anti schema. It does this by distinguishing between goals and means and by recognising that a number of different attitudes can be taken to each. As a result it also marks a shift away from a rule-based model of action in which action is portrayed as the product of attachment to values and is produced by following institutionalised rules which derive from and are legitimated in terms of those values. Instead, a decision-making model is assumed in which pupils select adaptations to school according to their goals and the means available to achieve them. This seems a far more promising basis for the explanation of pupil activity; even if, as we want to argue in the remainder of the paper, further development of this model is required if we are to advance our understanding of the complexity and diversity of pupil behaviour.

Problems of the adaptation model

The problematic nature of 'official' goals and means
With the adaptation model, as with the pro/anti scheme, the primary axis of pupil orientation is still presumed to be conformity to or deviance from school values. As a result, the complexities involved in the notion of 'school values' are neglected. Woods recognises the likely variation in 'official' goals, but he does not build this into the model, perhaps because this would render it even more complex than it already is. It would involve theorising the possibility that, for example, a pupil could simultaneously be a retreatist in relation to some official goals, intransigent towards others, and a conformist with regard to others. It means examining how pupil activity varies in different circumstances and we would also need to explain how pupils and teachers cope with the resulting 'inconsistencies'.

Figure 10.1 *Revised Typology of Modes of Adaptation in the State Secondary System*

GOALS

MEANS	Indifference	Indulgence	Identification	Rejection without replacement	Ambivalence	Rejection with replacement
Indifference	Retreatism			Retreatism		
Indulgence		Ingratiation	Ingratiation			
Identification	Ritualism	COMPLIANCE	Compliance			
Rejection without replacement	Retreatism			Retreatism		
Ambivalence	*Colonization*				OPPORTUNISM	
Rejection with replacement	*Intransigence*					Rebellion

KEY

Capitals: typical of earlier years
Italics: typical of later years
Arrows: some typical movements

In our view, though it probably gives a final blow to the elegance and force of the Mertonian model, such complexities cannot be ignored. One small sign of hope that this will not leave us in the mire but lead to a more satisfactory model is that we can expect that schools in different locales within the education system, and teachers at different points in the organisation of a particular school, will project *systematically* different values and conceptions of the pupil role. These variations will be the product of, among other things, situational adjustment,[11] the moral division of labour within and between schools,[12] and the work of missionary movements.[13]

Pupil orientations will be related in some way to the particular conceptions of 'success' and proper pupil behaviour to which the pupils are exposed. Though this relation may be quite complex, involving multiple and shifting adaptations, pupil orientations will thus be distributed in systematic ways across different locales of the education system and school.

However, this does not exhaust the influence of variations in 'official' values on pupils. Even within a single classroom the teacher acts towards pupils differentially, and indeed the attitude displayed toward the same pupil may change somewhat over the course of a particular lesson. It is, in the first place, such displays that pupils will respond to, not abstract values; though it is likely they will interpret and evaluate these displays in terms of such values.

Finally, we can only note here the differences which may arise in views about what are legitimate and illegitimate means to school success. These will vary with the versions of teaching to which the pupils are exposed.[14] And, of course, pupils also have their own views about this. Indeed, condemnation of the 'swot' and the 'teacher's pet' are not always restricted to pupils, they are sometimes also voiced by teachers.[15]

The assumption that 'official' values/goals are the primary feature of the school environment for pupils
This assumption seems rather implausible. Pupils have various latent identities and cultures which they bring with them to school. Class cultures are the most obvious examples, but equally there may be gender-specific and generational orientations,[16] and perhaps also child culture.[17] Furthermore, these different latent cultures may be interrelated in various ways producing multiple subcultures. The use of traditional sociological concepts such as the local-cosmopolitan distinction can also be productive. Thus, in Willis's work there is a hint at one point of the contrast between national (cosmopolitan) and localised adolescent subcultures.[18]

Of course, because pupils are dealt with in batches, the potential for the generation and maintenance of alternative conceptions of status becomes much greater than it would be were each pupil taught in isolation from others (as in home tutoring).[19] For this reason, it is actually misleading to regard class, gender, generation, etc., simply as latent identities. To the extent that any such identity becomes a key orientation for some pupils, it is made manifest and has an important presence *within* the school. This can occur in another way too. It has been noted by Woods, in another context, how aspects of latent pupil cultures are incorporated and mobilised by teachers for the purposes of maintaining order.[20] A consequence of this is that part of a pupil's response to school may be a response to mediated forms of his or her own latent cultures. This opens up an intriguing area of research: the way in which pupil adaptations are accommodated to by schools and how, through these accommodations, these adaptations act back on themselves.

We can even playfully speculate, reversing the Merton and Cohen models, that conformity to 'official' goals might sometimes be the product of failure to succeed in other subcultures. This might explain, for example, the academic success of some working-class pupils.[21] It might also be that, as with deviance, 'success' can be amplified by the process of social interaction.[22]

The important point is that we must begin from concrete description of the orientations of pupils rather than by imposing prior assumptions about what the key features of their environment are and how they react to them.[23] If we do this we may well find a group of pupils strongly committed to 'academic success' for one reason or another, and perhaps also another group whose activities are centrally organised around opposition to school. But these two groups would probably only account fo a small number of pupils in any school, the perspectives of the remainder not being explicable simply in terms of conformity to or deviance from school requirements.

Adaptational careers

It is clear that Woods assumes that middle-class pupils are more able and more likely to conform than others, and there is some evidence for this. However, his model does not provide any basis for explaining why particular conformist and deviant adaptations are likely to be adopted by particular kinds of pupil.[24] In this sense it has less power than Merton's original, where different social locations are specified as conducive to different adaptations: notably, the working class to innovation and the middle class to ritualism. We have suggested earlier that systematic variation in exposure to 'official' values and norms may provide some basis for the explanation of differences in pupil adaptation. But this could only be the sole source of such differences if we assumed a direct, unmediated, relationship between 'official' goals/values and pupil adaptations. That would be to abandon one of the most important advances made by the adaptation model: recognition of the role of pupil decision-making.[25] Even so, we expect to find some kind of relationship between the official and unofficial cultures pupils are exposed to and their orientations.

The development of Merton's model has not been restricted to its application in the sociology of education. Thus, for example, in their work on delinquency Cloward and Ohlin (1960) have added an important new element which can be fruitfully applied and developed in the field of pupil adaptations. The central point they make is that Merton assumes that particular adaptations are freely available for actors to adopt. Thus, for Merton, the crucial factor determining which adaption is adopted is the nature of the contradiction between goals and legitimate means experienced by the actors. Cloward and Ohlin argue that adaptions have to be learned, and thus that an equally important determinant is access to others who can socialise the actor into a particular mode of adaptation.

While we may not want to press the argument too far, since then it becomes difficult to account for the emergence and development of adaptations, this is clearly an important point. Indeed, we reached it earlier by another route in talking about the way in which batch treatment had the potential for turning latent into manifest cultures. Thus, for example, working-class culture is not simply something working class pupils are able to draw on as a result of their out-of-school experience. To the extent that they act on it, and even celebrate it, within school, working-class culture has an intra-school presence to which middle-class pupils must adopt some attitude and through which they can gain access to it. However, the perspectives of other pupils may not only facilitate the adoption of a particular adaptation, as Cloward and Ohlin suggest, they may also prevent it, or at least make it very difficult. For example, a pupil may be faced with a choice between working for his exams or keeping his friends.[26]

This argument can be developed further. Thus, it seems likely that some adaptations to school would require negotiation with teachers to create the space for them; and this may be more or less possible at different places within the education system and within a particular school. Indeed, we should perhaps treat pupil adaptations as involving not only conceptions of how the pupil himself should behave, but conceptions of social order that, if successfully negotiated, become a working consensus or contract.[27] We can speculatively illustrate this by reanalysing some data provided by Willis (1977, pp.11—12):

[In a group discussion on teachers]

Joey   [. . .] they're able to punish us. They're bigger than us, they stand for a bigger establishment than we do, like, we're just little and they stand for bigger things, and you try to get your own back. It's, uh, resenting authority I suppose.

Eddie   The teachers think they're high and mighty 'cos they're teachers, but they're nobody really, they're just ordinary people ain't they?.

Bill   Teachers think they're everybody. They are more, they're higher than us, but they think they're a lot higher and they're not.

Spansky   Wish we could call them first names and that . . . think they're God.

Pete   That would be a lot better.

PW   I mean you say they're higher. Do you accept at all that they know better about things?

Joey   Yes, but that doesn't rank them above us, just because they are slightly more intelligent.

Bill   They ought to treat us how they'd like us to treat them.

[. . .]

Joey   [. . .] the way we're subject to their every whim like. They want something doing and we have to sort of do it, 'cos, er, we're just, we're under them like. We were with a woman teacher in here, and 'cos we all wear rings and one or two of them bangles, like he's got one on, and out of the blue, like, for no special reason, she says, 'take all that off'.

PW   Really?

Joey   Yeah, we says, 'One won't come off', she says, 'Take yours off as well'. I said, 'You'll have to chop my finger off first'.

PW   Why did she want you to take your rings off?

Joey   Just a sort of show like. Teachers do this, like, all of a sudden they'll make you do your ties up and things like this. You're subject to their every whim like. If they want something done, if you don't think it's right, and you object against it, you're down to Simmondsy [the head], or you get the cane, you get some extra work tonight.

PW   You think of most staff as kind of enemies [. . .]?

—   Yeah.

—   Yeah.

—   Most of them.

Joey   It adds a bit of spice to yer life, if you're trying to get him for something he's done to you.

There are a number of different ways of interpreting this passage, none of which can be securely established, including Willis's claim that it displays 'entrenched, general and personalised opposition to "authority" '. One alternative interpretation is that what we have here is a conflict between two forms of authority; indeed we may even be able to formulate it as a conflict between charismatic and legal-rational authority. On the one hand, there is the teacher who demands obedience from pupils on the basis of his or her institutional identity. On the other, there are 'the lads', or some of them, for whom authority has to be earned and maintained in interpersonal interaction. On this reading 'getting him for something he's done to you' is not simply a reaction against what they regard as the teacher's illegitimate authority claim, but is simultaneously action on the basis of their own conception of legitimate authority, which involves competing for status in interpersonal interaction.[28]

Academically oriented pupils will also have certain ideas about what a teacher should and should not do, in what kind of circumstances and for what reasons; slanted, no doubt by their own particular interests. Furthermore, built into such conceptions are notions of the limits within which particular attitudes operate: thus the compliance of 'academic' pupils may only operate so long as the teacher does not claim control over areas not regarded as within the legitimate domain; and so long as he or she is thought to be competent. If these limits are transgressed, compliance may be replaced by intransigence or rebellion.

The exclusive focus on goal-directed behaviour
The adaptation model is a general sociological theory which has been applied to many specific fields. It is a rudimentary form of decision-making theory, but it is a version which is rather limited in scope, only providing for combinations of specific attitudes to a single set of goals and a single set of means. As a result, it is incapable of incorporating some of the other general sociological models which, while inadequate as complete accounts, may capture some aspects of pupil activity not amenable to the adaptation model. An example is mass society theory which, deriving from Durkheim, conceptualises modern societies as having a low level of social integration with individuals cut from one another and lacking any sense of purpose and direction.[29] One is struck by the similarities between the comments of school refusers about the anonymity and loneliness of life at school and the tenets of this theory.[30] It also fits the general complaints about boredom at school which are often voiced by pupils. Taken at face value at least, this suggests that the mass society model may have some application to pupils. One possibility is where a pupil is committed to academic success but finds the work he or she is required to do isn't relevant to this goal. Where this is not a shared experience paving the way for collective alternatives, the pupil may well come to feel bored, isolated and restless.

Goffman's discussion of adaptation to total institutions, in which inmate behaviour is a reaction to the loss of civilian identity and status, represents another model which we may be able to draw on in explaining pupil perspectives.[31] Thus, for example, it does seem that with recent changes in attitudes to children and in the social organisation of the family,[32] there may be a mismatch between the way pupils are treated in school and outside: outside, certainly among some strata, they are increasingly treated as 'semi-adults', whereas the school's authority relies to a considerable extent on their being 'children'.[33] Goffman's work also has the advantage of focusing attention on organisational structure as well as 'organisational goals'. The significance of the organisational structure of schools has been rather lost in the shift from the deviant-conformist scheme to the adaptation model.

If it is indeed true that these alternatives to the pro/anti and adaptation models do offer distinctive contributions to the understanding of pupil activity, any new model in this area should be capable of incorporating the relevant aspects of them.

An interactionist alternative

There is one other key approach to the explanation of pupil behaviour which should be mentioned here: the work of Furlong[34]. Unlike the previous two models, which are derived from normative functionalism, this is interactionist. As one would expect, therefore, instead of starting with a theory about possible orientations to society, Furlong begins at the level of social interaction and stresses the importance of pupils' definitions of the situation for their behaviour on different occasions. He emphasises the variability of pupil behaviour across different contexts, in particular according to pupil evaluations of the teacher as strict or soft, effective or ineffective.

If one monitors the behaviour of the same pupil in different circumstances, the existence of considerable contextual variability soon becomes obvious; the 'disruptive' pupil is not 'disruptive' all the time and 'conformist' pupils often deviate from school requirements.[35] Furlong sets out to explain this variability by pointing to the importance of mutual support among pupils, employing the concept of interaction set': 'those pupils who perceive what is happening in a similar way, communicate this to each other, and define appropriate action together'.[36] And he documents some of the considerations which underly a pupil's perception of 'what is happening' and thus provide the basis for the development of interaction sets.

The great advantage of this approach is that it begins at the level of action and sets out to describe the actions of pupils and the perspectives on which these are based. It is because of this focus that Furlong detects variability where the other two models assume consistency. However, the model hardly begins to provide a viable alternative to these other models. Even at the level of action, the approach is schematic, giving no account of why a pupil might on one occasion join in a 'disruptive' interaction set and on another occasion ignore it. Even more importantly, Furlong's model does not relate the perspectives of the pupils either to their goals and values or to the structure of the school, let alone the society in which they find themselves. Thus we have no idea why pupils are interested in 'effective learning' or how their position 'one from the bottom' in the streaming system shaped the kind of teaching they were exposed to and their own orientations to schooling.

In a summary, then, while it points us in the right direction, Furlong's paper only takes us a few steps on the way.[37] In the next section we attempt to build on this work in such a way as to make possible the incorporation, albeit in modified form, of the deviant-conformist and adaptation models.

Towards another model

We can only begin to sketch the outline of a more satisfactory model here. An essential starting point is to recognise the different levels of abstraction at which the model must operate. The first two approaches discussed in this [paper] work at the level of general adaptations to school. It seems to us that working solely, or even primarily, at this level is unsatsifactory for both methodological and theoretical reasons.

Methodologically, it tends to result in a reliance on interview data since in interviews participants can themselves provide generalisations about their own and others' behaviour across different settings. But the danger of an exclusive reliance on participant accounts are well known.[38] To take one example, Woods (1979) documents his concept of ingratiation with the following piece of data:

Karen	If Jane does something, she gets ignored. If she don't do anything she never gets told off, all the teachers favour her.
Susan	She's so *good* in lessons, behaviour and work. She does *more* than they give them, she does *extra* work. If we have a film, she'll watch it, whereas others might talk a bit. If we have a book to read, she'll do it in a couple of days, and pointedly go and ask teacher for another one.
Liza	She goes up the library every lunchtime. She used to creep round.
Karen	If we do anything wrong, we get shouted at. If Jane does it, it's 'Oh Jane, do stop please dear'.

Susan	She copies in maths to get ahead, and gets ratty if she falls behind. She's not so good in maths, so she has to copy to keep up. She says 'Come on, let's have a look'.
Liza	She *always* does homework, so never gets into trouble.
Susan	She had a cousin from France who come over, she was flouting her about.
Karen	One teacher said, 'This is a girl who's going to get on in life'. It makes you sick.
Liza	Reading a passage in French, she'd volunteer. Beefy would say 'I think you've done enough, Jane.' She'd say 'I want to do it, I want to.'
Karen	Mr England told her 'Oh Jane! You should have been in the top stream, you know!'—as if she didn't know.
Liza	Beefy asked her 'Will you look after the library for me?' 'Oh yes sir' she said, 'certainly sir, thank you very much sir'.

What we have here are pupils' typifications of another pupil and these are, of course, an interesting topic in themselves. But we cannot assume that these typifications represent an accurate analytic account of Jane's action in school or of a particular kind of adaptation some pupils adopt. The case would be stronger if, in addition, we had Jane's own account of her orientation to school. But even that would have to be supplemented by observer description of her behaviour in school if we were to establish that Jane's general adaptation to school is that of ingratiation. It may be that ingratiation like deviance is not something anyone does all the time and that to formulate it as a general adaptation is misleading.[39] Certainly Woods provides no data to allay such doubts.

Focusing solely or primarily at the level of general adaptations to school is also problematic from a theoretical point of view: it is a central and well-established finding of interactionist work that actors do not react directly to general situations or social structural locations. Rather, they build their actions to deal with the particular configuration of circumstances that they perceive to be facing them at any moment in time.[40] Thus the actions of pupils in relation to moment-to-moment changes in their situation must be a central element in any model of their activity. Indeed, this level has a certain priority. At this level, when we talk of say, retreatism, intransigence, etc., we are describing the intentions of pupils or at least our analytical descriptions are not far removed from those concrete intentions. When, on the other hand, we talk of general orientations to school, we are generalising about pupils' typical actions across a wide range of circumstances. Such generalisations are necessary, but they *are* generalisations; they are dependent on prior analysis and documentation at the more concrete level. Furthermore, it may not always be possible to specify a particular general adaptation adopted by a pupil: he/she may not have a single dominant mode of adaptation, but rather display a collection of orientations to various aspects of, or situations in, school.[41]

We must begin, then, as does Furlong, with the analysis of pupil action, identifying the intentions, motives and perspectives which underlie it. Once we do this we can see that at any moment in time a pupil is faced with choice from a range of different possible courses of action. For example, with whether to attend to what the teacher is saying, talk to a neighbour, carve his or her name in the desk, or make some initiative in the lesson, perhaps in an attempt to sidetrack the teacher on to something more interesting. Each of these lines of possible action will have certain actual and perceived consequences. These will be evaluated as payoffs or costs, in terms of both extrinsic and intrinsic gratifications, including identity implications.

Operating at this level it is possible to specify a much more unequivocal definition of conformity. We can conceive of the teacher as, in the course of teaching, setting up frames, projected patterns of joint activity which specify the proper behaviour of pupils. Frames vary in scope and several may be operative at any one time. Thus some will be virtually all-pervasive, specifying the appropriate behaviour of pupils at any time; though there may be occasions, for example, school trips, visits to the games field, etc., where even these are relaxed. Other frames are much more specific, being relevant to particular lesson phases [42] or relating to just one segment of a phase. An example of a very specific frame is where the teacher asks a question. This demands pupil behaviour which at other times during the same phase is illegitimate: it requires pupils to talk publicly to the teacher and the rest of the class, albeit in an 'appropriate' manner. Directives play a similar role in specifying a certain form of action pupils are to engage in.[43] It is in terms of such frames, and specifically in terms of the frames operative at any particular point in time, that we can define pupil conformity to school requirements.

However, while, in many versions of teaching, the teacher is the only classroom, participant who has an automatic right to set up frames, in practice pupils also propose frames, and sometimes these 'come off'. Much classroom deviance amounts, whether intentionally or not, to the proposal of an alternative framework to that the teacher is operating. Such alternatives frames may be public, classroom wide, or they may be more localised, being confined to those who are sitting close to one another.[44] Where this occurs the other pupils are faced with a choice between conforming to the 'deviant' frame, joining a 'disruptive' interaction set, or conforming to school requirements and being seen to conform by fellow pupils as well as the teacher. It is at such times that the issue of being a conformist or a deviant, a 'lad' or an 'ear'ole', becomes particularly salient.

However, it is unlikely that such decisions are made on the basis of criteria which are simply momentary. In his article on interaction sets, Furlong points to some of the criteria which the pupils he studied seemed to employ. However, underlying such typifications of teachers must be some basic concerns which make these particular aspects of teachers relevant to the pupils. Of course, we cannot assume a single integrated set of such concerns nor can we assume that these concerns are derived from school values or even from an inversion of school values. We indicated earlier the complex nature of 'school values' and the diversity of other influences likely to impinge on pupils. Furthermore, it is also clear that the salience and implications of these concerns will vary across different contexts in the schools; for example according to the reputation of the teacher or the composition of the pupil audience.

The field of possible actions facing a pupil, and the costs and gratifications associated with different lines of action, will also change over time. Thus, we must take account of the way in which pupils re-evaluate their positions over time and adjust their orientations to changes in their situation. Some of these changes will occur independently of the actions of the pupil. Others may be consequences of his or her own previous actions: for example, adopting a particular line of action frequently involves building up commitments which change one's situation in such a way that it becomes more and more costly to act in any other way.[45]

One particularly important kind of consequence linked with lines of possible pupil action is identity implications. It is not just social scientists who make generalisations about the typical or general orientations of particular pupils. Both teachers and pupils do this too. In adopting a particular line of action a pupil must take into account the way others will interpret and react to his or her actions, since this may have important consequences for what options are open in the future. Of course the relationship between actions, identity ascription, 'societal reaction' and the options available to an actor in the future is fairly loose. Performing a particular action does not automatically result in the acquisition of a particular reputation, and having a particular reputation does not absolutely determine how others will act towards you. But there is a tendency for each to follow from the other.

The pupil may also make sense of his or her action in terms of a conception of own identity and biography. Even so, we should not assume a great deal of consistency over time and across contexts in the behaviour of pupils. Not only will a pupil's assessment of the feasibility of achieving particular goals vary across different situations but, more than likely, his or her assessment of the *desirability* of the different goals will also shift. And, of course, he or she may frequently be faced with dilemmas: as we noted earlier, the existence of a deviant interaction set forces choice between open 'conformity' and 'deviance'. Such crises may have important implications both for a pupil's sense of self and for how he or she is treated in future both by fellow pupils and by the teachers.

How the pupil evaluates the desirability and feasibility of different courses of action, how dilemmas are resolved and thus the general drift in his or her school career (if there is one) may well be influenced by the gatherings and groups in which he or she participates. The structure of the school—whether pupils are streamed, banded, setted or taught in mixed ability groups and how they are allocated to classes—is obviously of considerable importance here, as are the informal groupings which develop within and across school classes. However, we cannot assume an isomorphism between the adaptations pupils adopt and the interaction sets or groups in which they participate.[46] Pupils may interact with their fellows for many reasons, not necessarily because they share values or even goals.

Conclusion

In this chapter we have reviewed the currently available models for the interpretation of pupil activity: the pro/anti subculture model, the adaptation model, and Furlong's interactionist approach. The first two models have considerable scope but fail to account for the complexity and subtlety of pupil behaviour revealed even in the evidence of those who have employed them. On the other hand, Furlong's model, while it certainly begins to take account of the contextual variability of pupil behaviour, is very limited in scope: it seems stuck at the level of description. In the final section of the chapter we have sketched a slightly different approach which should provide a basis for the integration of these various models. While it *begins* at the level of the intentions, motives and activities of pupils, it nevertheless also allows for the *explanation* of patterns of pupil behaviour in terms of the structural features of the school and the wider society. A pupil's social class position and position within the school will have consequences for the lines of action available to him or her and the costs and benefits associated with these. But the operation of these factors only works through, and can only be identified and documented in, the more shifting moment-to-moment features of school process.

Acknowledgements: We'd like to thank Peter Woods for his comments on an earlier draft of this article.

Notes

[1] A curious feature of this influence, however, has been the dominating influence of subcultural and adaptational models deriving from normative functionalism rather than interactionism. For exceptions, see Furlong (1976) and D. H. Hargreaves (1976).
[2] For example, Lacey (1970), Marsh, Rosser and Harré (1978) and Woods (1978a) and (1978b). Delamont (1973) and (1976) are exceptions to this, taking the form of straightforward applications of interactionist theory.
[3] See Bernstein (1977).

4 Matza (1964). Also, we can expect differences between the values and norms teachers project and those they live by.

5 Merton and Barber (1963); Lang (1977).

6 Goffman (1971).

7 For Miller (1958) delinquency, like crime, is the product of conformity to working-class culture. Cohen (1955) treats it as the product of a youth subculture centred around the inversion of middle-class values. This is produced by status frustration on the part of the working-class boys who do not have the resources to succeed in middle-class terms. However, despite their differences, both Miller and Cohen employ the contrast between two sets of values to explain contrasting behaviour: conformity and deviance. Paradoxically, therefore, both 'straight' and delinquent youth are treated as conformists, albeit to different sets of values and norms.

8 Merton (1957).

9 In this respect his version of functional analysis is an advance over that of Parsons which fails to provide any systematic basis for the social production of deviance. See Parsons (1951), ch. 7. For a critique of Parsons along these lines which, curiously, doesn't mention Merton's work see Lockwood (1956).

10 Woods (1977); Woods (1979), ch. 3.

11 See Becker (1977).

12 For an application of Hughes's concept which has particular potential in this context see Emerson (1969).

13 See Bucher and Strauss (1961).

14 For an attempt to differentiate versions of teaching see Hammersley (1977).

15 The issue of the perceived legitimacy of different routes to school success is an important area for investigation.

16 See Mannheim (1952).

17 Speier (1976); Silvers (1977).

18 Willis (1977), p. 38.

19 See Wheeler (1966).

20 See Woods (1977) on fraternisation.

21 For other, but not necessarily incompatible, explanations of this see Jackson and Marsden (1962), and Lacey (1970).

22 This is one possible explanation for Rosenthal and Jacobson's (1968) findings.

23 This is, of course, a central tenet of interactionism.

24 He does, however, make the important suggestion, following Wakeford, that some of the adaptations tend to occur at characteristic points in pupils' school careers.

25 Though it should be said that the model stops well short of any analysis of the *process* of decision-making.

26 See Turner (1983).

27 See Geer (1977) and Werthman (1977). The classic discussion of negotiation is of course Strauss *et al.* (1964). Also see Strauss (1978).

28 Another plausible reading is that some of 'the lads', including Joey, don't object to teacher authority as such, only to the degree or particular range of authority the teachers claim; for example, their attempts to control aspects of personal appearance.

29 See Bramson (1961), Kornhauser (1959) and Shils (1975).

30 See Lang (1977) on school refusers.

31 Goffman (1968). Later proponents of the adaptation model have incorporated some of the adaptations pinpointed by Goffman but not his basic model.

32 Shils's (1975) notion of the displacement of charisma in modern societies seems particularly promising as an explanation for these changes.

33 See Hammersley (1976) for the manipulation of the notion of 'child' in bolstering teacher authority.

34 Furlong (1976). See reading 9 in this volume.

35 Turner (1983).

36 Furlong (1976), p. 27.

37 The same judgement applies to Delamont's (1976) application of this approach.

38 See Deutscher (1973).

39 Matza (1964) points out that deviants are never deviant all the time, they spend most of their lives conforming. He argues that this misconception has led to the incorrect presumption that deviants are a different type of person from conformists, for example having a different physical make-up, or personality.

40 See McDermott (1976) for documentation of this at a very detailed level.
41 Of course, some of those working with the adaptation model have recognised this, notably Peter Woods. But the adaptation model cannot deal with this problem because it focuses exclusively at the level of general adaptations to school values. While Woods recognises the complexity of pupil activity and of the situation they are responding to, he does not develop the model to cope with this complexity. In this sense his account amounts to a normative functionalist model dressed up in loosely fitting interactionist clothing.
42 For the concept of lesson phase see Hargreaves, Hester and Mellor (1975).
43 This concept of frame is an interactionist reformulation of the more structuralist notion of frame used by Sinclair and Coulthard (1975) and Goffman (1975). Also, see Hammersely (1981).
44 Though even the latter may encourage other localised side involvements elsewhere in the classroom.
45 See Becker (1977) for this concept of commitment.
46 This is an inevitable result of adopting a decision-making rather than a rule-based model of action.

References

Becker, H. S. (1977) 'Personal change in adult life', in Cosin, B. R. *et al* *School and Society* Routledge and Kegan Paul, London, 2nd ed.
Bernstein, B. (1977) 'Class pedagogies: visible and invisible', in Bernstein, B. *Class Codes and Control,* Vol. 3, Routledge and Kegan Paul, London, 2nd edn..
Bramson, L. (1961) *The Political Context of Sociology.* Princeton University Press.
Bucher, R. and Strauss, A. (1961) 'Professions in process', *American Journal of Sociology,* Vol. 66, January 1961, pp. 325–43, reprinted in Hammersley, M. and Woods, P. *The Process of Schooling,* Routledge and Kegan Paul, London.
Cloward, R. and Ohlin, L. (1960) *Delinquency and Opportunity,* Free Press, New York.
Cohen, A. K. (1955) *Delinquent Boys,* Free Press, New York.
Delamont, S. (1973) 'Academic conformity observed'. Unpublished Ph.D thesis. University of Edinburgh.
Delamont, S. (1976) *Interaction in the Classroom,* Methuen, London.
Deutscher, I. (1973) *What We Say/What We Do,* Scott Foresman, Illinois.
Emerson, R. M. (1969) *Judging Delinquents,* Aldine, London.
Furlong, V. (1976) 'Interaction sets in the classroom', in Stubbs, M. and Delamont, S. *Explorations in Classroom Observation,* Wiley, New York.
Geer, B. (1977) 'Teaching', in Cosin, B. R. *et al.,* *School and Society,* Routledge and Kegan Paul, London, 2nd edn.
Goffman, E. (1968) *Asylums,* Penguin, Harmondsworth.
Goffman, E. (1971) *The Presentation of Self in Everyday Life,* Penguin, Harmondsworth.
Goffman, E. (1975) *Frame Analysis,* Penguin, Harmondsworth.
Hammersley, M. (1976) 'The mobilisation of pupil attention', in Hammersley, M. and Woods, P. (eds), *The Process of Schooling,* Routledge and Kegan Paul, London.
Hammersley, M. 'Putting competence into action', in P. French and M. Maclure 1981 (eds) *Adult-Child Conversation,* Croom Helm, London.
Harary, F. (1966) 'Merton revisited: a new classification for deviant behaviour', *American Sociological Review,* Vol. 31, No. 5.
Hargreaves, D. H. (1967) *Social Relations in a Secondary School,* Routledge and Kegan Paul, London.
Hargreaves, D. H., Hester, S. and Mellor (1975) *Deviance in Classrooms,* Routledge and Kegan Paul, London.
Hargreaves, D. H. (1976) 'Reaction to labelling', in Hammersley, M. and Woods, P. (eds) *The Process of Schooling,* Routledge and Kegan Paul, London.
Jackson, B. and Marsden, D. (1962) *Education and the Working Class,* Routledge and Kegan Paul, London.
Kornhauser, W. (1959) *The Politics of Mass Society,* Free Press, New York.
Lacey, C. (1970) *Hightown Grammar,* Manchester University Press.
Lang, T. (1977) 'School experience—more sociological ambiguities', in Woods, P. and Hammersley, M. (eds) *School Experience,* Croom Helm, London.

Lockwood, D. (1956) 'Some remarks on "The Social System", *British Journal of Sociology,* Vol. VII, No. 2.

McDermott, R. P. (1976) 'Kids make sense: an ethnographic account of the interactional management of success and failure in one first grade classroom'. Unpublished Ph.D. thesis, Stanford University.

Mannheim, K. (1952) 'The problem of generations', in Mannheim, K. *Essays on the Sociology of Knowledge,* Routledge and Kegan Paul, London.

Matza, D. (1964) *Delinquency and Drift,* Wiley, London.

Marsh, P., Rosser, E. and Harré, R. (1978) *The Rules of disorder,* Routledge and Kegan Paul, London.

Merton, R. K. and Barber, E. (1963) 'Sociological ambivalence', in Tiryakian, E. (ed.) *Sociological Theory, Values and Sociocultural Change,* Free Press, New York.

Merton, R. K. (1957) 'Social structure and anomie', in Merton, R. K. *Social Theory and Social Structure,* Free Press, New York.

Miller, W. (1958) 'Lower class culture as a generating milieu of gang delinquency', *Journal of Social Issues,* Vol. 15, pp. 5-19.

Parsons, T. (1951) *The Social System,* Routledge and Kegan Paul, London.

Rosenthal, R. and Jacobson, L. (1968) *Pygmalion in the Classroom,* Holt, Rinehart and Winston, New York.

Shils, E. (1975) *Centre and Periphery,* University of Chicago Press.

Silvers, R. (1977) 'Appearances: a videographic study of children's culture', in Woods, P. and Hammersley, M. (eds) *School Experience,* Croom Helm, London.

Sinclair, J. and Coulthard, M. (1975) *Towards an Analysis of discourse,* Oxford University Press.

Speier, M. (1976) 'The child as a conversationalist: some culture-contract features of conversational interactions between adults and children', in Hammersley, M. and Woods, P. (eds.) *The Process of Schooling,* Routledge and kegan Paul, London.

Strauss, A. *et al.* (1964) *Psychiatric Ideologies and Institututions,* Free Press, New York.

Strauss, A. (1978) *Negotiations,* Jossey Bass, California.

Turner, G. (1983) *The Social World of the Comprehensive School,* London, Croom Helm.

Wakeford, J. (1969) *The Cloistered Elite,* Macmillan, London.

Werthman, C. (1977) 'Delinquents in school', in Cosin, B. R. *et al., School and Society,* Routledge and Kegan Paul, London, 2nd edn.

Wheeler, S. (1966) 'The study of formally organised socialisation settings', in Brim, O. G. and wheeler, S. *Socialisation after Childhood,* Wiley, New York.

Willis, P. (1977) *Learning to Labour,* Saxon House, Farnborough.

Woods, P. (1977) 'Teaching for survival', in Woods P. and Hammersley, M. (eds) *School Experience,* Croom Helm, London.

Woods, P. *E202 Schooling and Society,* Unit 11 Pupil Experience, The Open University Press, Milton Keynes.

Woods, P. (1978a) 'Relating to schoolwork', *Educational Review,* Vol. 30, No. 2.

Woods, P. (1978b) 'Negotiating the demands of schoolwork', *Journal of Curriculum Studies,* Vol. 3.

Woods, P. (1979) *The Divided School,* Routledge and Kegan Paul, London.

PART THREE

Pupil Perspectives

11

The delinquent group

D. H. HARGREAVES

[. . .] The delinquent group was dominated by Clint of 4C, since this boy was the best fighter, the 'cock of the school'. He was a fairly tall but slender boy. His hair was very long, emulating the style of the Rolling Stones, the 'pop' group he most admired. According to the eleven plus examination he was one of the most intelligent boys in the school, with an I.Q. of 110. He had been a borderline case for a place in a Grammar School. On arrival at Lumley he was naturally placed in the A stream, but by the end of the first term, allegedly due to persistent misbehaviour, considerable enmity had developed between Clint and the form teacher of 1A. As a short, sharp shock, he was temporarily demoted to 1E, and then replaced in 1B. His form position in the examinations at the end of his first term was 27th out of 30 boys. In 1B he joined Clem. He fared no better in the B stream; his next four form positions were 2nd, 6th, 21st and then 30th. He was thus moved into the C stream, where he remained until he left the school at Easter 1965. In the C stream his academic position began to drop more sharply; 18th out of 28, 16th out of 26, 18th out of 23, 21st out of 23. Had he remained at school for the Summer Term 1965 he would probably have been demoted into 4D.

How did he become the dominant member of the delinquent group? His rise to power was a slow process. He needed to find companions with similar values, which was not possible until he had declined in the streams.

> Clint used to be very quiet when he was at the other [Junior] school. He changed in second year. He began going with that gang. Then he started going up town and things like that.

> He was very quiet in first year. Then in third year when he came in our class he started. Well, you see he got with all his pals in third year, the ones that he goes with nights. They was all separated when Clint and Clem were in 2B. Clem came down with Clint and Drac come up and they all got together.

> Clint was pretty quiet when he first come. When Clint and me (62) went down to 3C, we started going round with Drac and then he started going round and all that, picking on little kids. Drac, you know, well he was a bit of a bighead. He's gone quiet now 'cos he's scared of Clint.

These comments are from boys who were with Clint in 1A and 1B. They will attest to the fact that Clint changed from being a fairly quiet boy, and that this change was associated with a change of friends. During the second and third years, the nucleus of the delinquent group began to take shape, especially when many of the key members found themselves in 3C. At this stage, Drac dominated the group.

> Drac was cock of third year. Clint wasn't a good fighter then.

It seems fully confirmed by my discussions with other boys and teachers that it was not until the third year that Clint began to assert himself, though of course the demotion from the A stream to the B stream brought him into immediate contact with Clem as reported above. Later they became two of the leading delinquent members of 4C. The change in Clint was noticed by boys in the A and B stream. As one 4A boy said:

> In 1B I used to go around with Clint. He was all right. He's sensible on his own. He was on the borderline of the eleven-plus at the other school. He's clever. He could have been good at sport and all that, but he just won't go that way. It's the teachers' fault really. 'Cos he was in 1A. But because he was a bit bad they put him down into 1E. If they'd kept him in 1A and kept him clever and that, he could be cock of the school now, like, but sort of be good. Clem's another like that. He was all right in second year. I used to get on with him. It's just that when they got older they think because they can fight they have to be bigheaded. He was clever, Clem. He came near the top. He was top the term after I went into 1A. And the teacher said, 'If you're top again next term I'll put you in the A class.' He should have been put up that time. Then after that he started mixing with the bigheads and he thought, 'If I can go down, I'll be with my friends then.' Next term he was bottom and got put down.

The facts are correctly reported here. Clem was indeed top and then bottom of the B stream, and thus shows a similar academic decline to Clint. The boy who reported this was one of the most shy members of 4A, and certainly no friend of either Clint or Clem. That he should describe the change in attitude and behaviour in these two boys so vividly, supports the contention that as they began to decline in the streams, and thus progressively alienated from the staff and the academic goals of the school, group attitudes began to take a negative turn. Life in 3C, when Drac began to play his dominating role, marks the real beginnings of the delinquent group.

The evidence of the duration of Drac's reign as 'cock' is conflicting. Some boys claimed that he had been the best fighter since the first year: others dated it only from the third year. It appears that it took at least some two years for Drac to establish himself in this position. The conflicting dates of origin may result from the differential perception of his dominance, i.e. the diffusion of the knowledge of his fighting ability spread slowly and unevenly through his year group. And secondly, it appears that being 'cock' does not bear any significance to members of any one year group until the third year, when boys learn that the fourth year has a definite cock and pecking order of fighting ability. This explanation is intended more as a suggestion. It is impossible to trace back the real origins; but this suggestion does account for the conflicting reports.

Drac's reign in the third year was not permanent. Partly this may be due to the fact that although he was a tough, wiry boy he was also rather short, and by the third year many of his peers were becoming very much taller and stronger than he. Secondly, and this may be causally related to the first point, Drac's growing self-assertiveness led to unpopularity as he began to alienate them by his aggresiveness. By the beginning of the fourth year, when I arrived at the school, Drac had fallen into a decline of unpopularity.

> Nobody talks to Drac now. Everybody used to be scared of him at one time. Now they stay away from him.

> He was always playing dirty tricks on you. And spitting.

> We fell out with Drac once when he kept beating up little kids, so we all just didn't bother with him.

> Drac was hard in third year, but he's gone soft now.

> Drac stopped going with me [Derek] and Clint. We didn't want him so we kept telling him to shift. And he had no one to go with except the little kids. Then some of the others started going with him.

There must have been a number of events which led to this ostracization of Drac. A typical event seems to have been:

> Drac got hold of Don's towel and wiped his feet on it. He cleaned his shoes on it and so did Derek. But Derek didn't do it till after Drac. Don got him for it and beat him up and he was going to get Derek, but I don't know if he did.

Don confirmed this story.

> [Drac] used to pick on everyone, worse than Clint does. Take money off them. He used to take two shillings a day off—. And cigs and everything. He used to try and pick on me and beat me up. Then one day he got my towel and wiped his feet all over it. So I was that mad that I cracked him one. And then Clint stopped going with him so he had no one to go with. And he had to go with little kids. Then one night he got drunk and started crying that no one would go with him. So we all started going with him. So we all started going with him again and he's all right now.

It does not seem that there was any dramatic single event or fight by which Drac was replaced as 'cock'. Rather, his general unpopularity, the fact that Don did retaliate, and possibly his unwillingness to accept fights from others simply led to his decline. The ostracization of Drac, was not, so far as I was able to check, an immediate or sudden event.

But the decline of Drac marks the rise of Clint, just as later the decline of Clint coincides with the reintegration of Drac. Clint did not replace Drac by any single event. There seems to have developed some general consensus among members of the group that he was 'cock'. This process seems to have three elements. Firstly, Clint was able to spread his claim to the title on the basis of several small incidents. For example, at the end of the third year, simultaneously with Drac's decline, Clint was involved in a fight with a fourth year pupil.

> He beat up a prefect last year. It was me and—. Clint came and asked us for a penny or summat. And the prefect tried to chuck him out, you know, and Clint pushed him back like that and a fight started and Clint cut all the top of his [the prefect's] head and it started to bleed. He had to have stitches in it. Clint was hurt an' all, but he won.

This victory must have considerably enhanced Clint's claims to superior fighting ability. But this alone was insufficient to grant him the title. It does not demonstrate his ability to fight everyone else in his own year. The second element therefore is the fact that no other single boy was willing to ask Clint for a fight. This lack of challenge acted as a support for Clint's emergence. The third factor is that Clint more than any other boy made himself highly *observable* as 'hard', or tough, by a process of systematic self-display. As one A stream boy put it:

> People are afraid of you if you go swaggering around the playground threatening everybody.

This is precisely what Clint did.

We can see then that the emergence of a 'cock' is not just a matter, at least prior to the fourth year, of simply displacing the reigning cock. The leadership may change by a much more subtle process. Although fighting ability is by far the most significant factor, achieving a reputation by isolated fighting events, lack of adequate challengers and self-display are important factors. By the end of first term of the fourth year, Clint had fully established his reputation. This was clear from my attempts to find out *how* Clint had become cock of the school. He himself was very uninformative about the matter, but others came to my aid.

> I don't know *how*. It's just the way you act really. It's just their reputation, if you know what I mean. Like Clint. It's not because he's fought everybody in the school. It's just the reputation. He can probably fight Don, so the rest think he can fight them.

> It's just got round that Clint is the best fighter. But you don't know really 'cos they've never had him a fight.

> Clint must be the best fighter 'cos he can beat Don and he can fight Clem too. Everyone says so.

Don of 4D was generally agreed to be 'second cock'. The next four or five positions were not sharply defined. Everyone knew the names of the boys occupying these ranks, but the actual order was not agreed. This was because the boys were friends; the fights by which definite positions could be determined did not take place. Although fighting ability was a major criterion of informal status in the delinquent group it was not the only one. Don, the 'second cock' held informal status rank 5 in 4D. This is because high informal status is partly determined by closeness to Clint. As we shall see, Don was not well-disposed to Clint, and was somewhat ambivalent in his relationship with him. Derek of 4D was Clint's closest friend, and it was Derek who held the top informal status rank in 4D. Even though Derek was not one of the five best fighters in the fourth year, his close friendship with Clint granted him high *associated status*.

Changes in the 'pecking order' can, however, occur when one boy offers to fight another. If the superior fighter declines to accept a challenge, the two boys change ranks. If he accepts, a fight ensues, and the winner obtains the higher rank. Likewise, if the leader or 'cock' feels in danger of being replaced, he can forestall the potential threat to his position by asking the challenger for a fight. Drac had done this in the third year.

> Clem came into our class. He should have been cock, him. I asked him for a fight but he wouldn't have one.

In this way Drac anticipated and defeated a rebellion before it could take place. And similarly, Clint maintained his superiority over Don, his nearest potential rival.

> Clint must be the best fighter 'cos Don won't have him a scrap. Clint's the best fighter. Then Don comes next. They've never had a fight, but Clint's the best fighter 'cos Don won't have him.

Yet Don was not scared of Clint, and was *known* not to be afraid.

> Everyone's scared of Clint, but I don't think Don is.

And this fact was known to Clint. He no longer tried to be very aggressive towards Don, who pointed out:

> Clint's changed now. You couldn't say nothing to him then [in the third year], you know what I mean? He'd turn round and crack you, but now he's all right.

But at the same time, Don did not want to challenge Clint.

> I don't want a fight with Clint. 'Cos if he beat me he'd be a big hero, like, wouldn't he? And I wouldn't want to beat him. 'Cos then I'd be first and I wouldn't like that.

This remark looks superficially like a justification of cowardice. This is not so. Don was very popular among the boys, and was frequently compared with Clint.

> Don's better to get on with. He doesn't know whether he can beat Clint. He'd have a good go though. No one else could have a go.

> I wish Don would beat Clint. 'Cos he's not a bighead. He's not always going round beating people up.

> [If Clint and Don had a fight] it might be a close fight that. 'Cos Don's a good scrapper. It might be a draw, I don't know. But I think Don would put up a good fight if he had to take him on. Clem says he won't have him a fight.

> Don's smashing to get on with. You've no need to be frightened of him 'cos he won't touch you.

> Don's about the best one. He never bothers anybody. But he's not frightened of anybody in the school. He acts more like a grown up, does Don. If he's got some toffees

he gives you some, but the rest won't hand none out. But they expect you to hand yours out.

Don was indeed a much more mature boy than Clint. He commanded loyalty from other boys and became popular because his fighting ability was not used to dominate. Moreover, he was able to see, as shown in the earlier quotation, that becoming 'cock' would endanger this popularity. On numerous occasions he seems to have been tempted to fight Clint, both for his own self-esteem and in order to 'tame' Clint. But his fear of becoming an unpopular 'cock' restrained him. It is not that unpopularity is inherent in the position of 'cock'. The 'cock' is of high informal status because of the power he is able to exert over others, even against their will. 'Popularity' is a different dimension which is concerned with personal preference and the ability to elicit and maintain sympathetic relaionships. Don was more popular than Clint; he received eleven choices from 4C and 4D boys on the 'friends' question, whereas Clint received only six. It seems that to maintain fully his position as 'cock' the occupant must combine high status in terms of both power and popularity, even though power is the primary prerequisite. That is, the 'cock' must *legitimate* his authority in that the followers accept him not only because he can force his will upon them, but also because they willingly consent to his exercise of power because they like him. The fusion of these two dimensions of power and popularity was no mean task for the reigning 'cock'. The potential risk of unpopularity in being 'cock' was explained clearly by Drac, who in describing Clint elucidates his own failure to acquire popularity as 'cock'.

> I'm glad I'm not cock now. You know, they don't seem to like you when you're cock of the school. They don't like Clint now 'cos he's a bighead 'cos he's cock. They all say Don will be able to fight him, so Don's waiting for him to start on him but he hasn't said owt to him yet. If he says owt to Don, Don's going to get him. Clint thinks he's friends with him, but Don doesn't like him. He's too bigheaded, you know. Some little kids come up to him and he cracks them and everything. But Don, you know, all the little kids can punch him, you know, act the goat with him, but he won't do owt.

Clint, by his indiscriminate aggression, began to follow the same fate as Drac and lost the support of his followers.

> Everyone knows Clint 'cos he's cock, but he's not popular, 'cos no one likes him, you know what I mean? I don't see why he should go round bullying people like he does just 'cos you can fight them. Taking money off them and all that. He's bigheaded.
> (Don)

> I liked Clint more in third year. Now he seems to be jumping on everybody, you know, and putting them on the floor and all that. And hitting them. I've seen him kick people in the face and start his nose bleeding.

> They're all frightened of Clint. I used to go with him for about two years, but then I stopped going with him 'cos he nutted me.

> I don't like Clint much now. He's got too bigheaded. And he was dead mad when I started talking to Drac again.
> (Clem)

> You can't tell with Clint. One minute he's talking with you and then the next minute he's saying 'Shut up'. He's like that all the time.

All these comments are from members of the delinquent group taken in the second half of the Spring Term. The same trend is followed by Chris his reciprocated first [friendship] choice. [. . .] The two boys always sat in adjacent seats for a term and a half. When this ceased, Chris explained:

I don't like him much now. He's always messing around. He's all right outside school but I don't like him in school. He asked me to sit next to him when we first come in this class. But I didn't really know him and he didn't know me. I liked him for a time. But then he began messing around and doing things, you know, so I just moved away. I said, 'I'm just going sitting somewhere else near the radiator 'cos it's cold,' and then I stayed there. He's been more friendly since I stopped sitting next to him.

Up to this point the stress in the description has been on the conflicts and instability of the group. This emphasis, while essential to a full analysis of the group, fails to give adequate weight to the co-operative and integrative activities of the group, which could be daily observed, especially during lessons. One further example would be the 'exortation racket', which followed in the Drac tradition. All non-members of the group were potential victims.

Like Derek, he came up to me and said, 'Lend us a penny.' I said, 'What for?' He said, 'To go to't Cavern.' I said, 'No' but he didn't bother and he turned to [my friend] and showed him 1/5d and said, 'Look I've cadged this today.'

Clint lets you off if you've only got a penny like and you need it for your bus fare or summat. But if you've got any more he'll take some. He might even take half. And if you don't pay you get smashed.

They say, 'Have you got a penny?' And if you say, 'No' they search your pockets. They search your pockets and you can't do nowt.

Membership of the group thus had a protective function: it insulated a boy against aggressive attacks and exortation. But not all the group members were involved in extortation. Don was a notable exception, and this fact may have contributed to his loss of informal status, and an increase in his general popularity.

The majority of the delinquent group had a Court record and were involved in current petty crime. Many of the accounts were very similar to those reported by members of 4B, such as the *collective* nature of the commission of the crimes. But there are important differences. In the B stream the main form of theft is incidental and petty. Cigarettes, sweets, cakes, minerals and small trinkets from multiple stores are the most common of the articles stolen. Although this also occurred in the delinquent group, there are important differences. Firstly, criminality is more purposeful and organized. Rather than taking place, as was the case in 4B, 'on the way', on an incidental basis, it is planned beforehand and often a special journey into the town is made. And when the boys get there, they arrange more carefully who will play which role.

I generally go with someone else. You wouldn't go on your own, not up town. They suspect you more if you're on your own. If you're on your own you can't just pick them up and put them in your pocket 'cos you don't know who's watching. But when there's two of you one can just walk round and look who's there. You go in separately and meet again when you come out.

They learn by experience which shops are 'easier' than others.

I've nicked lots of small things out of Woolworths. The last few Saturdays I been down to town with them. But I must stop going with them. I had all the stuff on me. Like—, he had all those stolen records in a bag and the floorwalker—I know her—she started to follow him. But if they'd caught me I'd have got done. I told them when they were in this cafe that she was following us.

They won't let you in—'s now. They keep their eye on them with long hair. A bit ago they used to leave all the records on the counter and you could easily shove them up your jacket.

—'s is supposed to be the hardest place; they prosecute.

In addition, the quality of the stolen articles tends to increase in price. Clothes—significantly—become a major item of interest. This is perhaps partly because the home fails to provide them and partly because of pressures to be fashionable.

> Shirts from up town. You just pretend you're looking at them like that then you drop two on the floor and as you're picking one up you put one down your pants. A mate of mine just put a jacket with a leather collar on, took the tab off, and just walked out. No one stopped him.

> —'s nicked everything he's got on. His pants, his corduroy jumper, his shirt and all that. He spends the money his mam gives him and then tells her he's bought the clothes.

> I folded two pairs of pants up and went into the changing room, wrapped one pair round my waist and took the other pair back. Then I put my jacket on and put my coat over it and just walked away.

In 4B I could find little evidence of acts of 'malicious damage', a common element of delinquency, though I am certain that it did take place on a limited scale. In the delinquent group such acts were fairly common.

> We were once near the canal and there was this big boat. I was going to push it in but it was dead heavy. A big canoe sort of. And it fit thirty odd people. So we shoved it in the canal and it turned over. A bloke run and phoned the cops and they all came so we jumped on the boat and got across. About four of us got away. We was hiding in this grass, but—got caught.

> Last night—got this tin and went like that and threw it through this window. Then we ran away.

> Once when we was going by the chip shop—kicked a window and it went in. So he ran out and I was the last one and the others were all in front so he just got hold of my coat like that and I just hit his hand and let go.

> Sometimes when trains came past we'd throw stones at the windows. Me and—, we got stopped by this plain-clothes copper, he got hold of—and me and took us in this car, and he didn't get our names until we was in the car. I wanted to run away but we couldn't. I had to go to Court. Another mate of mine used to climb up the signals and make dents in them with a brick, you know. We got done for that as well and we had to pay £4.

I found that whilst many of the boys were happy to discuss their various thefts, they were curiously reticent about acts of malicious damage. It was as if they felt some shame about such gratuitously destructive behaviour. Two boys told me that they thought the majority of the delinquent group were involved in such acts but they thought that some were simply afraid to tell me about it. Another frequent misdemeanour was to obtain entry to a cinema secretly without paying:

> You open the toilet doors and pretend you've been in. Or you can get in from the outside doors. You've only got to get a piece of wire in the door and pull it. At the—you open the door, go up some stairs, and just before the screen there's a curtain. Well, you've got to crawl on the floor by this curtain and get into a seat. They got—the other day just as he was getting into a seat.

Of course, some of the boys were able liars and would be completely unscrupulous in avoiding blame and guilt.

> I'm always the one that gets caught. I got done nicking some mouth organs. He asked my name so I told him another lad's name. He's in a home now. He stole £170 from a pub.

The delinquent group contrasts with the B stream boys in that only from the former did I find frequent attempts to rationalize their delinquency.

> You see kids pinching off the milk cart. It's natural. They can't help it. Some people deserve it though. You go in one shop and they have things all over the counter.

> It's not wrong to nick things out of shops. They've got more money than us.

But they were not complete fools: they knew how the dice were loaded against them and played the game accordingly. They relied on the fact that firms caution more often than they prosecute.

> Once I leave school and start work I'm going to be dead careful. 'Cos if you get caught then, you go into court and get done. When you're at school it's a matter of you can get done or you can't get done. That's why a lot of lads do pinch. You see more kids at school pinching than grown ups or owt like that.

And of course the drama of delinquency, for all its dangers, had a romantic aspect which gave identification with gangsters and commanded the attention of the group.

> They took us to this cop-shop and it was just like a gaol. You know, there were all bars and they kept locking all the doors. We was like real convicts.

The home atmosphere of some members of the delinquent group seems to have been more permissive than of boys in higher streams. [. . .] In such cases, the home acts as a reinforcer of the group norms.

> I only swipe cigs off my dad. If he catches me he just tells me to put them back.

> My dad caught me smoking once. He comes in and I was sitting in this chair. He was going to batter me but my mam says, 'Oh, they all do it so why shouldn't he?' My mam gives me cigs, sometimes.
> (Clem)

But Clem also reports that his parents were not permissive about drink.

> I went home drunk the other week. Well, I wasn't exactly drunk, you know, it had wore off. But my face was all red. And she wanted to know what I'd had and she found out and she went to the pub for my dad and he come out and kept me in.

One boy in 4D was taken to Court for taking a motor-bike without the owner's consent, with the additional charges for driving without a licence and insurance, etc. The police visited the parents, and when the police had gone the father's first remark to his son, as it was reported to me, was:

> Hadn't you got the bloody sense to dump it?

The father was not concerned about the delinquent act *per se*, but its unintelligent commission.

But let us be clear on this point. I am not claiming that from the evidence of this study that the delinquent group members come from homes which are more supportive of a delinquent sub-culture—though such may be the case. The evidence about home background in this study is extremely slight. Rather, there is *some* indication that *some* of the delinquent group come from homes which seem supportive of criminal tendencies, especially since some of them had fathers and brothers with prison records. But this was also true for some of the non-delinquent members of higher streams. The point here is that the relation between home background and delinquency is not simple, and cannot by itself provide an adequate explanation. The present argument is making an obvious point: that where the home is less orientated against criminal tendencies, entry into the delinquent group and an acceptance of its norms will be considerably facilitated.

Our central concern is with the informal processes in the group and the pressures it mediates. The forces exerted by the delinquent group on its members are difficult to detect, since many of the key situations were not open to observation. But a number of examples are available.

> On Saturday, 64 says to 70, 'Have a cig.' He says, 'No.' So he says, 'If you don't have a cig you don't come round with us no more.' So he says, 'Right give us a cig.'

Here the group exerts pressure on a boy to practise a behaviour which is proscribed by home and school alike. Unless he conforms to the group he will be rejected. Even if on such an occasion a boy is not threatened with direct rejection, he will be teased or scorned for being 'soft', an effective taunt for bringing deviants into line with group practices.

98, an aspirant, that is unreciprocated, member of the A clique in 4D became increasingly unpopular with the staff during his last year at school. He was regarded as having become very 'silly' and 'stupid'. The boy was aware of it himself. In his own words:

> I'm more cheeky now. I used to dead quiet when I first come.

He had learned that being quiet did not earn recognition from the group: he needed to be visibly and actively conformist to the norms of the group.

> 98 goes round slapping kids necks. He's mad, him.

> 98's gone bigheaded. It's only 'cos he thinks he's started to be one of the cocks of the school.

To be seen to be conforming thus requires a boy to *over*-conform to some extent. And the kind of behaviour which is practised can only be learned from imitation of the boys with high status. Let us consider the boy of status rank 14 in 4D.

> When I first come, well they thought I was dead quiet, never giving cheek and they used to pick on me but when I started giving cheek they started treating me like anyone else.

This is the *negative* side of the process by which the group punishes the boy since he refuses to conform. This is followed by the *positive* side by which the boy begins to acquire the norms of the group and demonstrate them behaviourally. He continues:

> When I heard Don answering back [to the teachers], you know, then I got started. Once I got six slippers for answering back. He [the teacher] told me to come back after dinner. And I had to do a test and he said, 'If it's not finished you'll have to do it at 4 o'clock', but I didn't go back and he says, 'Why didn't you come back?' and I said, "Cos I din't want to' and I said I couldn't and then he gave me four and I says 'I hope this'll refresh your memory', and I said, 'Get lost', and he hit me again.

In this way a boy can change his concept of the pupil role to conformity to group expectations but to deviance from teacher expectations. Because the group rewards him more than the teachers do, the group norms become more attractive than those of the teacher.

It will be evident that the delinquent group would frequently be involved in conflict with the teachers. On a number of occasions the incompatibility between teacher expectations and group norms was made quite explicit. We shall consider two examples.

The first took place on the last day of the Easter Term when most of the delinquent group were leaving school. On a number of occasions two members of the group had told me what they intended to do to certain of the less popular teachers as their Parthian dart to the system. I regarded these as verbal outlets for their aggression, and assumed that none of them would materialize on the day. None of these plans did: but another plan was accepted.

All the boys in the group bought fresh eggs during the lunch hour. These were concealed in their pockets during the last afternoon when the boys are allowed to play records and games with their form teachers. On these eggs the boys drew pictures of a particular master at whom these eggs were to be thrown after the final Assembly. However, one teacher spotted one of the eggs and confiscated it. On observing that one teacher's nickname was written on it, he quickly guessed the purpose of the eggs and informed the Headmaster, who then summoned all the leavers into the Hall. He had questioned the boy who was found with the egg in his possession, Chris, and also Clint and two of his main followers, 62 and 79. His attempts to extract the truth from these boys met, of course, with complete failure. some of the boys I had felt very uncomfortable and out of place because of my *short* protests and warned them that they would not be given their Leaving Certificates until after the final Assembly and told them (falsely) that without these Leaving Certificates they would be unable to get a National Insurance Card or a job. Anyone who showed the slightest sign of misbehaviour would be refused a Certificate. The plot was thus foiled, but the hostility towards the teacher who was the object of the scheme was increased. As soon as the boys received their Certificates, they rushed out of school, armed with some of the remaining eggs and other missiles and waited for the teacher to drive his car off the school premises. Fortunately for the teacher, he was able to avoid the crowd of some fifty or sixty boys awaiting him.

The second illustration is much more illuminating, in that it represents not one isolated event, but a continuous clash between the standards the teachers wish to impose and the norms of the delinquent group.

At the time of the study many of the 'pop' groups playing 'beat' music had long hair styles—the Beatles, the Rolling Stones, the Kinks and so on. Throughout the town many teenage boys imitated these styles. It is not surprising, therefore, that at the beginning of the Autumn Term 1964 a few boys in the fourth year arrived at school with long hair. The origin of this fashion, which by the middle of the fourth year had spread to many high status boys in the B stream, was in the delinquent group.

> Clint says, 'I'm going to get my hair flicking up', so I says, 'I'm going to let mine grow too', so he says, 'O.K.' So then we started letting it grow and then everyone did.
> (Derek)
>
> There was only three of us grew it long at first. There was me, Clint and Derek. But 105 had his hair long before it come out in fashion, I think. I just grew mine long but they thought they'd look hard if they didn't have it cut.
> (112)
>
> I wasn't going to grow it long at first and then they all said, 'Are you going to get your hair cut?' so I let it grow long. I'd rather have it short now but I'm not going to get it cut. I'd look a right nit.

Many of the older boys had been wearing jeans in school for some time and the staff had made regular but not entirely successful attempts to ban jeans in school. Although the Headmaster was aware that the Local Education Authority would not support his refusal to accept a boy in school because of wearing jeans, he announced in Assembly that jeans were against the school rules. This rule was strongly resented by many boys for several reasons. Several other schools in the area did not enforce rules against jeans at school. Some felt that when the fashionable narrow trousers were worn at school they tended to become shapeless very quickly. Also some boys possessed only one pair of trousers and wished to keep these as a 'best' pair.

A few days after the beginning of the Autumn Term, the Deputy-Headmaster called the top four informal status boys of 4D out of their classroom and told them that he would not tolerate this flouting of the school rules and that in future they must wear trousers to school. He explained to me afterwards that he hoped in this way to nip this incipient revolt in the bud. Yet the wearing of jeans continued intermittently, so a few weeks later one of the teachers asked for guidance on this matter at a Staff Meeting. The Headmaster pointed out that they could expect no support from the L.E.A. for their policy, and that the staff must therefore use informal sanctions against the wearing of jeans. All privileges would be withheld from offending pupils. One teacher pointed out that the offending pupils were the ones who in any case did not want privileges. The Head teacher retracted his remarks and stated that a boy must not be penalized simply because he wore jeans at school.

Many of the staff were not satisfied by this. Lengthy, informal discussions took place in the Staff Room and over lunch. The most vociferous members of staff were strongly opposed to jeans and long hair, and expressed their opinion in no uncertain terms. They argued that long hair was unhygienic and encouraged the spread of lice in the school; that it was dangerous, especially in the school workshops; that it was very unsightly and effeminate.[1]

By November, when a second Staff Meeting was held, many tempers had been roused. As a result the Headmaster authorized the use of informal sanctions against the offenders. They were to be excluded from participation in the school concert, and from school visits. He also said, 'They'll get no help from me and I shan't give them a reference when they leave.' One of the teachers strongly objected to this policy, arguing that the academic development of the children was the school's real function, not the determination of styles of dress. No other teacher supported this objection, though one teacher expressed his agreement to me privately. The Deputy Headmaster countered the objection with a justification of the policy on the grounds that these boys were in any case disobeying their parents by having long hair and jeans and that the boys concerned were simply trying to be awkward in school. It was suggested that a long haired member of 2A should be transferred to the E stream 'as an example' but this was not in fact carried out.

The more general policy was put into effect. Boys with long hair or jeans were excluded from school visits, though this affected very few boys since only 4A and 4B were involved in these visits. The few offenders in these upper streams tended to capitulate and conform to teacher expectations as the year progressed. (One persistent deviant in 4A stayed at school for a fifth year, but since one master refused to teach him unless he had his hair cut, he left a few weeks after the beginning of his fifth year.) Teachers constantly made adverse and derogatory remarks about long hair and jeans. Such comments usually took the form of ridicule or an attempt to shame the pupils for their 'scruffy' appearance. Most of the teachers seemed almost completely unaware that such pressures would be unavailing since group norms were much more attractive and compelling than teacher expectations.

At the end of the Autumn Term the local Inspector of Schools attended the school's Carol Service, and criticized the appearance of many boys. This caused the Headmaster to instigate a sort of 'purge' on jeans and long hair, and on lack of cleanliness, which he tended to see as synonymous. In an announcement to the whole school he said that boys who came to school in a dirty state in the Spring Term would be sent to the Chief Education Officer with a note to the effect that he, the Headmaster, would not accept these boys in school until they were more presentable. He also repeated that those boys with long hair could not expect a reference from him when they left school. He stated publicly that offenders would be excluded from extra-curricular activities. Finally, he indicated that such boys would experience great difficulty in finding an employer when they left school.

At lunch that day a heated discussion ensued amongst the teachers. The majority agreed that long hair was a sign of anti-social behaviour and must be stamped out. Two teachers thought that long hair was a part of an adolescent phase and bore little relevance to the teacher's function.

The Spring Term marked the beginning of concerted opposition to jeans and long hair. On the first day of term boys with jeans were excluded from Assembly and lectured about the matter. One fourth year teacher openly admitted that he had caned six boys for having hair over their eyes and would continue to do so daily until they had it cut. The application of informal sanctions continued. The Headmaster wrote on one boy's report to the Youth Employment Officer, 'Has long hair.' The Headmaster refused to let boys with long hair have time off school to visit their future employers. He told the low stream boys:

> Make yourself look normal. Make your appearance normal, instead of being like nothing on earth, or you'll not get a job. If an employer has two lads to choose from, he'll pick the normal one, not you.

One teacher began cutting the hair of these pupils, an act which caused considerable dismay amongst the boys. The teacher did not, perhaps significantly, cut the hair of the leaders of the delinquent group, but of low status boys. However, one irate parent complained to the Education Offices about this, and the matter was hastily hushed up. The less drastic pressures continued. Bert of 4B was not allowed to sell flags in a local cinema for charity because the Headmaster considered that the boy's appearance would give an unfavourable impression of the school. It was on these grounds that several high status low stream boys were forbidden to attend the Leavers' Service at a local Church at the end of the Spring Term.

The teachers who disagreed with the Headmaster's policy formed a very small minority. One part-time teacher spontaneously told me that he disagreed with the policy for two reasons: firstly, the rule against jeans and long hair provided a means for the boys to express their antagonism to the system; secondly, the rule was arbitrary, since dirty trousers were considered more acceptable than clean jeans. Other teachers would not follow this argument.

As a researcher I tried to avoid becoming involved in the argument, but when my opinion was asked I felt it best to be honest and express my disagreement with the Headmaster's policy. I pointed out that when I had visited a local beat club with some of the boys I had felt very uncomfortable and out of place because of my *short* hair. On these grounds, we should appreciate that the club was more attractive to these boys than school, so we could not expect to win. Secondly, although I agreed that it was part of the teacher's duty to make the boys clean and tidy, I did not feel it was part of the school's function to dictate styles of dress. Thirdly, I stated that the Headmaster had informed me, after a visit from the school nurse, that with exceptions it was not the boys with long hair who tended to carry lice, since they washed their hair frequently. Finally, I suggested that long hair was perhaps a symbol of the boys' rejection of the school's values and that our opposition would only exacerbate this rejection. These arguments were hotly refuted by many teachers who were present.

Conflict between staff and boys continued. The Deputy Headmaster refused to consider Don for appointment as a prefect because of his long hair, despite support for his candidature from several teachers. As one teacher said:

I don't care a damn over his long hair, but if that's the school policy it's O.K. by me.

One boy in 4C who as an aspirant member of Clint's group, was offered ten shillings by his mother and the same amount from his grandmother to have his hair cut short. His refusal in spite of these incentives is an interesting index of the symbolic importance of long hair in aligning him so visibly with the delinquent group.

Most of the delinquent group were leaving school at Easter. Few of them made any real attempt to secure employment. Part of this was their reluctance to have their hair cut. One boy in 4C did have his cut prior to an interview with a prospective employer a few days before the end of term. He was, of course, excessively teased by both teachers and peers. Derek had his hair cut short on the evening after he left school. He was not willing, one might infer, to let teachers or pupils see that he was willing to abandon his long hair in order to get a job. He maintained his opposition to the last.

Notes

[1] There is little doubt that some of the teachers perceived long hair in boys as a threat to the masculine sex role. It is possible that in this respect they betrayed their own sex role insecurity.

12

Making sense of school

H. GANNAWAY

[This paper on pupils' views of their teachers, was written while the author was a student teacher in a London comprehensive school. It was submitted as his main education essay for a Post-graduate Teaching Certificate. -Editors]

[...] I have divided my analysis into three sections which I introduce briefly below. Some draw upon ideas which I am sure are shared with many pupils, while some are based on ideas which are mainly my own.

Order and authority
One of the topics most mentioned by pupils was how they related to teachers in the area of order and discipline. In other situations I came to see that this had connections within the wider area of choice and decision making in the school.

The ideal teacher and his subject
Central to Nell Keddie's (1971) paper 'Classroom knowledge' is Becker's notion of the ideal pupil as conceived of by teachers. This made me wonder whether the evaluation of teachers by pupils might be similar, i.e. do pupils rate teachers according to the degree to which the teacher acts in harmony with the pupil's own notions of what is 'expected' or even 'good' teacher behaviour?

Work and boredom
'Boring' is certainly one of the most common words in pupil vocabulary. (Blishen, 1969, p. 10) says of his school pupil writers: '[boring] is the word that unites all the essays that allow themselves to be freely critical'. But, as a teacher, I have in the past been aware that pupils' use of this word differs from my use of it. What do they mean? How do pupils rate 'good' activities in school and how do these evaluations compare with 'official' ones?

Order and Authority: 'Will the real Mr Teacher please make us sit down?

It became clear to me that, for some pupils, the most important parameters for evaluating not only the performance of teachers in school, but also their own enjoyment as pupils, were order and discipline. John frequently made comments of this sort when asked about teachers. Once, when I asked 4X how they would describe an ideal teacher, the following conversation took place:

John: One who has a laugh with you.
Ann: And one that understand you.
John: And one that won't let you get too stroppy ... and stops the lessons getting boring ... he doesn't let the class get all stroppy and do what they want ... and, wait a minute, whether he's human. Right, didn't sort of sit here on a desk, right? He didn't sort of, you know, sort of being mucked about ... sort of doing what we wanted him to go.
Ann: ... took advantage of him.
John: Yeh, yeh, we didn't take advantage of her ... swearing at her and things like that.
Obs: You prefer someone who doesn't let you do that?
Ann: Yeh.

Similar statements were made at other times by other pupils. Altogether they led me to the view that there is a widely held picture of two extreme types of teacher: the soft and the hard, if you like. In operation, the difference consists in whether he can keep order or not. This order relates to various preventative measures: not allowing rudeness, maintaining control over the physical layout of the room (e.g. movement of desks), controlling noise and preventing unauthorized movement about the room (or outside the room) by pupils. In another lesson where the class had been discussing the possibility of making a film about the school it was said (this conversation is reconstructed from written notes):

Teacher: What sort of lessons are you going to show?
Pupil: Ones with soft teachers. Before the teacher comes in, pellets flying about and all that.
Julie: No, you want to show different teachers: ones you play up and ones where you sit down.

This type of 'playing up' is not always accidental or motiveless. On one occasion John explained how a class will 'push' a teacher to 'see how far he will go'. The tactics for this activity are unauthorized talking, walking about and contravening all the other norms of an ordered class. This is not done in the form of an all-out attack but rather a steady process which seems to be a very important part of meeting a teacher for the first time and establishing a relationship. What is required is that the teacher shows some signs of what he considers to be acceptable behaviour and what is not. The teacher's performance can have fairly important results for the class and for the teacher. Tony recounts a failure:

Tony: . . . last year 3M (laughter) there was one teacher, a Mrs G. and she was coming in the first week and everyone was chatting as she said, 'Be quiet' and no-one took any notice of her at first until she ran out of the room. *(Talk by class).* We swapped over for a Mr M. and he isn't very tough like . . . but he kept us quiet. You know: 'I'm the teacher. I'm taking the lesson. You can either get out or listen'. So you kind of kept quiet while he was in there.
Keith: We had a laugh in that class last year *(laughter).*

Stories of teachers who had at the first attempt failed to keep order and either left the school or ceased to teach the class (which in a large school can amount to the same thing from the pupils' point of view), recurred in several discussions. I attempted to find out what attitude the pupils had, on reflection, to these teachers. (It is interesting that these stories always referred to teachers who no longer took the class and never to someone teaching them at present.) When I asked whether they would want to include in the film (which, as I have already mentioned, they were planning to make about the school) a scene of the female teacher crying, there was general agreement that it was all right to show pranks, but showing that was going too far. One way of shedding light on the stories of the 'non-starter' and the pupils' apparent embarrassment about it, is to see the 'non-starter' as part of a mythical structure in the Levi-Straussian sense of a story or stories which represent conflicting extremes of accepted behaviour or social structure and by which the 'middle way', as represented by the hero, is to be ascertained. (I will deal with the other extreme—woodwork teachers—below.) The hero, or embodiment of the 'middle way', I have referred to as The Ideal Teacher who is a very difficult person to describe, both for pupils and teachers, as he represents a fine balance between conflicting opposites, namely, freedom and control. The nature of this conflict is very complicated and sometimes leads to apparent contradictions. In a myth, the extremes are a way of indicating the conflicting values that the hero finally manages to encompass. The extremes are all, in some sense, desirable, but individually inadequate. The 'middle way' shows how they can find valid expression.

I suggest that the 'non-starter' represents, for the pupil, freedom carried to absurd extremes. The teacher (who, in the accounts, is invariably a young woman) fails even to establish a presence in the class. The game cannot really begin. In a 'normal' situation the teacher establishes his presence, his personality and his codes of behaviour, by means of his responses to the disruption techniques and to the other happenings in the classroom. In a normal situation the process is seen by the pupils as 'natural' and quite straightforward. It is worth noting that there are few teachers who, in the course of initiation into the profession, have not encountered a similar definition of the situation presented to them by one of their superiors, in words such as: 'You've got to let them know who's in charge right from the start'. This may even be formalized into an official instruction or piece of advice. Here it would seem that both 'sides' have compatible definitions of the situation. Both see the first meeting as an occasion when rules are laid down. It is not difficult to see why, from the point of view of the pupils, the 'non-starter' comes as a great shock and may even raise feelings of guilt. In a successful situation, the question of guilt never arises; the structure of the process is unproblematic although the actual outcome may be uncertain in terms of what sort of relationship emerges.

Perhaps pupils who adopt disruption tactics see it as a necessary ordeal for the new teacher. The primary test of a real teacher is: can he keep order? I find it difficult to make any other sense of the following statements from John:

Obs: Supposing in a class the teacher picked on one of the class, all right? I know that people . . . kids in a class do get upset when that sort of thing happens and they resent the teacher doing that and yet you all seem to think it's a really great laugh when this happens to a teacher. *(Laughter).*

John: Well, that's the way it is, isn't it?

Obs: Is it? do you mean it's O.K. for a teacher to do it to kids as well? *(Calls of NO.)*

John: Yeh, but it doesn't work that way, does it?

Obs: Tell me what you mean.

John: It's all right for us to muck a teacher about and make her cry *(laughter from class)* and that . . . but as soon as she starts on us it's not all right, you know? *(Laughter and noise.)* That's the way it is, isn't it?

Obs: Perhaps this is not quite the thing to say, but does that not seem to you a little unfair?

John: Of course it's unfair!?

On another occasion John said: 'Some teachers are weak and some teachers shout all the time'. Teachers' shouting was frequently mentioned by pupils, referring to House Heads and others mainly in posts of responsibility. Whenever this topic was raised, there was nearly always a body of opinion to contradict such statements and to counter them with a comment like: 'Oh, but he's nice when you get to know him'. After a time I realized that there were some teachers who frequently had stories told about them shouting or losing their tempers which no-one ever contradicted: they were all woodwork teachers. Some of these stories are remembered from four years previously and concerned teachers who had now left the school. Here is an example (and a fairly mild one!) from James:

James: We was in the craft room with Mr C. and he was telling us to shut up but we kept going so he got hold of his saw and he whammed it down on the bench and it went flying and hit him on the head *(laughter from class)* and he was swearing!

The structure of these stories is fairly consistent and concerns the woodwork teacher's unsuccessful attempts to keep order or to discipline someone. The teacher loses his temper and takes some wild action which rebounds upon himself, making him appear ridiculous and adding to the lack of order. Other examples of these stories concerned a woodwork teacher who, in a fit of temper, had thrown a chisel at his bench and pierced right through his attendance register; and another about a teacher who had, in an enraged attempt to discipline a boy, lifted him by the shoulders to sit him on a bench and in the process was (accidentally?) kicked in the groin by the boy.

Whenever these tales were recounted they too, like the 'non-starter' stories, evoked laughter which I would describe as partly embarrassed and guilty. Mike's reaction to James' story about the woodwork teacher (above; Mike had been present when the incident had occurred) was very untypical; but, even though it bordered on the sympathetic, it too was greeted with further laughter:

> Mike: I never thought a teacher was human until I heard him swear . . . because he didn't seem sort of . . . right *(laughter)* . . . I couldn't imagine him going home and sort of . . . having a house . . . a car and everything like that until I heard him swear and then I felt sorry for him. He was standing all on his own talking to a goldfish. *(Laughter).*

I suggest that the reason stories such as these were greeted with laughter from a class which at other times showed that they were very sensitive to human feelings, is because the 'mad woodwork teacher', like the 'non-starter', gives rise to grave doubts among the pupils. Neither is capable of providing a secure relationship for the pupils, or of assembling meaningful order for the class. Despite the apparent levity accorded to these tales, they are really very moral in the sense that they are concerned with the basic quality necessary to establish a relationship with a teacher. As mythical opposites, the 'non-starter' and the 'mad woodwork teacher' are essentially caricatures and express only one feature of a personality. The former is female, passive and cries; the latter is male, over-active and aggressively temperamental. It is tempting to see these as extreme sex-role stereotypes. Both of these failures were contrasted unfavourably with the good teacher who can keep order.

Our 'hero' then is someone between these two poles, a complex character capable of generating freedom within an ordered framework. Although being able to keep order is a necessary quality, it is only the start. For instance, a teacher who is able to keep order but is too strict is also frowned on:

> Phil: *(replying to the question: what makes a teacher human?)* If a teacher treats you like a human being and jokes with you . . . *(inaudible)*. But if he's strict with you and goes by the book we think 'we don't like you' so we'll give him trouble.

The idea of 'having a laugh' is a very important one; the phrase was used very often by many pupils. Formality is definitely frowned on. John's first response to the question about the ideal teacher was 'one who has a laugh with you'. This idea of having a laugh is a complex one; it is an interaction between class and teacher which preserves a finely balanced tension, allowing the class to push the pace while the teacher holds invisible reins.

The Ideal Teacher and his Subject: 'Oh, to be in English . . .

I wish now to look at some of the other ways in which pupils rate or evaluate their teachers. This is a complex subject, as the evidence which I have shows a high degree of interconnection between the ratings. It was fairly easy to isolate the idea of 'order' in the last section, as I feel that *most* pupils see this as a necessary preliminary evaluation: if a teacher does not pass the order-test then he does not go forward to be assessed on any other criteria. I have said that humour and flexibility seem to be the key to the order-test but how do these relate to other evaluations. who are the *good* teachers?

I will start from the end and refer to [. . .] where Ann says her Geography teacher was 'a good teacher but she does drag on a bit'. The class teacher translated 'drag on a bit' into 'a hell of a bore' and this new expression was accepted by Ann. They threw this problem about a bit and finally Ann withdrew from the debate with 'she teaches you things but it's boring . . .'. These statements from Ann were clearly taken to be problematic by the class teacher, whose comments imply that he feels that the terms 'good teacher' and 'boring' are mutually contradictory. Ann, however, sees no difficulty: the teacher does teach you things but they are boring things. I think that this evaluation is closely related to the 'have a laugh' versus 'sticking to the book' criteria. The Geography teacher seems to have been one who stuck to the book and who could be seen by Ann to be doing a good job *per se* but neverthless *she was boring.* That a teacher could be a good practitioner of his art and yet bore his pupils is probably an idea which would appal most teachers, but then Ann is not a teacher. Why should the pupil want to address the *teacher's* philosophy of teaching? When the class teacher asked the pupils how they would recognize a teacher if one came into the room (. . .), the first reply he received was 'because he'd start teaching you things'. In the context of the analysis which the teacher seems to have been trying to develop, this statement may sound tautological, which may be why it was not followed up by the teacher. But subsequently none of the pupils actually came up with any deeper analysis of the word 'teach'. So, a teacher is someone who teaches you. The identification of teachers and strategies of teaching are not susceptible of consideration in the abstract.

I want now to move on to another aspect of the evaluation of teachers: the subject that they teach. Some weeks after Ann had made her statement about the Geography teacher I raised the matter again with her and in the course of her reply she said:

> Ann: With a subject like Geography . . . it's boring itself. She's teaching it to you . . . she's a good teacher but the subject's boring.

However, she went on to talk about Geography lessons she had had at a previous secondary school which had been interesting. The teacher, a woman, was described as 'terrific'—Ann had come top in Geography 'because she was such a good teacher'. When I put it to her that this contradicted her previous statement that Geography was always boring she explained that in her previous school she had become involved in what they were learning about the products of various countries. She prefaced these remarks with the words: 'I know it sounds funny but . . .', as though anticipating that the class would not believe this tale of interesting Geography lessons. John then remarked that it was the teacher that made all the difference to a lesson and the rest of the class seemed to agree with this. It was said that a good teacher is *one who understands the pupils.*

As I listened to accounts of various teachers and their personalities I began to realize that for many of the pupils there is one subject where the sort of problems which Ann outlined for Geography did not apply. That subject is English. In English the situation is almost exactly the reverse; both the subject matter and the teachers are interesting. It is almost as if one has to be a really *bad* teacher of English in order not to be rated highly by the pupils, and a number of reasons were given for liking English teachers. It would appear that English lessons and teachers represented a happy coincidence of agreeable features, so that many pupils find something good about the lessons. And this fact also, that many pupils come to the lessons in pleasant anticipation, may contribute to their success.

For Mike, as for some others, English was contrasted with Maths, a contrast which Mike sees in terms of the freedom of expression and variability allowed in English:

Mike: English is sort of about what you think. But in Maths you can't. There's just sort of one answer and that answer's right. But in English you could have about four or five answers which are correct.

Obs: So you prefer English on account of that, do you?

Mike: Oh yeh, because English is sort of more free . . . because in Maths if you get the answer right then your answer's the same as everyone else's but if they ask you in English what do you think of . . . uh . . . that Warhol bloke . . .

Teacher: Oh yes, Andy Warhol.

Mike: . . . someone might say, 'he's great' and someone might 'he's stupid' but to you that answer's right.

Success in Maths means conformity, whereas success in English can mean that you establish the uniqueness of your personality by expressing your individual opinions on a topic.

As it happens, the English teachers in the school are nearly all under thirty and the majority of women. They nearly all dress fashionably and very informally. Pupils often made general statements about the age of teachers' and attributed different characteristics to young and old teachers.

John: Young teachers are more adaptable, old teachers go by the book.

This is a context in which pupils made far more detailed analyses of lessons that we saw previously. Mike, talking about two of his past English teachers, said:

Mike: If a teacher's not too remote . . . like we had this Miss L. last year and she was sort of like an overgrown one of us—dressed like us and everything and you could really sort of talk to her. But, was it the year before, we had another English teacher and it was all English composition. English speaking and things like that.

Obs: Oh, so you would like someone to be as much like you as possible?

Mike: Yeh, yeh, but . . . *(class laughter)* well, not too aloof. Not too far departed, sort of thing.

Later on he added:

Mike: She was like us but if she wanted to be firm she could be.

Not only was Miss L. seen as having more pleasing personal characteristics and as being close to the pupils in age, or at least manner, but also, this was all related to her work in the classroom. I note that Mike contrasts Miss L.'s dress and her easy manner of speaking with the English composition and speaking lessons of the other teacher. Who can fail to picture the difference between 'really talking to her' and ' 'English speaking'? Miss L. is a part of the content of her lesson in a way that the other teacher is not.

Another aspect of teacher evaluation which relates especially to English teachers is the use of the teacher's christian name by the pupils. In the problem of how close the pupils wanted their teachers to be to them. Most of the examples cited by the teacher and the pupils were English teachers and both Keith and Phil said that they would incline towards calling an English teacher rather than another subject teacher by his first name, according to Phil, 'because they've got the right ideas'. It is almost as if English represents an outpost for some pupils; and the English teacher is a man or woman apart. At no time did I ever hear of English teachers having discipline problems. In addition, I heard more accounts of the actual *content* of English lessons (books read, subjects discussed, etc.) than for all other subjects put together. In fact I rarely heard mentioned the content of any other subject lesson.

One exception to this was Mike's sustained critique of Environmental Studies [. . .] which I think throws some light upon his liking for English. I quote part of it below:

> Mike   When we first come to this school and they told us what subjects we were going to to I was really baffled because I didn't know what Classics was. I had no idea, and at one stage I thought it was classical music . . . They didn't tell you what you were going to do. It was just put on a plate. I went into Environmental Studies with my eyes shut and didn't know what that was going to be. I thought it was going to be almost identical to this [*i.e. Social Science*] . . . Environmental Studies: I thought; well it's environment so it's going to be about where you live but it isn't really. It's all sorts of things . . . [*And on the question of whether it makes sense 'doing' Eskimos*] . . . but it doesn't [*make sense*] in a practical way because no-one here has ever lived in an igloo, I don't think, so they can't really compare it with us, can they? . . . We're doing Aborigines next week [*class laughter*] and how can you keep an Aborigine, an Eskimo and our lives sort of . . . one thing . . .

Mike's main cause for concern seems to be that he does not understand the structure of the subject. The reasons for this are probably complex but the fact remains that he cannot make sense of what he is doing. At the outset he had an idea of what Environmental Studies would probably be, but this was very soon confounded by the departure into 'Eskimos'. He criticizes the study of Eskimos on fairly utilitarian grounds (as he had previously criticised Religious Education):

> Mike: Well, that wouldn't help you in any job at all, not being a vicar, because you wouldn't want to learn about other religions, would you even . . .

But this is a parameter that he does not apply to English. This to me is a paradox; as I look at it, the uselessness of building igloos seems analogous to the uselessness of discussing Andy Warhol. So why does Mike not say that English is 'no use to you'?

My conclusion is that for Mike, and perhaps for other pupils as well, the 'utility test' has to be seen in the context of all the other tests that pupils apply to teachers and their lessons. In the diagram I have attempted to put together the tests Mike applies along with tests I have derived from other pupils. I have set them out in linear form because, for the first two stages at least, it does work that way. Of course, I am not saying that pupils actually do evaluate their lessons this systematically. The diagram is primarily a model for me to make sense of the judgements that are made. It may seem at first sight that the tests passed by good teachers are very simple (not easy, but simple). For instance, can a teacher really go into a class and say, 'Oh yes, I understand you', and pass the test? Obviously not—the tests are more subtle than that. I think that in the assertion that a teacher 'understands' pupils we have a form of shorthand, signifying that the teacher is acceptable on a number of counts which are subsumed under the heading 'understanding'. For instance, the actions of a teacher who continually sets written work would not be classed as 'understanding' actions. The *things* that a teacher has to do to become an understanding teacher are very important and I will go on to discuss them in the next section.

I will end this section by mentioning briefly a survey being carried out by some sixth formers as part of their 'A' level Sociology course. The survey aimed to discover how pupils perceive and evaluate their teachers and lessons. The survey was still uncompleted when I left the school but a pilot study had been done on two groups of fourth years (none of them in 4X). One of the questions asked them to choose from a list of about thirty words and expressions those which described their favourite teacher (they could add words if they wanted). The words most frequently chosen were, first, 'has a sense of humour' and, second, 'understanding to pupils'. I felt this lent support to the conclusions I had reached from observation of other classes.

Work and Boredom

This is one of the hardest parts to write. This is because I am piecing together statements and ideas drawn from various situations and people and also because [. . .] I am sure that the rationale which pupils apply to activities in school is very different from any rationale that teachers are used to. In this section I attempt to highlight some of these differences. When it is also borne in mind how many teachers, teaching methods imply a complete ignorance of these differences, it can surely be left to the reader to imagine how they contribute to misunderstandings and confusions in the teaching process.

I include the transcript of a fairly lengthy section of a lesson*[. . .] because the evaluation of activities is considered throughout. The conversation ranges across a number of topics but it is nevertheless something to which the group returns repeatedly. The course of the lesson prior to the beginning of the transcript had been roughly as follows: the teacher had asked the class a number of questions to do with the way a teacher positions himself in the classroom, how desks are arranged and what these things might signify about the teacher and his understanding of his role. The responses from the class were not enthusiastic and I made a guess that they could see no point to the lesson. That is where the transcript starts. I want to examine three areas of the lesson and they are connected to three individual pupils and their views: first, Mike and his comments on the content of lessons; second, Phil on the subject of getting out of school; and third, Tony on the subject of having to come to a school.

We have already seen how Mike attempted to make sense of the Environmental Studies course, how the change from Eskimos to Aborigines struck him as quite arbitrary and meaningless. In addition, when I presented him with an 'official' explanation for studying Eskimos he reluctantly replied that it sounded O.K. 'on paper'. He then added that practical comparisons can only be made on the basis of practical experience. So Mike has two problems: first, that no-one has ever told him, in terms that he can understand, why he is studying Eskimos and Aborigines, and second, when presented with my suggested 'teacher's' rationale for the course of study, he found it unacceptable. No wonder he is confused. He seems to be someone who needs a sensible rationale for his activities—I think that of all the pupils I spoke to, he spoke about motives and reasons more than any other. But for Environmental Studies he can find no rationale. Another statement where Mike shows the gap between his own construction of reality and those of his teachers is where he says of his teachers:

> Mike: You don't start at the beginning, you sort of start at the middle and end at the beginning and things like that. You get so confused.

words which should surely be hung over the entrances of all Colleges of Education.

I must pause here to admit that I find Mike's words very disconcerting, and the thought that there might be others like him very worrying. For he is not a miscreant or a trouble maker. He is fairly strongly motivated to learn and seems from his statements very anxious to make sense of what he is doing so that he *can* learn. And yet the school is not explaining itself, even in its own terms, well enough for him to

*Not in this version–*Editors*.

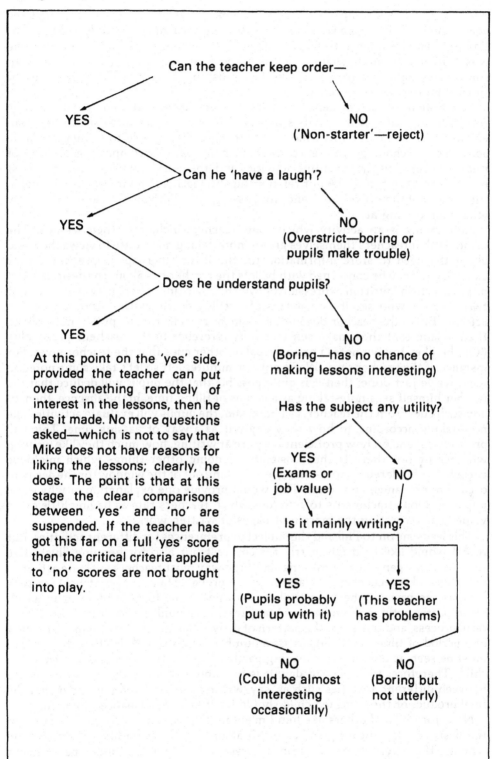

Figure 12.1   *An evaluation scheme for teachers*

understand what is going on. Nobody told him enough about Classics for him to be able to distinguish it from what he knew about classical music; nobody told him that Environmental Studies was different from Social Science; nobody told him why he was studying oriental religions. If the school's courses are not making sense to someone as highly motivated as Mike, how must they be getting through to some of those who require more coaxing?

I am drawn by such evidence towards the conclusion that many pupils must be forced to evaluate their activities in school by some more intrinsic, rather than extrinsic, rationale. By this I mean that if pupils are unable to evaluate routine activities in school by reference to some philosophy encompassing an idea of relevance between those routine activities and 'the world outside', then they must evaluate them in the context of relationships to teachers and to each other, and in the context of their own preference for passing time. Perhaps an example will show what I am driving at.

Note-taking is an activity which some teachers include in their lessons. The meaning that teachers themselves give to note-taking may relate to views they hold about the need to store information for the future (perhaps in preparation for exams), or it may be concerned with beliefs the teacher has about the desirability of pupils practising written expression or even handwriting. There may even be one or two teachers who see it as a means of 'settling down' a class after some other activity. But if the teacher does not explain *his* reasons for the pupils' note-taking then I claim that they make sense of it by reference to the teacher's personality ('Oh, he likes to give notes') or to verbal or other cues that the teacher gives. For instance, if the teacher says, 'We've got five minutes left so let's take some notes on what we've just done, then it is quite possible that the pupils will deduce that the teacher himself sees note-taking as a means of filling time. In the absence, then, of any such cues from the teacher, as I have said, the pupils will evaluate activities like note-taking according to how they enjoy it as a way of passing time. This will probably depend on how proficient they are at writing, how much they like writing, whether or not there is the possibility of doing other things which might be curtailed or hindered by note-taking (e.g. looking out of the window) or the desire to occupy one's hands, and so on. This would provide one explanation of why some pupils develop attachments to activities which teachers rate as having little or no value (e.g. decorating the margin of pages of written work).

This leads me on to Phil and the subject of preferences for different activities. But first I would like to make, partly for contrast but also for genuine illustrative reasons, some general propositions about the way most teachers evaluate activities in school and especially in the classroom. It is probably fair to say that most teachers have as the basis of their practical organization some form of philosophy which incorporates notions about *learning*. Many teachers would say that learning is a long-term process, and therefore the pattern of daily activities must be set in the context of a period of time stretching across a number of years, and also that this pattern must be seen as deriving its meaning partly from the future goal of the educated child. Therefore, from day to day, it is probably necessary to achieve a balance between different activities such as, say, writing and discussion, in order that the final product of the educated child should itself be a well balanced compound.

Now, for Phil and others like him I maintain that activities are not evaluated on the basis of such future goals as much as on other criteria like enjoyment and whether the activity makes sense in the present. I am in no position to be confident or precise in my suggestions of these criteria, but what I will do is piece together ideas from Phil and from other people to try to show how some preferences are made. Here are some of Phil's ideas summarized.

1 Work is better than school because you have more responsibility and because you get paid.
2 Any school activity which takes you out of school is a good thing.
3 Going on trips to new distant places is better than going to local places which you have already visited on trips.

To this I will add Tony's comment [. . .] that the discussion activity is a good thing, being 'better than writing'. It is clear that the practical purposes behind such statements are different from those of most teachers. Using the above statements and others that I heard in school from pupils, I have made up a 'popularity table' of activities. As with my chart of 'teacher-tests' this does not aim to represent the views of any individual, although when I presented it to one group of fourth year pupils no-one disagreed with it substantially. The table starts with highly valued activities and proceeds to low:

1 Not being at school. (This is, strictly speaking, not one activity but a residual category taking in such things as weekends, evenings, part-time jobs, absence from school through sickness or truancy.)[7]
2 Going out on school trips: new places preferred.
3 Film shows in school, or other 'events'.
4 Classroom discussion
5 Listening to tapes in class.
6 Reading in class.
7 Writing in class.

This list is subject to modification at times, which affects the basic rating: each activity is rated as interesting or boring and this may cause a shift in preferences so that an interesting class discussion may be preferred to a boring film. Writing is not only bottom of the table but is also the only activity that is always referred to as 'work'. A distinction is commonly drawn between writing and talking, the former being work and the latter not work. This I believe is the basis of Ann's despairing: 'That means we'll have to *work!*' [. . .] when she thought she would be taken for Social Studies by Mrs. T. [. . .].

To get another comment on the preferences of activities in school we should look at the statements from Tony [. . .] concerning the fact that school is compulsory. This factor affects greatly how Tony sees the possibilities for choice within the school. He says:

> Tony: You've got to go to school. If I didn't come to this lesson, they'd have me down the House Head's room and everything . . . 'Why didn't you turn up?' . . . I can't say: 'I was bored'.

It is worth noting that in this dialogue the teacher does not accept Tony's distinction between work and school on the grounds of freedom (Tony says: 'you don't have to go to work, you can go on the dole or something like that'), though, literally speaking of course, he is quite correct: what other occasions are there in a person's life when they are compelled legally to take part in activities in this way for such lengths of time? For me, however, this is not the most significant factor in Tony's attitude. I would rather draw attention to the fact that he offers the compulsory nature of school as a reason for him to submit to all the procedures within school without much complaint. He says he cannot complain about the lessons. Throughout [. . .] the lesson [. . .] the teacher was trying to encourage critical comments about the processes within school, but with no success. Tony said that it was no use even going to another school, as one would only get the same lessons there. (Unknown to Tony,

the Social Science department was co-operating with the Social Science department
of a nearby school to produce printed resource material more economically for them
both to use!) This was, for me, one of the most apparent expressions of the gap
between teacher and pupil models. The teacher implies that changes can be made in
the school structure, that individuals can act to improve their circumstances. Tony,
on the other hand, says that you cannot change the school. I was frequently told by
pupils of occasions when they had tried to express some opinion about the running
of the school or tried to negotiate some improvement, only to have the attempt
defined as naughty behaviour by the staff. I also frequently heard staff complaining
to each other about the difficulties *they* experienced in getting the smallest thing in
the school changed.

John also made statements like Tony's about the compulsory nature of school and
I found one of them very worrying. It occurred in one of 4X's discussions about
Education where the teacher had been asking some points about the use of
Education to develop cultural values and national identity. The teacher had related
how the British had exported their own Education system as part of the process of
colonization during the British Empire, with the result that Africans in African
schools would be learning English constitutional history. The teacher asked, rather
rhetorically, what right the colonists had to do this and John replied as follows:

John: I hate school but I have to sit here and take it all, so I don't see why they shouldn't
        teach the Africans English history.

I have no doubt that most teachers would think it extremely distasteful that John
should see his own classroom experiences as being analogous to a process of
subjugation. I hope that they would also worry that the compulsory nature of school
might be helping develop attitudes of intolerance outside the school.

For John and Tony the fact of *having* to come to school seems to foster an attitude
of total rejection and undiscriminating criticism of what goes on in school. This
seems to be connected to the high rating given to any activity involving getting out
of school. At times I thought that John did not care about anything that went on in
school so long as it did not involve him, activities being rated according to how little
they impinged on him.

This brings me back to the word 'boring'. I think many teachers have difficulty
coping with the term as used by pupils. Aside from the tendency teachers have to see
the use of the word as implying a *personal* criticism of them, I think the main problem
is that teachers tend to evaluate their lessons according to the pedagogic content
while pupils, as I have said before, evaluate the lesson by other criteria which have
more to do with their own enjoyment. All very puzzling: if the Mikes of this world
say a lesson is boring, it may be because they don't understand what the content of
the lesson means; for the Phils it may be because they don't like writing; whereas the
Johns may say it because they hate school.

I wish now to look more closely at the use of the term 'work' and I shall make some
comparison between school and employment. I shall refer to them as 'schoolwork'
and 'jobwork'. Pupils quite frequently made comparisons between the two. Ann said
[. . .] 'I think you ought to get wages for coming to school' and John said [. . .] 'It
would be better if schools sort of taught you a trade'. From these and other
statements I suggest that some pupils think of school and jobwork in comparable
terms. I can set out the comparison as follows:

1   Their parents go to jobwork for a certain number of hours each day and the
    pupils go to school. In both cases it involves massing people together in specific
    places to perform common tasks.

2 The organization of time in schools and factories is similar in some respects: 'work' interspersed with shorter periods of 'free' time. The 'work' is usually less enjoyable than the free time.
3 The 'work' in both schools and factories involves the performance of routine activities which in both cases may be very repetitious and, insofar as it does not engage the individual's *own* preferred creative or recreative interests, it may be boring, especially in view of the length of time spent on it.

The Social Studies department of the school had prepared some material in work packs for a course on the sociology of work. These packs began with the information that the pack was about 'work'—not school work but *real* work, eight hours a day, five days a week . . . '. I maintain that for some pupils, like John and Tony, this is not seen as an important distinction between schoolwork and jobwork. Both are seen as similar as regards routine and boredom (though Phil did say that there was more responsibility at work, a belief which may be held by others). The *important* difference between school and jobwork is that the former is compulsory while the latter is not and that for jobwork you get paid money, an immediate reward for your activities, whereas in school you do not. Also, for many young people the entrance into work marks the change from childhood to manhood: *men* work.

It is not only in the Social Studies department that there are attempts to convey a definition of school which separates it from jobwork. In other schools I have often seen attempts to indicate to pupils that school is preferable to jobwork. Statements such as 'How do you think an employer would react to that sort of behaviour?' are made to show that a pupil has more freedom than an employee. But if the teachers in school fail to take note of the compulsory nature of school and its importance to pupils, then they will also fail to see that for some pupils an equally pertinent comment to the one above might be this one from a pupil: 'How do you think the workers would react to behaviour like *that* (from an employer)?' In addition to this, the school frequently contradicts itself about the alleged comparison with jobwork. In some contexts, usually when the staff demand adherence to some activity or standard of behaviour, it is stressed that school is work. One teacher in the Social Studies department would frequently chastise latecomers to school with a comment such as 'If I can get here on time why can't you?', which was frequently met with a reply from the pupil: 'But this is your job', to which the teacher would reply: 'It's *your* job as well'. Exit pupil mumbling, 'But you get paid for it'.

This sort of double-bind forms an authority trap which many schools fail to recognize. At home the pupils are under the authority of their parents who tell them they should go to school to 'work'. At school they have the *in loco parentis* authority presenting them with conflicting ideas about school and work, with power to compel them to accept certain forms of behaviour and certain activities. As the schools go about their business of developing patterns of behaviour which may be acceptable to employers, it is possible that they are creating real confusion in the minds of their pupils, or at least those who are open to this sort of persuasion. On the one hand school is contrasted favourably with jobwork, and yet the word 'work' is used to describe school activities rated most highly by the school [. . .].

References

Blishen, E. (1969) *Roaring Boys*, Hamish Hamillton.
Keddie, N. (1971) 'Classroom knowledge', in Young, M. F. D. (ed.) *Knowledge and Control*, Collier MacMillan.

13   The meaning of trouble

E. ROSSER AND R. HARRÉ

[. . .] Our participants fell into two sharply distinguished groups, from geographically distinct areas and having somewhat different ways of life. Those we call group A lived in a recently constructed industrial suburb of a middle-sized country town. Their parents worked in a very large factory where 'industrial relations' were bad. Many families in this suburb had emigrated from other parts of Britain but not usually in the lifetime of our participants. Without detailed sociological investigation, it is difficult to make sweeping statements about the parental society of group A participants, but we think it can be said safely that the result of the mixing of markedly different British sub-cultures was a fairly anomic and bland common sociality. Our participants attended a large comprehensive school, which had been built at the same time as their industrial suburb. The speech of our group A participants tended to a widespread use of glottal stops, of unstressed consonants and non-standard vowels, though only one spoke in a marked regional dialect. Most of them were not taking exams at the time of their discussion with us but they had made some attempt on the examination system in the past, at the CSE level, one having succeeded in as many as eight subjects.

Our second group, B, lived in a country town but one which had very little industry. They attended a new local comprehensive and were the first-year intake brought in to begin the school. The parents of our participants worked mostly in predominantly managerial jobs. Our participants' speech tended to be careful, with only a trace of local accent. They were much engaged in the taking of examinations, and over half had recently taken from six to nine O levels and the rest from three to seven CSEs. Unlike our group A participants, group B had well-articulated conceptions of future careers and the steps needed to achieve them.

For group A, neither school nor home were considered 'serious'; that is, people participating in these social places were not living fully in accordance with the official rhetoric for that type of institution. For most of these pupils, official tasks such as learning seem to involve highly conventional behaviour fulfilling a meaningless ritual. This is not just an arbitrary theory they have developed but is derived from their seeing themselves as having been written off. 'They [the teachers] sort of couldn't care less if you were going to leave at the end of the fourth year. All their time was spent on the ones that were going to stay on, so ones that were going to leave were never there and nobody sort of worried about them.' Several of these pupils clocked in at the beginning of the school day and then left. One even went off to work.

The more academically oriented group (group B), on the other hand, were more willing to accept the official school rhetoric. These pupils came largely from supportive families whose parents had primed them for success in school in general, and as a means to a professional career. 'I've been brought up to think that school-work comes first, you know, if you want to get anywhere.' In addition, this group experienced a school atmosphere close to their expressed ideal, and had the considered advantage of being the first-year intake in a new school. 'You got a lot of responsibility. A lot is expected of you but think there's more advantages than disadvantages. I think it encourages people. You want to achieve what people expect of you.'

Despite the differences between the two groups, their criticisms of school organization and atmosphere had much in common. Furthermore, both groups judged their teachers by reference to a similar set of criteria. To their way of thinking, classes were not disorderly and anarchic but rule-bound, and these are the same classes which teachers and journalists describe in terms of total chaos.

Our students shared a system of justification for what they did which involved two major components: the first, an elaborate categorization of occasions of offence, the second, some quite specific principles by which retribution for the offence was meted.

The first category of offence was rather vague. In the home it was widely referred to as 'getting on my nerves' (A) or 'going on' (B). For group A, that phrase was occasionally used in school, but much more frequently the pupils referred to the same category of generalized offence at school as 'being boring'.

The second category of offence involved more specific actions. We would identify them in our form of speech as 'forms of contempt'. A somewhat generalized offence which occurred in both home and school was recognized as 'treating me like a kid'. Group B seemed more fortunate in this respect, having teachers who did not offend so frequently. 'They [the teachers] speak to you as a person, not as a little kid as they do in junior school. They speak to you more like they would do at college, more like you're somebody . . . as if you know something. It builds your confidence.'

Another more specific form of contempt was being given teachers who for one reason or another were classified as 'a load of rubbish', 'useless'. Both groups agreed that poor teachers were those who 'treated teaching as a nine to five job, after that forget it. They don't pay any attention, do what they got to do and get out'; those who 'go on as if they were never young and did things we do'; those who 'feel it's below them to explain', or were unable to put the subject matter over well.

It was important to them to be recognized as persons each in their own right. It was thought to be deeply contemptuous to be treated as anonymous. 'If you're just another person in the classroom you don't get on half as well.' Not surprisingly, the failure of group A's headmaster to know their names was deeply resented. 'You can go in there and he'll say, oh yes, and try and think of your name. He doesn't know who you are but he'll say he knows you. He doesn't know any individual apart from the ones that are in there every day.' Group B said of their headmaster, 'He takes an interest in you, which helps.' We came to see that group B recognized in their teachers, and in their school situation as a whole, many of the qualities which group A found to be lacking in theirs.

One of the worst categories of offence was indecision or weakness of will by those they expected to be strong. Although both groups considered it 'natural to play the teachers up', this proposition was qualified by group B who felt that playing around was 'worse' in the third and fourth forms, 'not so bad in the fifth year', and that unruly pupils were 'not in the O level group'. For the O level people, and those who just wanted to work, mucking around was seen to be unfair both to them, because it held them back, and to the teachers; 'they seem to think they're there to punish the people. They're there to teach. If you don't want to listen, get out.' Playing up was also seen by group B to take a different, more subtle, form in the later years.

> 'It's more trying to get the better of him or her. I suppose it helps both, doesn't it really, because if you're trying to catch the teacher out that means you've got to know your lesson pretty well, because otherwise if you try to catch the teacher out and yet you've been proved wrong, you've had it really. For the teacher, it's quite easy to snap back at you, and the teacher's always on his guard.'

Both groups made it clear that the 'soft' teacher's offence was to provoke more playing up. 'The more meekly they reacted, the more we go on. Well, those that could stop us did so in the earlier years and we never played them up again. Those that didn't, that was it for them.' These young people found mere feebleness by those they expected to respect particularly offensive. Part of the explanation we think is that it is perceived as a way of not taking them seriously. For example, in the home, 'He's not like a father as you'd sort of think as a father . . . well, they're supposed to be protective aren't they. He couldn't care less what I do as I long as he knows where I am, I mean, you know, if I said I was going to an orgy, he'd say, oh allright, as long as I know where you are.' In the same way, teachers who the pupils felt should 'show they're the boss,' but were unable to do so, received rapid and at times violent retribution.

Equally, if not more offensive, acts were those where someone who had been feeble 'comes on strong' and then, when challenged, gives in. Examples of this form of insult appeared both at home and at school for group A, but only at school for group B, for whom parental discipline seemed to be more effective. In group A we have the father who, after conniving at a fifteen-year old daughter going out every night for eight consecutive weeks, tried to assert his authority. She answered back ('it's allright, I've got him under my thumb really') and he abandoned his position, giving her a pound for spending money. Or the soft teacher who attempted to assert her authority and was condemned, not for trying to be strong, but for being unsuccessful.

> 'She tried kicking me out of the classroom. I'd been mucking around. And none of my mates liked that. They just started getting mad with her and chucking blackboard rubbers, smashing up the lightbulbs and everything, and in the end she just went in to the store cupboard, crying her eyes out, and we locked her in'.

The offence of weakness on the part of teachers seems to be very much bound up with the pupils' own theories about the value of discipline. Not only did they disrespect parents and teachers for not meting out punishment when deserved, but it was clear that they wished for discipline in the structure of their everyday lives. Although group B expressed a great liking for the friendly relaxed atmosphere of their school, they were nevertheless critical that it was often too lax. This viewpoint was reinforced by the observations of those pupils who had attended grammar schools for a while and had found the 'stuffy' regimes, where 'you don't have any feelings towards somebody . . . where you have to sit in silence in neat rows' to be distasteful. Discipline to our people was seen to be essential. 'Well, if I do an essay, I like it to be marked. Whereas if the teachers just don't mark it, just give a comment, or just tick it, I tend to get lazy'. 'It's an unusual thing to say, but I think probably if it was stricter it'd get better results.' 'There's no discipline. Well, if there was people would learn something a bit more'. Both groups agreed overwhelmingly on the necessity to strike a balance between freedom and natural behaviour and complete rigidity in the classroom. 'You know you want someone who's pretty strict but who'll let you feel a bit free.' 'I think you've got to hit a medium where in the class it's not so strict. I mean silence doesn't help, but too much talk tends to hold you back.' A good teacher, in their view, 'is someone who'll take a good joke but will make us work', 'subtle control, everybody's happy and you don't realize you're getting the work done.'

A third category of offence is that of overt insult. Our pupils regard this category as very much less wounding, largely, we think, because in these offensive stances they are being treated as equals. These involve arguing, verbal insulting, and, in the case of group A, hitting.

Finally, there are offences of unfairness. Recognition of pupils as individuals was a major concern. A deeply wounding cause of offence involved a teacher or parent treating a student in a manner which suggested that he or she was the same sort of person as an older sibling who had either offended in some way or was being offered as a worthy model. 'Other teachers got it in for me because my brother [a trouble-maker] went there before me.' 'I'm a bit rowdy and I'm compared with him and that annoys me. He's done so and so, he's got so and so . . . and I, you know, feel as if, well, I'm not exactly thick, I think, I'm just that little bit lower. Well, when he did his exams he did O levels, whereas I'm doing CSE's.

Unfairness was also seen to stem from the helplessness of their position as children/pupils as opposed to parents/teachers, where, by definition, parents/teachers, hold ultimate authority. As such, pupils often felt themselves 'put down', trapped in their position.

> 'On my report they write that I'm a bit too chatty, that I talk too much to everybody, friends and teachers. One comment on it said, "I talk to the teacher, that is good." Well, I'm the one who gets everyone else going . . . it starts the discussion. And another comment said, "I tend to wear the teacher's patience talking." So I said to them, well, if I didn't talk you'd say I was withdrawn, and they didn't know how to answer that. It's true.

In the home we see this offence operating in the way parents make moral judgments for their children and dictate their choice of friends.

> 'I had a boyfriend . . . and my parents didn't like him, so they broke it off . . . the boy had come for a visit with his prospective second stepfather and my parents didn't like the boy, well, they liked him, but they didn't like his parents. Well, they thought they were lower class. They didn't like their background. D— had been in a home for children for three years. He [Dad] wrote to his stepfather and said he didn't want me to see D— again. I liked them.'

There are a number of principles of retribution which are used to explain the sorts of response which the offences bring forth. These fall into two broad categories: principles of 'reciprocity' and principles of 'equilibration'. A principle of reciprocity requires that one gives back whatever one has received, so that in a simple case of verbal insult one returns verbal insult or on being hit one hits back. As one girl put it, 'And if they turn nasty, well, we can turn nasty too.' Hitting as a form of interaction was largely unknown to group B both at home and at school.

In the second main form of reciprocity the reciprocal action does not take the same form as that insult. The phrase most commonly used for this by group A was 'storming out', but the reaction of walking out was shared by both sets and we have many accounts of such occasions; but because there is less freedom of action at school, this, unlike simple reciprocity, seems to be confined to home. Protection of self seems to be involved in walking out. Our people didn't want their parents to see they had been upset. 'Then if I want to feel upset, I'll go and feel upset somewhere where they can't see me.' 'Well, I try not to [show emotion] anyway, you know. You put on a good front as you might say, you know.'

In categorizing the occasions of offence, we emphasized the importance that the pupils attached to forms of contempt. But the principle of reciprocity is not applied in dealing with this kind of offence: they do not see themselves as returning contempt for contempt. The accounts seems to involve an equilibration; that is, when they feel themselves put down, treated without seriousness, they behave in such a way as to restore themselves as mature beings. This then defines the form of their response.

Over and over again we find that in talking about such an occasion they describe themselves as making a dignified or non-demeaning withdrawal into a silence. 'I just go quiet and that annoys them even more.' 'Yes, ignore them, I'm very good at that. I just switch myself off, play some Pink Floyd in my head, look at the ceiling.' 'I just wait until they've finished, you know. It just happens like an alarm, or something, and it's going to keep going until it's finished, and that's it. Might as well not have happened, you know.'

There are occasions when equilibration is achieved by some positive action. We see the girl who is indignant with her father 'for ever warning me about coming home pregnant' not only retaliating verbally, 'What do you think I am? Do you think I just stand on corners and wait for them to go past or something?', but also using her indignation to provoke his fury by pretending that the pain of a suspected ulcer is in fact a sign of pregnancy. 'Anyway it plays up now and again, and I goes, "Oh, my stomach" and I say, "Oh Dad, I'm pregnant." He goes up the wall.' Nevertheless, withdrawal, rather than positive action, seems to be the most frequent response, as they account for their lives, and the commonest means by which equilibration is achieved. This suggests that forms of contempt are perhaps the commonest readings which our people give to things which happen to them, and which they can attribute to the actions of others. It is not surprising, therefore, to find Tim Devlin quoting the teacher as saying, 'The worst thing they did was to ignore you completely.' Looking at it through their rhetoric, of course, they were not ignoring their teacher at all. From their point of view they were restoring a measure of dignity, conceived to have been taken from the, by withdrawal into injured or strategic silence.

Who are the arbiters of the propriety of social action? Both sets of participants, as might be expected, refer to their peers as the audience and critics before whom their dramatic performances are staged, and whose judgment they defer to. There is a faint hint, which we have been unable to follow up, of one or two members of each group having a special prominence in this regard. Peer arbitration is clearly described in the two following extracts:

'The situation demands it, I suppose. You can't very well sit there. You've got a whole class of thirty-five people sat round absolutely mucking about, chucking books, ripping up books, everything like that and the teacher stood out in the classroom writing a load of work down on the blackboard. You can't really work, so you've got the choice. You either stand up and walk out and go to a different class, or you join in. If you walk out of the class you get called all the names under the sun, "Cissy" and "Pouff" and all that crap, so you just join in . . . Anybody that works in a lesson that you doss about in, that you know you're going to doss about in, that's it, you get called "Ponce" and everything'.
'I'm what's generally known as a "creep' actually. But there are "creeps" and "creeps". J—, he's known generally just as a "swot". He is a "swot" so he takes that position. I'd be defined as someone who works hard but who can also fool around.'

But additionally, and given the enormous importance attached to the equilibration of dignity, it is not surprising to find a form of self-arbitration, where what they have done and said is judged by reference to their own conceptions of the integrity and dignity of themselves, regardless of 'popular' opinion, or the arbitration of specific others.

In one respect members of school A showed a marked difference in arbiters from members of school B. Parents and teachers count for nothing as arbiters in group A. Their judgments of propriety are scorned or ignored, and their good opinion is not sought. Group B, however, take parents' views of propriety fairly seriously, though they certainly do not take them as absolute in the arbitration of proper action and correct portrayal of character.

A typical group A reading of attempts at parental authority ran thus:

> 'Theirs is the old-fashioned style. Do everything by the book, the book's it and that, you know. That's life and you should go by that and there's no other way. But I want to live my life how *I* want to live it . . . My Dad keeps on how his life was hard and everything and I should have the same. It just gets on my nerves and I just get up and walk out and don't come back at all for two or three days.'

Relationships between group B people and authority were very different: 'I respect my parents because they respect me and I don't cause trouble or anything.'

And the clear acceptance of the parental standards by the speaker shows in:

> 'We don't row. We never row except when my brother's home. It's my mother and brother usually. They get on very well, but it's just that sometimes my brother gets on her nerves. She likes everything to be just so. She likes everybody to eat properly and not to make a noise. And he is very rowdy. He is a very rowdy, unruly person, and so Mum's always raising her voice at him.' (What about You?) 'Oh, it's easy to keep in line.'

And is equally clear in:

> 'When I was going out with a bloke, Mum said, "Be in by ten", and I thought, "Well, they've let me go out with this boy, why can't they let me have a bit longer, you know?" And of course if I came in late they said, "We'll chop it down.". So therefore, that way I think it's right because I've got to learn that I've got to come in at a certain time.

However, in certain circumstances the claim to at least an equal place in decision-making does emerge: 'Me? I'm a back-room lawyer in many respects. My sisters won't stand up for themselves. However, I do. I don't stand on any decision if it's unfair. I won't accept it.'

The accounts we have analysed so far are concerned with short-term cycles of offence, retribution and reciprocity. The orderly and rule-bound action-sequences whose structures we have revealed above are over in a matter of minutes. But both groups describe occasions of much longer term cycles of interaction. An adult moves a proposal of some sort, involving an offence of some kind. The long-term cycle involves four phases.

(i)   violent rejection of the proposal as *insulting or demeaning*.
(ii) arguing from some basis, constituted as rational for the occasion, against the proposal,
(iii) a withdrawal in the course of which the challenged persona is maintained according to a local convention (e.g. door slamming, head-tossing, etc., the fine structure of 'storming out'),
(iv) ignoring the offence because no resolution is possible: experience has told them that none of the reactions shown in the previous phases is in any way effective against a repetition of the offence.

We see this cycle in a description given by one boy as a result of his parents 'getting on at him'. At first he reacted.

> 'Violently . . . just generally went mad, strolled in and out when I wanted. Didn't work at home. Just walked in, dumped my stuff, got changed and walked straight out again. Cheeky and things like that.' (And after a while) 'Oh, I just played along then, let them think they was having a good time . . . Just let them get on with . . . They had upset me but they didn't realize it. They put me into stinking moods sometimes. I just don't care any more . . . They can do what they want. I'm never at home.'

The structure of the discussion phase (ii) is different in the two groups. As the dominant organizational theme of the discussion, group A report such matters as accusations, counter-accusations, castings of the other into demeaning categories and the like, while the *issue* is not addressed. Group B, on the other hand, report the second phase as dominated by rational criteria, and the issue is addressed seriously. A further empirical study should be made to reveal the conceptions of rationality involved, since we cannot take it for granted that they will be 'logical' in the strict sense. [. . .]

[. . .] On the basis of this study, we can offer some tentative suggestions about the 'problem of disorder in our schools'. Official explanations such as 'the decline of the family' do not seem to fit the 'reality' revealed in the speech of our participants very well. The central issue for them seems to be the unseriousness of the institution and its practices and the depersonalization and contempt meted out to those who see it as such. The clash between the effect of the unrealistic present school-leaving age, the available curricula and the school scene as viewed from within generates a 'trialectic' of contempt, depersonalization and reciprocal retaliation which underlies and is the meaning of 'disorder' from the viewpoint of our participants. The school itself, which is, after all, a comparatively new social invention, is officially construed according to a conception of disciplinary and academic relationships which is very hard to sustain against other and conflicting renderings. Something has to give. Perhaps the 'school' could become a community resource, where those who *seek* knowledge and skill could find it, regardless of age and official attainments. And the apprenticeships to violence, which our schools now offer as a major part of the informal curriculum, particularly to those whose physical maturity is denied by the official theory of schooling, could be eliminated from the real curriculum, by letting those who will go free.

14   Delinquents in schools: a test for the legitimacy of authority[1]

C. WERTHMAN

In the recent sociology on juvenile delinquents, the school is characterized as the major instrument and arena of villainy. Cloward and Ohlin suggest that lower class delinquents suffer from unequal 'access to educational facilities',[2] Cohen points to their 'failures in the classroom',[3] and Miller and Kvaraceus argue that a 'conflict of culture' between school administrators and lower-class students is precipitating delinquent behaviour.[4] Although there are many differences between contemporary sociological portraits of the lower-class juvenile delinquent, the same model of his educational problem is used by all authors. Regardless of whether the delinquent is ambitious and capable,[5] ambitious and incapable[6], or unambitious and incapable,[7] the school is sketched as a monolith of middle-class personnel against which he fares badly.

Yet data collected by observation and interviews over a two-year period on the educational performances and classroom experiences of lower-class gang members suggest that pitting middle-class schools against variations in the motivation and capacity of some lower-class boys is at best too simple and at worst incorrect as a model of the problems faced by the delinquents.

First, during middle adolescence when the law requires gang members to attend school, there seems to be no relationship between academic performance and 'trouble'. Gangs contain bright boys who do well, bright boys who do less well, dull boys who pass, dull boys who fail, and illiterates. To cite a single example, the grades of thirty 'core' members of a Negro gang, the Conquerors, were equally distributed in the sophomore and junior years of high school. Four of the gang members are illiterate (they cannot read, write, or spell the names of the streets they live on); twelve consistently receive Ds and Fs on their report cards; and fourteen consistently receive Cs or better. Four are on the honor roll. Yet all thirty were suspended at least once a semester during the tenth and eleventh grades, and the average number of suspensions received per semester was above two. There was a general tendency for the illiterate and dull boys to get into more trouble than the better students, but none of them was immune from difficulty. Twenty-two of these thirty regular members spent some time in jail during this period. Differences in access, success, and failure thus did not seem to have a determinate effect on 'trouble' in school—at least among the Conquerors.

Second, difficulties occur only in some classes and not others. Good and bad students alike are consistently able to get through half or more of their classes without friction. It is only in particular lessons with particular teachers that incidents leading to suspension flare up. This suggests that schools are not as monolithic as most contemporary sociologists have argued. Moreover, it suggests that something more specific about teachers than being 'middle class' produces problems, just as something more specific than being 'lower class' about gang members produces the response.

The problem

For events in high school classrooms to proceed smoothly, students must grant teachers some measure of authority. Although teachers are in a position to overlook a great deal of extra-curricular student activity in classrooms, they cannot ignore everything. Some modicum of order must be maintained if anything resembling a process of education is to take place. Most teachers thus find themselves in the position of having to act on definitions of improper behaviour and hope that students will stop. The authority of teachers is put to a test in this act of communication.

Authority becomes a stable basis for interaction only when those to whom commands are issued voluntarily obey.[8] Students in classrooms, like all parties judging claims to authority made by others, must therefore decide whether treatments received at the hands of teachers are based on grounds that can be considered legitimate.

Most students accept the authority of teachers to pass judgment on practically all behaviour that takes place in classrooms. The teacher is seen as a person who can pay legitimate official attention to everything that happens inside the physical confines of a school plant.[9] Since the authority of teachers is accepted at face value, most students can make sense of the specific actions teachers take towards them. Any specific action is interpreted as an instance in which this general rule is being applied.

This is why, for example, most students do not question the grades they receive. They accept the norm that teachers have the authority to grade them. This authority is more or less traditional. A report card signed by the teacher is accepted on much the same basis as are proclamations of war signed by kings. Neither are required by their subjects to give strict accounts of the decisions they make because the prerogative to make them has been granted in advance of the act.

Gang members understand the treatments they receive in no such way. They do not *a priori* accept the authority of any teacher. Final judgment on the conferral of legitimacy is suspended until it is discovered whether or not authority is being exercised on suitable grounds and in a suitable way. The burden of proof lies with the teacher.

Since teachers exercise authority in a variety of ways, becoming a 'delinquent' depends in large measure on whether these various claims are accepted. This is why gang members are frequently 'delinquent' in one class and ordinary students in the adjoining room. This paper analyses accounts of classroom situations in which gang members received unacceptable treatments, refused to recognize the authority of teachers, and were labelled 'delinquent'. These accounts are compared to classroom situations in which the treatments received were considered soundly based, the authority of teachers was accepted, and gang members remained ordinary students.[10]

Gang members make decisions to accept or reject the authority of teachers on the basis of four criteria. First, they evaluate the jurisdictional claims made by teachers. Some teachers not only insist on the physical presence of students but also expect a measure of intellectual and spiritual 'attention' as well. These teachers frequently take issue with behavior such as sleeping on desks, reading comic books, talking to neighbors, passing notes, gazing out of the window, turning around in chairs, chewing gum, and eating peanuts. Gang members do not *a priori* grant teachers the right to punish this behaviour although good reasons for ceasing these activities are often accepted.

Second, under no conditions can race, dress, hair styles and mental capacities receive legitimate official attention. Failures on the part of teachers to accept these rules of irrelevance often contribute to denial of authority.[11]

Third, gang members are extremely sensitive to the style in which authority is exercised. The frequent and consistent use of the imperative is perceived as an insult to the status and autonomy of those to whom this form of address is directed. Teachers who 'request' conformity are more likely to achieve desired results.

Ultimately, however, the decision to accept or reject the authority of teachers is made on the basis of a weightier concern. Teachers who consistently violate conceptions of proper jurisdiction, irrelevance rules, and modes of address will not find gang members particularly co-operative architects of authority. But the grounds on which teachers make their formal and semi-public evaluations of students tell a more important tale. Grades can be based on a number of criteria, not all of which gang members find legitimate. Moreover, the fact that they get a grade tells them nothing about the basis on which the judgment was made. They must discover the general rule used by particular teachers to assign grades with only a single application of the rule to go on.

Gang members thus find themselves in a rather serious bind. They *must* figure out the general basis on which teachers are assigning grades because their future behaviour depends on what they discover. They cannot walk away from the claims made by teachers to possess authority.

Hypotheses

Their task, however, is not hopeless. Gang members do know *something* about the basis on which a grade might have been assigned. In fact, given what they know about their situation, they reduce the rules teachers might be using to four.

First, the grades might be given out fairly. Although as a rule gang members have no idea how much knowledge they possess relative to other students, they have a general idea of how 'smart' they are relative to others. They judge the intelligence of the boys and girls they know personally, and they estimate the intelligence of strangers from the contributions they make in class. They thus generate a set of expected frequencies on the basis of the hypothesis that bright boys will do better than dull boys.

(Is there any relationship between getting into trouble in school and getting good grades?) Naw. Take likes Charles. He in my classes. He bad outside, and he doing well in school. There ain't no difference. Let's put it like this. Friday, Saturday, Sunday, that's the nights for fucking, drinking, driving, fighting, killing, doing the shit you want to do. There's a lot of guys like Charles in my classes that gets A's on their report cards in school, but when they on the outside, the hell, they bad! They crazy! Dice, drink, shoot people. (How about the ex-President of the Club? How does he do in your classes?) Johnny's smart. Johnny's got a good brain. He doing good. Everytime I see Johnny, he always got his books. He goes to the bathroom—smokes cigarettes and shoots dice like all of us—but you don't see that man cutting no classes. I swear to God, I think he really got a swell mental brain. (How about the rest of the club?) It just that some people lazier than others. Just like Donald. He in my classes. I ain't got no more brains than that man. I may know a little more than he do from the past things, but as far as class is related and all, I don't know no more than him. The class is just as new to me as it is to him. Now if I can pass that class, he can pass that class. He didn't pass this time. He flunked. He got a F. He got a F in all his classes. I passes those classes with flying colors, with a C. That's average. I always get average grades. I don't look for no A's and B's. (Do you think you could get A's if you tried?) I doubt it. I don't see racking my brains to death to get no A on no paper. Cause I feel like a A ain't nothing. A C will get you just as far. I mean truthfully I think the highest grade I could ever get was a D. (How about Carson?) He's not smart. He dumb. I mean he goofy. He just ain't got it up here, period. We gonna get kicked out. (What for?) Fighting, gamblin, cutting classes, nasty attitude. (How about the guys who don't get in trouble. How do they do?) Just like us. Some of them smart, some of them stupid. I mean there's a couple dudes in my classes that's born to be somebody, people with straight A's like Johnny, and then there's the real stupid ones. They just sit there all quiet, get to class on time, never gamble, smoke or nothing and they flunk. You might say we got smart ones and they got smart ones just like we got average ones and they got average ones and we got dumb ones and they got dumb ones. Everybody born on this earth ain't got the same brains.

Second, their response to the presumed authority of the teacher may enter into the grade they receive. They are conscious that the grade is a source of power, and they understand that it may be used as a weapon against them. When teachers use grades as sanctions in this way, gang members perceive it as discrimination. On the basis of the behavior observed in class, gang members divide their fellow students into those who *a priori* take as legitimate the claims to authority made by teachers and those who do not. (As a rule, the latter category is filled with friends.) Expected frequences are thus generated under this condition also. The distinction between scientists and sell-outs lies at the heart of what gang members consider the essential difference between their kind of person and 'squares'.

There's some teachers that treats everybody differently. He always get wise with the studs that ain't gonna take no shit, and they real nice to the people that just sit there, the people that kiss ass behind him. He give the good grades to the ass-kissers and he give us bad grades cause we aint't gonna suck up to him. (Are there many kids in class who kiss up to teachers?) Yeah. There's enough. Like this one girl, she's kiss behind everybody, and the President of the school! He'll eat you if you ask him to! The bad teachers give the kiss-asses good grades and make us eat shit. They always looking for the ones that run errands, shit like that. (What kind of people are the ass-kissers? Do they wear any special kind of clothes?) Some of them come looking like a farmer or something. Jeans. Or maybe they wear a tie or something. They not like us. We come to have a good time in school as well as sometimes learn something. Some of those boys don't even enjoy parties and things like that. They allergic to girls. They just poopbutts.

The third dimension that may affect a grade is the amount of power possessed by particular students. The sources of this power stem from the possibilities of physical assault on teachers and an ability to keep a class in constant turmoil. Delinquents thus hypothesize that teachers may award grades on this basis. The boys define this possibility as 'bribery'.

(Are there any teachers who give you good grades because they are afraid of you?) Yeah. Like Mr F. He say, 'Aw, come on, why don't you give us a break or something.' And all the lady teachers, I won't let them go with nothing. Like these teachers say, 'You do me a favor and I do you one. You straighten up in class and I'll make your grade better.' Shit like that. If you control that class, you gonna get a good grade. They afraid of you or they want you to stop fucking up the class. I control a lot of those classes. (What do you do when the teacher tries to make a deal with you?) I don't take shit. That way they gotta keep giving me a good grade. They try to con me, but I ain't going for it. Like that stud that kicked me out of class yesterday? He tell me, 'Come on, why don't you be a good guy? I'll give you a good grade if you be quiet. Why don't you go on and give me a break?' I said, 'I sure will, right on your neck!' When you get a good grade, sometimes you know the teacher is afraid of you. That's why he give it to you.

The final alternative is that grades are randomly distributed. This is a distinct possibility in large classes such as gym where teachers cannot possibly interact personally with all participants. Some students become visible of course, either as athletes, delinquents or 'flunkies'. But it is quite possible for a particular boy to be graded on the basis of the way his name happens to strike the teacher when he sees it printed on the report card.

> When I think I deserve a C and I get a D? That's when I'm gonna bitch. I'm really gonna have something to say about it. Cause when I feel like I got a better grade? And get something lower? I feel like that teacher either prejudiced or he just, you know, he just don't give a damn. He just go down, read your name and everybodies' name, and go A, B, C,—A, B, C. He get to a special name. 'Well, I don't like this fellow, I'll give him a C. I don't like him. I'll give him a D.' You know, so on and so on. Shit. That's like they do in gym, seem like to me. Every damn time it seem like my report card came up to be a C. I don't mind a C if I have to get it, but I seen the gym teacher, you know, in the office. They have a whole stack of report cards. Now how a gym teacher gonna look at your name and go straight down the line, just put a grade on? Like he going A, B, C,—A, B, C. And he just throw them away! And if he run across a name he know real good? Somebody that, you know, real tight with him? Go out for all the sports? You know, he flunky for him. Work around the gym. Shit like that. You know you gonna give him a B or something. Somebody that deserve a B, he gonna give a C or D. All kinda shit like that.

Thus before grades are handed down, gang members construct four alternative hypotheses or rules about the basis on which teachers evaluate them. Given what they know about the student population being graded, they make predictions about how fellow class members will be marked under three of the four alternative conditions. They know that the grade they receive will be a single case of one of these four classes of rules, but the single grade they receive will not tell them *which* rule the teacher is using. Their problem is to discover it.

Methods

As soon as the grade is handed down, gang members behave like good social scientists. They draw a sample, ask it questions, and compare the results with those predicted under alternative hypotheses. The unit of analysis is a *set* of relevant grades. The one received by a particular student is only a single member. No interpretation of a grade can be made before the others are looked at.

The sample is not selected randomly from the class. The class contains types of students constructed from the knowledge on which the predictions were based. Gang members thus divide the class into four basic sub-groups: bright students who recognize the authority of teachers; duller students who recognize the authority of teachers; bright students withholding judgment about teachers; and dull students withholding judgment about teachers. The latter two types are like himself. They are his friends. If the gang member conducting the inquiry possesses power, this dimension will also be of concern.

As soon as the grades are delivered to the students in class, representatives of all types are sampled. First, gang members typically ask their friends what they received, and then others in the rest of the class are interviewed. Most of the 'poopbutts', 'sissies' or 'squares' will usually show a gang member their report card. Refusals to reveal grades are often dealt with sharply.

> (How do you know how the teacher is grading you?) Sometimes you don't man. You don't know whether the stud bribing you with a grade, whether he giving you a bad one cause you don't kiss behind him, or whether he straight. Or maybe he like the gym teachers that give out the grades any which-way. (But how do find out what basis the

teacher is using?) Well, you gotta ask around the class. Find out what other kids got. Like when I get my report card? I shoot out and ask my partners what they got. Then I go ask the poopbutts what they got. (Do they always let you look at their report cards?) They can't do nothing but go for it. Like they got to go home sometime. I mean we shoot them with a left and a right if they don't come across. I mean this grade shit is important. You gotta know what's happening. (Why?) Well, shit, how you gonna know what the teacher like? I mean if he straight or not.

After the grades have been collected, the process of analysing data begins. Final conclusions can be reached at this point, however, only if the teacher has previously provided an account of the grounds being used to grade. Some teachers voluntarily provide these accounts and others do not. Although there is considerable variation in this behavior among teachers, the variation is not random. Teachers who believe that their authority in the classroom should be accepted *a priori* are less likely to volunteer the basis of which they judge students. In fact they are less likely to offer explanations of any action they take. Claims to authority are often demonstrated by not having to account for all decisions made.

On the other hand, some teachers are careful to make visible at all times the basis on which they grade. These teachers understand that they have certain students who will not accept authority in advance of proof that it is being legitimately exercised.

(What made this teacher fair?) He'd give the class an equal chance to be graded. Like he'd say, 'How'd you like to be graded on this? Class average, individual, or what?' And you know, let's say half the class want to be graded on class average and the other half on individual. He just take the group out like that, you know, and he would grade you as such if that's the way you want to be graded. I mean I felt that the teacher real fair. See, after the first report card, after he see the grades wasn't too good? He asked us how we would like him to grade, and what we would like him to do. (The grades from the first report weren't very good?) No, they weren't so hot. Cause, you know, he wanted to see how his approach did and how we would react to it. Anyway, the results wasn't so hot. Anyway, he gave us a choice. So I felt that was helping them, helping me, and that he seemed fair.

In addition, teachers who attempt to bribe certain students will also signal the basis on which they behave in advance of the grade. If a gang member receives a better grade than the one he expected relative to other students, he suspects a 'con'. He thus reviews his previous relationship with the teacher. If the teacher has offered him a good grade in return for good behavior, he has sufficient grounds to conclude that the grade he received was based on his power to control the class.

(How do you know when you get a good grade whether you deserved it or whether the teacher is trying to buy you off?) When they tell you personally. You know, we was in the class by ourself when they told me I could get a good grade if I stop being a troublemaker. Like Mrs C. Like in class she told the whole class, 'If you be quiet you get a good grade!' You know, everybody get a C or something on their report card. But she told me privately, I guess maybe cause I was such a troublemaker. When I see what everybody else got? And I see that they all fail or get something else? I know I got the grade cause I control the class.

Similarly, if the teacher has recently left him alone in class regardless of what he has done, he concludes that the teacher is afraid of him. In this case also he thinks that the teacher is trying to buy control.

(How do you know when you get a good grade because the teacher is afraid of you?) After you ask around the class, you know, you see everybody that shoulda done bad done bad and shit like that. and you got a good grade? Well, sometimes that teacher just leave you alone. I mean you be talking and everything and they won't say nothing. Then you know he afraid of you and he afraid you'll fire on him [slug him] if you get a bad grade.

If teachers provide the rules used to grade students in advance of the grading period, regardless of whether they are using fair criteria, bribing, or discriminating, gang members do not need to request information in order to find out what is going on. As soon as they receive their grade and compare it to others, they 'know what's happening'.

But if gang members need more information to discover the rule being used and it has not been provided in advance of the marking period, they will go to the teacher and ask for an account of the grade they received. This event typically takes place a day or two after report cards have been handed out.

If a gang member is given a grade he thinks he deserves relative to others, he suspects that the grades have been awarded fairly. But his suspicions are based only on the perceived relationship between grades and mental capacity. He can only confirm his suspicions by checking with the teacher. Moreover, if the gang member suspects that the grade is fair, his request to have the grade explained is uniformly polite.

The teacher's response to a request is crucial information to the gang member. If he receives an account of his grade and the account is at all reasonable, he concludes that the teacher is grading fairly. The very fact that the teacher provides a reason at all predisposes him to conclude that the criteria being used to pass and fail students are on the 'up and up'.

> After we got our compositions back I went up to him you know. I asked him about my composition. I got a D over F and I ask him what I did wrong. He told me that he could tell by the way I write that I could do better than what I did. And he explained it to me, and he showed me what I need to improve. And he showed me, if I correct my paper, I would get a D, a straight D instead of that F. O.K. And I got the D for half the work. But anyway he showed me how I could get a regular D and pass his class. I mean I feel that teacher was helping me. I mean he was showing me a way I could pass the class and how he was grading everybody. I mean the way he explained everything to me, I knew he was straight, that he was grading fairly.

Similarly, if a gang member receives a lower grade than expected, he suspects that teachers are using grades as a weapon to award those who accept their authority and punish those who reject it. Again, he can come to no final conclusions about the rule being used to give grades until he checks with the teacher.

If the gang member feels there is a possibility he is being discriminated against, he *demands* an account of the grade. He typically asks, 'What the *hell* did I get this for?' Moreover, since each gang member is in a slightly different position with respect to mental capacity and power, they all approach the teacher alone instead of in groups, even though they compare notes carefully after the encounter has passed.

> See, me and that man, we always be fighting. Maybe because of my attitude. See, a lot of teachers grade you on your attitude toward them and not your work. And like sometimes you be talking, you know, and he say, 'Why don't you hush! Shut up! I told you once or twice already not to be saying that in class!' Everybody else be talking. He say, 'Trying to get smart with me?' 'No', I say, 'I ain't trying to get smart with you.' He say, 'What are you trying to do? Start an argument?' And you know, I get tired of copping pleas. 'Hell yeah I'm trying to start an argument!' So he say, 'If you keep fooling around I'm going to lower your grade.' On the report card, the dude give me a D. I told that son of a bitch today, I know damn well my work better than a D! Cause all my tests have been C's, you know, and everybody else getting a C. I'm hip to shit like that, man. Then he gonna tell me, 'Well, I grade on the notes and the homework more than I do the

tests.' I say, 'Well, what kind of a teacher are you? What bull shit you got on your mind?' I cussing at him all the time. That man don't move me! He bore me! He get on my damn nerves! He look up at me. 'You trying to start a fight?' I say, 'I'm gonna start the biggest fight you ever seen! I want my grade changed!' And he say, 'Why don't you go sit down?' 'No man, I ain't gonna sit down till you straighten my grade out! You show me my grade in the book and I show you. I know I got a C!' And he just say, 'Go on and sit down before I call the boys' dean to come up here and get you.' I say to myself, 'I can't get suspended no more. If I gets suspended again, I fucked. I never will pass.' So I went and sit down. That nasty ass motherfucker just don't like bloods.

If a gang member receives a bad grade and finds the teacher frightened and apologetic, he concludes that grades have been awarded randomly. The gang member reasons that if the teacher is frightened during the encounter and grades had not been given randomly, he probably would have received a better one.

Like my gym teacher today. That fucking freak! F? Aw hell no! Nobody get no F in gym. And I stripped every day! My gym suit wasn't clean every Monday. That's just three points minus. All right. Six weeks times three is eighteen. Right? Eighteen points minus out of a hundred. How the hell you gonna get a F?. And I stripped every day. All right then. So I went in there and told Mr C. I say, 'Now look here, the man gave me a F! I stripped every day. My gym suit wasn't clean every Monday. I took a shower after class every day. Now why I get a F?' He looked in the book. 'Oh, I guess he made a mistake. I'm not sure cause I wasn't with you all during the six weeks so I give you a D.' So I say, 'Look man, I don't think a D's fair either. I think I ought to get a B or C just like everyone else.' 'Well, I'll give you a D and you'll get a better grade next time.' All the time I was talking to him he had his head in a book, and when he looked up it seemed like you could see in his eyes that he was almost scared. You know. Didn't want to say too much. It seem like almost everything you say, he agrees with you and make you look like a ass. 'Yeah. Yeah. That's right, that's right.' Stuff like that. And you know that some of the things you be saying you know is wrong. You'd be expecting him to say, 'No, that's wrong.' You know. And he'd be agreeing with everything you say. He just say, 'Well, do things right next time and I'll go on and give you a better grade.' Something like that. Then he say, 'I sorry.' He apologize to you. Shit like that. That's how you know a teacher is scared of you, and if he scared of you, he going to give you a better grade than you deserve, not a worse one! That gym man! They don't know what they give you. They just hand them out as they come up. I finally say, 'O.K. Fuck it!' You know. I didn't want no F so I took the D. And I say, 'Well look here, man, I hope to hell I don't have your stupid ass for a gym teacher next term!'

If he is dealing with a teacher who believes it is not necessary and in fact demeaning to explain decisions to students, the gang member may receive no answer at all. His search is then frustrated, and he has been directly insulted. This frustration and anger is typically reflected in loud and obscene outbursts directed at the teacher. This is a 'classic' scene in the folklore of a delinquent gang. After blowing up at the teacher and storming from the classroom, he comes to the conclusion that he is being discriminated against, regardless of whether or not this is in fact true.

(How did Tyrone get kicked out of school?) Putting down the teachers. He didn't feel that he was given adequate grades for a term paper or work that he had passed in. He went up and told the teacher to get fucked. She went up to the Dean of Boys, and he tell Tyrone that he'd have to let him go. (Were you in his class?) Yeah. (Did you see him tell off the teacher?) Yeah. I was standing right behind him. (What happened?) Well, see we get these papers back and Tyrone, he start asking everybody what they got. So he go up to this one stud, Art, and he say, 'You see Mrs G., that bitch, she gave me a F. What's the story?' Art say, 'She gave me a passing grade.' Tyrone say, 'Shit. You don't do a damn thing. How come you pass and I don't?' Art say, 'I don't know man. Maybe she don't like you.' So Tyrone goes up to her. He said, 'What the hell's going on here? Why I get that F? I felt the answer to this question was right! I think it's right!' She said, 'Well, no, it

isn't. I'm sorry.' He say, "Why ain't it right?' She say, 'I corrected it the way I saw fit.' He
say, 'Well shit! Why ain't it right?' She say, 'Uh, would you stop using so much profound
(*sic*) language. I'll have to tell the Dean.' He say, "Tell the fucking Dean! He ain't nobody!
Aw fuck you!' She told the Dean, and the Dean kicked him out.

It is important to point out that not all gang members are able to learn something
about the rules teachers use to grade by using this procedure. The illiterates or
relatively dull students who expect F's even under the fair condition, and the bright
gang members who expect As and Bs, are in a further bind. The F students cannot
distinguish between the fair case and the case of discrimination, and the A student
cannot distinguish between the fair case and the case of being 'bribed'. Unlike the F
student, however, the A student will be particularly sensitive to discrimination.
Gang members who fall in these two categories use other grounds to decide
whether or not to co-operate with teachers. The procedure being discussed here
thus works best for average students, those who can learn something by receiving
As and Fs. Most boys, including gang members, however, fall into this category—at
least while they are attending school.

Conclusions

Once gang members have either requested or demanded accounts from teachers,
they have all the materials needed to come to a conclusion. The accounts that
teachers give or fail to give furnish warranted grounds for understanding one
aspect of what goes on in the classroom. The gang member has discovered the class
or rule being used to grade and thus can understand the single grade he received.
Once having discovered the rule, however, he then faces the question of what to do
about it. It is in the decisions he makes about his future course of action that we
discover the essence of the delinquent.

If he concludes that he is being either discriminated against, bribed, or treated
randomly, he does not modify his behavior. Even though he becomes aware that
'kissing ass' will get him a better grade, he does not avail himself of the technique. He
is prevented by his sense of morality. The tactic is considered illegitimate. After all,
he reasons, 'If I go for that shit I might as well stick to the streets and pull some big-
time action!'

(So you know your attitude toward the teacher gets you bad grades sometimes?)
Yeah, sometimes it does. (Why don't you change your attitude?) I wouldn't
go kiss up to them motherfucking teachers for nothing! Shit! They prejudiced
or they gonna hit you over the head with that fucking grade so you gonna kiss up to
them? Well no! We supposed to be graded on what we know. Right? Ain't that supposed
to be how it is? Damn teachers are something. I tell you they ain't got shit but a racket
going, man. Motherfuckers get down there and kiss them God damn principals' asses,
the bosses asses. That's the last motherfucking thing I do! I wouldn't go kiss that damn
horse's ass for nothing! I wouldn't do shit for that man. If I go running over there, I'm
gonna feel funny. Cause I'm always getting in trouble. What if I go running over there
and ask him, 'Look man, why don't you help me out in gym. Tell this man to kinda
lighten up on me cause he kinda fucking my grades around. I ain't for all this shit. I know
I'm doing right.' You know. Shit like that. He gonna say, 'Lee, you always want favors,
but you never want to do nothing in return. You're always messing up in class.' And
this and that and the other shit. I'd rather be raped, man. If I go for that shit I might as
well stick to the streets and pull some big time action! Shit! If I gonna be corrupt? If I
gonna get me a racket going like that, shit, I ain't gonna waste my time sucking up to no
teachers! I gonna pull some big time shit.

Practical applications

How do gang members act in classroom once they decide that a teacher's claims to authority are illegitimate?

While gang members remain in school, either before graduating or before being kicked out, they do not comply with the grounds teachers use to treat them. This fact explains much of their delinquency in the classroom. If they feel that a teacher is discriminating against them because his claims to authority are not being granted, they are careful to avoid all behavior that implicity or explicitly recognizes this authority. Raising a hand in class, for example, is a gesture used by students to present themselves as candidates for speaking. Implicit in the gesture is an understanding that the student may not be called on. The gesture implies further that the teacher has the authority to grant speaking privileges in class. If a student raises his hand, he thus implicitly makes the authority of the teacher legitimate. This is why gang members refuse to raise their hands in some classes and prefer interjecting comments without being recognized. This behaviour would no doubt be treated by some theorists as a rude and unruly by-product of 'lower-class culture'. Lower-class or not, the behavior has its reasons.

> I'm not the quiet type in that class [California history]. Like when we're having a discussion or something? I don't go for all that raising your hand. Cause everybody else on the other side of the room might—while the teacher asking you a question?—well the one that just went by, people probably still discussing it. And you might want to get in on that. And you just come on out and say something, and he tell you to get out of class. Well that shit ain't no good, man. So you know that kinda get on my nerves. But I don't mind getting kicked out of class. That ain't no big thing. I feel like—that class I got now?—if I try hard I can pass. My citizenship may not be worth a damn, but I can pass the class. (Do you always forget to raise your hand?) Hell no! I raise my hand in Civics and some of the other classes. That's interesting. But California history ain't shit. It's easy. It's simple. It's just that teacher. He a punk! He just ain't used to us. He just don't understand bloods [Negroes]. I don't raise my hand for that freak! I just tell the dude what's on my mind.

The time and circumstances that surround entering and leaving class also have implications for the implicit acceptance or rejection of authority. If a student consistently comes to class on time, he implicitly gives teachers ground to assume that he accepts both their authority and the legitimacy of school rules. This is why gang members frequently make it a point to arrive five minutes late to class. It is no accident that gang members are suspended most frequently for tardiness. Not only is tardiness an affront to the authority of teachers but it also flaunts the claims to authority made by the school system as a whole.

> We came in late to class today because he threatened us. He see us between fifth and sixth period when he was supposed to be going to one class and coming from another. We was on our way to his class. I was standing by my locker. My locker right next to his class. So he come up to me and say, 'Lee, you tell Wilson that if you two come late to class I'm gonna get you both kicked out of school.'
> So I went and told Bill, and we made it our business to be late. We walked in about five minutes late. Knocked on the door. He opened the door. Just went in and sat down. I looked him in the eye. Would have put a ring around it if he'd said too much. The door comes in through the back. We made a little bit of noise sitting down to make sure he see us. We giggled and laughed a little bit to make sure he noticed we were there. We try to remind him that he supposed to kick us out. It was almost to the end of the period before he kicked us out.

Gang members also have the choice of leaving class before the bell is rung, when the bell is ringing, or when the class is formally dismissed by the teacher. When they occasionally leave class before the bell is rung, they flaunt the authority of both the teacher and the school.

> (What do you do when you discover that the teacher has been grading you unfairly?) Lots of times we just get up and walk out. Like you say, 'Oh man, I'm tired of this class.' You just jump up and walk out and shut the door. (What do the teachers do?) Mostly they just look at us and then resume with the rest of the class and don't say nothing. (Why don't they report you?) I guess they be glad for us to be out of their class.

More frequently, however, they wait until the bell rings to leave class instead of waiting for a sign of dismissal from the teacher. This act implicitly accepts the authority of the school while explicitly rejecting the authority of the teacher. When this happens teachers who feel they have authority to protect often take action.

> After class, as soon as the bell rang, everybody jumped up. The teacher said, 'Everybody sit back down! You're not leaving right now!' So Alice jumped up. She starts walking out.
> He say, 'Alice, go sit down!'
> Alice say, 'Who the hell you talking to! I'm tired of school. I'm going home!'
> She walked to the door. He grabbed her. She looked at him. 'I'm gonna count to three, and if you don't get you hands off me . . . No, I ain't even gonna count! Take your hands off me!'
> He took his hands off. He say, 'We're going to the office this minute!'
> She say, 'You going to the office by yourself unless you get somebody else to go down there with you!'
> And so she walked away. So she was down talking to some other girls, and he say, 'Alice, would you please come!'
> She say, 'No! And stop bugging me! Now get out of here!'
> I didn't see all of the argument. I just went off and left. When I passed him I said, 'Man, you ain't nothing!'
> He looked at me. Then he say, 'One of these days you gonna get yours.'

In addition, gang members are careful never to use forms of address that suggest deference. 'Yes Sir' and 'No Sir' are thus self-consciously stricken from the vocabulary.

> And you know like in some classes the teacher tell you don't say 'Yes' and 'No'. It's 'Yes Sir' and 'No Sir'. They would have to whip my ass to make me say that. I don't go for it. Shit. They don't call me Mr Lee! Teacher once tried to tell me to say, 'Yes M'am'. I say, 'All right you call me Mr Lee.' I don't like it. I feel if I did, I'd probably feel funny saying 'Yes Sir' and 'No Sir' to somebody. (How would you feel?) I'd feel like I was a little old punk or something.

But of all the techniques used by gang members to communicate rejection of authority, by far the most subtle and most annoying to teachers is demeanor. Both white and Negro gang members have developed a uniform and highly stylized complex of body movements that communicate a casual and disdainful aloofness to anyone making normative claims on their behavior. The complex is referred to by a gang member as 'looking cool', and it is part of a repertoire of stances that include 'looking bad' and 'looking tore down'. The essential ingredients of 'looking cool' are a walking pace that is a little too slow for the occasion, a straight back, shoulders slightly stooped, hands in pockets, and eyes that carefully avert any party to the interaction. There are also clothing aides which enhance the effect such as boot or shoe taps and a hat if the scene takes place indoors.

This stance can trigger an incident if a teacher reacts to it, but it is the teacher who must make the first overt move. The beauty of the posture resides in its being both concrete and diffuse. Teachers do not miss it, but they have a great deal of difficulty finding anything specific to attack. Even the mightiest of educators feels embarrassed telling high school students to 'stand up straight'. As the following episode suggests, teachers typically find some other issue on which to vent their disapproval.

The first day I came to school I was late to class so this teacher got smart with me. He didn't know me by name. See a lot of people have to go by the office and see what class they in or something. Like there was a lot of new people there. So you know I was fooling around cause I know nothing happen to you if you late. Cause all you tell them, you tell them you got the program mixed or something.

When I came into the class you know I heard a lot of hollering and stuff. Mr H. was in the class too. He's a teacher, see. I guess he had a student teacher or something, you know, because he was getting his papers and stuff. So Mr H. went out. Well this new teacher probably wonder if he gonna be able to get along with me or something. Cause when I came in the class, you know, everybody just got quiet. Cause the class was kinda loud. When I walked in the class go quiet all of a sudden. Like they thought the Principal was coming in or something.

So I walk into class and everybody look up. That's natural, you know, when somebody walk into class. People gonna look up at you. They gonna see who it is coming in or something. So I stopped. You know, like this. Looked around. See if there was any new faces. Then a girl named Diane, she say, 'Hey Ray!' You know, when I walk into class they start calling me and stuff. They start hollering at me.

I just smile and walk on. You know. I had my hands in my pocket or something cause I didn't have no books and I just walk into class with my hands in my pockets a lot of times. I mean I have to walk where I can relax. I'm not going to walk with my back straight. I mean you know I relax. (What were you wearing?) About what I got on now. I had a pair of black slacks and a shirt on but they weren't real high boots. They came up to about here.

Then I looked over at the teacher. I see we had a new teacher. He was standing in front of the desks working on some papers and doing something. He looked at me. I mean you enter by the front of the classroom so when you walk into the classroom he's standing right there. You gotta walk in front of him to get to the seats. So then I went to sit down. Soon as I passed his desk he say, 'Just go sit down.' Just like that. So I stop. I turn around and look at him, then I went and sat down. (What kind of look did you give him?) You might say I gave him a hard look. I thought you know he might say something else. Cause that same day he came he got to hollering at people and stuff. I don't like people to holler at me. He was short, you know, about medium build. He might be able to do a little bit. So I say to myself, 'I better sit down and meditate a little bit.'

So I went and sat down. I sat in the last row in the last seat. Then he say, 'Come sit up closer.' So I scoot up another chair or two. Then he tell me to come sit up in the front. So I sat up there. Then you know a lot of people was talking. A lot of people begin telling me that he be getting smart all day. You know Studdy? He a big square but he pretty nice. He told me how the teacher was. And Angela start telling me about how he try to get smart with her. He say, 'This is where you don't pick out no boy friend. You come and get your education.' I mean just cause you talk to a boy, that don't mean you be scheming on them or nothing. It just that you want to be friends with people.

Then he say something like, 'You two shut up or I'll throw you out on your ear.' So he told me he'd throw me out.

So I say, 'The best thing you can do is ask me to leave and don't tell me. You'll get your damn ass kicked off if you keep messing!'

Then he told me to move over on the other side. See I was talking to everybody so he told me to move away from everybody. And so I moved to the other side. He told me to move three times! I had to move three times! And then he got to arguing at somebody else. I think at somebody else that came in the class. You know, a new person. So while he was talking to them, I left out. I snuck out of class.

So I walk out the class. Went out in the yard and started playing basketball. We were supposed to turn in the basketball out there so I took the ball through the hall on the way back in. I was gonna go back out there and play some more. See I had the ball and I passed by his class and I looked in. I seen him with his back turned and I didn't like him. That's when I hit him. I hit him with the ball. Got him! I didn't miss. Threw it hard too. Real hard!

It is easier for teachers to attack the demeanor of students directly if the encounter is formal and disciplinary. If a gang member is 'sent' to someone for punishment, the teacher or principal he appears before often makes demeanor an issue. In the following incident, a gang member is suspended for ten days ostensibly because he faced the music with his hands in his pockets and the touch of a smile on his face.

> Miss W., she sent me to Mr M. cause I cussed at her. When I came to class he was talking to some gray boys [white boys] and he called me in. He talked at me like he gonna knock me out. Talked about fifteen minutes. He wasn't coming on nice. He got right down to the point. 'I think you know what you're in here for. I think you know what you did fourth period concerning Miss W.'
> I say, 'Yeah, I know what I done.'
> And so he just sat down and went on and talked. He told me to sit down. I was already sat down. I had my hands in my pockets. He told me to take my hands out of my pockets. (Why?) I guess he wanted my attention. I was looking down at the floor and he told me to look at him. I look at him and look down at the floor again. He didn't say nothing then. And I walked out the woodship and I just smiled. And he say, 'Come on back here! I want to talk to you again.' So I went back there. 'What was that smile for? That little smile you gave.'
> I say, 'Ain't nobody can tell me if I can smile.'
> He said, 'You smiling as if you gave me a bad time. You didn't. I gave you a bad time!'
> So he told me to go on down to the Principal. He told me the Principal was gonna suspend me for ten days. (Did he?) Yup.

Yet when gang members are convinced that the educational enterprise and its ground rules are being legitimately pursued, that a teacher is really interested in teaching them something, and that efforts to learn will be rewarded, they consistently show up on time, leave when the class is dismissed, raise their hands before speaking, and stay silent and awake.

> I mean I feel like that teacher was helping me. I mean he was showing me a way I could pass his class. And then all the time he was telling me, you know, he was leaving me with confidence that I could do better if I wanted to. Like I mean he'd be up in front of the class you know, and he'd give the class an equal chance to be graded. I mean I felt that the teacher was real fair. Cause some of the people that were slow, he would help. I mean he wouldn't take off time just for that few little people but he would help you. He'd give you confidence. Tell you you can do better. That man used to have a desk full of people. Everyday after class you know there be somebody up there talking to him. Everybody passed his class too. He let you know that you wasn't in there for nothing.

Notes

1 This paper is part of a larger research project done with Irving Piliavin on delinquent street gangs in San Francisco. The project was initiated by the Survey Research Center at the University of California on a grant from the Ford Foundation and was later moved to the Center For the Study of Law and Society where funds were made available from the Delinquency Studies Program sponsored by the Department of Health, Education, and Welfare under Public Law 87-274.
2 Cloward, R. A. and Ohlin, L. E. (1961) *Delinquency and Opportunity*, Routledge and Kegan Paul, p. 102.
3 Cohen, A. K. (1956) *Delinquent Boys: The Culture of the Gang* Routledge and Kegan Paul, p. 115.
4 Miller, W. B. and Kvaraceus, W. C. (1959) *Delinquent Behavior: Culture and the Individual*, National Educational Association of the United States, p. 144. See also Miller, W.B. (1958), Lower-class culture as a generating milieu, of gang delinquency *Journal of Social Issues*, vol. 14 for a more explicit statement of this position.
5 Cloward, R. A. and Ohlin, L. E. (1961) op. cit.
6 Cohen, A. K. (1956) op. cit.
7 Miller, W. B. (1958) op. cit.

8 Barnard, C. I. (1938) *The Functions of the Executive* Harvard University Press, p. 163.

9 This assumption is widely shared by both sociologists and gang members. Hopefully we will someday put it to a test.

10 This model of events is based on the assumption that regardless of how students are behaving in class; they can only misbehave if a rule about proper conduct is invoked by teachers. It is in this sense that 'social groups create deviance by making the rules whose infraction constitutes deviance, and by applying those rules to particular people'. See Becker, H. S. (1963) *Outsiders*, Collier-Macmillan p. 9.

11 For a general discussion of the problems created by contingent or purposive infraction of irrelevance rules see Goffman, E. (1961) *Encounters* Bobbs-Merrill pp. 17–85.

15   Negotiating the demands
of schoolwork

P. WOODS

Introduction: the experience of work

The central official activity of school life is without doubt 'work'. School rituals, pedagogical orientations, examinations, and careers are all geared to its production. Yet we have no direct studies of what this phenomenon 'work' means to teachers and pupils. There are several that make certain official assumptions about pupil categories,[1] which means we do not know how central they are; some that take a true ethnographic approach, but mainly with counter-cultural groups, whose main aim and activity is in the avoidance of work and its replacement;[2] and some that are connected with the approaches to it.[3] In all of them, the central experience (if indeed there is one) seems to be taken for granted.

In this article, I examine the phenomenon as encountered during a participant observation study in a secondary modern school. A great deal of the activity is taken up with 'negotiating' as teachers seek to maximize pupil efforts, and pupils often to minimize them. I use the term 'negotiation' here as in Strauss *et al.*[4] Strauss and his colleague showed the importance of informal arrangements, often contrary to official policy, in the running of a hospital, but the concept is applicable to all institutional life, including schools.[5] These negotiations are marked by much skill, ingenuity, diplomacy, effort and study on both sides—the very qualities one might look for in an idealized notion of 'work'.[6] Through their study we might get closer to that mysterious central activity. In a previous article, I illustrated the importance for the pupil's interpretation of the status of the work, and the mediatory relationships with the teacher.[7] Here, I shall try to focus more closely on the experience.

One way to represent the experience of the pupils I encountered is by the four categories along the dimension in Fig. 15.1.

Type of work:	Hard work	Open negotiation	Closed negotiation	Work avoidance
Pupil adaptation:	Conformists	Colonizers		Rebels

Figure 15.1

'Hard work' implies full commitment, and is practised by conformists.[8] 'Work avoidance' at its extreme implies total lack of commitment and is where the real counter-cultures flourish. However, the majority of pupils are mostly to be found somewhere in between indulging in 'open' or 'closed' negotiation. Both arise from partial commitment and hence a mismatch between teacher and pupil aims. Open negotiation is where parties move some way to meet each other of their own volition, and subsequently arrive at a consensus. Closed negotiation is where the parties independently attempt to maximize their own reality in opposition to and conflict against each other, and each makes concessions begrudgingly, and only if forced. However, they do make concessions, unlike the 'work avoiders'.

From all these positions, the experience of work is somewhat different, and in the rest of the article I shall try to describe the three categories containing work for both pupils and teachers, concluding with some speculations on the forces that lie behind a possible 'shift to the right' along the dimension in Fig. 15.1 in pupils' accomplishment of schoolwork, when teachers perpetually seek a shift to the left. I should make clear that I am talking about categories of work, rather than individual pupils, who can move among them according to subject, teacher, and time of day, though pupils often have a predominant mode.

Open negotiation

Command of the process of negotiation is at the heart of being a successful teacher. Quite often, if the teacher overdoes concessions, the pupils will demand more and threaten to take over the lesson. It is also to be reviled as offending the norm: 'He's a bit of a queer teacher. He's not like a proper teacher. He doesn't tell you off'. If not enough concessions are made, pupils might become resentful, and potential colonizers might be turned into rebels. What the standard lesson consists of then, is a number of checks and balances, prompts and concessions, motivations, punishments, jollyings, breaks and so forth, as the teacher displays professional expertise in getting the most out of pupils, while the pupils, seeking basically the comfort of their own perspective with reality, will tend to react according to how the teacher's techniques mesh with that reality.

One of the most common gambits the teacher makes is to offer to do a great deal of the necessary burdensome work and to 'carry' pupils along. For the pupils this is what I would term 'distanced work', because the pupils themselves are a long way from its point of origin. The most common illustration of this is teacher talking—pupil listening. It has many variations, including the standard question and answer, board work and doing experiments. Pupils are constantly reminded of the terms of the contract:

Example 1
>   Teacher: I'll do the algebra for you now. There are six methods of factorization, give me one. [No hands go up, a certain lethargy.] I'll make you do the lot if you start yawning! [Several hands go up.]
>   Teacher: Formulae are getting longer and more complicated, and your memories are getting worse. So what do they do? Give you the formulae to take in with you! There's not enough practice learning or memorizing these days. Do you have to remember passages in English Literature? [They shake their heads.]

Example 2
>   Teacher: [During an experiment on expansion of liquids.] I'm going to record the results now [noise increases in class]. I gather some of you would rather *write* the whole double period!

Example 3
>   Teacher: I've talked enough, now I think its time you did some work. I'm going to give you four essay titles, choose one and make a start in these last 20 minutes. You can get half your homework done if you get your minds on it.

In this last example there is a double bargain. The teacher has 'worked' for 20 minutes of the scheduled 40-minute period, while the pupils took things easy. Now it is their turn. Furthermore, extremely valuable leisure time in the evening is offered as an extra inducement. Another element appears in this example:

Teacher: [After a few admonitions at the beginning of lesson, and one pupil getting moved up to the front.] I'm going to start with a promise, or two. In the second period we'll have a film—if you're good, and work well this first one! Then I thought next week we'd go out and do the nature trail in the forest [pupil talking]. I think you're adopting a very anti-social attitude, and that became apparent the moment you walked through the gate this morning. [Quiet, but a ripple of noise again.] Now don't let me have to nag!

Thus, not only do pupils stand to gain pleasurable experiences if they comply: if they do not, they will earn the teacher's wrath and precipitate what Furlong's pupils called 'trouble' which at all costs they sought to avoid.[9] Individuals might get 'shown up'[10] or verbally (even physically) assaulted.

Teacher: If I hear another burble from your stupid little mouth, I shall push your head through the top of that desk! [With nose an inch from pupils', and eyes wide and unblinking. Ghostly quiet in room, and they go on writing.]

Thus bargaining tactics of the teacher are not always pleasant ones.

Sandra: I think some of the teachers are frightening. They frighten you into working. I don't think it should be like that really. I'm frightened to walk into some lessons.

Lessons frequently proceed in this way, with pupils exploring the boundaries of tolerance, and teachers continually defining them, though in ways that accord with general and particular teacher –pupil norms and rules.[11] What is being bargained for is often 'control' rather than 'work'. Here the distance between the pupil and 'work' is at its greatest. That is to say that there may be no passage through the pupil of the teacher-initiated activity whatsoever, even though there might be an appearance of it.[12]

The extreme bargain derives from situations where children do hardly any 'work' at all, and teachers have long since given up trying. But because teachers can cause 'trouble' and kids can be extremely awkward, both trade appearances for tolerance. Much 'work' in the school day therefore is counterfeit. No productivity rates are required, there is no factory line, no next stage in the process waiting, and for non-examination forms, no examinations. The only kind of productivity rate demanded by 'supervisors' is a semblance of work and a semblance of good order [. . .].

[. . .] There is a great deal of 'play' in pupil work. Teachers, who are interested in pupils' *learning* by whatever means, or if that is completely impossible, keeping them occupied in as pleasant a way as possible, often devise games as part of their teaching strategy. Teachers thus provide curriculum forms to compensate for the basic curriculum, the relevance of which, for many pupils, is not clear. This is one of the paths to 'good relationships'. Those teachers high on the pupils' list in this respect were adept at humanizing the basic drudgery with departures from routine, attention to individuals, skilful use of laughter, converting 'work' to 'play', and so on.

They will sell such activity to the pupils as 'play' both as a learning enterprise in itself and as a balance to more grisly business. Thus: artwork, pottery, craftwork, needlework, domestic science, science experiments in the labs—such activities could often more appropriately be classified as play. Pupils might seek to transform any dull activity into play. For example, in one physics lesson observed, pupils were set four problems of balance to work out. The class proceeded with these in a mood of happy and casual industry, chattering in groups, sorting through the problem, but with frequent and cheerful digression to the state of the football league or the current pop scene.

'You can't expect much from these' the teacher told me. 'If you wield the big stick, they rebel. At least like this we stay friends, and they do learn something.' Some pupils thus are perceived as having 'limits' in their capacity to do schoolwork. Some need extending, others need indulging. As for the latter there is much play, games and laughter. If the teacher can incorporate some of these elements into his programme, rather than allowing them a subterranean illicit existence, he might achieve some learning via the back door as it were. At worst, he will achieve a *modus vivendi* and a spirit of sociability.

Some teachers thus deliberately construct the learning process as a game. After all, it is not self-evident *why* one should have to learn about Roman villas, upland sheep, the area of an annulus, the Citizen's Advice Bureau, how to make a canoe, the principle of levers, similes, and so forth. Thus a rather dry social studies lesson on 'educational expenditure' was relieved by sending pupils all over the school to get essential information from the caretaker, the cook, the secretaries, and so on. A history lesson on strip farming was lightened by allocating the class character parts in a medieval village. A project on housing, was spiced by sending pupils around householders with a questionnaire. The point of the Citizen's Advice Bureau was incorporated into a strip cartoon). They were certainly not 'work'.

Hard work

If negotiating more tolerable degrees and forms of work is the main activity, there are times when pupils do *hard* work. 'Copying notes from the board', for example, can be extremely 'hard work' for some pupils. The difficulty lies in the mental effort required in concentrating on the task, and in the act of writing. What has become easy and second nature to some, almost a natural extension of the self, to others poses the greatest problems:

> He gives us loads and loads of writing.
>
> What I don't like is when they get on about your writing.
>
> 'E makes us do a load of writing' . . . I don't mind the drawin', but writing'—huh!

This might not be perceived as hard work for the pupils by teachers since they have devised the notes and written them on the board or dictated them. More likely are they to put into this category work that more obviously requires a stirring of the mental processes and some initiative on the pupil's part, and that releases them, the teachers from the effort of production. Thus, working from work cards, doing exercises—this kind of set work, which involves some form of problem-solving on their own initiative, is the ultimate in pupil hard work to many teachers. So it is, of course, for many pupils. I joined in one group activity with some 'deviant' fourth-year boys, based on a comparison of two housing estates. We had to find answers to a list of questions from the evidence presented in the form of photographs, statistics, tenants' comments etc. I taped this discussion, and playing it back to them several days later, one remarked. 'Cor! We was workin' 'ard then! That's the 'ardest I've worked all term!'

What made this 'hard work' for these pupils was the extent of application of mind needed to grasp the series of problems, the *creative* task of coming up with ideas in interaction with the elements presented to produce solutions, all of which made it an individualistic effort. Contrast this with the routine procedures of 'distanced' work, which can either be a drudge in calling on one's powers of attention, but nothing else (e.g. interest), or euphoric in permitting its sublimation in some other activity.

The greatest physical effort I witnessed at Lowfield was in the gym, especially circuit training, which involved press-ups, shuttle-running, sit-ups, bench jumping, and rope climbing, all performed, of course, against the clock. The staff certainly perceived this as work of the first order. It involved application, determination and the utmost investment of one's physical resources. 'Old Gary Simpson, he works, but he never seems to be on his beam ends' (P.E. Teacher).

The games' teacher's approach was framed in a 'workish' rhetoric. Thus, in games, pupils were often urged to 'work'. 'You must work for it' was often impressed on them. The techniques were ground out to them in forceful terms: 'Serve, Dig, Catch! Serve, Dig, Catch!' Games involved skill, which requires practice, but other gym activity tests the limits of human endurance. Some pupils have an instinctive fascination for this especially after the boredom and distance of classwork, and will rally group support to push an individual on, as when they all shouted Gregory Beech up the rope for a third, very painful, time within 60 seconds at the end of his circuit training.

However, this does not constitute work for the pupil. For him, it is a respite from the usual school chore, an opportunity to expend a great deal of bottled-up energy in a direction that he can comprehend. For some pupils therefore it comes under an *opposing* category—that of 'sport' or 'games'. It is perceived as a peripheral activity within the school's official programme, but in some pupils' lives, it is central—'the best part of the week'—but as 'play', 'sport', 'leisure', uncontaminated by the alienating characteristics of 'work'.

Most 'work' is done by the examination classes. The rest of the school do very little 'work' in proportion to their other activities over the week. There was frequent reference to this divide. Exams meant 'work' for both teacher and pupil. 'No exams' let them both off the hook:

[. . .]
> *Vera:* I thought that was the only time we really worked hard, for exams. The rest of the time we was just told to do some work and that was it. Then when it come to the exam and they mentioned that, we was all working very hard and I found it difficult really.
>
> *Dianne:* As you get nearer the end of the school, you more aim for something than during your first years an' that. So you do work harder.

[. . .]
Much of this work is seen through the medium of relationships with the teacher concerned. But what of the activity itself? Mostly I got the impression that pupils felt they were 'shovelling away at a giant slagheap'[13] This applied even to the supposedly 'creative' work of CSE projects and English essays. This is illustrated in one way by the quantification applied: 'I got a bit bored when I was doing the Geography project and I couldn't decide what to do and had to do about 40 sides, and after about 10 I was fed up with it'.

The same applied to the English 'folder':

[. . .]
> *Shirley:* I quite liked English actually. Miss Dickens, she's a nice teacher. The only trouble I had was with essays. You know, we had to do a folder for CSE, and we had to keep changing our teacher, because Mr Johns had to take us in the fourth year, and he'd come in once a week, and we had to do essays every weekend, sometimes two a weekend, and it really got us down a bit.

But mostly, for examination pupils, work consisted of attempts to commit to memory slabs of knowledge by various means of varying tedium.

> *Dave:* The metalwork homework was to copy 10 pages out of a book, and that took three to four hours.

P. Woods:	Was that usual?
Dave:	Every week, for a year.

[. . .]

Daphne: I would have been much happier taking fewer exam subjects, because there's so much forcing you to do what you don't want. Then you try to cram more in at the end, and that was too much. Especially physics, I found that very hard, and chemistry.

I found few expressions of 'enjoyment' of work.

[. . .]

Elaine: I didn't mind English, but I wouldn't say I enjoyed it.
Julie: It's just something you had to do. You had to do it, you couldn't get out of it.
Kate: I don't think its been really hard work. I mean when people go out to work, I bet they find it a lot harder than at school.

The demands of examinations appears to militate against the personal relationships so highly regarded by pupils. What seems fairly clear is that there is a misfit between demands and resources. Suddenly and dramatically between the easily negotiated calm of pre-exam work and the rather exciting prospect of remunerated, independent, responsible and meaningful employment, comes this period of peculiar pressure, for which it was difficult to find a consistent rationale.

Shirley: I thought the normal homework during the year was quite interesting—maths and English I didn't mind doing them. But at the end when it gets towards exams, it gets you down a bit. They say you've *got* to learn this, you've *got* to learn that, or you won't pass your exams, and things like that.
Christine: When you start going over things all over again, that's what I don't like.
Caroline: Well, it was out of proportion. Physics we had hardly any homework, and we didn't learn much. In French we had a couple of hours every time, and we don't have the time to do that in one evening, we've got other subjects.
Beryl: You're supposed to spend an hour for each subject, but physics, you can do that in a quarter of an hour, French would take us three hours.

This work has a mechanistic quality:

Debbie: I don't like geography because it's all on the blackboard all the while, and I can't stand the teacher so . . .
Angela: He doesn't speak to you as . . . well, I dunno . . . 'e kind of treats you as machines really [yeah]. Its 'come in' he'll say, probably talk about something; not very often, its usually straight out of a book or atlases, or off the board.

Also it seems to squeeze out those other (non-work) areas of school life that make it a humane institution. So that, for some, it is the total impact of the exam programme that impinges:

P. Woods: What will be the thing you remember about school most of all?
Heidi: Hard work.
P. Woods: Hard work?
Heidi: Yeah, no end of homework in the evening, especially in French.
Shirley: Teachers tend to push you too much in the fourth year, they watch everything you do, and generally keep getting on to you all the while.
Caroline: Yes, and, you know, a bit strict with you, they don't let you have no freedom whatsoever.
Barbara: It starts the first day of the fourth year. We have homework sheets every month. If we miss one lot of homework or two lots of homework we get 'unsatisfactory' and if you get two 'unsatisfactorys' you have to see the year tutor and get told off by him, get put on report and everything. Really gets us down. That's why half of us don't do it really, to rebel against them, I think [laughs].

[. . .]

Closed negotation

'Open negotiation' takes place together. It is a joint activity, based on a certain amount of good will towards each other, recognition of the value of co-operation, and belief in the possibility of consensus. But sometimes teachers and pupils take action independently of the other either in a spirit of less than goodwill or resignation, or in adapting to the circumstances that have been negotiated, thus engaging in the activity that I have called 'closed negotiation'. For pupils, this includes skipping homework, pooling knowledge and resources, cribbing, skiving, tricking the teacher into doing it for them, or simply 'mucking about'[14]. It is the most popular replacement of routine 'distanced' work, which can sometimes be a drudge, but on the other hand can often be euphoric in that, since it involves no interaction with the self, it permits its sublimation in some other activity.

If teachers do not collude with them, and connive at the 'working game', as described in the previous section, pupils will sometimes take the initiative in transforming the activity of work into an activity of play. Thus there is a great deal of playing at working, and playing at listening. Intricate class and individual games, which the teacher might detect as 'a lot of fiddling with pen and rulers' abound. There is a great deal of pretending to work while doing something else. [. . .] [for example] time passing and time-filling, not as an adjunct to a larger purpose, but as an overall end in itself. This is earmarked by endless performances and rituals around the distribution, collection and finding of rulers, pencils, paper. The term, day, period is there, inevitably, and it is more necessary that it be 'got through' than it is the syllabus, especially with regard to non-examination classes. Sometimes this is an *ad hoc* adjustment to the contingency:

> *Notes* = 10 *October, periods 7, 8, fourth year art and pottery.*

> Jack Lester is forced to take the fifth year art group in the T.D. room for the second two periods, where he's on a hiding to nothing. That group sits around the table in there. Philip gets on with his—which he's been doing all term—passing the time. Kim is reading *Mad* and Possee is with his mates S.R., L.S., and J.T., who've been 'lobbed out' of pottery. Jack is meandering aimlessly around, also time-passing. Having discussed the *Planet of the Apes* and the *Six Million Dollar Man*, I say I'm going to see fourth year art. 'I'll wander up with you', said Jack, 'for something to do'.

[. . .]

The critical nature of time, as ruler of content, is often conveyed by teacher comment to pupils, perhaps filling a space in one lesson by talking about the next subject which 'will take us up to half-term'. Or, by, inversely, talking about the compartmentalization of knowledge and how it is geared to time:

> That's got 'maturity' done. Now we'll go on to 'availability'. We've only got 'curiosity' after than, then we'll call it a day.

In these examples teachers and pupils are similarly affected. In the following example different constructions of reality are more obviously in play.

> *4th year set 5, maths observation: Excerpts from lesson*

> Noisy lot. First few arrivals are quite jocular with Len. David asks 'What are we doing to today Sir?'

> | *Len:* | Decimal division this afternoon, page 46. |
> | *Harry:* | Oh these aren't too bad, sir. |
> | *Len:* | Right now, pay attention everybody, just like you did yesterday. [Len explains how to divide decimals.] Tell me what you do Jane. [General commotion while Len tries to explain division of decimals.] Just shut up talking when I'm |

talking, will you, you have the chance of talking when you're working. Listen
to me now! Now pack up this chatting and turning round will you!!

Fiona:	What do you do with the decimal point, Sir?
Amanda:	Which sides goes which, Sir?
Derek:	What page are we on, Sir?
Len:	The idea of this introduction is to tell you how to do it, so stop asking questions! . . . Now, when dividing, you move the decimal point two places to the left.
Amanda:	Right, Sir?
Len:	No, *left!*
Amanda:	That's what I meant Sir, right, left, sir.
Len:	You said *right!*
Amanda:	I meant you were right, Sir!
Sheena:	I said left Sir, I *did!*

(Later)

Sheena:	Oh Sir, do we have to do these?
Len:	Yes, you do, it's very important. [He explains some more.]
Sheena:	You haven't moved the point.
Len:	You don't have to with this one.
Sheena:	Oh, it isn't 'alf' ard, Sir! [Len explains more more.]
Sheena:	Can I have another piece of paper then?
Len:	Well you shouldn't have started yet!
Sheena:	I did, I thought we 'ad to!
Len:	I've been here explaining, how do you know what to do before I've explained it?
Sheena:	That was before I knew!

(Later)

Amanda:	Sir is that right?
Len:	No, that's not right! Look, you're all working, and half of of you don't know what you're doing! Why don't you put your hands up and ask?
Sheena:	Init 'ard?
Len:	No'it's not hard, it's ever so easy, it should've been done in the second year!
Christine:	Who invented the decimal point, Sir?
Len [to me]:	I thought I'd give them something easy to do so I could get on and mark their books—blimey!
	[The lesson continued in this vein.]

Clearly there is not much agreed consensus in this lesson. It is a good example of
'closed negotiation'. Teacher and pupil attribute different meanings to the lesson.
The teacher keeps trying to impose a formal structure in the traditional mould, and
keeps resolutely to it despite its apparent failure. The pupils play with the teacher,
pretending at the game of learning, contriving fun and jokes out of it where they
can, and devising their own amusement where not. The teacher's complete
immersion in his own paradigm was shown at the end when he confided to me 'that
wasn't too bad. They worked quite well in that lesson'. Most of the pupils, however,
had played their way through the two periods.

In 'negotiation', teacher and pupils usually manage to arrive at a 'core' universe of
meaning which has properties recognized by all parties to it. Perspectives, to some
degree at least, lock into each other at certain points. In other areas of school life, as
in the example above, teacher and pupils remain firmly within their own 'sub-
universe of meaning'. The physical points of contact are mentally transformed into
matter appropriate to the sub-universe.[15]

Conclusion: cultural lag and structural fault

Approaches to 'work' in school show a variety of perspectives. Teachers would say
their aim is to accomplish learning, and that to learn, pupils have to work. Some

pupils work hard, those with total commitment, very hard. The majority, however, at my study school had less straightforward attitudes to work. The teachers moved to meet these in various ways from the almost continuous urging and enticing to work that went on in assembly, lessons, speech day, headmaster's office, reports, etc., and the parading of ideal models to a variety of adaptations to pupils' own adaptations or recalcitrance. The extreme example of this, very pervasive at this school, centred on 'survival'[16] Much activity, therefore, was a product of teacher striving and pupil recalcitrance—negotiating, bargaining, with teachers persuading, forcing or kidding pupils to work, doing most of it for them, chivvying them along, creating atmospheres of obligation, with pupils passing the time, playing, working the system. Some teachers and pupils spent their whole time thus engaged, and this therefore was the measure of their work.

More 'hard work' was to be found among the examination forms, but it was a strange activity, at times difficult, tortuous, and much disliked, not at all involving the ingredients of 'fulfilment'—opportunities for choice, decision, acceptance of responsibility, self-determination and growth. This 'work' was often the opposite of these, suppressing rather than encouraging them. There is a great deal of talk of work as a commodity, matched with notions of quantified capabilities.[17] Teachers compose imperatives like 'proper amounts', 'fitting into periods', 'finishing before the bell', 'what these kids can or can't do', 'the need to catch up', 'that's that subject done'. As Bernstein notes 'Children and pupils are early socialized into this concept of knowledge as private property. They are encouraged to work as isolated individuals with their arms around their work.[18]

An interesting yardstick on close personal meanings of work today is provided by Fox.[19] Much condensed, these are:

(a) provides an organizing principle
(b) services sociability needs
(c) sustains status and self-respect
(d) establishes personal identity
(e) provides a routine
(f) distracts from worry
(g) offers 'achievement'
(h) contributes to a cause.

For many pupils, at my study school only (b) and (e) of this list would appear appropriate, with possibilities of (c), (d) and (g) in 'fringe' school activities like games, the official programme being actually counter-productive in respects (a), (c), (f) and (g). This might only appear reprehensible if we regard work as *the* central life interest. But as Bell notes, 'for the modern, cosmopolitan man, culture has replaced both religion and work as a means of self-fulfilment, or as a justification . . . of life'.[20] The organization of life in the modern industrial society has brought about a heavy investment for the individual in the private sphere.[21] Thus the most *meaningful* activities to many of these pupils were those which made sense within their own culture, and which pertained to the 'private' sphere—'childcare' to the retreatist 5L girls, 'social crafts', swimming, and other sports to the intransigent 4L boys. But even for many of the conformist strivers, there was a 'distance' between them and their work, so that all, to varying degrees, support the contention that 'Man, once *homo faber*, and at the centre of work, is now *animal laborans* and at the periphery of work'.[22]

This, of course, is just as true of teachers. And if work is a kind of secondary 'going through the motions' for many teachers, with its compartmentalization, systematization, subservience to time, then it can hardly be anything different for the pupils. For when teachers try to convert the business, whether for integrating or motivational reasons, into a more 'progressive' enterprise, it ceases to be work, and becomes 'play—either a familiar kind of adaptation to the work scene, or a component more in keeping with the private sphere.

This general trend, common to all, is complicated by the class factor. The same group perspectives I identified on a previous occasion are apparent to some extent.[22] When turning to future occupations, as well as subject choice, it is the human face of work that concerns those from a working-class background—personal security to be sure, and the means for the enrichment of the private area ('good money', 'in the dry'), but also the desire to be with friends, the camaraderie, the good 'relations' among all concerned. The other perspective, less evident in this article, contrasts in its extra-personal criteria, its careerist, professional keynote and its tendency toward total commitment and matching role with person. The first aims at securing the best possible conditions for toleration purposes and maximizing the adaptive techniques. 'Fulfilment' will be elsewhere. Society is not 'their' domain, but is run by and for others—those of the other perspective.[24] As with regard to subject choice, so too with work and future career, family perspectives are reinforced by the school, equally paradoxically against the apparent intent of the teachers.[25]

The majority of pupils at my school were from working-class backgrounds, and this article shows how the influence of modern industrialism is reinforced among examination and non-examination forms alike. Pulled apart in some ways, by for example, the hierarchies of work, which possibly channelled them along different routes into the occupational structure, most brought the same basic criteria to the experience of work. Part of the answer lies in the roots of the working-class culture from which they come. The process of adaptation to work goes back many years, and the cultural forms it has given rise to have deep roots, and are very pervasive. As Fox argues, 'Generations of the working-class subjected to this pattern of work experience, have made a 'realistic' adaptation to it by relinquishing or by never bothering to take seriously aspirations towards intrinsic satisfaction'.[26] Like the factory, school is not an area where they can 'make something of themselves'.[27] And the 'deskilling' of the working-classes has led to a contempt for work. There is an 'experimental' separation of the inner self from work', and it is 'the sensuous human face of work as prepared for unofficially . . . in the school, much more than its intrinsic or technical nature, which confronts the individual as the crucial dimension of his future'.[28] One of the keystones of this work culture is the aim to secure the best possible conditions for toleration purposes, while personal fulfilment will be found elsewhere.

Here, then is a possible explanation for the emphasis on relationships. The cultural forms that envelope the pupil in his life outside school, among which he was reared from birth, and through which he constructs his meanings of life, and particularly certain generalized attitudes to work are reinforced in school. Attempts to oppose these, however well intentioned, are restricted. Those elements that are valued within their own culture, are, however, highly esteemed.

> P. Woods: Do you keep your work in a folder?
> Posser: Yeah, all them sort of pouffy things.

Folders, projects, exercises, writing, reading, homework, indeed all mental work as such, are 'pouffy things', not only not for the likes of some of them, but oppositional and threatening, and therefore to be resisted. Whenever the full extent of their machismo is promised satisfaction, as in games, they will perform wholeheartedly. There is dignity to be won in the gym or on the field; enemies to be resisted in the classroom. But where the agent of that enemy force, the teacher, accords with certain strands in their culture, as in the emphasis on social relationships, and sheer indulgence in the delights of sociation, the gap will be bridged. The teacher–pupil relationship is not all conflict by any means. At times it rises to great heights of togetherness, but, at least with these pupils, it is based not on the manifest role of the school, work, but something that is often seen as an oppositional force to work, in that it has no other purpose than the immediate production of pleasure. The official programme is not just middle-class. It is childish, kid's stuff. To these pupils, there are not many connections between school and work. School is for kids; almost a separate compartment of life, a glorified crèche for adolescence. Work is for adults.[29]

It should be said that within this broad, general trend, there are many individual differences, encouraged by a certain amount of differentiation in the occupational world. There are related differences in commitment—for example, as one goes up the occupational hierarchy, more of one's 'self' is invested in the job.[30] There are differences among teachers in commitment, and vast differences between teachers and pupils. Among the pupils also, there are degrees of involvement. Some are thoroughly attuned to school, others totally opposed. This said, the general trend remains clearly evident.

All this illustrates one of the biggest paradoxes about school, in that it is often held to be in the forefront of knowledge, in its efforts to develop skills and abilities and to open minds, yet is one of the biggest victims of cultural lag in this society. Teachers go on preaching the virtues of the Protestant Ethic, with its emphasis on ambition, hard work, and deferred gratification, but the structural parameters of society no longer make these viable propositions for most people. 'Work' has undergone a metamorphosis, little any longer involving the totality of the person. It is by and large a nagging necessity, to which people have adapted over the years, developing new meanings which are filtered through to their children direct from their first-hand objective experience of work and participation in work cultures, which helps perpetuate 'the cycle of inequality'.[31] No amount of teacher advice and persuasion can scratch the surface of this massive influence. They instinctively know this, and thus their exhortations seem to have an unreal quality. This suits their own ambivalence, for they, too, are subject to the same structural forces. Teacher's 'work' is not exempt from modernizing forces which have rendered it an intermixture of pedagogy, professionalism and survival.[32] They are thus in the curious position of sponsoring an ideology they neither follow themselves nor is any longer appropriate for the structural situation of their charges. It persists because it is associated with the self-perpetuating practices and beliefs that have been mustered by their teachers in defence against the exigencies of the job which themselves have become standardized.[33] The cultivation of a work ethic—that work is intrinsically satisfying and rewarding—is a useful strategy when they have to co-ordinate and control subordinate labour. When a disjunction is perceived between this view and reality, it might be concluded that it is the content of the programme that is wrong, rather than their view of it, or that pupils are defective in their powers of appreciation.[34]

Thus pupil 'work' (schoolwork) is not a straightforward matter of application to a task in hand, but the product of a series of adjustments to the exigencies of the moment, and these adjustments are strongly influenced by background cultural factors. The teacher, in turn, responding to the demands of professionalism and the needs dicated by the conditions of work (resources, space, numbers etc.), makes the requirement of the pupil even more esoteric. Schoolwork is therefore unreal for many pupils, and they duly transform it into something more meaningful—play or sociation. In this form they can live with it, even enjoy it. But work of the old-fashioned order has lost its structural supports and its accomplishment therefore will not be a result of a pure state of application, but a product of negotiation, bartering, adapting and manoeuvring. A cynical view might hold that that is not inappropriate training for adult life in the modern world. A more optimistic line would be to set in hand ways and means of bridging the gap between intention and practice in more positive fashion. That would have to take less account of 'ideal' notions of work, and more of the cultural supports which sustain pupils and which grow out of the conditions of real work actually experienced by their families and fellows.

References and notes

[1] See, for example, Morton-Williams, R. and Finch, S. (1968) *Young School Leavers* Schools Council Enquiry 1, HMSO; Smithers, A., Avis, G. and Lobley, D. (1974). 'Conceptions of school among pupils affected by the raising of the school leaving age', *Educational Research*.

[2] Willis, P. (1977) *Learning to Labour*, Saxon House; Furlong, V. (1977) *Anancy Goes to School: a Case Study of Pupils' Knowledge of their Teachers* Woods, P. E. and Hammersley, M. (1977) *School Experience*, Croom Helm; Woods, P.E. (1976) 'Having a laugh: an antidote to schooling', in Hammersley, M. and Woods, P.E. (eds) *The Process of Schooling*, Routledge and Kegan Paul.

[3] See, for example, Nash, R. (1976), 'Pupils' expectations of their teachers', *Research in Education*; and Gannaway, H. (1976) 'Making sense of school.' in Stubbs, M. and Delamont, S. (1976). *Explorations in Classroom Observation* Wiley.

[4] Strauss, A. *et al.* (1964). *Psychiatric Ideologies and Institutions*, Collier-Macmillan.

[5] Delamont, S. (1976) *Interaction in the Classroom*, Methuen.

[6] See Anthony, P. D. (1977) *The Ideology of Work*, Tavistock.

[7] Woods, P. E. (1978). 'Relating to schoolwork: some pupil perceptions,' *Educational Review*.

[8] This typology of pupil modes of adaptation comes from Wakeford, J. (1969) *The Cloistered Elite: a Sociological Analysis of the English Public Boarding School*, Macmillan.

[9] Furlong, V. (1977) op. cit.

[10] Woods, P. E. (1974) 'Showing them up in secondary school', in Chanan, G. and Delamont, S. (eds.) *Frontiers of Classroom Research*, NFER.

[11] Werthman, C. (1963) 'Delinquents in schools: a test for the legitimacy of authority.' *Berkely Journal of Sociology*, Vol. 8, No. 1, pp. 36–60; Blishen, E. (1966) *Roaring Boys* (Panther; Rist, R. (1970) 'Student social class and teacher expectation', *Harvard Educational Review*, Vol. 40, No. 30.

[12] Dumont, R. V. and Wax, M. L. (1971) 'Cherokee school society and the intercultural classroom', in Cosin, B. R. *et al.* (eds) *School and Society*, Routledge and Kegan Paul.

[13] Taylor, L. and Cohen, S. (1976) *Escape Attempts: the Theory and Practice of Resistance to Everyday Life* Allen Lane, p. 203.

[14] Woods, P. E. (1976) 'Having a laugh: an antidote to schooling', in Woods, P. E. and Hammersley, M. *The Process of Schooling*, Routledge and Kegan Paul.

[15] Berger, P. and Luckman, T. (1966) *The Social Construction of Reality*, Penguin.

[16] Woods, P. E. (1976) 'Teaching for survival', in Woods, P. E. and Hammersley, M. (eds) *School Experience*, Croom Helm.

[17] Young, M. F. D. (1979) 'Curriculum change: limits and possibilities', *Educational Studies*, Vol. 1, No. 2.

[18] Bernstein, B. (1971) 'On the classification and framing of educational knowledge', in Young, M. F. D. (eds.) *Knowledge and Control* Collier-Macmillan.

[19] Fox, A. (1976). *The Meaning of Work*, The Open University Press.

[20] Bell, D. (1976) *The Cultural Contradictions of Capitalism*, Heinemann.

[21] Berger, P., Berger, B. and Kellner, H. (1974), *The Homeless Mind* Penguin.

[22] Seligman, B. B. (1966) *Most Notorious Victory: Man in an Age of Automation*, The Free Press.

[23] Woods, P. E. (1976) 'The myth of subject choice', *British Journal of Sociology*, June.

[24] Willis, P. (1977) *Learning to Labour*, Saxon House.

[25] Ashton, D. N. and Field, D. (1976) *Young Workers*, Hutchinson.

[26] Fox, A. (1976) op. cit., p. 24.

[27] Ashton, D. N. and Field, D. (1976) op. cit. (Note 25).

[28] Willis, P. (1977) op. cit. p. 102.

[29] Carter, M. (1966) *Into Work*, Penguin, p. 70.

[30] Berger, P. L. (1973) 'Some general observations on the problem of work', in Berger, P. L. (ed.) *The Human Shape of Work*, Macmillan.

[31] Fox, A. (1976) op. cit.

[32] Woods, P. E. (forthcoming). *The Divided School*, Routledge and Kegan Paul.

[33] Lortie, D. C. (1975) *Schoolteacher*, University of Chicago Press; Rosenbaum, J. E. (1976) *Making Inequality*, Wiley.

[34] Anthony, P. D. (1977). *The Ideology of Work*, Tavistock, p. 289.

16   Goodies, jokers and gangs

A. POLLARD

Introduction

This paper is concerned with the perspectives of children in their final year at an 8–12 Middle School.[1] The school was situated in a predominantly working-class area on the perimeter of a Northern textile town. Data was collected at 'Moorside Middle School' over a period of two years using ethnographic methods. With regard to the children this included observation, a sociometric analysis and extensive use of interviews which were carried out with the partial assistance of a child interviewing team.[2]

The present paper is particularly focussed on children's attempts to 'cope' with school life and on their immediate interests in the classroom. Of course, the greatest potential threat to children's coping in school is associated with the power of the teacher, and it has been argued (Pollard, 1979) that they orient their actions with particular regard to this power. However, it is necessary to break down the assumption of homogeneity which the unproblematic use of the category 'children' implies. This is attempted in the present paper which reports on the tendencies and parameters of children's perspectives through the identification of three analytical 'types' of friendship group. These range from those children who were 'good' and normally conformed to teachers' wishes, through 'jokers' who would 'have a laugh' with teachers and commit acts of 'routine deviance', to those 'gang' members who acted more with regard to peer-group expectations than to those of the teacher.

Goodies, Jokers and Gangs

We can begin the analysis by considering the three types of child group which were identified. The sociometric analysis yielded twelve friendship groups, distinctions between good groups, joker groups and gang groups were derived from comparison of the perspectives of children in these groups, particularly regarding their attitudes to themselves, to other children and towards teachers and school. There were clear differences between the children in such groups. Children in groups that other children termed 'good groups' regarded each other positively as 'sensible', 'fair' and 'friendly' and regarded groups which they called 'gangs' very negatively for their 'roughness' and 'destroying' behaviour. Groups which I termed 'joker groups' puzzled at the quietness of Good groups, regarded each other as 'good fun' and 'sensible' but were also clear about the 'bigheaded', 'thick' 'roughness' of gangs. Gang groups condemned Good groups as 'soft' and 'goodie-goodies' and Joker groups as 'show-offs' and 'big heads'. Whilst their own gang was regarded as 'great' other gangs were usually labelled as 'soft', 'rubbish' or 'cocky', thus reflecting the extent of inter-gang rivalry.

Using such data it was possible to construct an inter-group sociogram to represent the children's social structure. In Fig. 16.1 the sizes of each group are represented by the area of the group's symbol. This shows the nine children in Good groups, thirty-eight in Joker groups and twenty-eight in Gangs.

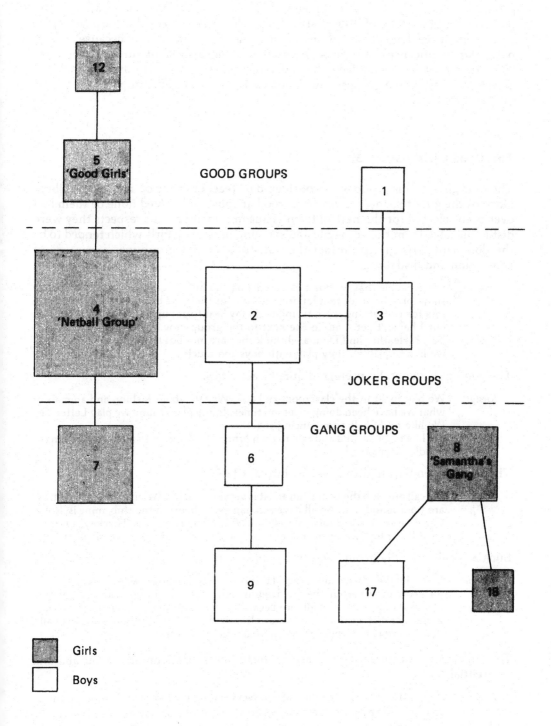

Figure 16.1 *An intergroup sociogram.*

The ethnographic data which documents the perspectives of each of the twelve groups is too extensive to be included in full in this paper but an illustration of the perspectives of a group of each postulated type is essential. For this purpose I offer data from three friendship groups of girls—a choice made not because of any particular significance of the girls' perspectives to my argument but simply because girls' perspectives have tended to be under-represented in the literature in the past. So here we have three groups—the 'Good Girls', the 'Netball Group' of 'jokers' and 'Samantha's Gang'.

The 'Good Girls' (Group 5)

The four girls in this group were considered by teachers to be of 'moderate ability'. None of the girls felt themselves to be good at sport and indeed none of them had ever been selected for the netball team. Thus in two important respects they were distinguishable from the academic and sporting netballing girls which tended to be the dominant girls group. In fact their attitude to that group was a mixture of admiration and disdain:

> *Linda:* Some people that we don't like are Paula and Julie—they talk too much and are show-offs. Some of that lot dress too old for their age but they are all in the top sets for everything. I am trying to do my best to get up to the A set for English but I haven't yet. I am in the next to top group now.
> *Kirsty:* Tessa, Heather and Donna—I think they are nice but they don't like the things we like to play at, they play with boys too much.

The good girls generally preferred quieter activities.

> *Kirsty:* We like to sit in the classroom and talk. We talk about fashion and animals or what we have been doing in lesson times. In the playground we play Letter Tig. We like to do ballroom dancing together.
> *Linda:* We like to sit around and talk to each other. We sometimes all play games in the middle playground.

The girls had constituted themselves into a 'Club':

> *Linda:* We call our club the Lion Club and it is very successful. We are all friends in it. We are honest and fair. We all have nicknames for being in the club, mine is 'Rory', Caroline's is 'Little Boots', Mandy's is 'Shelly' and Kirsty's is 'Thackey'. Ours is a friendly group, we never fall out, or if we do it's only because of silly things.

Such a 'small, friendly group' was distinguished from a 'gang':

> *Caroline:* In school there are many gangs. I think it's terrible being in a gang because when we grow up we would be involved in some kind of trouble with the police.
> *Kirsty:* I think gangs are not at all nice because they are rough and I am nearly always getting bashed in so I have to stay clear of them. I do not think it is fun at all. I hope there is not going to be any more gangs made.

The attitudes of the girls to school and to the teachers was generally favourable and deferential:

> *Kirsty:* School tries to help us a lot and you feel very good when they encourage you to do things. They try to help you with your work for instance when I was in the first year I could only write a few sentences in real writing but look at me now.
> *Linda:* School rules are fair because they are good for us or for our own safety so they are fair really. I think children should be good in school because it helps everyone so that the teachers don't get in a bad mood.

Caroline: I think school helps us a lot because if there was no teachers we would never learn anything and when we were up to the age of getting a job we would not know a thing about it or what to do, or if you worked in a shop you would not be any better off because you would get shown up.

However, the girls were not at ease with teachers, as Kirsty commented:

Kirsty: Talking to a teacher is very hard. If you know what to say before you still get so nervous that you just mumble something out and hope for the best and to get it over and done with. At home it is more relaxed but at school it's easy to get the words all jumbled up which is very embarrassing and it's very hard to show that you are not that way really. It's horrible, and you feel as though you are going to cry about it anytime, but you can't.

As with the boys of Group 1, another 'good' group, these girls were hesitant about having a laugh and wished to avoid getting into trouble.

Kirsty: You should only laugh really when the teacher is laughing, then it's alright, but in some of the lessons we get people messing about all the time. Having a laugh is a good thing sometimes 'cos it brings out the happy side of you and makes you cheery and bright, but we shouldn't do it too much at school or we'll never get any work done.

Mandy: We don't like getting into trouble because when we get told off we get upset. It's not very nice 'cos you don't know what to do. Usually we try and keep out of trouble then it's OK.

It was this reluctance to get involved with any form of deviance which had led to the group being termed as 'goodie-goodies' by many of the other children. The girls appeared to have countered this position as a minority and 'out' group *vis-à-vis* the majority of children, and also their only moderate academic success, through the closeness of their friendship, the protection of their 'Club' and by their determination to avoid trouble either with 'rough gangs' or teachers.

The Netball Group of 'Jokers' (Group 4)

This was a large group of twenty girls and the sociomatrix showed that it was made up of numerous interlocking and chaining trios and pairs. Ten of the girls were in the school netball team and practised regularly at dinner-time. Eleven of the group were in the choir and all four girls House Captains were members of the group. They were almost all regarded as being 'bright' academically.

The Netball Group of girls was very comparable to the other main 'joker' group, the Football Group of boys (Group 2). They were similarly successful both at sport and academically, and their perspectives on many issues were very close. For instance, they both regarded themselves as 'sensible' and showed disdain for some other groups. Here are some comments from the girls:

Jo: There's us lot, er . . ., you could call it the netball team and their friends, and then there's the other lot which is Samantha's [Group 8], Janine's [Group 7], people like that. It's two different bands, and really we're always against one another— there's a difference.

Donna: People in the first band, they seem to be sensible, they do work, they like the teachers and everything, but the others . . . they cause trouble—I don't know, you can't really understand it, but they don't seem to like the teachers. They act about and they're always getting into trouble.

Becky: We like to be able to be doing activities such as netball, choir, Gym Club, and helping teachers. We think we are too old to play games as it seems to be silly to us. There are also groups of people that go round together like Jenny's and Janine's [Group 7]. These girls are very silly and play silly games. Sometimes they get very bossy and begin to boss people around. I don't like gangs because they're always bother causers.

In the playground Netball Group members almost always played netball when a court was available. A few of the girls would also usually be involved doing telephone duty, 'helping teachers' or 'doing a job'. Others 'just walked around.:

Jo: The thing that we like doing is just walking around about the school—touring round, talking and watching everything.

Louise: We don't exactly do anything much, we like to go around together and see what's going on, and we talk a lot about school and what we'll do when we get home and things like that.

Sometimes games were more active:

Gill: We like playing with a ball and skipping and playing out in the playground. We like to talk and have a good laugh. Sometimes we play chasing with the boys or watching them playing football.

The 'boys' referred to by Gill above were, of course, members of the Football Group. However, the girls had clear conceptions of the parameters of 'respectable' behaviour with boys. For instance Becky commented on the activities of two 'gang' members:

Becky: Last night I saw 'em necking in the corner. It's getting out of hand. It's disgraceful.

In lesson times the girls generally wanted to do their work, learn and 'get a good education'. However, as with the Football Group they enjoyed a fairly close rapport with many teachers which was one of the main distinguishing features of the 'joker' group.

Jayne: See, I've found out with Mr Matthews and all the others that are friendly, you get on well with them and get on with your work . . . and Mr Jackson, when we didn't do our work and we hadn't got time, he didn't play heck with us as Mr Smith would have done.

Tessa [Interviewing]: Do you think all teachers should be like that?

Jayne: Yes, but you've got to get it done, you haven't just to leave it.

Julie: You haven't to joke about as much as Mr Matthews does sometimes tho', he doesn't let you get on with your work sometimes.

Julie's comment above shows the girls' concern to be 'sensible' and not prejudice their learning, but at the same time they were very keen on having a laugh to overcome boredom:

Becky: It's boring being in General Studies, when we have to stop and think, you're looking around the room you've nothing to do, thinking, wondering what to do, run out of ideas, looking at the paper, sighing and can't think properly, thinking of something else and can't concentrate on what you're doing—you need a laugh.

Jayne: We can have fun with most of the teachers. Like in Maths we have fun and if the teachers were strict the lessons would get boring, everybody would start fidgeting and they would not listen. If we have a laugh at school we can, sort of, be normal, and it's more relaxing instead of having to be a little Miss Innocent.

There was also a good deal of talking in lessons and note writing about school work and other interests.

Carol: In lessons we usually talk to each other or me and Julie sit next to each other so we talk, and Donna sits near so we sneak across and talk. In sewing Julie is with Louise so I get with Donna and Hazel so we can talk.

Thus the netball girls took the overall view that:

Donna: Children should be good in school, but not good all the time because we can't all be goodie-goodies.

In most cases their rapport with teachers led them to like them and respect their authority:

Jo: Teachers can joke with us and it's good fun. The school rules are for our own good and they're usually fair. In these ways school helps you and learns you all it can so that you grow up well educated. To help teachers learn you you should be good and help the teachers by being quiet and obedient.

Tessa: Like Mrs Graves, if you've been really naughty she'll give you the slipper but otherwise she'll just shout at you—or sometimes she'll just leave you but if you carry on after a period she'll give you a smack or whatever. I think that's right. Teachers can't be patient all the time, they have to teach us.

However this respect did not prevent them condemning teachers who exceeded their perceived authority, particularly by 'picking on people' or 'going mad':

Jayne: I don't know, I think when teachers pick on people and go mad it's probably because they've been arguing with their husband or wife at home, or there's been summat happening at home and they take it out on the children, they come to school because it's the law. It's not fair that some kids get upset by teachers when they're just in a bad mood.

In circumstances of being told off the friendship group was important both as audience and support, with the event being retrospectively taken to build solidarity.

A.P.: Well how do you feel about a telling off? Does it matter?

Tessa: It matters alright 'cos you know you've got into trouble—you go bright red and when you go back sitting with your class you try to talk, to be cheerful with your friends, but they know that you've got into trouble and you're blushing an' that. You try to laugh about it and everybody's looking. Some folks say . . . 'I'm not bothered' . . . and they get on with their work, and eventually they get right happy and laugh about it when the teacher's not there and in the playground.

The girls tended to have fairly traditional attitudes regarding gender. For instance they allowed the initiative for most classroom laughs to come from the boys and the desire to be seen to be 'sensible' often took the form of 'clearing up' for teacher, thus mirroring dominant domestic expectations. A New Year's resolution from a jotter read:

Dawn: My New Year's resolution is to help my mum by keeping my bedroom tidy and as well to help Mum to do the shopping and to help her to do the washing because I like washing.

However some were conscious of iniquities in the roles which they were allocated:

Jayne: My Dad, he says . . . 'Look you'll get a chance for choice when you grow up, so you'll get the chance not to wash up when you grow up but you've got to do it now'—and my brother, he always get out of stuff like that, all he has to do is fill the coal hod and then he can go out and play as long as he wants, and he could do that when he was our age and that's all he had to do. Now we're our age we have to clean up, wash up and all sorts.

A.P.: And why do you think that is?

Jayne: It's 'cos he's lazy.

Tessa: It's 'cos we're girls.

Thus in summary, this large group of girls were intelligent, were successful at work and got on well with teachers. They enjoyed a laugh but considered themselves to be 'sensible' in terms of doing their work, playing nicely, being 'kind', dressing appropriately, helping teachers and not 'going too far' with boys. They were popular with most of the other groups and with the teachers. They participated in a large number of school activities and clubs, and were particularly good at sports.

Samantha's Gang (Group 8)

The members of this group of seven girls were the least successful academically of the girls. However, the most distinctive features of the group were their relatively greater 'roughness' and their very uneasy degree of cohesion. One of their perennial activities was that of falling in and out of friendships with each other:

> Tina: I have a good group of friends when I don't fall out with them. Katherine is always falling out with me and going off with Carly. If that happens, like, she has pinched my friend, then Carly is a fat cow. When I am friends with Susan, just because I am small for her age, she always pushes me around and blames me for things, but Lucy, if we are friends and we play hitting one another it's good fun. But if I hit her too hard she will not play at all. She can be a baby sometimes.

Some more quotations will give the flavour of other activities:

> Samantha: Carly is good fun. Every time we go in for dinner she always put her foot in the mud and kicks it in our hair and sometimes on our clothes. One day Louise got it right up her skirt and all on her face. Then we try to do it back to her but it's hard to get her.
>
> Lucy: Our gang is very exciting. It's an exploring group. We like going to Mecca Ice Skating. We have a marvellous time falling and bumping into one another.
>
> Katherine: In the classroom we like to chase each other. We run through Mr Taylor's room and hide in Mrs Clark's. Sometimes we run round Mr Matthews' and through the kitchen. When we catch whoever is running we pretend to put them in our powers and then they must count to 20 and come after us.
>
> Carly: Our group always likes to have fun, like we play off-ground-tig or chasing or teasing someone. We like running down the banking or over the grass near the staffroom.

One of the most significant activities was that of 'braying' or 'gobbing' members of other gangs, and being 'got back'. Most of this fighting was with the girls of Group 18, Sarah and Diana, or the boys of Group 17, Malcolm, Robert, Nigel and Andrew. Sometimes the fighting would involve alliances between, or with members of, these groups with consequent variations in attitudes to them:

> A.P.:   What about Nigel and Robert . . . that lot? [Group 17]
> Samantha: They're awful.
> Lucy: They can be rough and nasty.
> Tina: Like when I was friends with Sarah and we was going home and Malcolm brayed me, just for no reason at all.
> Samantha: He said it was because she'd told Robert to gob him.
> A.P.:   Do you like playing with these boys?
> Carly: Yea, especially when I'm not friends with these [referring to Tina, Lucy and Samantha].
> Tina: But he, Nigel, he comes over to our table and starts teasing us . . .
> Samantha: . . . and being rude.
> A.P.:   What does he say?
> Samantha: He calls me awful names, I'm not saying them.
> Carly: Sometimes they call her 'Sticklesons'.
> Samantha: Oh that's nothing, it's rude what they call me, four-lettered ones.

A.P.:   Does it get you upset?
Samantha: Yea, but we get our own back later.

With regard to the boys there was some excitement, concern and teasing at their
intentions.

Samantha: Well y'know what they want don't you? Like when Malcolm and Tina went in the
woods, and Nigel, well he went chasing after Carly and touching her up, you
know.

Such activities generated much teasing and thus more 'gobbing' and 'braying' to 'get
back at' the teaser. 'Sexy' jokes and rhymes were also a source of amusement. For
instance, a rhyme from Katherine's jotter:

Eh by gum,
Can your belly touch your bum,
Can your tits hang low,
Can you tie 'em in a bow,
Can your balls go red,
When you rub 'em on your bed,
Eh by gum,
    That's it!

Samantha's gang were often involved with other groups, apart from those
mentioned, except for occasional insult-exchanges with Janine's Terrors (Group 7).
Groups like the Netball girls were regarded as a 'rubbish group' and 'big heads' but
Samantha's gang were not completely immune to other opinions and did feel it
necessary to neutralize their own relative lack of school achievement.

A.P.:   What about Tessa's groups? [Group 4, Jokers].
Samantha: Well, they're swell heads, just because they're in the top groups 'n that, but . . .
Katherine: . . . yea, they think they're 'brains' just because they've got more brains than
            other folk.
A.P.:   Do you think that's true?
Samantha: No, no.
Tina: Like Liz, she's a good worker.
Liz: I'm not, I'm not.
A.P.:   What do you mean?
Liz: I try but I never get anywhere.
A.P.:   Why do you think that is?
Samantha: Well like, they get help, like Carol, her Mum's a teacher so she's got a better
            chance than us lot.
Liz: It might run in their family to have brains.
A.P.:   Do you think it's right that they should be in the top groups?
Samantha: No, but we're not bothered.

Many of the other children were also regarded as being privileged and 'posh' in their
home backgrounds.

Carly: Lots of people act as if they are posh, just because they go on holidays each year
        and buy expensive things for their homes and make their kids look nice and take
        them to school in the car thinking one of the teachers should see her, and try to see
        how her child is getting on at school. Most people act as if they were posh but put it
        on an' show off about something new. They ask their Mums if they can have this,
        that and the other. They try to get the nicest present for a party. But them who are
        not that well off, they act normally. They admit that they do not get very much but
        they are still thankful for what they have got. If you have a lot you can't have very
        much more so I don't care really.

This disdain for many of the children at school meant that Samantha's gang were
'prepared at times to upset them as well as teachers.

> *Tina:* One good laugh we had was in games with Samantha because we kept slowing our team down and when it came to skipping together we kept falling over and having a right laugh and everybody was looking at just us and getting narky but we had a great laugh.

As with other groups the girls would have a laugh in lessons when they got bored or 'couldn't be bothered to do any work' but they were more prepared than many groups to laugh *at* a teacher or despite a teacher:

> *Anna:* If we have a laugh and the teacher's in a bad mood well that's hard lines, we don't care.
>
> *Lucy:* You can have a laugh about something and then if someone gets told off you can have a laugh about that 'cos it's only a warning. That gives you a laugh too when you get into the playground.
>
> *Carly:* When Mrs Jones caught us fooling about and my boot wouldn't come off, she said 'you two are making fools of yourselves' and I was laughing all the time when I bent down to put my boot on and then she said—'Let's hope you come in a better frame of mind tomorrow', and we was laughing all the way home.

Attitudes to teacher authority and school rules acknowledged a degree of well-meaning intent but were clearly unfavourable in many other ways:

> *Anna:* I think some teachers try to be fair and some are stinking ratbags and are always on to you. The school rules are not fair because if someone starts trouble and you bash them up then teachers interfere and you get into big, big trouble. The school tries to help you sometimes but they treat us like dirt so at other times they don't try to help us one little bit. If we were good in school there would be no fun at all.
>
> *Tina:* If you can't spell they learn you how and if you can't write properly they will learn you how to do but when we get done and they shout at us, it's not fair.

The girls were particularly incensed if they felt they were being 'picked on'.

> *Katherine:* Teachers are too bossy. They always stop me and Lucy sitting next to each other in lessons or they might keep us in.
>
> *Samantha:* Sometimes they tell us off for nothing, so then we should not be good, we should get our own back on them, not let them get us into trouble for nothing.
>
> *Liz:* I hate Mr Smith, he shows off too much and he shouts too much and he's always picking on us.

In summary, Samantha's gang could be regarded as having anti-school values in many ways. Compared with the other groups of girls they were relatively unsuccessful both academically and at sport. They were less popular. They caused more 'bother' in school and 'got done' more often. They had less respect for teachers and they looked forward to leaving school to get a job.

Parameters of Classroom Action

Clearly the children in 'good', 'joker' and 'gang' groups have very different perspectives on many aspects of their school life. However, I want now to focus more specifically on the ways in which they seek to cope in the classroom. In order to do this I will draw on a symbolic-interactionist view of the negotiating processes which take place between children and teachers in classrooms. In this perspective it is argued that negotiation leads to the establishment of particular definitions of the classroom situation (Stebbins, 1981; Ball, 1980) and that these provide guides for the action of the participants. Further, because of both the teachers' and the children's perceived necessity of 'coping' with daily life in classrooms, it is suggested that they routinely accommodate their definitions of the situation into a 'working consensus'. This represents a set of shared social understandings which structure and frame the classroom context in terms of routines, conventions and expectations and it takes its dynamic from the power of the children to threaten the teacher because of their numbers and from the power of the teacher to threaten the children because of their role and authority. In that each can pose a threat for the other the working consensus should be seen as a mutual accommodation and, in this sense, it represents a 'truce' rather than a consensus—an acceptance by both parties that the other has the power or resource to threaten their own ability to 'cope' and 'survive' (Woods, 1977) in the classroom situation. Of course, we then have to reject that implied assumption of child homogeneity and to analyse the parameters of the action decision of particular children. If this is done, using the analysis of types of group which has been presented, it yields Fig. 16.2 below.

Child position in social structure	Actions derived from the working consensus		Actions derived from peer culture
	Conformity	Routine deviance	Rule framed disorder
'Good' groups	——————→		
'Joker' groups	——————————————→		
'Gangs'	——————————————————————————→		

Figure 16.2 *Parameters of action decision*

Both the good group members and the joker group members are indicated here as acting within the bounds of the working consensus. However, the gang group members are shown as being prepared—in some situations—to act outside those understandings. What we have here then are three characteristic or 'ideal types' of child coping strategy, an important and formative component of which stems from the quality and nature of the child's interaction with the teacher. The parameters of children's action are thus determined to a significant extent by the actions of their teacher.[3]

Children's Interests-at-hand

Up to this point in the paper I have used the term 'coping' without much clarification. Yet it is a crucial concept for it provides a link between the discussion of the parameters of children's action and the analysis of children's interests in the immediacy of the classroom which forms the second half of the paper. In my use of the term 'coping' I have again drawn on symbolic interactionism and in particular on Mead's (1934) conception of 'self' with its social and biographical origins. Following symbolic interactionist analysis 'self' should be seen as a core concern for any actor. Thus in the classroom context 'coping' can be defined by how closely each participant can satisfy this concern—both from the presentational point of view, which is associated with the actors' role, and from the more personal point of view, which is associated directly with their biography. This attempt to satisfy the concern for self in the immediacy of classroom events can then be analysed in more detail using the concept of 'interests-at-hand' for it can be argued that interests-at-hand represent various facets of self which are juggled in the ebb and flow of classroom processes to produce an overall level of satisfaction for self—and hence of 'coping'. The remainder of the paper thus seeks to identify the major interests-at-hand of the children at Moorside and, in doing so, to distinguish between the priorities of goodies, jokers and gangs.

In the beginning of this task we must remember a crucial fact of the social situation within a classroom which is that two relatively distinct social systems exist beside each other. The official system of the school with its hierarchy, rules and particular criteria of evaluation exists alongside the children's own social system which may appear to be less formal but also has its own hierarchy, rules and criteria of judgement. In lessons the official school system is represented by the teacher whilst the children's own social system is represented by each child's peers. To which party and to which social system should each child refer his or her actions, and with what consequences?

I would suggest that the most important factor in each child's solution to this dilemma is their structural position within the school and class and therefore that their solutions can be seen as being patterned around the Good, Joke, Gang distinctions. It seems to be the case that Goodies conform to teachers and the offical school system during lessons, whilst Gangs tend to reference their actions more to their group of peers. The success of Jokers lies in their skill and flexibility in bridging both types of social system. I am thus arguing that Jokers are able to square their reference groups in both systems in ways which Goodies do not attempt and which Gangs would not attempt.

From the analysis of the Moorside data it was possible to identify particular issues which were salient to the children. These appeared to be bound to their instrumental concern with prediction and control in their classroom and could thus be grouped by purpose, which made it possible to infer interests. This procedure yielded six groupings and it seemed analytically useful to draw a distinction between the primary interest of 'self', which has several facets, and more secondary interests, which are 'enabling interests' in an essentially means-end relationship. These interests are shown in Table 16.1 below.

Table 16.1   *The interests-at-hand of children in classrooms*

	Primary interests-at-hand	Enabling interests-at-hand
Self	• Maintenance of self image	Peer group membership
	• Enjoyment	Learning
	• Control of stress	
	• Retention of dignity	

Of course, it is possible to argue that most children in primary schools share these interests-at-hand in classroom contexts and indeed I would want to do so drawing on a number of other studies. However, for reasons of space I have continued here on the Moorside children.[4]

'Self-image': a facet of the primary interest of 'self'
As we have seen the children at Moorside had clear images of their own identities. These were related in many ways to their friendship groups. The Good groups thought of themselves as 'kind', 'quiet', and 'friendly', the Joker groups believed

themselves to be 'clever' and 'good fun' but 'sensible', whilst the Gangs regarded themselves as 'tough' and 'rough'. These identities were further highlighted by denigrating concepts such as reference by Joker groups to Gangs as 'thick, silly yobs' or by Gangs to Joker groups as 'snobbish, creeping, pansies'.

It was clear that when interacting in their classrooms the children would act to maintain their self-image *vis-à-vis* their peers, often even when other interests were threatened. Perhaps the most regular and obvious instance of this was the number of Gang members who would assert their toughness by defying teachers and 'taking' the punishments and sanctions which followed. Clearly children have to manage their self-image in ways which are advantageous to them and this presentational problem can be acute in the classroom when the expectations of peers and the teacher or parent may clash. Maintaining their self-image and sense of identity in this context is an ever present concern.

'Enjoyment': a facet of the primary interest of 'self'
Enjoyment here refers to the degree of intrinsic self-fulfilment to be obtained from interaction with other people. Children will hope to experience a sense of positive reward from interactions so that they are supportive of self.

Of course there are many forms which such enjoyment can take but one which stands out in the literature, as at Moorside, is that of 'having a laugh'. As Woods has put it:

> [. . .] pupils have their own norms, rules and values and [. . .] their school lives are well structured by them [. . .] In their lives, laughter has a central place whether as a natural product or as a life-saving response to the exigencies of the institution—boredom, ritual, routine, regulations, oppressive authority.
> (Woods, 1976; p. 185)

However, not all 'laughs' are oppositional. Humour in the classroom also often enables teachers and pupils to step out of their role and to express themselves and to communicate in less guarded ways than they might usually adopt. As such, humour can also be seen as a source of reinforcement and development of teacher–pupil relationships, in that to share and 'get the joke' reasserts and constructs the 'culture of the classroom' (Walker and Adelman, 1976) and thus gives security to all 'members' within that setting.

Stebbings (1980) has noted that for teachers humour is both a strategy used for control and form of self-expression. 'Having a laugh' can be seen for children in similar terms. It can be a strategy of opposition which challenges teacher control or it can be enjoyable as a form of collective relaxation. At Moorside the different types of friendship groups had characteristically patterned aspirations. In the case of Gangs, their greatest enjoyment appeared to come from forms of action which were essentially oppositional to teachers. Thus, they emphasized incidents of 'causing bother' and 'mucking about' as highlights of their experiences and they liked the excitement from such activities as 'cheeking off' teachers or playing at 'dares' in lessons. Joker groups also enjoyed excitement but appeared to derive it in lessons from less disruptive actions such as sending notes or drawing in jotters. Rather than 'act daft' and 'cause bother' they would derive their greatest enjoyment from 'having a laugh' with teacher participation and they also reported enjoying lessons which were particularly 'interesting'. Good groups also emphasized enjoying 'interesting' lessons and mentioned enjoying lessons sometimes when teachers 'told jokes'. In most instances, however, their great desire to avoid stress meant that they felt most relaxed in ordered, routine and predictable lessons.

The references to enjoyment from 'interesting lessons' of course relates to the other main source of positive reward for children—the sense of self-fulfilment produced by success and achievement in learning. At Moorside many children, particularly in Joker and Good groups, wanted to succeed in academic terms—after all these were the official, adult criteria by which they would be evaluated and by which to some extent they evaluated themselves. The key to this though was balance. Children wanted teachers who would 'have a laugh' *and* 'teach things'.

'Control of Stress': a facet of the primary interest of 'self'

The main source of stress for children in classrooms derives from teacher power and the evaluative context of schooling. For 'good' groups at Moorside stress avoidance seemed to be a particularly prominent interest-at-hand, largely, I would argue, because their self-image as quiet, studious, and conformist was undercut with few defences if rejected by a teacher 'getting mad' with them. They were also vulnerable and relatively defenceless if in conflict with other groups of children. They thus tended to be wary and to concentrate on 'avoiding trouble'. In contrast Gangs almost needed stress by which to assert their 'toughness'. At the same time though, few children actually sought out, say, a severe telling-off from a teacher. If such a thing occurred, then it was used to build the tough identity but it was not enjoyed in itself. Joker groups were also concerned to avoid stress, be it from academic failure or acts of deviance. They very much disliked being told off because it negated the type of relationship which they tried to establish with teachers. At the same time, though, it is clear that a lot of their 'good fun' and 'enjoyment' was derived from juggling with the risks of 'getting done' by teachers. If their judgements were correct then routine teacher reactions would not result .n much stress. Indeed, spice and zest would be added to classroom experiences from such 'exploration of the limits' without serious sanctions resulting.

Stress is thus a double-edged interest-at-hand. Usually children seek to avoid the potential stress to which they are permanently subject because of teacher power and because of the constant evaluation of their learning. However, there is no doubt that other sorts of stress are wilfully introduced by children from time to time as a source of enjoyment and as an antidote to routine or boredom.

'Retaining dignity': a facet of the primary interest of 'self'

This was one of the important interests-at-hand for all the groups of children, being crucial for the preservation of self-and peer-group esteem. Of course there is a close relationship between dignity and perceived 'fairness' and this was particularly clear at Moorside. Thus teacher actions and censures would be constantly assessed by the children for legitimacy. 'Getting done' could therefore be accepted without loss of dignity if it was 'fair', but if the teacher went 'mad' and particularly if they started shouting and denigrating a child, then this would be regarded as a most 'unfair' assault by all the children. Other, more specific, threats to dignity came from being 'picked on', or teased by teachers as well as by having one's name forgotten. Being picked on was felt particularly deeply as a personal attack by the Gang groups. It was regarded as unfair because it was seen to arise from unusual levels of teacher surveillance and from particular attention being directed towards them. Slightly, being 'shown up' was recognized as a specific act of depersonalization intended to set an example. For instance,

> Malcolm: He only showed me up like that in front of everyone just to make me look stupid ... and just to try to make us all learn the notes better. He's always getting on at us for it and just 'cos I couldn't answer his questions he picked on me.

On the other hand, being teased was something which the Joker groups seemed

particularly conscious of. The girls related that one teacher often teased them about boyfriends which in some cases upset them because it made them 'go all red and look silly'. The relatively quiet members of Good groups were the main group of children who reported having their names forgotten. They clearly regarded this as insulting and resented it.

With regard to retaining dignity *vis-à-vis* the other children similar issues seemed important. The inter-group rivalry at Moorside was reflected in mild forms of teasing and in more serious episodes of name calling or fighting similar to that recorded by Sluckin (1981) in Oxfordshire primary schools. In all cases though the children's comments on such incidents revealed both defensive and aggressive actions to be forms of assertion of particular self-identities with particular group associations. The defence of personal dignity thus seems to be a very prominent interest-at-hand for children in all school contexts.

'Peer group membership' and 'learning': two enabling interests

It was suggested earlier that peer group loyalty and learning should be seen us enabling interests rather than as facets of the primary self-interest. They thus take on the same role for children as order and instruction do for teachers (Pollard, 1980), in that they articulate between the social ascriptions of respective reference groups and facets of the primary interest-at-hand of the participants. In the case of teachers, order and instruction can be seen as the two main aspects of their role expectation, which they have to come to terms with if they are to avoid external pressure. However, order and instruction are also the means of achieving a satisfactory level of satisfaction of more personal interests. In the case of the children, peer group membership and learning seem to relate to the social ascriptions of the child culture and social system and of the adult educational culture and wider society respectively. As such they reflect the ambiguity of each child's structural position and of course to some extent they offer alternative ways of enabling the primary interest-at-hand to be satisfied. They also pose severe dilemmas for the children when they come to make strategic decisions concerning action and to juggle with their interests in the dynamic flow of classroom processes.

Peer group membership

At Moorside peer group membership was linked to both the assertion and defence of self. Enjoyment, laughs and 'great times' almost exclusively derived from interaction between the children and their 'mates' or 'friends' with or without the positive participation of the teacher. A supportive audience was thus crucial and could only be guaranteed by the secure membership and solidarity of a peer group. Peer group 'competence' sometimes had to be proven if a child was to avoid being rejected as 'wet' or 'stupid' but would of course vary in its nature depending on the type of group. Group membership was also of defensive value both against the threat from teachers and from other children. The solidarity which existed within groups provided a powerful resource for individuals in exposed situations both in the classroom or playground. Group members were expected to 'stick up' for each other and certainly one of the worse actions imaginable was to 'snitch' or 'tell tales' on a friend. Peer group solidarity was a particularly important interest for gang groups because of the consequences of their frequent rejection of teacher authority. Children's concern to be seen as a full and competent member of their peer group can thus be seen as an enabling interest in the context of their primary concern to protect their self and 'survive' the variety of situations at school which they encounter.

Learning

Whilst the enabling interest of peer group membership responds to the children's social system, the interest of 'learning' is a primary means of coping in the adult evaluation systems of teachers and parents. Teachers and parents expect children to 'learn'. Thus one way of satisfying them and of negotiating their power and influence is simply to do just that. However, within children's social structures there will be considerable variation in the degree of commitment to this strategy. For instance, at Moorside the children would constantly assess the 'cost' of trying to learn by evaluating how 'interesting' or 'boring' the lessons were. Of course there were variations not only in those judgements but also in the responses then made. Good groups might consider a lesson as 'boring' but put up with it anyway, accepting it as 'good for them' and not wishing to compromise their identities with their teachers. Joker group members would be more inclined to attempt to direct the lesson into more 'fertile' activities whilst Gang members would be likely to attempt to subvert the lesson directly. Good and Joker group members reported far more intrinsic satisfaction from lessons than Gang members. The latter were far more likely to see lessons as a 'waste of time' or time spent on 'doing nothing' unless a direct link with future work possibilities was drawn. They thus generally had a more exclusively instrumental approach than the other, more academically successful, types of group. Obviously their perceived academic 'failure' meant that learning did not seem to provide anything more than a very limited means of enabling them to cope with their situation. On the other hand, for Joker group members their success at learning earned them the credit with teachers and parents with which they were able to relax and cultivate laughs. For the Good group members the studious sincerity of their attempts to learn enabled them to accomplish lessons without incident.

Of course academic achievement feeds back directly to the development of each child's identity and self-concept so that to learn in lessons is not an interest-at-hand simply by virtue of the need to accomplish the particular situation. It is linked to the maintenance and development of self-image, to enjoyment, to stress-avoidance and to dignity—facets of self which, though experienced with immediacy, accumulate over time into more established identities. Thus not only teachers but each child himself comes to 'know' who is 'thick' and who is 'bright', and of course so do other children. This last point is of considerable significance for it influences children's friendship groups and the nature of interaction within them considerably. Learning is thus an important interest in terms of developing a particular identity for children within their peer group though its main significance as an enabling interest clearly stems from its articulation with teacher concerns and with the official curriculum and purposes of school.

Conclusion

We can finally consider how these child interests-at-hand—maintaining self-image, enjoyment, control of stress, retaining dignity, peer-group membership and learning—might be used in the immediacy of classroom situations to produce forms of action. As a consequence of the understandings negotiated between the teacher and children and which form the 'working consensus', it is possible to see classrooms as being 'rule-framed' (Pollard, 1980). The nature of the rules 'in play' at any point will vary depending on the particular configuration of time, space, purpose and personnel and it is evident that contrasts in particular types of rule-frame situation will not affect all child interests in the same ways. The levels of satisfaction of different interests are unlikely, therefore, to vary together, and various degrees of imbalance in interest satisfaction will result. For instance, for a 'Joker' a low frame humorous interlude in a lesson may well be extremely enjoyable and offer many opportunities for establishing a strong identity as a peer group member, but it may also result in very little learning and a great deal of stress if called to account finally by the teacher. The point which I want to argue, therefore, is that the three major child interests of self, peer group membership and learning, whatever their relative prominence or nature for each type of group, are mutually interrelated in the way in which they affect coping. For each individual coping in the long run depends on evolving viable strategies by which to accomplish their structural position and hence must derive from some form of accommodation with it, in which an acceptable *balance* of self, peer group membership and learning is necessary.

I would suggest that the types of group which have been identified represent different types of solution to the problems posed by school life. The situation is difficult for children. Some will seek to cope with it by conforming and seeking to 'please the teacher' as much as possible; some will reject the whole experience, treat it as an attack on their self-esteem and resist it; some may try to negotiate their way through the situation by balancing their concerns with those of the teacher. Thus we have the strategies of the 'good' groups, the 'gang' groups and the 'joker' groups. One important consequence is the possibility that the adoption of particular strategies by children may result in further reinforcement and elaboration of the associated identity from interaction with teachers and from organizational amplification. Child adaptations and perspectives of the sort which I have been considering could therefore lead into an analysis of typing and 'career' and hence become directly related to the major sociological issue of the role of schooling in social reproduction.

Notes

[1] The paper forms part of a broadly based interactionist analysis which is reported elsewhere (Pollard 1981, forthcoming). It directly parallels an account of teacher interests-at-hand (Pollard, 1980).
[2] For a methodological account see Pollard (1984).
[3] For a fuller account of the implications of this model see Pollard (1979).
[4] See Pollard (forthcoming) for a fuller account which incorporates other research on primary school pupils.

References

Ball, S. (1980) 'Initial encounters in the classroom and the process of establishment' in Woods, P. (ed.) *Pupil Strategies*, Croom Helm.
Mean, G. H. (1934) *Mind, Self and Society*, University of Chicago Press.
Pollard, A. (1979) 'Negotiating deviance and "getting done" in primary school classrooms", in Barton, L. and Meighan, R. (eds) *Schools, Pupils and Deviance*, Nafferton.
Pollard, A. (1980) 'Teacher interests and changing situations of survival threat in primary school classrooms', in Woods, P. (ed.) *Teacher Strategies*, Croom Helm.
Pollard, A. (1981) Coping with deviance: school processes and their implications for social reproduction. Unpublished PhD thesis, University of Sheffield.
Pollard, A. (1984) 'Opportunities and difficulties of a teacher-ethnographer: A personal account', in Burgess, R. (ed.) *Field Methods in the study of Education: Issues and Problems*, Falmer Press.
Pollard, A. (forthcoming) *The Social World of the Primary School*, Holt, Rinehart and Winston.
Sluckin, A. (1981) *Growing up in the Playground*, Routledge and Kegan Paul.

Stebbins, R. A. (1980) 'The role of humour in teaching: strategy and self expression' in Woods, P. (ed.) *Teacher Strategies*, Croom Helm.

Stebbins, R. A. (1981) 'Classroom ethnography and the definition of the situation', in Barton, L. and Walker S. (eds) *Schools, Teachers and Teaching*, Falmer.

Walker, R. and Adelman, C. (1976) 'Strawberries', in Stubbs, M. and Delamont, S. (eds) *Explorations in Classroom Observation*, Wiley.

Woods, P. (1976) 'Having a laugh, an antidote to schooling', in Hammersley, M. and Woods, P. (eds) *The Process of Schooling*, Routledge and Kegan Paul.

Woods, P. (1977) 'Teaching for survival' in Woods, P. and Hammersley, M. (eds) *School Experience*, Croom Helm.

17   Friends and fights

B. DAVIES

Introduction

The analysis of friends and fights derives from recorded conversations with a group of children aged ten to eleven years, which took place at their school over a period of one year. The conversations on these tapes are generally about topics the children themselves wished to discuss: problems they were currently having with their various schoolteachers and with each other. Over a period of time, as their classroom lives were disrupted by the arrival of new teachers, and their classroom lives were disrupted by the arrival of new teachers, and their social lives were disrupted by the on-going squabbles they had amongst themselves, I began to see how these squabbles made sense from their point of view. Closer analysis of the tapes revealed the complexities involved in verbal exchanges where one 'comes to know' what the other means, and also reveals the creative work involved on the part of researcher and researched in producing sensible constructions given the available information—this is discussed and demonstrated in Davies (1978). While cognisance will be taken of this dimension in this paper the central interest is with the coherence of what the children do, given their perspective.

The advantage to the researcher of the squabbles the children had amongst themselves was that they created in natural form the sort of situation Garfinkel (1967) was after when he had his students disrupt the order of things to find out what was being taken for granted about the social order before the disruption occurred. The disruptions described by the children of my study were different in a significant way from Garfinkel's in that they were considered to be part of the normal order of things rather than abnormal events. The transcripts I have chosen generally deal with the disruptions. [. . .]

[. . .] The advantages of looking at children's accounts of their interactions, with an eye not only to the substantive meanings developed but to the function of those meanings in relation to developing and maintaining the world as an apparently sensible place, can be demonstrated by a brief look at a piece of research on friendship were description is the central purpose. Opie and Opie (1959) examine children's accounts in order to describe from the child's point of view what a friend should be. They state that boys' are definitely realists. The characteristic they most want in a friend is that he should like playing the same games that they do.' They note that girls are more concerned with 'presents, birthday cards, lending things and sharing sweets,' and are 'highly conscious of their friends' appearance.' (p. 323). So far so good. They then go on to quote from children's essays on friendship:

> Another thing about John is that he is sensible and nice. Whenever we are playing rocket ships he never starts laughing when we get to an awkward point.
> I like David because he is a good sport and kind to animals. At games he never cheats, and he sits out if he is out.

The Opies then go on, almost as an afterthought to explain the frequency of breakdown in children's friendships in terms of their gregariousness:

> Children's friendships are far from placid. Perhaps because of the gregariousness of school life they make and break friends with a rapidity disconcerting to the adult spectator.
> (p. 324).

This notion of gregariousness leading to a disconcerting amount of making and breaking of friends shows rather less insight than is usually displayed by these authors. They have noted the fact that children like other children who play the same games but ignored the specific mention by the children of *the way the games are played*. The way things are done, if viewed from the children's point of view, takes on a significance not immediately obvious to adults who are usually only conscious of what appears to be incessant and needless squabbling. *

As with the children the Opies studied, correct and incorrect behaviours were mentioned frequently by the children in my study. You should not, they claimed, 'get the snobs', 'get the cranks', 'lie', 'tease', 'show off', 'pose', 'bash up people', 'be piss weak', 'get too full of yourself', 'want everything your way', 'be spoilt', 'dob' or 'be stupid'. On the other hand you should 'play properly', 'share', 'be tough', 'stick up for your friends' and 'know each others feelings'. An independent study of friendship conducted by one of my students (Fox, 1977) revealed the following qualities of friends. For boys a friend was someone who 'does things for you', 'doesn't pick on you', 'helps you with work', 'plays with you', 'defends you', 'tells the teacher what he thinks'. For girls, a friend 'plays nice', 'doesn't tease', 'is good at school', 'plays properly and takes turns' and 'doesn't leave you on your own.'

It is obvious from these lists that children can quite readily produce very definite ideas on what they like and don't like in other children. To search out the functions of these words should throw some light on their meanings. It is worth noting that their functions are all the more elusive to adults by virtue of the fact that some of these words do not belong in the adult vocabulary. For instance posing, dobbing, getting the snobs or the cranks were all new terms for me. There are probably many functions of friendship for children—its mechanisms are non-obvious to the adult, and almost defy rendering into adult terms. However, as I have struggled with the conversations, listening and re-listening, two central themes seem to me worthy of closer analysis. These are that a friend should *be with you* and he should not *pose*. They both relate to the vulnerability experienced by the children if they do find themselves alone at school—vulnerability in terms of not knowing how to operate alone within the system of the school and vulnerability in terms of defencelessness in the face of other children who may be posing. Posing seems to be concerned with building or maintaining a positive self image, often (unfortunately) at other's expense. Since posing means showing one's self to be better than someone else, this is not surprising. Taking these two themes, one can re-organize the statements made by the children somewhat differently.

1. *Appropriate behaviours for a friend*
    Plays with you, plays properly, plays nice, takes turns.
    Helps, does things for you, is good at school work.
    Sticks up for you, is tough, tells the teacher what he thinks.
    Knows your feelings, shares.
[Thus a friend is someone who sticks by you, who knows how to cooperate and who will share their world with you.]

2. *Inappropriate behaviours for a friend*
    Posing, showing off, being too full of yourself.
    Wanting everything your way.
    Picking on you, teasing you.
    Leaving you on your own.
    Being stupid.

[A non-friend will use you to big note himself by putting you down. He will use you as the butt of his hard won superiority. He will not co-operate with you over maintaining the world as a sensible place.]

3. *Ways to let others know they have behaved inappropriately.*
   Leave them on their own.
   Get the snobs.
   Get the cranks.
   back back
   be piss weak, dob

[Since friendships and proper behaviour within friendship are so important, strategies for maintaining appropriate behaviour are developed, the most powerful of which is probably the first.]

Note the overlap of behaviour in 2 and 3. What are inappropriate behaviours for a friend are appropriate behaviours for friends who have behaved inappropriately.

Conversations with Children at School

One of the questions I asked the children related to their memories of first days at school. My interest in Aboriginal children had prompted me to ask about these first experiences since I believed that their first experience of school would be more traumatic than that of White children, since Aboriginal culture is markedly different from White culture (McKeich, 1974). But White children also found their first day at school memorable and traumatic not only at this very first school but each time they went to a new school. [. . .]

[. . .] Anyone entering a new situation is bound to feel some uncertainty, fear and vulnerability if they do not know how to conduct themselves as a competent person. It seems from the children's accounts that *friends* can change the situation from one of uncertainty to one which is tolerable and maybe even enjoyable. Roy, an Aboriginal child describes his first school as a good one because all his cousins and friends were there. In contrast, his first day at the school he is now at, was bad until he caught a glimpse of his friend who lives next door.

First Day at School

1 B.D.: So you can remember your first day Roy?

2 *Roy:* Um, yeah.

3 B.D.: What can you remember about it?

4 *Roy:* Um, when I first came here, I was a bit shy, then when you know the teacher, Mr Bell or someone took me upstairs and um, and then I saw Henry, because he lived next door, and . . .

1 Since he had been at the school for a couple of years, my question suggests he may not remember his first day.

2 The question is answered literally.

3 I produce a new question.
As Malcolm (1977) has noted, hesitance in Aboriginal children's replies leads teachers (or in this case the researcher) to multiply their questions, a tactic he claims they do not like, at least in the classroom situation, since it focuses too much attention on them.

4-8 Again the same sequence is reported: feeling bad, contact with teachers, and bad feelings alleviated when a friend is found. Henry and Roy both live on the same Aboriginal reserve.

5 *B.D.:* What did you feel when you saw, what was his name, Henry?

6 *Roy:* Yeah.

7 *B.D.:* Yeah, what did you feel when you saw him?

8 *Roy:* . . . well . . . um . . . ah . . . you know, I wasn't scared when I seen Henry you know? 'Cause this was when I first came to this school. That's all.

8 His 'that's all' tells me that he has had enough of that question.

9 *B.D.* What about the first day of the school at M [town] what was that like?

9 So I change the tack.

10 *Roy:* That was better than every school I went to, 'cause all my friends were, all my cousins were mostly there.

10 Roy can talk with much more enthusiasm about a situation where he had nothing but pleasure.

11 *B.D.:* Yeah, and so what, was this school mainly just for Aboriginal children?

11 A well-informed guess.

12 *Roy:* Yeah, mostly, and my cousin Sam, he used, we used, to fight all the time . . .

12 Said with obvious delight at the pleasurable memory.

[. . .] Friends not only alleviate the uncertainty which stems from being new and alone but via companionship and co-operativeness go on providing the means for warding off the vulnerability which attends being alone. Being *with* your friend then is important. Moreover the more advantaged children have contingency friends ready for emergency situations where their friend is absent or where their friend offends them in some way. If they withdraw to their contingency friends their bargaining power over their 'best friend' is quite high. In the following transcript Vanessa relates a tale of misery. Inadvertently she failed to be with her friend Pat when Pat thought she should be. Unfortunately for her Pat had contingency friends to withdraw to and she is now left alone in turn. The conversation was continually interrupted by some disruptive children, but with minimal prompting from me Vanessa tells her tale.

Contingency Friends

1 *B.D.:* O.K. I want to ask Vanessa how it turned into a horrible day.

1 Vanessa had earlier claimed that the day had started out well but it was now horrible.

2 *Vanessa:* Oh we were playing up in the bike shed and I came down because, um, I wanted to come down just to sit on the bike [*unclear*] and when I came down and the bell rang while I was putting my bike away and I was saying, and I was talking to Pat, I was saying something to Pat and she went [*pulls face*] and ever since then, ever since the bell she won't talk to me.

2 Vanessa left Pat simply to do something she wanted to do and Pat took offence. Vanessa was taken by surprise.

3 *B.D.:* And you don't know why she did that Vanessa?

[. . .]

3 I ask Vanessa for a causal explanation of the event.

4 *Vanessa:* I haven't had an answer.

[. . .]

4 Her reply is in the terms that matter to her. She has sent a message to Pat.

5 *Vanessa:* If I go away and do something and I don't stay up with her she gets the cranks.
[. . .]
6 and she goes off to Linda or Mandy and then we're not friends.
[. . .].
7 I do everything she wants and I can't do anything I want, has to be all her [. . .]. [*20 minutes*]
8 *Sally:* Pat is your friend.
9 *Vanessa:* No she's not. Sally if you go in before me will you ask her if she's my friend 'cause I haven't had an answer back yet.
10 *B.D.:* You mean she's cranky with you? And who have you got for your friend if Pat is not your friend?

11 *Vanessa:* Nobody.
12 *B.D.:* Betty. Betty just said she's your friend.

13 *Vanessa:* Yeah I know but I got no one to talk, no one, 'cause Betty's with Mandy mostly or . . .

14 *Betty:* You gotta be kiddin'
15 *Vanessa:* But I'm with no . . . I just gotta sit around and do things myself.
[. . .].
16 *Vanessa:* Pat was good you know, good and I, I've got really nobody in, ah, this school because the teachers are all against me. Mr Hunt especially.

5 She then replies to my earlier question.

6 She explains the contingency friendship plan.

7 There is an imbalance in the friendship as to who calls the tune.

8 Sympathetic reassurance from Sally.
9 Ambivalence in Vanessa. She isn't a friend at the moment though she may relent and therefore they will be friends.
10 This indicates I have just cottoned on to the fact that Vanessa and Pat have fallen out. The surrounding conversation had been distracting me from paying attention to Vanessa. I now ask who her contingency friends are.

12 Betty is 'friends' with whoever happens to be around. She explained in a separate conversation with me that her friend is whoever is doing anything interesting. She had noted Vanessa as her friend at the beginning of the conversation simply because Vanessa was there doing something interesting [talking to me].
13 Vanessa knows Betty will not do as a friend again for unstated reasons. She claims it is because Betty is friends with Mandy, but Betty's response shows this to be false.

Note here that an offer of friendship from Betty does not solve the problem. Betty is notorious for not allying herself with anyone in particular, the others constantly criticize her for her behaviour and according to her accounts she hates sitting around talking anyway. (Her learning of the teachers' ideas of acceptable behaviour has apparently been more successful since she is well liked by the teachers.) Certainly she is no substitute for Pat, and Vanessa's misery at losing her friend makes life look very bleak indeed. Physical removal of oneself from one friend to another is one way of letting your friend know that her behaviour was inappropriate. For this technique to work however one must know who one's contingency friends are.

The distress that Vanessa experienced when Pat left her need not have been so acute if she had had a contingency friend ready for the emergency. In the follow up transcript Roddie and Gary are quite happily together on the contingency plan.

1 *B.D.:* You two are good friends at the moment are you?

    .1 I assume this because they have come in together and seem to be getting on well.

2 *Garry and Roddie:* Yeah.

    2 They agree.

3 *Roddie:* Oh no, we don't hardly get around together, but we are friends, good friends.

4 *Garry:* Ah, before we used to but now we don't.

    3 Roddie is not happy with straightforward agreement. They are friends with a difference.

    4 They were good friends once.

5 *Roddie:* We are good friends but . . .

6 *B.D.:* You've always been good friends?

7 *Garry and Roddie:* Yeah.

5 *B.D.:* But you don't hang around together all that much?

9 *Garry and Roddie:* No.

    5-10 They still are good friends but the friendship is only mobilized when things go wrong between Roddie and Richard. Note the continual reiteration of the fact of their friendship which is necessary to counterbalance the qualification of contingency which is being described.

10 *Roddie:* Oh, but you know when I have a row with Richard or somebody, you know, I'll go to Garry and Garry'll come to me and I'll go to Patrick or some of them.

    10 Roddie has a string of contingency friends he can call on, unlike Vanessa who could think of no one.

Withdrawal to contingency friends does not spell the end of friendships. Negotiations such as that engaged in by Vanessa where messages are sent via others to find out if the friendship is still on, take place fairly soon after the withdrawal. In the following transcript Suzie is quite upset because her best friend Mandy has withdrawn from her. Many will not open negotiations—she has the snobs—yet Suzie feels relatively certain that Mandy is still her best friend.

1 *Terry:* At the moment Mandy has got the snobs . . .

2 *Suzie:* With me.

3 *Terry:* Because, we don't know what happened.

4 *Linda:* Aw, something about Graham Hurley or something.

5 *Terry:* Hurley, yeah and at the moment she's a real, you know snob.

    3-5 For a reason not entirely clear she has withdrawn from Suzie. Note that the children search on their own initiative for a causal explanation on this occasion.

6 *Suzie:* Yeah, because see Terry wrote on a piece of paper, 'What's the matter with Mandy' because he didn't want to say it in front of her and Mandy, I think she still is my best friend, but she, see, she thinks I hate her now because Terry wrote this and was something else, and she hates me now, and so does Betty Eggart. I never really did like Betty and that, because she's sort of spoiled.

    6 Terry wrote a note to Suzie about Mandy. Since Terry and Suzie are only recently friendly, this may have sensitized Mandy to potential rejection. So she has withdrawn and allied herself with Betty on the contingency friendship plan. This is one of the rare times when Betty is noted as someone's friend—if only a contingency friend.

7 *Terry:* she's a spoilt brat!

8 *Suzie:* No. She's a show-off. She doesn't leave you alone, she came up to me the other day, I asked Mandy if she liked a drink of my drink and anyway, Betty, thinkin' she was smart, she was eating this apricot or somethin' and put the seed in it, just because I took it out and put it on the seat she comes up and punches me.

    7-8 Betty is again noted as unacceptable, though how to characterize her unacceptableness is difficult. It is easier to illustrate it with an example of her behaviour which speaks for itself.

[. . .]

The centrality of *being with your friend* for friendship then is illustrated through the effects that leaving your friend can have. Children do not like to be left alone but will leave their friend alone if it seems appropriate to do so. The contingency friendship plan is vital for the success of this strategy. Moreover contingency friends increase the bargaining power of those children who know they will not be left alone if their friend choses to leave them in the event of a disagreement or fight.

Posing

The awfulness of posing was the other central theme to be counterpoised with the idea of not leaving one's friend. The first form of posing to be discussed is that which manifests itself as teasing. Teasing is at once a form of social control as well as a means whereby one sets oneself and ones' own style up as being better than that of the victim. One is generally safe from teasing where one's friends are concerned. In fact a friend who teases you could no longer really be counted as a friend. The following transcript is about teasing and the powerful effect it can have. Behaviours which are appropriate at home must be avoided at school since they lead to teasing. Teasing does not seem to have any friendly or joking overtones. It is seriously aimed at those whose behaviour is seen as unacceptable. Unacceptable behaviour falls into two categories:

1 Acting badly towards your friend (e.g. leaving her alone, writing notes about her to someone else); or

2 Appearing to be better than anyone else (e.g. posing, flirting).

Teasing is generally directed at this latter category, though it can be directed at behaviour which is simply different from everyone else's and therefore contravening more general rules of acceptable behaviour. (Reduced vulnerability goes with everyone agreeing to be the same. Someone who appears not to need to be the same is a threat.) The following transcript shows a readiness to change

1 *B.D.:* You are more responsible at school?	1 Linda has claimed she is quite different at home from at school. She is having trouble formulating the difference so I make a suggestion.
2 *Linda:* Yes, at home I sort of do everything, I sorta show off a bit at home.	2 She agrees but subsequent conversation indicates I am off beam.
3 *Suzie:* Yes!	3 Suzie has witnessed this behaviour at home.
4 *Linda:* I don't show off at school 'cos, you get called . . .	4 The reason she is different at school is that she would be teased if she didn't modify her behaviour.
5 *Terry:* 'Poser! Poser!'	5 Said in a sing, song teasing voice.
6 Linda: Yeah, 'Poser! Poser!' Or if you are a flirt they call you . . .	
7 *Suzie:* Yeah and they call ya, they say . . .	
8 *Linda:* 'Flirt! Flirt! Flirt!' something like that . . .	8 Chanted in a teasing voice.

9 *Suzie:* And if you're goin' round with a boy or somethin', talkin' to him or somethin' like that and somebody says somethin' about you or somethin', and your family's going around with a boy and you also those people would say . . .

10 *Linda:* 'Oh now you've got a boy-friend'.

11 *Suzie:* And the people who are going around with a boy will just say 'You're jealous'.

12. *B.D.:* So what the other kids say about you at school has a big effect on what you are at school?

13 *Suzie:* Yes, see, whenever I'm being called a name or somethin' like that, I dunno what happens, but it feels horrible.

14 *Linda:* I sorta really go, I sorta really get the snobs.

15 *Terry:* Yeah, me too.

16 *Suzie:* And Betty comes up and says, 'Don't get the snobs'.

9 Suzie explains you can even be teased however for aspects of your home life which are unavoidable.

10 Sing song teasing voice.

11 But there are words you can use to define yourself.

12-15 The recognition and acceptance of the power of social pressure is quite strong.

16 So if you are teased and withdraw, that too is worthy of more teasing.

So the teaser attacks the person he fears is setting himself up as a poser in the first place. Teasing is at once a fear of the possible superiority of the other and an attempt to place the teaser in the superior position.

1 *B.D.:* So posing is being sort of smarter than everyone else?

2 *Terry:* Yeah, showing off.

3 *Linda:* Yes, you just have to be the best.

4. *Terry:* Sometimes Graham will say "Aw don't pose' when he's posing, oh, sometimes, I'll pose on my bike and he'll pose chucking wheel stands on his sisters' bike, and he'll go down skating and pose. I just say 'Oh don't pose Graham' anyway he just takes no notice of me.

5 *Suzie:* Well that's what you should do, take no notice.

1 Posing is a word which was quite new to me at the time.

4 Posing is something Terry admits to doing himself and admits to criticizing others for. He further criticizes Graham however for not being affected by the criticism.

5-6 Suzie finds this commendable, however, and Terry agrees. After all, if you are going to pose, you should learn to ignore those who don't like it.

Posing sometimes takes the form of physical violence. Fist fights were not uncommon among the boys and the girls. If your friend is tough and bashes others up then you are all the safer since he will most likely defend you when necessary, so to be tough is admirable. On the other hand you may be on the receiving end of the toughness in which case it is no longer perceived as admirable. The tough guy from the point of view of the loser and perhaps the loser's supporters is seen as a pose—someone who is fighting to big note himself. To be seen as a pose does not feel very good—the word in itself can act as a form of social control to prevent someone from posing. Paradoxically then the tough guy in a fight can find himself either admired or despised or even both.

1 *James:* In Wilkins he's a poser because he can beat me in a fight.

1 To win a fight is to be a poser (or to
run the risk of being called one). That
is, James may mean that he poses
because he wins or the very fact that he
wins makes him a poser by definition.

2 *B.D.:* Mm, hm.

3 *Vanessa:* So's Mandy because she
beats me.

3 This applies to the girls as well.

4 *Garry:* And Terry! God he's a pose.
Ian Wilkins, when everybody's around
he gets in and fights me and beats me
just so everybody'll get around 'im and
be his friend and that.

4 Winning fights and posing calls for
admiration and friendship—at least
so it seems from the loser's point of
view.

5 *Vanessa:* 'N, have a look.

5 Everyone will look at your being
beaten.

6 *B.D.:* So if you're tough, everybody
likes you.

7. *James and Vanessa:* Yeah!

8 *B.D.:* What happens if you're not
tough?

9 *Vanessa:* Nobody likes you.

10 *Garry:* Yeah, they call you chicken.

10. Moreover you will be teased about it.

11 *Vanessa:* They call you words that
wouldn't be very good to say on tape.

12 *Garry:* They call you chicken.
[Laughter].

13 *B.D.* What do they call you?

14 *Garry:* They call you chicken, they
go 'Pk, pk, pk, pk.'

15 *Suzie:* No, they go like this, 'Aak! pk!
pk! pk!'

16 *Garry:* They call you p.o.o.f.

17 *Vanessa:* They do, that's what they
call you.

18 *Garry:* They hit you on the
shoulder.

19 *B.D.:* So it's the tough people who
know that they are tough who go
around bullying the people who aren't?

20 *Garry:* Yeah. Say I was Richard and I
was fightin' her, Richard's come up and
hit her there. Just there.

20 Garry explains that Richard, a high-
status person, can get away with things
that he Garry couldn't expect to get
away with.

21 *B.D.:* For no reason?

21 Interpreting the indignation in
Garry's voice.

22 *Vanessa:* The word they get around
calling you is deadshit and that's not
very nice really.

23 *Garry:* I call people deadhead.

So to be weak is potentially quite devastating. If you are beaten by someone and are
weak about it you risk some fairly unpleasant teasing. Garry, in the following
transcript has just been bashed by Roddie. He does not blame Roddie for this since
that would be being weak, instead he poses himself by telling a tale of his own
prowess.

1 *B.D.:* So sometimes you get on OK
with Roddie?

1 Garry and Roddie were contingency
friends.

2 *Garry:* Yeah we get on a lot of the
time.

3 B.D.: Why is it so important to him to prove he's so strong?

3 Another tale of Roddie's prowess has just been told. This time of Roddie over Garry.

4 Garry: I don't know, everybody reckons they're strong sometimes.

4 Garry recognizes posing as something everyone must do sometimes.

5 B.D.: Yeah.

6 Linda: Strong in which way?

7 B.D.: Everybody or just boys. or . . .

8 Linda: Betty, Mandy, Suzie.

9 Garry: Girls, everybody. Everybody reckons they're tough some time in their life. Like my cousin, he's only as tall as me and he's 16 this year, he reckons he's great in soccer and everything, and the other day he scores a fight with me and he went home, he went home, he had a bleedin' nose all blood was comin' out of his nose.

9 For example he is tough because he beat this 16 year old cousin in a fight. [Gary makes himself sound very tough in this story. The boys in Willis's (1977) study noted with some surprise how tough they sounded when they read the draft of Willis's book. These choices of stories to illustrate one's toughness are, as James points out (in statement 10 below) attempts to present oneself in as impressive a light as possible without straying too far from the facts, i.e. he is posing.]

10 James: You're just posin' 'cause you won!

10 Telling a tale (if colourfully) of your own prowess is in itself posing.

11 Garry: He always starts fightin' me.

11 Garry only has a lame defence prepared.

12 B.D.: But why is it that everybody needs to prove or to show that they're smart or tough?

13 Jane: I don't know, they just wanta pose.

14 Garry: Yeah, that's all.

13-16 It is a basic need—it does not really require explanation.

15 B.D.: But why do they?

16 Jane: They need attention.

17 James: They'll get no friends— everybody won't like them.

17 But it won't always work. You may get attention but there are some who won't like you for it.

18 B.D.: How do you mean?

19 Garry: Oh well, say I went up to Richard and I could beat Richard in a fight and if I was Richard and Richard was me, and Richard started fightin' with me and I hit him and no-one else liked me because he was all their friends, then I'd have no friends.

19 The meaning of the explanation is elusive, I think because it assumes Richard is popular. I know this yet don't feel I can assume it.

20 B.D.: Yeah, but its not a good idea to fight because you might lose friends.

21 James: Sometimes you fight 'cause you've got to prove you're tough.

21 But basically it is something you need to do.

22 Garry: Yeah sometimes.

22 Though not always.

So who can do what to whom depends on their popularity and status. Richard is exceedingly popular with everyone. He is well liked by both the girls and the boys. He is never seen a pose and when he fights, it is because he has to—at least that is how it is perceived by Roddie: 'He just stops out of it, we 'ardly have a fight me and Richard, only unless its called for.'

In order to know what constitutes acceptable behaviour in any given situation it is necessary for the children to have a clear idea of who has the right to call the tune. In the following transcript Roddie describes the origin of a current disagreement between himself and Simon. Both of them are Richard's friends. Richard and Simon are both part-Aboriginal, a fact which creates a bond between them which on occasion over-rides the bond between Richard and Roddie. Simon uses a technique of walking away from Roddie when Roddie is being disagreeable. Richard follows Simon which indicates that Simon's standing is higher than Roddie's with Richard. Roddie wants to beat Simon in a fight to restore this imbalance.

1 *B.D.:* What's been going on between you and the others the last few days?

1 I have heard rumours of a fight.

2 *Roddie:* Oh, a big row up. Pow, crash, bang!

2 Enthusiastic tone of voice.

3 *B.D.:* What happened?

4 *Roddie:* Oh, um, Simon?

4 Roddie, aware that I am not as familiar with his world as he is, always checks whether new information is clear to me.

5 *B.D.:* Mm.

6 *Roddie:* I think you had him in here before?

7 *B.D.:* Yeah, oh wait a minute have I talked to Simon? No I haven't talked to Simon.

8 *Roddie:* Oh, no, he's in another class. Well, see he wants it all his own way and if I said that I'm goin' on his side, or goin' with Richard and, um, he don't like me? So he just . . .

9 *B.D.:* So if you are friendly with Simon then Richard doesn't like you? No?

9 I am obviously confused at this point.

10 *Roddie:* See Richard always goes with Simon.

10 Roddie interrupts his story to provide the necessary information.

11 *B.D.* Oh yeah, Simon.

11 I then remember Richard mentioning Simon as a friend.

12 *Roddie:* Yeah.

12-13 Having got that straight enables Roddie to go on.

13 *B.D.:* Yeah.

14 *Roddie:* Well, um, see we was playin' soccer there and I come onto Richard's side, and Simon said 'Go on the other side' and I said 'I want to be on Richard's side the same as you do'.

14 Simon attempts to manipulate the situation in ways Roddie does not like.

15 *B.D.:* Mm.

16 *Roddie:* An' then he just walked off and he expected us to follow him. Richard followed him but I didn't. That's how it all started.

Roddie needs to find some way of getting back at Simon since he resents the power Simon has over Richard and the use he makes of it to put Roddie down. After getting sidetracked onto a fight between Roddie and Richard, where Richard had punched Roddie for supposedly saying something bad to Roy, another Aboriginal boy, Roddie explains that fights don't mean the *end* of a friendship, they are, like the contingency friendship plan, strategic moves inside the friendship.

17 *B.D.:* So what did you think of that?

17 That is, of the fight with Richard.

18 *Roddie:* Nuthin. It's always normal, every year we have about three or four fights through the year.

19 *B.D.:* Do you? What you and Richard?

20 *Roddie:* Yeah and Simon.

21 *B.D.:* How long have you guys all been friends.

22 *Roddie:* Since we come 'ere. Over at D [*school*] we was friends.

23 *B.D.:* Were you?

24 *Roddie:* We've been friends for a few years. You know we had arguments and fights in between that, but we always come back together. [*Laughs a brief knowing laugh.*]

25 *B.D.:* Are you friendly again yet?

26 *Roddie:* Yeah, Not with Simon. I'm not with Simon. I wanted to fight Simon yes'd'y, but he wouldn't.

27 *B.D.:* Why did you want to fight him?

28 *Roddie:* Aw, cos 'es the one that always starts it.

29 *B.D.:* How does he start it?

30 *Roddie:* Cos see Simon's never liked me. And I sorta *try* to make friends wif 'im, and 'e just won't, and he just goes orf and Richard follus i'm. An' then Simon, you know, starts callin' me things, names and that when Richard isn't around, but when Richard's around he crawls to us, because he knows Richard'll back up for him.

31 *B.D.* Mm.

32 *Roddie:* But when Richard's around he always wants to be friends with me.

31 *B.D.:* Mm. hm. But sometimes like when you play soccer he doesn't try and be friends with you?

34 *Roddie:* Mm. Richard made a promise that 'es not goin' with none of us.

35 *B.D.:* Mm. hm.

36 *Roddie:* And 'e said that's how its gunna stop. So me and Simon's gotta fight it out ourselves.

37 *B.D.:* Mm. hm.

38 *Roddie:* But see I was round the side, waitin' for Simon to come round and fight me. Just around there.

39 *B.D.:* Mm.

40 *Roddie:* And next minute I looked down an' there was Simon ridin' home on his bike.

41 *Roddie:* And he wouldn't come back either.

42 *B.D.:* Are you a better fighter than Simon?

18–24 Roddie is not offended that Richard hit him to the ground for something he actually had not done.

24 Roddie's laugh is one which indicated that he has a command of the situation with his friends; he knows how it all works so he doesn't need to worry unduly about the odd punch up.

26 The problem with Simon is not yet resolved.

30 Roddie describes how Simon capitalizes on Richard's following him. He asserts that Richard does not really know how bad Simon is. Incidentally, Simon's account of Roddie makes Simon sound innocent and Roddie the troublemaker.

34–36 That is, Richard will not be exclusively friends with one or the other. He is obviously fed up with the conflict so Roddie and Simon must sort out their differences without using him.

40 I laugh at the image of Simon rapidly retreating from a bad situation.

41 This is said with a grin.

42 If Simon was retreating it suggests he knew Roddie would win.

43 *Roddie:* I've tried him once, we both . . ., no one won 'cause the bell rang. Oh, I'm urgin' to fight him again but. I just wanna see 'oo can win.

43 But Roddie admits he doesn't really know if he can beat him. He may not have been retreating at all—Roddie's description may just have been a pose. Roddie is not necessarily angry with Simon but he does not need to know who is the stronger.

Simon's capacity to capitalize on Richard's friendship, and the knowledge that Richard will follow him if he walks away, and back up for him if he walks away, and back up for him in a fight, would be reduced if Roddie could demonstrate his physical superiority over Simon. Simon may well have recognized this as he made his speedy retreat down the road on his bicycle, if indeed that is what he was doing.

To sum up so far, the children have quite clear strategies for coping with unacceptable behaviour from each other. They can walk away from each other either with the intention of being followed or to seek out a contingency friend. They can tease each other and they can fight (or threaten to fight each other). These strategies do not spell the end of friendships: They are manoeuvres within friendships. Friends can walk away or fight with you and you can still count them as your best friend (after certain additional manoeuvres have been completed.) To fight someone however when it is not called for is unthinkable, as Henry, an Aboriginal boy, explains in the following transcript. The conversation takes place when Henry has just arrived back at school after some months of chronic illness. He explains that he will fight Roddie when the situation is right for it. At the moment they are friends, so fighting would be inappropriate. He is looking forward to the day when fighting Roddie will be appropriate.

1 *Henry:* I'm gonna drop Roddie.

1 Knock him to the ground.

2 *Roy:* You gonna drop 'm? Pick 'im up and drop 'im?

2 Roy is well liked for his sense of humour.

3 *Henry:* Sometimes you get me mad.

3 Henry is not in the mood for humour.

4 *Roy:* Roddie's better'n me and he's eleven, twelve.

4 Roy acknowledged that Roddie can beat him in a fight.

5 *B.D.:* So what are you going to do? Drop Roddie?

5 The expression is new to me.

6 *Henry:* I'll drop 'im.

7 *B.D.:* Why Henry?

8 *Sally* [Henry's sister]: Last time he made me real wild when Henry was at the Far West [*home for sick children*]. Um, Jennie got 'it by Roddie. And she kept cryin' that 'ed 'it 'er. And Roddie was sittin' down on the steps and I asked him, and I asked who hit her and I went over to Roddie and I said 'Roddie why'd you hit Jennie for?', and he wouldn't tell me no reason so I 'it 'im. Then 'e 'it me back and then 'e ran.

8 Sally explains that in the absence of her brother Henry, she had had to defend her younger sister. Defence of siblings and friends is top priority among the Aboriginal children.

9 *Henry:* 'Es scared.

10 *Roy:* 'Es scared that's why.

11 *Sally:* I reckon Simon's the best.

11 The knowledge Roddie wants as to who is best, him or Simon, is something others wonder about too.

12 *Henry:* I could drop Roddie.

12 Henry points out that he is stronger than Roddie.

13 *B.D.:* You're feeling mad at Roddie are you Henry?

13 I take Henry's continual assertion to mean he is annoyed with Roddie.

14 *Henry:* No, I'm not mad at 'im *now,* 'es   14–16 He finds my assumption rather
a friend now.   silly.
15 *B.D.:* But you could get mad at him
now?
16 *Henry:* I *could,* I *could,* I can't get mad
at 'im for no reason! You've got to 'ave a
reason.
17 *Sally:* Say Richard came up to my   17 Sally points out that he would have
sister and she was only five, and she   have punched him if he'd been in the
had a bashed lip, and 'e punched 'er well   situation she was in.
then what would you do?
18 *Henry:* Who? My sister?
19 *Sally:* Yeah, if it was your sister?
20 *Henry:* I'd punch 'im.
21 *Sally:* Yeah, right, so would I.
22 *Henry* I'd punch anybody.   22 Implied here is 'If it was appropriate'.

[. . .]
Conclusion

The children through their accounts recognize a wide range of appropriate and
inappropriate behaviours for different people and different situations. They seem
less concerned with consistency of action from individuals than they are with
consistency within given situations. They are not bothered for instance if a friend's
home behaviour is different from his school behaviour, or if friends display non-
friendly behaviour when the situation requires it. (If the situation does not require
such inconsistency in a person's behaviour, then inconsistency is unthinkable.) The
variables which seem to be important in the definition of any given situation are
status (who can call the tune), place (school, home, playground, classroom), who is
friends with whom and whether anyone is trying to pose as better than he is. This
detailed awareness of the definition of the situation and its power to dictate
appropriate behaviour may well be associated with the fact that schoolchildren
experience frequent and regular changes of situation over which they have little
control. They must pay close attention to the requirements of any one situation
such that within its own terms it becomes predictable. Once a situation is
predictable, then competent, appropriate behaviour is possible. Censure must fall
on those who threaten the reading of each situation.

Friends behave in predictable ways towards each other, thereby providing a
secure arena for competent behaviour. Even more basic than this though is that
friendship protects the child from the vulnerability associated with being alone.
This is sufficiently important for complex strategies to be developed to maintain the
friendship—not necessarily for love of the particular friend but because of the
functions it fulfills. Which brings us full circle back to the Opies. Children may
'make and break friends with a rapidity disconcerting to the adult spectator', but
that is perhaps because the adult spectator does not actually understand what is
going on. The friendships are in fact surprisingly stable. [. . .] What appear to be
breakages are, rather manoeuvres within the friendship so that the functions
friendship serves can be fulfilled. The children have developed words and related
concepts which describe or explain what it is they are doing. Insofar as these words
and concepts are alien to adults the children may be said to have a substantive
culture of their own. [. . .].

References

Cicourel, A. V. (1973) *Cognitive Sociology*, Penguin.

Davies, B. (1978) 'Contrasting Worlds of adult/researcher and child: resolution of a problem from different points of view.' Unpublished.

Fox, G. (1977) 'Friendships from the child's perspective'. Unpublished paper, The University of New England, Armidale. (Available from B. Davies, Centre for Behavioural Studies in Education, UNE, Armidale, New South Wales, Australia.

Furlong, V. (1976) 'Interaction sets in the classroom: towards a study of pupil knowledge', in Hammersley, M. and Woods, P. (eds) *The Process of Schooling*, Routledge and Kegan Paul.

Garfinkel, H. (1967) *Studies in Ethnomethodology*, Prentice-Hall.

Goodman, M. E. (1964) *The Culture of Childhood*, Columbia University, Teachers College Press.

Hammersley, M. (1977) 'School learning; the cultural resources required by pupils to answer a teacher's question', in Woods, P. and Hammersley, M. (eds) *School Experience*, Croom Helm.

Hargreaves, D. Hester, S. and Mellor, F. (1975) *Deviance in Classrooms*, Routledge and Kegan, Paul.

Harré, R. and Secord, P. F. (1972) *The Explanation of Social Behaviour*, Blackwell.

McKeich, R. (1974) 'The construction of a part-Aboriginal world.' Paper presented at The Australian Institute of Aboriginal Studies Biennial Conference, Canberra.

Mackay, R. W. 'Conceptions of children and models of socialization', in Turner, R. (ed.) *Ethnomethodology*, Penguin.

Malcolm, I. (1977) 'Interaction in the Aboriginal classroom: a sociolinguistic model.' A talk delivered to the seminar on Classroom Processes and Practices, West Australia Institute of Technology.

Mehan, H. and Wood, H. (1975) *The Reality of Ethnomethodology*, Wiley.

Miller, C. M. L. and Parlett, M. (1976) 'Cue-consciousness', in Hammersley, M. and Woods, P. (eds) *The Process of Schooling*, Routledge and Kegan Paul.

Opie, I. and Opie, P. (1959) *The Lore and Language of Schoolchildren*, Oxford University Press.

Rosser, E. and Harré, R. (1976) 'The meaning of trouble', in Hammersley, M. and Woods, P. (eds) *The Process of Schooling*, Routledge and Kegan Paul.

Speier, M. (1971) 'The everyday world of the child', in Douglas J. (ed.) *Understanding Everyday Life*, Routledge and Kegan Paul.

Speier, M. (1976) 'The child as conversationalist: some culture contact features of conversational interactions between adults and children', in Hammersley, M. and Woods, P. (eds) *The Process of Schooling*, Routledge and Kegan Paul, 1976.

Werthman, C. (1971) 'Delinquents in schools: a test for the legitimacy of authority', in Cosin, B. R. *et al.* (eds) *School and Society*, Routledge and Kegan Paul.

Willis, P. (1977) *Learning to Labour*.

Woods, P. (1976) 'Having a laugh: an antidote to schooling', in Hammersley, M. and Woods, P. (eds) *The Process of Schooling*, Routledge and Kegan Paul, 1976.

Index

Printed in the United States
by Baker & Taylor Publisher Services